Complete Guide to Test Automation

Techniques, Practices, and Patterns for Building and Maintaining Effective Software Projects

Arnon Axelrod

Apress®

Complete Guide to Test Automation: Techniques, Practices, and Patterns for Building and Maintaining Effective Software Projects

Arnon Axelrod
Matan, Israel

ISBN-13 (pbk): 978-1-4842-3831-8   ISBN-13 (electronic): 978-1-4842-3832-5
https://doi.org/10.1007/978-1-4842-3832-5

Library of Congress Control Number: 2018955901

Managing Director, Apress Media LLC: Welmoed Spahr
Acquisitions Editor: Shiva Ramachandran
Development Editor: Laura Berendson
Coordinating Editor: Rita Fernando

Cover designed by eStudioCalamar

Distributed to the book trade worldwide by Springer Science+Business Media New York, 233 Spring Street, 6th Floor, New York, NY 10013. Phone 1-800-SPRINGER, fax (201) 348-4505, e-mail orders-ny@springer-sbm.com, or visit www.springeronline.com. Apress Media, LLC is a California LLC and the sole member (owner) is Springer Science + Business Media Finance Inc (SSBM Finance Inc). SSBM Finance Inc is a **Delaware** corporation.

For information on translations, please e-mail rights@apress.com, or visit http://www.apress.com/rights-permissions.

Apress titles may be purchased in bulk for academic, corporate, or promotional use. eBook versions and licenses are also available for most titles. For more information, reference our Print and eBook Bulk Sales web page at http://www.apress.com/bulk-sales.

Any source code or other supplementary material referenced by the author in this book is available to readers on GitHub via the book's product page, located at www.apress.com/9781484238318. For more detailed information, please visit http://www.apress.com/source-code.

Printed on acid-free paper

In memory of my late grandparents Nathan and Lea Axelrod, pioneers of the Israeli cinema. Your memory is my inspiration.

Table of Contents

About the Author

Arnon Axelrod is a test automation expert, working as a senior consultant, architect, trainer, and lead of the test automation team at Sela Group. Arnon started programming his ZX-Spectrum when he was 10 and hasn't lost his passion for programming ever since.

After Arnon graduated with his B.Sc. in Math and Computer Sciences from Ben-Gurion University of the Negev in 1999, Arnon started to work for Microsoft as a Software Engineer in Test (SDET), where he was first exposed to the domain of Test Automation. Since then he has worked in several high-tech companies, mostly as a software engineer, until he rediscovered test automation from a new perspective. After working by Agile methodologies for several years, in 2010, while working at Retalix Ltd (later to be acquired by NCR Corporation), Arnon realized that effective test automation, and more specifically the Acceptance Test Driven Development (ATDD) technique, is crucial for delivering high-quality software rapidly and sustainably over time. While at NCR, Arnon established a test automation infrastructure that was used by over 100 developers and was running over 4,000 acceptance tests in less than 20 minutes.

In 2015, Arnon joined Sela Group, where he works now, with a mission to spread his knowledge to as many companies and individuals as possible, in order to help them develop quality software more effectively through proper use of test automation.

In his spare time, Arnon likes sailing, playing the piano, and singing in a chorus. Arnon lives in Matan, Israel, together with his lovely wife, Osnat, and their three boys: Ori, Elad, and Aviv.

You can follow Arnon Axelrod on LinkedIn, read his blog at `http://blogs.microsoft.co.il/arnona/`, or contact him directly at `arnonaxelrod@hotmail.com`.

About the Technical Reviewer

Bas Dijkstra is a testing and automation consultant and trainer. He specializes in creating and implementing automation strategies that support testing, starting with helping to answer the "why?" of automation all the way to writing effective automation solutions.

Bas delivers training on various subjects related to automation. He also regularly publishes blog posts and articles on various topics related to test automation, both on his website (https://www.ontestautomation.com/), as well as on other websites and in industry magazines.

Acknowledgments

First and foremost, to my wife Osnat – this book would not have been possible without the great support I got from you, and I know it wasn't easy! As much as I tried to not let this work affect our personal lives, I did leave you lonely for many long evenings and left you more of the house chores than I normally do. I don't think that it will make up for that, but I want to tell you one thing: I love you!

Next, I owe a big thank you to my direct manager and head of DevOps and Automation division at Sela, Shmulik Segal, who also supported me in this work and allowed me some precious time for working on this book, despite the fact that it had no economic justification. Shmulik, besides supporting me on this book, I appreciate you as a manager and as a person. You empower me to reach peaks in my career that I never even thought I could. And you do all of that very pleasantly.

I also want to thank Sasha Goldshtein, ex-CTO of Sela (author of *Pro .Net Performance* by Apress, 2012; and coauthor of *Introducing Windows 7 for Developers* by Microsoft Press, 2011), who tried to dissuade me from writing this book, but apparently failed. You were right at least about one thing: it took me much longer than I planned. But nonetheless you helped and advised me a lot, including recommending me to submit a book proposal to Apress.

Also, at Sela, I want to thank Zohar Lavy, who coordinates my schedule and helps me with many administrative tasks – it's a real pleasure working with you! To all the administrative staff at Sela for all the important and hard work you do behind the scenes; and to my skip managers and owners of Sela, David Basa, CEO; and Caro Segal, president of the Sela College; as well as Ishai Ram, VP Global, for leading Sela and making it such a great place to work at. And finally, for all of my talented coworkers – I learn a lot from each and every one of you.

To Carl Franklin and Richard Campbell, hosts of the ".Net Rocks" podcast, for expanding my horizons, making me laugh, and making my commute much more enjoyable. Carl, thanks also for creating the "Music to code by" collection that helped me stay focused while working on this book.

ACKNOWLEDGMENTS

I must also thank all of the people that actually made this book take shape: first of all to Bas Dijkstra, my excellent and highly professional technical reviewer for reading every sentence thoroughly and providing his invaluable insights, feedback, and suggestions for making this book better. Without you, this book would probably be a piece of crap...

And lastly for all of my editorial staff at Apress: Rita Fernando Kim, my coordinating editor for managing the progress of this work, and for providing valuable tips and advice for anything I asked or should have asked. To Laura C. Berendson, development editor, for helping me shape and present my ideas in the best way possible; Shivangi (Shiva) Ramachandran, editor, for managing this project; and for Susan McDermott, senior editor, for accepting my book proposal and believing in me in the first place. Thank you all!

Introduction

There are many great books about test automation, and particularly about best practices of Test Automation. However, there's no one size fits all. As I once heard someone saying: "'Best Practices' is always contextual: even something as common as breathing may be catastrophic if the context is free diving..."

Most of the books that I have read so far about test automation are aimed mainly for developers, focusing mainly at unit tests or at developer-written end-to-end tests. Some other books that I either read or know about deal with a specific test automation technology, methodology, or are simply just too outdated. While I tend to agree that the idea of developers writing the tests may be very effective in many situations, in reality it doesn't fit all organizations at all stages. Moreover, test automation is a tool that serves and affects nearly all stakeholders of a software development organization, including testers, product managers, software architects, DevOps people, and the managers of the projects, and not only developers. As every software organization and project is different, trying to adopt techniques, practices, and tools that don't fit the team's needs or skills can cause the failure of the automation project and in some cases even the failure of the entire software project.

The goal of this book is to give a broad view on the subject of test automation in order to allow the reader to make smart decisions upon his particular case, giving his constraints and the benefits he wants to gain from having the test automation, but also to provide detailed and hands-on guidance for building it effectively, at least for the majority of cases.

Who Should Read This Book?

As test automation affects nearly all stakeholders of software development organizations, and as this book attempts to cover nearly all aspects of test automation, this book is for everyone who's involved in the process of software development and is interested in knowing how to get more value out of test automation. This includes: QA managers, dev managers, developers, testers, architects, product managers (AKA business analysts, system analysts, or various other titles), DevOps people, and more. Ah, and of course test automation developers whose main job is to develop automated tests...

While most of the book is not too technical and is aimed at the broader audience, Chapters 11–14 are very technical and aimed for people who write code and are proficient with object-oriented programming (OOP). In particular – professional test automation developers. The code in this section is written in C#, but the ideas and concepts are transferrable to any object-oriented language. As C# and Java are very similar, there shouldn't be any problem for Java programmers to understand the code, but I'm also sure that programmers of other languages can understand the code or at least the main ideas behind it pretty easily.

In particular, I hope that many Dev and QA managers will read this book, as they typically have the biggest effect on shaping the methodology and working processes in their organization, which test automation should integrate with, and can help to improve. Having said that, this book also contains useful tips and techniques for non-managers for improving the methodology and working processes of their organization even without any formal authority.

How This Book Is Organized?

When I first sat down to start writing this book, I tried to think about the high-level structure of the book, but I found this task very baffling because it seems that almost any topic is related to many other topics. At that time, I couldn't find a clear and logical way to divide the content to high-level sections, so I ended up writing a "laundry list" of topics I wanted to cover and just started writing by letting the knowledge spill from my head down to the paper (or keyboard to be more precise...). Naturally I started from the most basic and general stuff and slowly built upon that with more and more chapters that are more advanced or specific. Because the topics are so interrelated, I often wrote a forward reference to a topic I was yet to write, and of course references from more advanced chapters to earlier ones. Eventually, like in a good Agile project (talking about cross-references... see Chapter 1 for more about Agile), the high-level structure of the book gradually started to emerge. At some point I realized that the book took a pretty logical structure consisting of two parts: The first part answers more of the general "Why" and the "What" questions, and the second one answers the more specific and technical "How" questions.

Generally, I encourage most readers to read the entire book from cover to cover. However, as this book aims at a broad audience, with different concerns, different starting points, interests, needs, etc., you might prefer to focus on specific chapters and skim, or even skip, others, optionally jumping back and forth to other chapters referred to from the chapter you're reading if you feel you need to fill in the gaps. Finally, keep this book within reach for later reference as the use of test automation in your organization matures and faces new challenges.

Here's an overview on each part and chapter in this book:

Part I: The "Why" and the "What"

This part covers the subject of test automation from many different aspects, but more in a "high-level" manner. This part is essential for those who don't have much experience with test automation and want to understand how it fits the big picture of software development, and where to start. This part will also help you understand what you can expect, as well as what you *shouldn't* expect from test automation. It is especially relevant for Dev or QA managers, as it discusses aspects like business structure, working processes, architecture, and more. It will guide you through many decisions that you'll have to make (which many people don't even consider!) and tell you what effect each decision might have. Even if you're not a manager and don't think that you have any influence over these things, I encourage you to read it in order to understand the constraints and advantages in your current situation, and to be able to communicate it better with your managers.

If you already have experience with test automation, this part can, and probably will, expand your horizons about the subject and show you alternatives and consequences of decisions you previously made less consciously.

Part II: The "How"

After you've gained the high-level understanding about the domain of test automation, it's time to roll up our sleeves and start writing some tests and the required infrastructure. After we write some tests, we'll discuss how to take it forward and to use the test automation most effectively in the development life cycle.

Conceptually, this part could be divided into two subparts (though this division is not mentioned explicitly anywhere except for here): Chapters 9–14 are written as a hands-on tutorial, in which we design and build a test automation system with few tests (using Selenium) for an existing open source project, and Chapters 15–19 provide guidance for using test automation in the most effective way, and how to get the most out of it.

Most of the chapters in the first subpart of Part II are very technical, while in the second subpart they are not. Therefore, the first subpart is more suited and relevant for developers, particularly test automation developers, with OOP skills, while the second subpart is relevant for everyone. For skilled programmers, I encourage you to follow along the tutorial step by step and do each step yourself, in order to *experience* it better. For non-programmers, I encourage you to skim over these more technical chapters in order to get the main idea behind them, even if not for knowing exactly how to implement it in your own project.

Here's a complete description of the chapters:

Part I:

- **Chapter 1: The Value of Test Automation** – this chapter discusses why test automation is needed and what its short-term and long-term benefits are.

- **Chapter 2: From Manual to Automated Testing** – this chapter discusses the differences between manual and automated testing and starts to set realistic expectations for test automation, as it's pretty different from just faster manual tests.

- **Chapter 3: People and Tools** – this chapter discusses who should write the tests and the automation infrastructure, and what the consequences of the alternatives are. In addition, it discusses how to choose the right tool according to these alternatives.

- **Chapter 4: Reaching Full Coverage** – this chapter sets realistic expectations for the long-term road map of the automation project, and shows how to start gaining precious value out of it long before the automation replaces most of the manual regression tests.

- **Chapter 5: Business Processes** – this chapter discusses how test automation is related to the business processes for developing software, and provides overviews for topics that will be discussed in greater depth toward the end of the book.

- **Chapter 6: Test Automation and Architecture** – this chapter discusses how test automation is related to the architecture of the tested system, and why it's important to adopt them to one another.

- **Chapter 7: Isolation and Test Environments** – this chapter discusses how to plan the automation and its execution environments to ensure that the tests are reliable and are not affected by any undesired effects.

- **Chapter 8: The Big Picture** – this chapter discusses the interdependencies between all of the subjects discussed in the previous chapters, mainly architecture, business structure, business processes, and of course test automation. It also discusses how all of these relate to business culture.

Part II:

- **Chapter 9: Preparing for the Tutorial** – this chapter describes the process that I'm going through in the tutorial, which is also applicable to most test automation projects. It also guides you how to set up your machine for following along with the tutorial.

- **Chapter 10: Designing the First Test Case** – this chapter teaches a specific technique for designing the test cases in a way that best suites automated tests.

- **Chapter 11: Start Coding the First Test** – this chapter shows you how to start writing the code for the first test. We start by writing a mere skeleton of the test in a way that will lead us to design and create a modular and reusable infrastructure. By the end of this chapter, our test compiles but does not work yet.

- **Chapter 12: Completing the First Test** – in this chapter we complete the work that we've started in the previous chapter. By the end of this chapter, we have a working test and a well-designed infrastructure to support it.

- **Chapter 13: Investigating Failures** – in this chapter we'll practice how to investigate and deal with a real test failure that occurred while we've got a new build of the tested system, and how to create a report that will help us investigate additional failures in the future.

- **Chapter 14: Adding More Tests** – in this chapter we'll add one more test, but also discuss how to go about adding more and more tests, while expanding and improving the infrastructure to support them, including support for cross-browser testing, support for multiple environments, and more.

- **Chapter 15: Continuous Integration** – this chapter (which starts the second subpart of Part II) discusses how to integrate the tests into a Continuous Integration (CI) build. More than the technical aspects, this chapter covers how to make it succeed as an organizational tool and provides advice for non-managers for how to gradually change the culture and processes of the organization for the best, by leveraging the CI.

- **Chapter 16: Acceptance Test Driven Development** – this chapter explains the benefits and how to implement the Acceptance Test Driven Development (ATDD) methodology, which expands on CI to encompass the entire development life cycle and help the team to become really effective with Agile.

- **Chapter 17: Unit Tests and TDD** – this chapter discusses the techniques that are traditionally attributed only to the application developers: unit tests and Test Driven Development (TDD) but are, in fact, an inseparable part of test automation.

- **Chapter 18: Other Types of Automated Tests** – this chapter discusses additional types of test automation, including performance and load testing, testing in production, Visual Testing, Installation tests, Artificial Intelligence, and more.

- **Chapter 19: Where to Go from Here** – this chapter provides some tips for how to continue to learn and improve in the domain of test automation.

In addition to these chapters, there are four appendices:

- **Appendix A: Real-world examples** – this appendix is supplementary to Chapter 6 ("Test Automation and Architecture") and provides four real-world examples of application architectures and their corresponding automation solutions.

- **Appendix B: Cleanup mechanism** – this appendix describes how to build a cleanup mechanism, which is described in Chapter 7 ("Isolation and Test Environments").

- **Appendix C: The Test Automation Essentials project** – this appendix describes the Test Automation Essentials open source project that I created, which contains many useful code utilities (in C#) for test automation projects.

- **Appendix D: Tips and practices for programmer's productivity** – this appendix supplements Chapters 9–14 with tips for increasing your productivity as a programmer. While these tips are relevant for any developer, I find it especially useful for test automation developers.

Happy reading!

PART I

The "Why" and the "What"

As this book is titled *Complete Guide to Test Automation*, it covers both theory and practice, both beginner and advanced topics, both methodological aspects and technical details, and more. After all, I attempted to address as many possible questions about test automation as feasible in one book.

The first part of the book tries to answer mainly the "Why" and the "What" questions, leaving most of the "How" questions to the second part. We'll start by answering why do we need test automation and what test automation is all about (and also what it isn't). Then we'll address many questions, dilemmas, and considerations (i.e., what option should I choose, and why) about test automation, which are important to anyone planning to start using test automation or improving an existing one. Finally, we'll look at the bigger picture and see how everything is related to the other.

Happy reading!

CHAPTER 1

The Value of Test Automation

As this book is about test automation, it makes sense to start by defining what test automation is. However, without proper context, the definition may not be clear enough and may lead to more confusion than understanding. In fact, this topic is so broad and diverse that it's hard to come up with a definition that is accurate, covers all the various types of test automation, and is also clear. My best shot for now would be something like "Using software to help in testing of another software," but then again – I'm not sure how helpful it is. So instead of focusing on formal definitions, the first part of the book is dedicated to examining this broad topic from multiple angles, and eventually it will be crystal clear what test automation really is. And equally important – what it isn't!

Why Do We Need Test Automation?

When I ask my customers what they expect to get from test automation, the most common answer is to reduce the time it takes to test the software before release. On the one hand, while this is an important goal, it's only the tip of the iceberg in terms of the benefits that you can gain from test automation. In fact, reaching the goal of reducing the manual test cycles usually takes a pretty long time to achieve. On the other hand, you may start to see the other benefits sooner. But let's first see why this basic goal of reducing the time for a test cycle became so important in recent years.

© Arnon Axelrod 2018
A. Axelrod, *Complete Guide to Test Automation*, https://doi.org/10.1007/978-1-4842-3832-5_1

From Waterfall to Agile Software Development

Even though some companies used test automation decades ago, it wasn't prevalent until recent years. There are many reasons for this, but without a doubt, the transition from the traditional Waterfall approach to the Agile approach contributed a lot to the need for test automation. In the traditional waterfall approach, software projects were perceived as a one-time thing, like building a bridge. First you plan and design, then you build, and eventually you test and validate the quality of the end product, fixing any minor issues that may arise. The assumption was that if the planning and engineering were done correctly, then besides some minor programming mistakes that could be easily fixed, everything should eventually work as planned. This approach requires us to verify that the end result behaves according to the specification only once. It is only when a test fails and a fix is made that the test should be performed again to verify the fix. If each test is done only once or twice, then in most cases it's much cheaper and easier to do it manually than to automate it.

Over the years, it became clearer that in most cases the waterfall approach does not fulfill its promise. Most software projects became so complex that it wasn't feasible to plan and close all the technical details in advance. Even in cases that it was feasible, by the time it took to complete a software project (which has typically lasted a few years), both the technology and the business needs have changed, making the software less adequate than it was supposed to be. For those reasons, responding quickly to customers' feedback become much more valuable than sticking to the original plan. Gradually, the majority of the software industry moved from one-time software projects, going through releasing new versions of the same software once every few years, to rapid delivery cycles. Today, some of the biggest companies on the Web deliver new features and bug fixes many times a day and even a few times a minute!

THE MANIFESTO FOR AGILE SOFTWARE DEVELOPMENT

In 2001, 17 thought leaders from the software industry formulated the **Manifesto for Agile Software Development**,[1] which states the following:

We are uncovering better ways of developing software by doing it and helping others do it. Through this work we have come to value:

Individuals and interactions over processes and tools
Working software over comprehensive documentation
Customer collaboration over contract negotiation
Responding to change over following a plan

That is, while there is value in the items onthe right, we value the items on the left more.

Kent Beck	James Grenning	Robert C. Martin
Mike Beedle	Jim Highsmith	Steve Mellor
Arie van Bennekum	Andrew Hunt	Ken Schwaber
Alistair Cockburn	Ron Jeffries	Jeff Sutherland
Ward Cunningham	Jon Kern	Dave Thomas
Martin Fowler	Brian Marick	

© 2001, the above authors

this declaration may be freely copied in any form, but only in its entirety through this notice.

Clearly, not all companies and teams adopt these ideas, but almost everyone who's involved in software developed today prefers to deliver new versions of the software more rapidly (and continue to deliver new versions over a long period of time), rather than delivering only a few versions in long intervals. This also implies that the changes between each release will be smaller than if you deliver a new version every few years. Naturally, software companies in sectors that are more missions critical are less prone to taking risks, and they will tend to keep releasing in pretty long cycles, but even many of them start to see the value in delivering more often, at least internally to QA.

---

[1]http://agilemanifesto.org/

Testing each version manually can take a lot of time, and that's an obvious reason why test automation became so important. But there's another important reason, too.

The Cost of Software Complexity

With every new version of a software, new features are added. As new features are added, the software becomes more complex, and when the software becomes more complex, it becomes harder and harder to add new features to it without breaking anything. This is especially true when there's pressure to deliver the new versions rapidly and not investing enough time to plan and to improve the quality of the code (as often happens in a badly implemented Scrum[2] methodology). Eventually, this causes the pace of delivering new features to decline, which is what we wanted to avoid in the first place!

Some of this added complexity is unavoidable. It would have existed even if we carefully planned and designed the entire software ahead. This is called *inherent complexity*. But most of the time, most of the complexity in a software exists because features were added quickly without proper design; lack of communication inside the team; or due to a lack of knowledge, either about the underlying technology or about the business needs. Theoretically, this complexity could be reduced if the software was carefully planned in advance as a whole, but in reality, it is a natural part of every software project. This type of complexity is often called *accidental complexity*.

Any complexity, be it inherent or accidental, comes with a cost. This cost is of course part of the overall cost of developing a software, which is mainly affected by the number of developers and testers, multiplied by the time it takes for them to deliver the software (multiplied by their salaries, too, of course). Accordingly, when the complexity of a piece of software grows, its cost increases because it takes more time to test everything, and also it takes more time to fix (and retest) the found bugs. Accidental complexity in particular also makes the software more fragile and harder to maintain, and therefore requires *even more* time to test and more time to fix bugs.

---

[2]Scrum is the most common methodology that is based on the Agile values.

Maintaining a Constant Cost

Figure 1-1 illustrates what we want to aim for: a constant cost while adding new features over time. However, adding new features generally means making the software more complex, which as we just saw, naturally increases the cost. However, two factors can help us keep a constant cost:

1. Make the cost of running the ever-growing regression test suite negligible.

2. Keeping the code very easy to maintain.

The first factor can be achieved if most of the tests are automated. However, the second factor is mainly affected by the accidental complexity, and it is much more challenging to control.

Having code that is easy to maintain means that the complexity that is added due to new features has very little or no effect on the complexity of existing features. This means that if we keep the complexity rise in a linear pace, we can still keep a steady cost, as shown in Figure 1-2. Clearly, we would like to preserve that ability to add complexity only for the inherent complexity (i.e., new features) and avoid wasting it on accidental complexity. However, in most cases in the real world, due to the accidental complexity, the complexity rises more steeply than linearly as we add more and more features, as shown in Figure 1-3. And as explained, this in turn also increases the cost of adding new features over time, as shown in Figure 1-4.

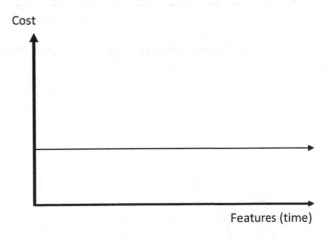

Figure 1-1. *Desired cost of adding new features over time*

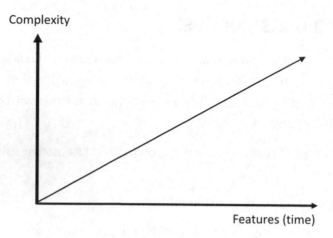

Figure 1-2. *The desired rise in complexity when we add more features is linear*

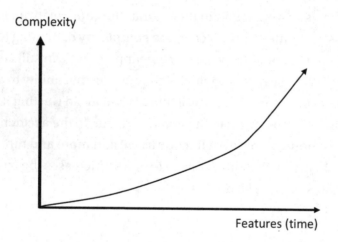

Figure 1-3. *The common case: complexity rises steeply due to the added accidental complexity*

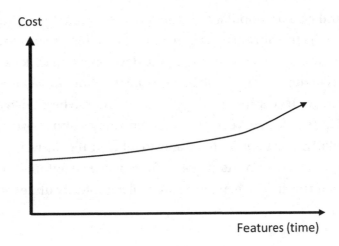

Figure 1-4. *The development cost in the common case: adding new features becomes more costly over time*

In most cases, stopping everything and planning everything from scratch, in order to reduce the accidental complexity is not practical. Even if it was, by the time the new version (which is developed from scratch) would reach feature parity with the old version, it will have its own accidental complexity...

Refactoring

So it seems that it's not feasible to keep developing new features with a steady cost over time, because accidental complexity is unavoidable. So are we doomed? Well... not really. The solution for keeping accidental complexity under control is called *refactoring*. Refactoring is the process of improving the design (or "internal structure") of a piece of software, without affecting its external behavior. In other words, it allows us to get rid of accidental complexity. Refactoring can be done in small steps, improving the design bit by bit without having to redesign the entire system. Martin Fowler's book *Refactoring: Improving the Design of Existing Code*[3] provides specific techniques to make refactoring

---

[3]Martin Fowler, *Refactoring: Improving the Design of Existing Code* (Addison-Wesley Professional, 1999).

in a safe manner. Today, most popular Integrated Development Environments (IDEs[4]) feature some automatic refactoring tools or have plug-ins that provide them.

But even with automatic refactoring tools, the developer can make a mistake, and introduce new bugs in the process, breaking existing functionality. Therefore, refactoring requires comprehensive regression testing, too. So in order to be able to keep a steady, fast pace of delivering stable new versions containing new features over time, we must be refactoring regularly. And in order to be able to refactor regularly, we need to test very often. That's the second important reason for having test automation. Figure 1-5 illustrates how refactoring helps keep the accidental complexity under control.

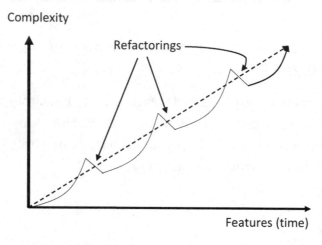

Figure 1-5. *Refactoring helps keep complexity under control*

Continuous Improvement

The thing that fascinates me the most about test automation is its relationships with all other aspects in the development cycle. Besides quality and productivity, which are obvious, test automation is also related to the architecture of the product, the business processes, the organizational structure, and even the culture (see Figure 1-6). For me, test automation is like a mirror into all of these things. All of these aspects have an effect on the test automation. But you can also leverage the reflection of these effects in the test automation to change and improve any of these aspects back.

---

[4]*IDE* stands for *Integrated Development Environment* and refers to a software that consists mainly of a code editor, a compiler, and an integrated debugger. Microsoft Visual Studio, Eclipse, and IntelliJ are some of the most popular IDEs for C# and Java.

In many cases, customers that already use test automation call me to help them with some problems they experience. These problems often manifest themselves at the technical level. However, when I come to them and help them analyze the root cause of the problems, they often realize that their problems are actually related to one or more of these other aspects. It's not always easy to fix these problems, but at least it brings the significance of these problems to their awareness, which is the first step to change.

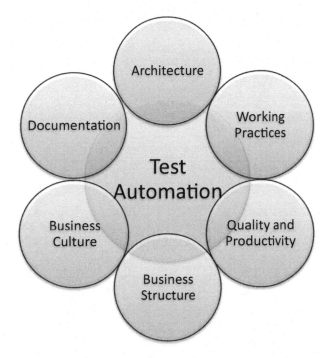

Figure 1-6. *Test automation is related to many other aspects of software development*

I hope that by reading this book, you'll be more perceptive to the effects that such problems have on the test automation you're building and be able to bring them to the awareness of the relevant people in order to make the necessary improvements. Of course, if your team has a culture of continuous improvement (e.g., perform retrospective meetings and really act upon them), then it will be easier to do. But even if not, remember that awareness is the key for making a change, and the test automation will help you achieve this even if you're a junior automation developer in a large and bureaucratic company (see Chapter 17 for more information about how to gradually change the culture of your organization to take more advantage of test automation).

CHAPTER 2

From Manual to Automated Testing

Let's face it: we're in the 21st century. There's no reason why any repetitive task won't be fully automated, especially in a high-tech environment! But still, a large portion of the manual tester's job is performing regression tests,[1] which is very repetitive. And obviously, doing it manually is much slower and error prone compared to what the computer can potentially do.

First Attempt: Record and Playback

So the first thought of anyone who wants to improve that process is to automate the manual tester's job. There are several ways to achieve that as we'll discuss throughout this book, but the most trivial one is simply to record the actions of the manual tester and then play them over and over again. The most common way to do it is by recording the user's interactions with the UI, but it could also be recording network traffic like HTTP requests or some other kind of data that is an indirect reflection of the user's actions.

If it was that simple, then we wouldn't need this book (and I probably had to find another job...). But in practice, things are not so trivial. Even though a big part of executing regression tests is highly repetitive, there is at least one very important part that is not repetitive whatsoever, and this part constitutes the entire essence of executing the tests. This non-repetitive part is the part of detecting the errors! While it's simple

---

[1]*Regression tests* are tests that verify that a functionality, which previously worked as expected, is still working as expected.

© Arnon Axelrod 2018
A. Axelrod, *Complete Guide to Test Automation*, https://doi.org/10.1007/978-1-4842-3832-5_2

to record the actions that the manual tester does and replay them, it's much trickier to detect bugs in an automated manner.

One naïve approach to automatically detect bugs is to compare the image on the screen to the expected image that was recorded. However, this approach has several drawbacks. Some of these drawbacks are merely technical. For example, there could be differences in screen resolution, differences in date and time that appear on the screen, differences in any data that appear on the screen but is not relevant to the test, etc. Some tools allow you to overcome these technical drawbacks by excluding the regions of the screenshots that may have legitimate differences from the comparison. A similar problem exists in the case of recording the HTTP network traffic, as some of the data may have legitimate differences. But then again, there are tools that help you specify which parts of the response to compare and which to exclude. But even if those technical drawbacks can be addressed by tools, there's still one big drawback that is inherent to the concept of record and replay: every legitimate change in the application will be considered as a failure, making it hard to distinguish between false positives and actual failures.

At this point you may think: "What's the big deal? We execute regression tests to ensure that everything keeps working as it did before!" So let me tell you this: if no one touched the code[2] of the *system under test* (or SUT in short), no regression would ever occur, and there's no point in spending time running either manual or automated tests. On the other hand, no programmer is likely to change any code unless he intended to make a change to the behavior of the application! Thus, there is a real value in executing tests only when things change, and therefore whenever we execute tests, we should expect that things have changed.

When we execute tests manually, we rarely think about these changes as an issue. Often the changes are minor enough that if we use our judgment and common sense, we can still relate the words that describe the test steps to the new behavior of the application, even if they don't exactly match anymore. We use this judgment and common sense that is based on our domain knowledge, communication with other team members, experience, etc., in order to assess whether a change is a bug or an improvement. However, a machine lacks any of these skills, and therefore it treats legitimate changes and bugs equally.

---

[2]For that matter, "Code" refers to any artifact that is part of the system and can affect its behavior. For example, if the list of countries in a database is not something that a user can and should be able to alter, then you can consider it as part of the code of the application.

If the expected results of your tests are too general (as in "exactly the way it was"), instead of reflecting only the specific information that is *important to test*, then your tests will fail much too often due to legitimate changes, rather than on real bugs. In other words, the ratio between false positives and real failures will be too high, which makes them less reliable! Without clear and concise expected results, you'd probably run into the following problems:

1. For every legitimate change in the application, you will keep getting the same failures for subsequent runs of your test until you'll re-record or fix the test.

2. When re-recording a test over and over again, there's a good chance that you'll have errors in the scenario you're recording. Obviously, there's a chance that an error will exist in the first recording and be fixed in the next one, but other techniques (that will be discussed later on) are more suited for gradually improving and solidifying the tests. Without the ability to solidify and stabilize the tests, people will start to lose trust in the test automation project as a whole.

3. Often a small change in the application affects many test scenarios. Even if the effect of this change is very minor to a human being, it causes many automatic tests to fail. For example, fixing a typo in a button's text, or even a removal of a redundant space, can cause many tests to fail if they all look for that button's text and click it as part of their scenario.

4. Investigating the result only according to the difference between the actual result and the expected result (whether it's a screenshot or other form of data that can be compared to the actual result) may not provide enough information that is needed to understand whether it's a bug or a legitimate change. In case it's a bug, it also doesn't provide enough information that can help understand what led to it. See Chapter 13 for more information about investigating failing tests.

The bottom line is that the effort you'll need to make in order to investigate the failures and to maintain the tests (re-record or fix them) will very likely go beyond the cost of manually executing the tests.

Getting the Most Out of Test Automation

Let's look at the other opposite: instead of looking at the goals of test automation from the perspective of what we have today (manual tests) and how we can automate it, let's take a look at the desired, ideal outcome of what's the *best we can achieve* using it.

Before we do so, let me clarify that while the picture I give here may be feasible to a few teams, for most teams it's not really practical as is. Nevertheless, it is feasible for most teams to get close to this, and get most of the advantages, given the right guidance and leadership (that can come from anyone, including yourself, even if you're not a manager!). Anyway, I want to give you an idea on what to aim for. In the rest of this book we'll talk about trade-offs and considerations that you'll have to make in order to get closer to the goal I'm about to suggest, but also be pragmatic and practical in what you'd probably achieve. Keep in mind though, that if you'll take it seriously, over a long enough period of time you can gain more traction to these ideas, which will get you closer to this goal. See Chapter 15 for more details and ideas of how to gradually change the culture of your organization to better utilize test automation.

So now, calm down, close your eyes and start imagining... Oh wait, keep your eyes open so you can continue to read...

Imagine that you have full coverage of automated regression tests that run altogether in few minutes. Imagine also that your team fixed all of the known bugs and all the tests are passing... Imagine also that every developer can run all of these tests on his own dev machine whenever he desired!

If that would be the case, how would it change the way you use your test automation when developing the next version, feature, or user story (see sidebar)? Would you still run it only nightly and investigate the failures the next morning? When you'll find a bug, will you just report it in your bug tracking system and wait until the end of the quarterly release cycle for the developers to fix it? I hope that your answer is "No"!

If the tests run so fast, then you can have them run automatically before every *check-in*[3] of every developer (which can be very frequent as well) and prevent the check-in operation in case one or more tests failed. This ensures that everything that resides inside the source-control repository always passes all the tests! This is the idea behind the

---

[3]*Check-in,* also known as *Commit, Push* or *Submit* is the operation of applying the changes made by a developer on his local machine into a centralized source code repository that is shared by the entire development team. These repositories are managed by source-control systems such as Git, Microsoft Team Foundation Server, SVN, Mercurial, and more.

concept of *Continuous Integration* (CI). See Chapter 15 for more on that topic. In effect, having full regression coverage that runs in CI prevents virtually all regression bugs from creeping in! So if you had no bugs in the first place, this process will prevent regressions from occurring too, allowing you to keep this state of zero known bugs virtually forever! In the rare case of finding a new regression bug (manually, after the developer checked-in the code), the bug can be first reproduced using a new automated test, and fixed immediately, to keep having zero known bugs.

Moreover, it encourages the developers to improve the *inner quality* of the code and the structure of the application, as they can freely refactor their code and still be easily assured that they don't break anything (see Chapter 1 about the importance of refactoring). This inner quality is often translated into external quality as well, as simpler code tends to have less bugs and is easier to maintain without introducing new bugs. In addition, code that is easier to maintain also means higher productivity, as it allows the developers to implement more and more features quickly, easily, and first and foremost – safely.

And what about new features? I won't get too much into details here (read more in Chapter 16 about Acceptance Test Driven Development – ATDD), but the main idea is that whenever a new feature is developed, its relevant tests are developed along with it and only when all the tests pass and no bugs are found in it, this feature (or User Story) is considered "Done."

I can hear your skeptical voice now saying: "That's really great… but it will *never* work on *my* team…" So let me convince you that it can: if you're applying these ideas from day one, this approach is fairly feasible and even easy. But you probably don't and indeed when applying them (much) later, it's more difficult to get there. However, in Chapter 4 I'll show you how you can gradually come close and gain most of the benefits mentioned above sooner. Also, in Chapter 15, I'll explain how even *your* team can make it. In that chapter I'll give you specific guidelines on how to show fast ROI to every stakeholder who might oppose and drive this change even if you're not a manager.

USER STORIES

A *User Story* is a term used in Agile software development, which describes a narrowly scoped requested feature. Instead of defining a comprehensive and detailed requirement document at the beginning of a project and then implement it over a long period of time, as is customary in Waterfall development, in Agile the approach is to add small features to the software incrementally. Each such added small feature or change is a user story. In some cases, a user story can also be a request to change or even remove an existing feature according to user feedback, and not necessarily adding a feature.

User Stories should be narrowly scoped, so that they'll be developed quickly and be able to get to the customer's hands (or at least the product owner's hands) early to get her feedback. However, even though a User Story should be narrowly scoped, it should still **give some value to the end user**. It often takes some practice and creativity to break down a big feature into such user stories,[4] but I very rarely found a feature that cannot be broken into user stories in such a manner.

Even though there's nothing preventing one from describing a User Story in great detail, the focus should be more on the general idea and its value to the end user, allowing the team to come up with their creative solutions for the problem.

It is common to define User Stories using the following template or something similar:

```
As a <role>
In order to <goal>
I want <a high level description of the feature>
```

For example:

```
As a site administrator
In order to prevent a "Denial of Service" attack
I want to be able to control the maximum number of requests per seconds from
each client's IP
```

Differences Between Manual and Automated Tests

Now that we understand that blindly mimicking the manual tester's work is not enough, and we also see that a successful implementation of test automation has some great benefits that you can't get from manual regression testing, we can conclude that manual testing and automated testing are essentially different. So let's dive deeper into the differences between the two. These differences are especially important to keep in mind when coming to implement existing manual test plans as automated tests.

---

[4]See http://agileforall.com/new-story-splitting-resource/ for some guidelines for breaking down big user stories.

In general, executing manual tests can be divided into two types:

- Exploratory testing
- Planned testing

Different companies and teams have different policies (whether these policies are strict and enforced, or only exist in practice) regarding who, when, and if planned tests are created and executed. Some teams focus primarily on exploratory tests plus maybe a few sanity scenarios that reside only in the head of the tester. This is more common in small, start-up teams or in small software development teams that are part of a bigger organization that is not software centric. On the other end of the spectrum, highly bureaucratic teams rely mainly on highly documented, precise planned testing.

Exploratory Testing

In exploratory testing, the tester is free to explore the system in order to look for bugs that were not thought of before. This type of testing has a big advantage when your goal is to find as many bugs as possible. In many cases, even when a tester follows a planned test, he's free and even encouraged to look around and do a little exploratory testing along the way of the planned tests.

Often people think that because automated tests can run fast and cover a lot in a short time, then they can find more bugs quickly by either randomly or systematically trying to cover many usages. If that's what you thought, I'm sorry to disappoint you that this is not the sweet spot of automated testing. In order to find bugs, the test should have a notion of what's expected and what's not. While a manual tester has this notion intuitively, a machine doesn't. If you think that you can formalize these rules in a simple way that can be automated, I encourage you to think again. In most cases these rules are as complex as the SUT itself... Remember that the sweet spot of automated testing is **not to find as many bugs as possible**, but rather to provide **fast feedback** about whether the system behaves in the way we expect, as defined in the tests.

On the other hand, there are cases where you can formalize some important (though very generic) rules about the boundaries of the possible outcomes of the system and create an automated test that goes over many possible inputs, either randomly or sequentially, verifying that the outputs are indeed in the expected range. If you try to write or modify such tests to verify some nontrivial rules, then you'll quickly end up complicating the test so much until the point that is difficult to analyze and to maintain. So you may want to use this technique only to verify rules that are simple to define and yet mission critical. In all other cases I would recommend simple tests that only verify one or few specific examples. This technique is called *property-based testing,* and the most prominent tool that supports it is QuickCheck, which was originally created in the Haskel programming language but was later ported to a long list of other popular languages, including Java, F# (which can be consumed by C# and other .Net languages), Python, Ruby, JavaScript, C/C++, and more. Because this topic is only relevant at rare cases, it is outside the scope of this book.

Another, probably more useful option, is to create semi-automated tests, or tools for the manual testers, which will help them cover many cases quickly, but leave the analysis of whether the results are as expected or not to the manual testers. I'll leave it to you to find when and where you can develop and use such a tool, as this is also beyond the scope of this book. Therefore, from now on, if not specifically mentioned otherwise, we'll talk only about *planned* manual testing and automation of these testing.

MONKEY TESTING – AUTOMATED EXPLORATORY TESTING

The term *Monkey Testing* refers to a practice of randomly hitting keys (or otherwise performing operations without understanding their context), like monkeys, or more realistically, toddlers, can do, and see if the program crashes or not. While this technique can be easily automated, it's usually not very effective for a few reasons:

1. You can only catch crashes (or errors that you explicitly look for), not any other bug, because you can't define the expected result for each action. Even if the program freezes (but does not crash), you probably won't be able to detect it, let alone determine if the application behaves in any sensible manner or not.

2.   Because the automation presses the keyboard and mouse blindly, the chances that it will do something interesting is pretty low. For example, it can get stuck for hours with a message box open until it will randomly press "Enter," "Esc," or click exactly on the "OK" button. Obviously, we can develop a bit smarter "monkey" that instead of sending random keystrokes only clicks those available buttons or menus. It will indeed resolve the message box problem specifically, but any other form or dialog that has some input validation will likely cause the same problem.

Considerations for Automated Testing

Now that we understand that automated tests are not very adequate for exploratory testing, let's see how planned manual testing is different from automated testing. In the following paragraphs, we'll analyze the main differences between the two and how these differences should affect our considerations when we come to plan an automated test as opposed to planning a manual test.

Preciseness

Manual (planned) tests are written by humans, in order to be consumed (read and executed) by humans. Not only that, but the consumers are usually other team members that know the application and the business domain and share pretty much the same pre-assumptions regarding the system and how it is used. I say here "other" team members, which is the better case, even though in the vast majority of cases I have encountered, mostly the tests cases are executed by the same person who wrote them. In those case, these basic assumptions are never challenged and the test cases[5] contain only the details that the writer *thought* he would need to *remind* himself about what he intended when writing the test case.

---

[5]The term *Test case* may be somewhat overloaded. For me, a test case is one test scenario that is composed of specific steps (actions) and verifications. Usually test cases are organized in *Test Suites*. A *Test Plan* usually contain multiple test suites, in addition to other details regarding planning, resources, etc.

21

All of these assumptions that the test case writer makes cause the manual test case to contain some vagueness. Humans usually don't have a problem dealing with some vagueness, but computers just can't. When writing automated tests, vagueness is simply not possible. Eventually the automated test (like any other computer code) must be precise and detailed in order for the computer to be able to execute it. It is very common that when converting manual tests to automated ones, many questions arise even about nuances that seem minor. However, every question must be answered in order to be able to automate the test, and that answer is baked into the code of the test automation and will be used every time the test will run! In fact, these questions often reveal more important and interesting bugs than the bugs that are found when the automated tests run.

Maintainability

As mentioned in Chapter 1, it's useless to execute tests on code that hasn't changed, and therefore you should expect the application to change almost every test cycle. This means that test cases must be changed often to reflect the changes in the application. However, in reality very rarely have I seen this happening with manual test cases. In most cases, the changes in the application are minor and the person that executes the test can pretty easily understand what has changed and how he should adopt what's written in the test case to the actual state. But as mentioned above, with test automation, every small detail matters; therefore the automated tests must be updated to reflect every change that may affect them. For example, suppose that our application has a "Save" command in the "File" menu, and one of the steps in a test case specifies that we should "click the 'File'➤'Save' menu." If at some point the "Save" command is moved outside the "File" menu onto a more visible toolbar button, then any sensible tester would understand that the step should now refer to the toolbar button rather than the menu item, even if the description of the step hasn't changed. However, an automated test would fail if it can't find the "Save" menu item as written.

Now that we understand that tests need constant maintenance, the most important question is how we can write the automated tests so that it's easy and fast to make those changes. Most of the chapters in Part II of this book deal exactly with this question.

Sensitivity to Change – Preciseness and Maintainability Put Together

From what I said above about preciseness, you probably think that automated test scripts[6] should, and even must, be full of very fine-grained details of every operation it should perform. On the other hand, the more you rely on such specific details, the more difficult it is to keep your test scripts up to date. So it seems that these constraints are in odds, and there's no way to achieve both of them.

Fortunately, preciseness does not necessarily mean bloating each script with all of the fine-grained details. All the details must be defined *somewhere*, but not *all* of the details must reside inside the *scripts* themselves. A test automation system is usually more than just a plain collection of test scripts, but it can, and should be built in a modular fashion, where some pieces contain the fine details, and the scripts are only a composition of these pieces.

You can think of it like the plans (drawings) of a car. When designing a car, there's no single drawing that contains all the details of the car. The car is a complex object that is composed of many smaller objects (chassis, body, engine, gear, steering system, wheels, interior parts, etc.), and each of them is composed of even smaller parts. There's probably one drawing that shows the "full picture" of the car, but with less details, and many smaller drawings that describe the details of each part. If all the details were in a single detailed drawing, and an engineer that designs the seats want to make a change (that doesn't affect its external dimensions), the entire drawing should have been updated!

Similarly, when composing automated tests, even though all the details must be flushed out before the test can run, not all the details should reside in one place, but rather be spread across several components (methods, classes, modules, etc.), which can be changed or swapped out without affecting the others.

Handling Failures

The first time a manual planned test case is executed, we may encounter many unexpected conditions that we haven't thought of when we wrote the test case. If we're well organized, then we'll probably fix the test case after that first time. When developing

---

[6]I use the term "script" here to describe a *single automated test case*, whether it is written in code, a scripting language, a record-and-playback tool, or any other form.

an automated test, a similar process happens during the *development* of the automated test, until the test passes at least once.

But after that stage, whether we're talking about manual tests or automated tests, unexpected conditions may still occur due to one of the following reasons:

1. A new bug in the product (regression).

2. A legitimate change (improvement) to the product that we weren't aware of.

3. Environmental problem. For example, a network failure, out of memory, out of memory, etc.

4. An event in the product that the test was not designed to handle. For example, suppose that the application shows a pop-up message every day at 16:00, reminding the user to back up his work. An automated test can pass consistently when it runs every other time, but if it starts a little before 16:00, then the pop-up message can cause it to fail. This is of course a simple example, but real applications have sophisticated logic that sometimes makes it difficult to think of all the conditions that can occur, and to address all of them appropriately in the test case. We can say that these gaps in the design of the test case are, in fact, errors in the test case itself. In case of automated tests, we can in fact call these... bugs in the tests!

5. Someone did something with the system before or during the test, which unintentionally affected the flow or result of the test. This "someone" can be another manual tester that ran some tests; a user or administrator that changes some settings; or another automated test that performed such actions. For example, if one test changes the password of a user that another test tries to log in with, then the second test may fail. Another example is when two tests run against the same server simultaneously and each of them tries to change some data that the other uses. This class of problems are called *isolation* problems and are somewhat similar to the previous kind of problems, but at least in case of automated tests, they usually indicate not only a bug in a particular test, but rather a problem in the overall architecture of the test infrastructure. Chapters 6 and 7 deal with these issues in more details.

While all of these conditions might happen both when executing a manual test and when running an automated test, the way they are *handled* is a key difference between manual and automated tests. Humans (manual testers) often distinguish between these types naturally and easily and know how to handle each of them accordingly. Even in case of a product bug, after the tester files the bug, in most cases he can continue executing the rest of the test case, maybe after performing some work-around or re-do the last few steps. On the other hand, in the context of automation, by definition, "unexpected" means that the computer doesn't know how to handle it!

Important note   Test automation may be able to handle the third type of failure reasons to some degree, but this is a very delicate topic. If you can identify possible events that may occur during the test execution, you may be able to handle them in the code in a way that will work around them and handle them similarly to what a user (or a manual tester) would have done. However, this should be handled with care, as on one hand, the goal of these work-arounds are to make the tests more reliable; but on the other hand, it's much harder to verify that the test itself handles all of these situations correctly, and therefore you may end up with the opposite effect: the tests would be less deterministic and eventually less reliable! Even though in some cases these work-arounds are worthwhile, you should thoroughly consider the alternatives discussed in Chapters 6 and 7.

SHOULD WE RETRY FAILING TESTS?

I sometimes find that people built a retry mechanism into their testing framework, so that it retries all of the failed test once or twice and only mark a test as failed if it has failed after *all* of the retries. To me, by doing so they're missing an important point. Failing tests tell you something: either there's a problem with your test code or with your application under test. Even if it's time consuming at first, those problems should be thoroughly investigated to find their root cause and handled accordingly to prevent them from reoccuring. Ignoring these failures by blindly retrying the entire test will probably leave your automation unreliable and potentially leave significant undeterministic bugs in the product, too! Let alone the extra time it takes to rerun those failed tests…

Length of a Test Case

The difference between the way that manual testers handle unexpected conditions and the way automated tests do, has a vast impact on the way that automation should be written: individual manual test cases are often somewhat lengthy and tend to cover a complete feature with all of its nuances in one test case. It makes a lot of sense for manual test cases to verify many smaller things "along the way" in order to save time when executing the test case. If there's a minor bug or something changed that affected these sideway verifications, the manual tester can often skip it and continue with the rest of the test case. However, if you automate such a lengthy test case as is, and it fails in one of the first verifications, it doesn't have the wisdom to decide whether it makes sense to continue or not.

Some automation frameworks allow you to report the failure and continue nevertheless. However, when a human tester encounters a failure, he usually decides whether it makes sense to continue, go back a few steps (and exactly how many) or completely abort the test execution, based on some understanding of the *nature* of the problem. I find that deciding at runtime solely upon the importance of the verification itself whether it makes sense to continue or not (without means to repeat or work around some last few steps) is not very reliable and consequently has the potential of hurting the reliability of the test automation as a whole! In particular, it's almost impossible to assure that the test behaves correctly in all of the possible failure conditions.

Other frameworks (including the vast majority of the unit-testing frameworks) take the approach that any unexpected condition that the test encounters causes the entire test case to fail and continue only to the next test case (rather than the next step). In my opinion, this is the safest and most reliable way to go. However, **this implies that tests must be short and should verify only one thing**, otherwise, a minor failure can block the more important parts of the test from executing. If you try to outsmart and make your tests "smart" about possible failures, you'd only make the things worse, because now you'll have a full-blown logic in your test code that you have no reasonable way to verify!

This also means that almost every verification should have its own test case! It may sound wasteful and cumbersome, but in the long run, you'll realize that this is the only way to keep your tests reliable and maintainable.

Dependencies Between Tests

Sometimes manual test cases are described with dependencies between them: execute test X only after executing test Y. In automated tests, because a failure in one test normally aborts that test and continues to the next one, we won't want the failure to affect the next tests. This means that we need to guarantee that every test starts from an initial well-known state. In other words, dependencies between automated tests are strongly discouraged. The exact details on the various options to enforce a clean start in every test is covered in Chapter 7

Logging and Evidence Collection

How the automation *recovers* from unexpected conditions so it can continue to the next test is one thing, but another important thing is *what to do about* these unexpected conditions. In case of manual tests, if at the time of execution, the tester encounters an unexpected condition and he believes that the problem lies in the application, then he usually reports a bug immediately before proceeding to execute the rest of the test case or skip to the next one. In the bug report, he usually describes what he has done that led to the failure and maybe some other facts he finds relevant. When writing the report, he should also try to investigate the nature of the bug by "playing around" to discover its boundaries.

However, when an automated test encounters an unexpected condition, the story is very different:

- As already discussed, automated tests treat any unexpected condition as a failure without proper ability to articulate the nature of the problem.

- Automated tests usually run unattended, and the investigation of the failures is done after the fact. This means that the investigation of the failure can only be done after some of the evidence was already lost or corrupted!

If the test reproduces the same failure each time and in every environment, one can run the test again on a different environment (e.g., his local machine if the failure occurred in a CI or nightly build), or execute its steps manually and investigate the failure this way. Even in this case, it would probably take some precious extra time. Nonetheless, in case the failure does not happen all the time, then it's highly important to have logs, both of the test and of the application, as well as any other evidence that may help investigate the problem. Such evidence can be screenshots or even a screen's video recording, DB snapshots, a web page HTML source, etc. Chapter 13 covers the topic of investigating failing tests more deeply.

SHOULD THE TEST AUTOMATION SYSTEM REPORT BUGS AUTOMATICALLY?

Even though I saw many attempts to connect test automation systems directly to the bug reporting system, and open a bug automatically when a test fails, it doesn't turn out to be a very good idea. First of all, as mentioned, all unexpected conditions may cause automated tests to fail, but not all of those failures are in fact bugs. But even if the bugs are assigned to a tester to analyze them first, there are many cases that a single error causes many tests to fail, causing extra overhead managing and tracking these piles of autogenerated bugs. For more details about the recommended way that bugs discovered by automation should be treated, see Chapters 5 and 15.

Trust

Mistrust between developers and manual testers is (unfortunately) pretty common: testers blame developers from writing crappy code, developers blame testers for opening bugs with too little or inaccurate information, etc. (and everybody blames product managers for writing unclear requirements, but that's another story... we'll see how ATDD helps with that, too, in Chapters 5 and 16). But eventually, everyone agrees that the other role is necessary and important.

When it comes to test automation, both developers and testers, as well as their managers, need to trust the machine. At first it may sound like a no-brainer: machines always produce consistent results, better than humans do! So why would it be hard to trust them? But as we discussed above, automated tests can fail due to a number of reasons and not only bugs. In fact, in order for us to trust the automated tests, we have to believe that:

- Tests fail only on real bugs.
- Tests don't miss bugs.

As much as we'd want and try to make these claims true, we cannot guarantee them. But with a good test automation suite, we can guarantee a softer version of these claims:

- Tests fail *mostly* on real bugs (and it's easy to investigate and determine the real cause).

- Tests don't miss bugs that they were designed to catch.

If you design your automated tests so that they are short and simple, as you should, then it's pretty easy to prove the second claim. But the first one is more difficult to achieve. This situation where the first claim is not met is manifested either when there are many tests that fail for a long period of time even though the basic functionality that is verified by these tests is working, or when tests frequently fail with an unexplained reason. When that happens, stakeholders (especially managers) cease to trust the results of the automated tests. When the results of the automated tests are ignored, and no resources are given to solve these problems, then pretty quickly the tests will become irrelevant and stale, collapsing all the investment that was put in building the test automation system!

Unfortunately, there's a large percentage of test automation projects that start with a lot of excitement but after some time fail to fulfill their promise, and then these projects die miserably. **Hopefully, this book will help you avoid this destiny and lead you into the destiny of success!**

Before diving deeper into the aspects of ensuring the success of the test automation project, let me add to some of the practices already mentioned, and highlight some more key practices that will help the automation project avoid the destiny of doom and rather reach its successful destiny:

1. Every failure, first and foremost automation bugs, must be treated and fixed ASAP! (more on that in Chapters 5 and 15).

2. Every failure should be investigated thoroughly to find its root cause. "Covering" for errors may solve short-term problems but may cause future problems that are harder to identify and fix (more on that in Chapter 13).

3. Tests should be built in a way that ensures consistent results. If the results depend on external conditions, when they fail the tendency would be to blame these external conditions and to avoid investigating the real cause (more on that in Chapters 6 and 7).

CHAPTER 3

People and Tools

As a consultant, most customers that call me to help them start working with test automation start with the questions: "Which tools are there?" and "which tools should I use"? If you're in that situation yourself, then you're probably asking this question too. The short answer to the first question is that there are a bazillion tools out there for test automation. Oh, and there's Selenium, too, of course, so there are bazillion and one. And the short answer to the second question is the classical consultant's answer: "It depends."

Choosing the Right Tools

Now in a more serious tone, even though there are indeed many tools, and almost every day I hear about a new tool for test automation (each of them promises to be "the next thing"), there are only few categories of tools serving different purposes. Some tools cover more than one purpose, and in most cases, you'll probably need a combination of tools. In order to know which tools are right for you, there are bunch of questions that you should answer first. While the question "which tool should I use" is a "how" type of question, the questions you should start from are the "whys" and the "whats." Once you answer these questions, the choice of tools will be pretty trivial in most cases. I'll describe the categories of these tools and the questions that you should answer further down this chapter. However, I encourage you to read at least the chapters in Part I of this book before you actually make a decision, as these chapters will help you *answer* those questions better.

While the rest of the chapters in Part I will help you answer most of the "why" and the "what"questions, I want to dedicate this chapter to one important question that is too often overseen, which is neither "why," "what," nor even "how," but rather a "who" question...

31

© Arnon Axelrod 2018
A. Axelrod, *Complete Guide to Test Automation*, https://doi.org/10.1007/978-1-4842-3832-5_3

Who Should Write the Tests?

Most of the time my customers already have an answer to this question, even though they didn't consider all the alternatives and their implications, simply because they're not aware of them! So let me describe the options and their implications. Note that there's no one right answer to this question, and every option has its pro's and con's, so you have to make your own choice, as best fits your organization.

Note that **even if you already have an automation team in place, I encourage you to still read this chapter**, as you'll gain a better understanding of the pro's and con's of the situation you're in, which will probably help you deal with them better. You may even want to consider changing or trying to influence your managers to change the decision in the long run.

Promoting Manual Testers or Inexperienced Programmers to Automation Developers

Sometimes manual testers with no or with very little programming skills hear about one of the record-and-playback automation tools out there and get very excited. They come to their boss and tell him that they can start building automated tests quickly and save a lot of time and money! This enthusiasm is great, and as a manager you may want to harness it, but please keep in mind what we already discussed in the beginning of Chapter 1: record-and-playback tools are easy to begin with but does not hold water for long.

Many manual testers have some background in programming. Some of them studied computer science or something similar in college or high school but ended up in QA for several years. Others simply played here and there with programming and are enthusiastic to write code. These people are often seen as great candidates for starting your test automation endeavors. Taking someone that you already know and trust, which has some basic programming skills, and already knows your system and the company is very compelling. There's no need to invest too much in training, and this opportunity usually really motivates this person! At first, the QA manager would probably decide that this person will dedicate only 20%–50% of the time to the test automation project and continue to do manual testing at the rest.

Of course, every person is different and I'm generalizing here, so take my words here with a grain of salt, and judge your own case for yourself. But in my generalized opinion, while some of these people may be appropriate as test automation team members once it's properly established, they're usually not the right persons to start building and establishing the test automation system. If you'd let them, they'll probably succeed at first, which will contribute to the perception that it was the right choice. But over time, maintainability and stability issues will start to occur and the project might begin to deteriorate.

At the early stages, the technical challenge of building automated tests that "do the job" is usually not so high. Some tools make it easy even for people without any programming background, but even writing automatic tests in code (e.g.. using Selenium) does not require high programming skills just to make it work. These tests would usually pass and may even find some interesting bugs.

However, after some time, some things might start to go not so well: the development of the application doesn't stand still. The application evolves, new features are added, some existing features and UI screens change, and some parts are re-written. From time to time, that inexperienced automation developer will find that some things in the application changed and he'll need to fix the automation accordingly. As long as these are very specific and small changes, he'll deal with it fine. But without proper planning and design, and without appropriate debugging skills, when the number of tests increase, some unintentional dependencies or assumptions can hide in the code of the test automation, which make the tests more fragile and less reliable. In addition, at some point the application developers will change something that may affect a big portion of the tests. In order to fix that the automation developer will need to rewrite large chunks of the tests. It will take a long time to fix, and regardless of whether the application works correctly or not, the automation is completely broken for a long period of time, in which time it doesn't provide any value.

As a lesson learned, he might ask the developers (and also involve his manager for that) to let him know in advance about every change that they're about to do that might affect the automation, so that he can prepare in advance. Unfortunately, this isn't going to work... Even with their best intentions, the developers are not aware enough or simply don't even know which changes that they make might affect the automation and which won't. On one hand they're making so many changes all the time, and on the other hand, they're not familiar with what and how the automation does, that it's really not practical from their side to know what can affect the automation and what doesn't.

Another problem that may probably happen if there's no one around with proper experience in test automation is that occasionally one or more tests will fail without a clear reason. The automation developer may first blame the tool, the network, or just the bad luck and try to run the test again. Alternatively, he may suspect that it's a timing issue and attempt to fix it by adding or increasing the delay between operations. Anyway, he runs the test again and it passes, hurray! But soon, besides the fact that the tests would be painfully slow due to the added delays, their overall stability will deteriorate and it'll become hard to tell the root cause of the failures. In this case, the entire value you are supposed to gain from the test automation is diminishing, as neither the automation developer nor the application developers can tell whether a failure is a bug in the product or in the automation. Eventually, this also leads to losing trust in the test automation.

If the automation developer is supposed to work on the automation only partially (e.g., 20%–50%) and keep doing manual tests the rest of the time, there are a few additional problems that would probably occur.

First of all, devoting a specific percentage of your job to one activity and another percentage to another activity is almost never practical. It's very hard to devote specific days of the week or long hour periods for one activity when you're in the same office with people that need your help in the other activity as well. And without dedicating specific days or hours, it's really hard to measure, both for you and for your manager, how much you really dedicate to test automation vs. how much you dedicate to the manual tests, which is always more urgent! In addition, specifically with test automation, writing the tests is only part of the job. At the minimum, you should also investigate the results and fix broken tests, and this takes time too. If you want to run the tests every night, the results must be investigated every morning! If you don't run the tests every night, then too many changes can take place between one run and the other, and it's harder to tell why something broke. If you fix or change something in the automation, you'll be able to tell whether your changes are correct only a few days later – will you remember what were you trying to fix, why and how? Probably not... It's also harder to make use and promote something that is not consistent. People (managers, developers, etc.) don't know whether to expect to get results from the automation or not, so they don't look for it, and therefore they don't pay too much attention to it anyway. Once again, the result is that people can't *rely* on the test automation and eventually lose trust in it.

Conclusion   People with some programming knowledge but no programming and automation experience may become effective test automation team members, but they need guidance! Test automation is a craft (discipline) of its own, requiring specific skills. It takes time, effort, and dedication to become good at it and therefore isn't something that can be done "on the side," even if you're the best developer ever

---

Splitting the Work Between Manual Testers and Automation Programmers

Another common approach is that few experienced developers develop the infrastructure and "building-blocks," and a bigger group of non-programmers or junior programmers use this infrastructure to create the automatic test scripts in a simpler manner. This approach has a tight relationship with the chosen tool, which can either be an off-the-shelf tool or a homegrown tool. Also, the kind of tool usually implies how much of the work can be done without writing code vs. how much requires coding.

I know quite a few teams that took this approach and are very happy with it. It allows you to involve all the original testers in the team in the automation project without having to teach them programming. In addition, the reality is that testers that don't write code are usually cheaper than programmers, and this also makes financial sense.

Later in this chapter I'll describe the categories of tools in more detail. And I will give a few examples for tools that support this approach. Most of these tools trade the need for writing code with the limitation to a specific way for interacting with the SUT. Examples of such tools are Ranorex® and SmartBear SoapUI®. While Ranorex works excellent with many UI technologies, it's not designed for any other kind of test. Soap UI, on the other hand, is dedicated only for testing systems by means of HTTP (and a few other) network communications protocols. Most of these tools allow both recording (whether of single steps or of an entire scenario) and/or manually composing and editing scripts, through an intuitive GUI or a simplified scripting language, which does not require real programming skills. They also typically provide some mechanisms that allow reuse of a set of actions, even though these are generally less flexible than true object-oriented code in that regard. These tools only require coding whenever you want to do something that the tool was not designed to do specifically. These tools typically come as a complete solution for managing the tests, executing them, creating reports, etc.

The ability to reuse composite actions and/or coded actions has another advantage besides the fact that it reduces the amount of work and maintenance: for every reusable component, you can give a descriptive name that describes what it does. This allows you to build the tests in a way that reveals your intent much more clearly, making the tests easier to maintain. In addition, you can use this technique to apply an approach called *Keyword Driven Testing* (or KDT in short). In this approach, the test scripts are composed only (or mostly) out of these reusable *building blocks* (or *actions*), each describing a *business action* rather than a fine-grained technical action. For example, an online-shopping scenario can be composed out of building blocks like "login," "add to cart," and "checkout." These building blocks can usually take arguments from the test script so that they can be used with different values or slightly different ways in different places. Because of the ability to use descriptive names, it makes the automated test scripts more *readable* and also easier to write and maintain. So even if a nontechnical business person looks at the test script, he can clearly see *what* it's supposed to do, without having to go into all the technical details of *how* these actions are performed. The names of the building blocks are sometimes referred to as "keywords" and therefore the name of this technique.

For some reason, I encountered quite a few companies that developed complete, sophisticated tools by themselves for this approach. Maybe the tools that were available when they started weren't appropriate.

Yet another variation on this is to write everything in code, but still spit the work between coders and non-coders, such that the coders create the "building blocks" as methods and the non-coders are only taught the bare minimum they need to know in order to call these methods from the tests.

Even though the KDT approach inherently takes advantage of reusability, its main drawback is the overhead and interdependency in the process of writing and maintaining the test automation suite as a whole. While composing test scripts out of predefined building blocks sounds very compelling, in reality the need to add or modify an existing building block is pretty frequent, which means that you can rarely write a test script without having to need a programmer to make a change or add a new building block first. But before the programmer can create or update the building block, he needs to know how you intend to use it, which you often know only when you start writing the test. In addition, the non-coder can only investigate failures up to a certain point, but if the problem lies inside the operation of a building block, then the programmer needs to continue the investigation too. Because the programmers that write building blocks are usually fewer than the number of testers that write the test scripts, these programmers become a bottleneck and potentially delay the process of writing and maintaining the tests.

Another issue that often happens in these cases is that in order to avoid the need to make changes to a building block, it's designed to be too generic. This can take a form of having too many parameters, or of having fewer parameters but that their values encapsulate a lot of information (e.g., using a comma-separated list) that can affect the behavior of the action in many ways. The use of such parameters may indeed minimize the required number of different building blocks, but is also very error-prone, and the person who writes the script should know the exact format of the data that the building block expects. At the end of the day, these "solutions" to the bottleneck problem end up making the test scripts more complex and confusing to write and maintain.

There's another category of tools that also makes a separation between the test scripts and their underlying implementation. Cucumber and SpecFlow are the common examples of tools that belong to that category (we'll talk more about in a later section). The main differences between this category and the previous one, is that these tools focus primarily on the *readability* of the tests, in order to use them primarily for documentation. Usually these tools are not technology specific, that is, they can be combined with other tools to provide abilities of UI automation, HTTP API (see sidebar later in this chapter), communication, or any other means for interacting with the SUT, though they require more coding than the tools in the first category. Because tools in this category also provide separation between the test scripts that don't require code writing and the implementation part that is purely code (and probably also because most of the tools are open source), many teams use them in order to apply a KDT approach, that is, allow non-coders to write the test scenarios and programmers to write building blocks. Unfortunately, while doing so they're missing the point of these tools, which is much more about making the scenarios *readable* as documentation, and less so to provide reusability. Advocates of the BDD approach (see later in this chapter) even say that the main purpose of these tools is to communicate the *requirements* in a verifiable way, and don't see testing as its main purpose. While there's a sweet spot where reusability and readability go together, if you'd try to stretch it too far to one direction, you'll compromise the other. In other words, the more you'd try to make the building blocks more reusable, eventually you'll compromise their readability and vice versa.

Using a Dedicated Automation Team

Probably the most common approach is to have a dedicated team (or one or two people if it's a small project) that is responsible for the test automation as a whole. The team members normally all write code and they're responsible for implementing the test scripts, the infrastructure and reusable code, as well as maintaining it, investigating the results, and improving the test automation system over time.

The big advantage of such a team is that they share knowledge and practices and reuse code without any boundaries. This is especially important at the beginning, as the infrastructure and practices are still being formed. Also, if the development teams are divided along the architectural and technology boundaries, like "client team," "server team," "DB team," etc., then it makes more sense to have a separate dedicated automation team that implemented end-to-end tests for the entire system. See Chapters 6 and 8 for more information about the relationships between test automation, business structure, and architecture.

On the other side, because this team is cohesive, they usually don't work very closely with the other developers. One of the consequences of this situation is that this team usually write tests after the features that they verify are done and pretty stable (after manual testers tested it at least once). Typically, they receive existing test scenarios that manual testers created beforehand and automate them, possibly after adapting them in one way or another for automation. However, this phase gap between the application developers and the automation developers yields some challenges:

1. If the code under test wasn't written in a testable way, it could be very difficult to automate it. In order to change this, the application developer should be interrupted from his current work and change the design of a feature he already implemented and that was even tested manually, which would very rarely happen...

2. Similar problems may occur if you find a bug at the time of implementing the automated test. If the manual tester already tested the feature, chances are that the bug you found is not critical, but it may impede you from implementing the automation properly. Again, the work of the application developer must be interrupted in order to fix this, and until this happens, the automation developer cannot continue working on that test.

Another drawback of this approach is that because the responsibility for investigating the failures is primarily of the automation team rather than the development teams, it may be very difficult to stabilize the tests. Every change that the application developers makes can potentially cause one or more tests to fail, and they usually won't care unless you prove that it's a bug. See Chapter 5 on the consequences of such business processes.

Having Dedicated Automation Developer(s) Inside Each Team

In development organizations where teams are organized around features rather than around technological or architectural boundaries, it often makes more sense to have one or two automation developers as part of each feature team. This is especially true if there's an organizational intent to cover every new feature (or User Story) with automated tests before declaring it done.

In this case, it's recommended that all the automation developers will have some formal means to share knowledge and code and ideas, and preferably there should be some senior automation developer who does not belong to any particular team, but his job is to provide guidance and supervise the work of the other automation developers from a professional standpoint.

Obviously, this approach does not fit well when automating existing, older manual test cases, as in this case there's no real collaboration between the automation developer and the application developer. If full coverage is still not in place, it can be useful to have a few automation developers work on the old tests, while other automation developers work inside the feature teams on new tests. See Chapter 4 on how to converge into full coverage while ensuring that new features are always covered.

In small organizations or teams, there can be one or two automation developers that work in conjunction with the application developers on the new features, while filling any gaps in regression tests in the remaining time.

The biggest advantage of this approach is that it's easy to keep the automation "green" as it's the responsibility of the entire team to deliver the new features with all tests working. In addition, writing the tests along with the development of a feature aids in ensuring that the application is testable.

Give the Developers the Ownership for the Automation

Some teams take the previous approach one step further and instead of having dedicated automation developers inside each feature team, they decide that the application developers will write and maintain the test automation. Traditionally developers do this with unit-tests (see Chapter 17), but there's no good reason why they can't do this with broader scoped tests too. In fact, the original advocates of the test-driven development (TDD) approach (namely Kent Beck and Martin Fowler) claim that they use the term "unit-tests" not only for a single class or method level tests but rather to test of any scope.[1]

---

[1]See the description of "sociable" tests at https://martinfowler.com/bliki/UnitTest.html. Other relevant references: https://martinfowler.com/articles/is-tdd-dead/ and http://www.se-radio.net/2010/09/episode-167-the-history-of-junit-and-the-future-of-testing-with-kent-beck/ (around minutes 22–26).

In my opinion this approach is excellent as long as all the developers (or at least a few from each team) have the necessary skills for writing good tests. The same way that some developers only specialize in "client" development and some only in "server" development, there are also "full stack" developers, and developers can have or not have the skills to write good tests.

In small organizations that have the adequate people, this can work out very well. However, I wouldn't easily recommend for a dev manager of a large organization to adopt this approach across the board, as not all teams may have people with the proper skills for that. My advice to that manager would be to find an expert (either external or internal to the organization) that can train and accompany **one team at a time** into this way of thinking and working. This is important because usually each team has different challenges and constraints, and a "one size fits all" approach can be very dangerous, leading to poor quality tests that are unreliable and harder to maintain. In addition, it is important to promote knowledge sharing and transfer among the teams, both in order to create consistent practices and to optimize the working processes, mainly through code reviews and pair programming.

The Variety of Tools

As already mentioned, I encourage you to choose the tool you need only after going through all the chapters in Part I of this book. However, now that we clarified that one of the most important considerations that affects the selection of the tools is how people are going to use them, we can start overviewing the variety of tools out there. Note that in most cases you'll end up using a combination of tools, as different tools answer different concerns, and together they provide the full solution. In many cases you'll also find that you need to build your own little tools (mainly for gluing other tools together),or forced to use some legacy homemade tools that were previously developed in your company. In the following sections, I'll classify the tools into categories, give a few examples, and discuss the considerations for choosing among them.

Classification of Tools

Before we go any further, I have to disclaim a few things. First, this classification is not conclusive or unquestionable, as many tools don't fall exactly into one category. Other people can classify the tools in a different manner. Even though some tools are similar, each has its unique features and characteristics, and many tools cover more than one concern and therefore can belong to more than one category. In general, most tools that don't require programming skills are more feature rich, while tools that require programming skills are often more targeted at a specific and narrow goal but are allowed to be combined with other tools easily.

Note that even though I'll give some concrete examples of popular tools in some of these categories, in no way does this aim to be a comprehensive list of all the tools in each category. The examples are mainly based on my own experience and knowledge, and I have no interest in promoting one tool over another. Finally and clearly, tools and technologies come and go. I guess that the concrete examples and specific feature descriptions will be outdated pretty soon after this book is published, but I also believe that in general, the classification itself and the main concepts will remain pretty much the same for a pretty long period.

IDEs[2] and Programming Language

Whether you choose to develop the automation by writing code or use a tool that is better suited for non-programmers, the automation developer will do most of his work inside an application that provides the main work environment. Using this tool, the automation developer will create and maintain the tests and mostly any other artifact that is part of the test automation system.

In case you've chosen to use tools that are better suited for non-programmers, these tools typically consist of their own specialized environment that is easier to learn and work with for non-programmers. So, in this case, there's usually no choice regarding the IDE, as it is simply the same application that provides the underlying technology that enables the test automation creation, editing, and running. However, note that even these tools usually either generate code in a general-purpose programming language that the automation developer can modify, and/or allow programmers to extend the automation by writing custom code modules. For that purpose, some of these tools provide their own IDE, but most simply allow the developer to use an external, common IDE (that are more programmer oriented) for editing these files.

---

[2]IDE is an acronym for *Integrated Development Environment*. These are applications that allow developers to write, edit, compile, and debug their code; and carry many other actions that are related to the development of the code.

If you plan to write the automation mainly in code, then you must decide also on the programming language. While most IDEs can work with multiple programming languages, and also most programming languages can be written using different IDEs, most programming languages have their own "natural" IDE. So, once you've chosen a programming language, choosing an IDE is usually pretty straightforward.

When it comes to choosing a programming language, there are a few considerations to take into account. First, while in most programming languages you can do pretty much everything you want, some other tools (e.g., for UI automation) work only with a specific programming language. For example, **Microsoft's Coded UI** only works with C# or VB.Net. You cannot write Coded UI tests in Java or Python. However, some tools, like **Selenium**, for example, are either supported by many different languages or have alternatives in other languages.

In case you're not restricted by the technology and you can choose among many programming languages, here are some considerations to take into account:

- First, it is highly recommended to use the same programming language that the other developers in the team use. For unit testing, this decision is obvious, both because it's the most straightforward way, and also because usually unit tests are written by the same developers that write the code of the system. However, this is recommended also for other types of automation tests. The main reasons for this is knowledge transfer, collaboration, and reuse of tools and utilities between the automation developer(s) and the product developers. I encountered a few companies where the sole automation developer chose to use a different language than the rest of the team (probably because he was more familiar with it), and later the company was "stuck" with that decision, having to go through various hoops in order to integrate it with the build system or other tools, sometimes after the original automation developer has already left the company. **Changing a programming language down the road is almost impossible!**

- Popularity – in most cases it is better to choose a popular, well-established language, than a niche one. Avoid choosing the "latest, newest, and coolest" language that very few have real experience with. (Also avoid choosing an anachronistic language for mostly the same reasons.) There are several reasons for that:

- Choosing a popular language will make it easier for you to recruit additional automation developers when necessary.

- It is easier to find help and tutorials on the internet, as well as frontal training.

- It has many more and better tools and libraries to choose from.

As of writing this book, the most popular programming languages are Java, C#, Python, and JavaScript. There's also an extension language to JavaScript called **TypeScript**, which is 100% compatible with JavaScript but adds a lot of important language features to it.

- Language features – while generally you can write any program in any programming language, and most languages have similar basic constructs (like "if" statements, variables, methods, etc.), each language has its own unique features as well as its limitations. These features and limitations can have a significant impact on the readability, reusability, and maintainability of your code! Some language features may come at the expense of other benefits that other languages might have. In particular, most languages have features that allow the programmers to *limit themselves from making mistakes*! While these features sometimes confuse junior programmers, it helps make the code much more reliable and robust by helping you to prevent mistakes. See the sidebar below for few examples of such language features.

LANGUAGE FEATURES COMPARISON

While this is not a comprehensive comparison between programming language features, it can give you an idea of what features exist in different programming languages and their benefits. Note that "languages features" are not the same as features of the core libraries of the language. While each language typically has its own set of core libraries that provide some basic services, like mathematical operations, lists, and common data structures, printing, file operations, date/time, etc., language features are more generic syntactic constructs that the compiler recognizes and that you can use to *structure* your code, regardless of what it actually *does*.

- *Strong typing* vs. *dynamic typing*. Strong typing means that the type of a variable or parameter must be explicitly declared, so the compiler can validate its correct usage right at compile time. In some languages, you can mix strong typing and dynamic typing. Java has only strong typing, C#, in mainly a strongly typed language but it also supports dynamic typing (via the dynamic keyword); Python and JavaScript only support dynamic typing. TypeScript also supports strong typing.

- *Encapsulation* – The ability to control the scope in which a variable or a method is accessible, usually by declaring members of a class as *public* or *private*. All object-oriented languages including Java and C# have this feature. So does TypeScript. JavaScript achieves this in its own unique way of declaring nested functions and declaring local variables in inner functions. Python doesn't have this feature.

- *Polymorphism or callback functions* – While polymorphism is considered one of the object-oriented tenants and callback functions are not, they enable more or less the same benefits. Simply put, it allows variables to reference data *as well as functionality*, and also to pass them to and from methods. This allows you to easily *extend the behavior* of the code without having to modify its core logic. All of the popular languages have at least one of these features. However, some scripting languages, especially languages that were created for a very specific purpose or tool, lack this ability.

- *Lambdas and closures* – This is the ability to define a method within another method, and to reference the local variables of the outer method from the inner method. Lambdas typically allow you to do the same thing using a shortened and more elegant syntax. C#, JavaScript, and TypeScript fully support closures. C#, TypeScript, and JavaScript ES6 also support the lambda syntax. Java and Python support the lambda syntax also, but their implementations of the closure concept are somewhat limited.

- *Multithreading* – The ability to execute code in parallel. While writing robust and reliable multithreading code is dead hard, and I encourage even experienced developers to avoid it if they have a choice, you can still take advantage of third-party libraries that use it. Java, C#, and Python all support it, but JavaScript doesn't. While JavaScript has some mechanisms that allow *concurrency* (using a concept called "promises"), it's not truly multithreaded. For that reason, if you use Selenium from JavaScript (WebDriverJS), your code becomes much more complicated and cumbersome, as well as more difficult to debug, relative to other languages. The *async and await* keywords, which are available in TypeScript and in JavaScript ES2017, make the problem somewhat less painful, but it still doesn't make Selenium code in JavaScript or TypeScript as easy to read and debug as in all other languages.

While Python has become pretty popular lately for test automation, probably due to its simplistic syntax and easy learning curve that helps non-developers get up to speed quickly, I typically don't recommend it due to the limitations mentioned above, though other considerations described above may tip the scales toward it. My own favorite programming language is C#, and that's the main reason I used it for the examples in part II, but I admit that it's mainly a matter of habit after all…

(Unit) Testing Frameworks

If you're writing the tests in code, you need a tool that will allow you to run the tests. While you can write all the tests as one simple command-line program that performs them in sequence and displays their results, a testing framework gives you an easy way to write and run individual tests. Then, either from a command line or a GUI tool, they allow you to see the list of tests, run them, and see which ones passed and which failed. Typically, you can select which tests to run: all, specific ones, or filter by various traits.

In addition, these tools also give you means by which you can ensure that tests don't interfere with one another, by writing special methods that get executed before and after each test, before and after a group of tests, and also before and after all the tests altogether. Some frameworks allow you to specify dependencies between tests, even though the benefit of such a feature is questionable, as it makes the tests serve two distinct purposes: initialization and testing, which don't go very well together and complicate their maintainability. In addition, it prevents running the dependent tests in parallel.

Testing frameworks are typically designed primarily for unit tests, but they suit just as well for integration or system tests. Therefore, don't panic by the term "unit test framework," which is normally used to describe these tools. Examples of such frameworks are: **JUnit** and **TestNG** for Java; **MSTest, NUnit, xUnit** for .Net; for Python you have the built-in **unittest** framework and **py.test**; and for JavaScript the most popular ones are **Jasmine** and **Mocha**.

All unit testing frameworks that I'm aware of are either part of an IDE or some a language development toolkit or are free open source projects. So, you don't have to worry about their price...

Note *Testing Framework* is sometimes also called *Test Harness*.

Assertion Libraries

In most frameworks, a test is considered "passed" as long as it doesn't throw an exception (i.e., as long as no errors have occurred when they run). However, a best practice is to perform some kind of verification at the end of the test, usually by comparing the actual result of the tested operation to a specific expected result. For that reason, most testing frameworks provide means to perform such verifications, using a simple mechanism called *assertions*. A typical Assert allows you to compare the actual result to an expected result, and to throw an exception in case the comparison failed, which consequently fails the tests. While most testing frameworks come with their own assertion methods, there are some dedicated assertion libraries that provide their own benefits. Some provide more specific assertion methods, for example, for validating HTTP response messages. Others are more extensible and allow you to define your own assertions, usually in a very readable and "fluent" manner.

Note Many testing frameworks also provide mocking mechanisms as well, and there are many third-party mocking libraries too. However, as these mechanisms are useful only for pure unit-tests, I see no point discussing these here. See Chapter 17 for more details about these mechanisms.

BDD-Style Frameworks

Behavior Driven Development (BDD) is a methodology that is derived from *Test Driven Development* (TDD, see Chapter 17), but adds to it an emphasis on bridging the gap between the natural language description of the behavior of a feature (which stands in place of formal specifications), and the tests that verify that the feature indeed behaves according to that description. For that reason, some call it *Executable Specifications*, or *Living Documentation*. Another aspect of this methodology is that the tests are used as the acceptance criteria of user stories, and therefore it is also called *Acceptance Test Driven Development* (ATDD). This methodology is covered in depth in Chapter 16.

The way this is normally achieved is using tools that allow us to write tests using sentences in natural language and map each sentence to a method that performs the operation described by that sentence. These sentences, along with their corresponding implementation methods, can be made reusable, which makes the documentation and the tests more consistent.

Simply put, BDD supporting tools provide a means to translate human readable specifications into executable code. The most popular BDD tool is **Cucumber**, which was initially developed in **Ruby**, and later was ported to many other languages, including Java and C# (where it is called **SpecFlow**). Cucumber uses a special language called *Gherkin* that consists of very few keywords followed by natural language sentences. Here's an example of a scenario in Gherkin:

```
Scenario: Cash withdrawal charges commission
      Given the commission for cash withdrawal is $1
      And I have a bank account with balance of $50
      When I withdraw $30
      Then the ATM should push out $30
      And the new balance should be $19
      And the charged commission should be $1
```

In the above example, the emphasized words ("Scenario," "Given," "And," "When," and "Then") are the Gherkin language keywords, and all the rest is a natural language. The methods are associated with these sentences using regular expressions, thus allowing you to specify parameters, like the amount values that appear in italic at the example.

Most BDD frameworks generate code for a skeleton of a unit test behind the scenes, using one of the existing unit-test frameworks, and using one of the popular programming languages. The generated unit test skeleton calls into other methods that *you* should implement, and each of them is associated with typically one natural language sentence in the Gherkin scenario, in order to do the actual work.

Another popular tool in this category is the Robot Framework. While the Robot Framework also supports Gherkin, it doesn't require you to do so. The Robot Framework comes with some built-in libraries for common actions, operations, and validations, and has a greater set of external libraries for various ways of interacting with the SUT (see the next section). And, of course, you can also write your own libraries in Python or Java.

Some other tools take a slightly different approach and try to provide means that allow you to incorporate the documentation inside the code of the test itself. Examples of such tools are RSpec for Ruby, Specturm for Java, MSpec for .Net, and also Jasmine and Mocha for JavaScript, which are also testing frameworks.

SUT Interaction Technologies

Whether you write the tests in code or another tool, the test must interact with the SUT somehow in order to test it. The most obvious way to do that is by simulating the user's interaction with the UI. But this is not always the best option (see Chapter 6 for more details about the pros and cons of testing through the UI). Sometimes you may prefer to interact with the SUT using HTTP, TCP/IP, or some other communication protocol; through the database; by creating, changing, or reading from files that the SUT uses; invoking command-line commands, etc. You can do most of these from code using standard APIs and libraries.

However, most UI technologies don't provide an easy-to-use API for simulating user actions, simply as the UI is intended to be used by the *user*, and not by another application... They sometimes provide such an API, but these are usually very low level, and not so easy to use directly from an automated test. In order to simulate user actions from the UI, you usually need a dedicated tool that is appropriate for automating the UI of that specific technology. The most well-known example of such tool is Selenium, which automates web-based UIs.

If you plan to interact with the SUT over HTTP and willing to write the automation in code, you can simply write your own code that sends requests and process responses just like any other client. This will give you the maximal flexibility and also the "feel" for what it takes to write a client application. However, because HTTP is a very popular way to interact with the SUT, there is a bunch of tools and libraries that aim to make it somewhat easier. Some of these tools are meant to be used from code (for example, **Rest-Assured** for Java), and some are stand-alone tools (for example, **SoapUI** by **SmartBear**). There are some tools whose main goal is to help sending and/or monitoring requests and see their responses through a UI, but also provide some means for creating macros or automated tests. However, because test automation is not their main goal, they're usually not the best suite for a full-blown test automation system. **Fiddler** and **Postman** are examples of such tools.

APPLICATION PROGRAMMING INTERFACE (API)

While most applications are designed to be controlled by users, through a *user interface*, some applications and software components are designed to be controlled by other applications (or software components). Also, many applications can be controlled both by users and by other applications. In order for an application to be controllable by other applications, it should expose an Application Programming Interface (API), which the other applications, which are the *clients* or *consumers* of the API, can use to control it. From a technology standpoint, APIs can come in many different shapes or forms, but conceptually, all APIs define the set of operations that the clients can invoke, along with their corresponding parameters, data structures, results etc. APIs should usually be well documented in order to make it easy for developers of client applications to use the API correctly, and to know what to expect from each operation. The technologies that facilitate applications to expose APIs can be categorized to these three main types:

1. Direct method calls – the application (or more typically a software component) provides a set of methods (and classes, in most modern technologies) that the client application can call directly, within the same process, similar to the way that the client calls its own methods.

2. Network communication protocol – the application defines a set of messages that it can exchange with the client, and their exact format. The application exposing the API typically runs as a separate process and often on a separate machine and can often serve multiple clients simultaneously. These days HTTP (or HTTPS to be more precise) is the most widely used base protocol upon which many applications expose APIs. These APIs typically define the format of the messages that it uses for requests and responses, according to an architectural style called REST (which stands for Representational State Transfer). They also typically use JSON (JavaScript Object Notation) as the underlying syntax for the data structures and message formats. A somewhat older style for HTTP APIs, which is still in pretty common use, is SOAP (Simple Object Access Protocol), which is based on the XML (Extensible Markup Language).

3. Remote Procedure Call (RPC) – this type of technologies is like a combination of the first two. With RPC, the application defines the operations it exposes through the API as a set of methods (procedures) and classes, similar to the

way it's done in the Direct Method Call. However, as opposed to direct method calls, RPC is used to call these methods from *remote* clients, in other processes and machines. The underlying RPC technology generates stub methods that the client can consume locally, which have the exact same signatures (method names and parameters) like the methods on the server that exposes the API. These stub methods serialize the name (or other identifier) of the method along with the values of its arguments into a message and sends it to the server over a network communication protocol (e.g., HTTP). Then at the server side, it parses the message and invokes the corresponding method along with its arguments. Windows Communication Foundations (WCF) can be used in an RPC fashion, Google provides the gRPC technology, and many services that expose REST API also provide a Language Binding for popular languages, which is the like the client-side only portion of RPC.

These three categories are only the main ones. An application can expose an API in other, less standard, ways too: for example, by reading and writing from a shared file, database, or any other mean that other applications can communicate with it.

APIs can be used for various purposes:

1. Operating Systems expose a rich set of APIs for its hosted applications. These APIs can be used to work with files, processes, hardware, UI, etc.

2. Reusable software components, or libraries, expose APIs that applications can use. Typically, this API is the only way to use these libraries. Such a library can be used, for example, for complex math operations, or to control some specific hardware device.

3. Plug-ins – some applications can be extended by third-party software vendors to provide more features for the application or integrate with other applications using plug-ins. For example, a text editor can expose an API that plug-ins can use for various purposes, like spell checking, integration with Source-Control systems, integration with email applications, and more. Sometimes the same API can be by the users to create macros, like Microsoft Office applications do.

4. Web services exposes APIs (typically REST APIs) to allow other applications to take advantage of it. For example, a weather forecasting website can expose an API that application vendors can use to integrate with it.

Record, Edit, Playback Tools vs. Code Libraries

Generally speaking, UI automation tools can be categorized either as "record & playback" tools or as mere code libraries that you can call from code. But in reality, it's more of a continuum rather than just these two categories. On one side of the continuum, we can find very "stupid" tools that record the mouse movements and clicks, and also the keyboard keystrokes, save them, and then let you play them back. Elders like me might remember the Macro Recorder tool that was included in Windows 3.1 back in the days... Fortunately, this tool is no longer part of Windows and similar tools are no longer popular. Needless to say, such naïve tools are very error prone, as they blindly replay the mouse and keyboard actions, without any notion whether something has moved, changed, etc.

At the other end of the spectrum, the operating system provides low-level APIs that let you interrogate the existing elements (or even pixels) that are displayed on the UI, and send messages to those elements, as if they were sent from the mouse or keyboard.

But there are many tools in between: first of all, most tools that record mouse clicks, don't just record the X and Y of the clicks or movements, but they rather try to identify the UI elements using one or more of their properties, preferably some kind of a unique identifier. In addition, they either generate code in a popular programming language that you can later edit, adopt, and maintain for your needs; or they generate a more high-level script, which is more oriented toward non-programmer, and that you can edit using a dedicated editor of the tool itself.

Note that almost all UI automation tools are either bundled with a tool that lets you inspect the elements in the UI of your application, and their properties, or is designed to be used in conjunction with an existing tool, usually supplied with an SDK of the relevant OS, which does the same thing. Here's a short description of some popular UI automation tools.

Selenium

This is probably the most popular test automation tool and is mostly suited for UI automation on web applications. Like all UI automation tools, Selenium allows us to mimic mouse and keyboard actions on behalf of the user and retrieve data that is displayed. Selenium has a few important advantages that make it so popular:

- It's open source (and therefore free);
- It supports a very wide range of browsers;
- It's available in many programming languages.

Selenium's main drawback is that it's designed primarily for browsers and has only a limited support for other UI technologies through external extensions. In addition, it is mainly designed to be used from code.

In order to allow the versatility of browser and also of programming languages, it is composed of two parts, each of which is interchangeable. These parts are:

1. Language binding

2. Browser driver

The language binding is the code library that provide the classes and methods that you can use from the code of your tests. Theses libraries are either compiled as in Java and C#, or pure source code libraries as in Python or JavaScript. A different language binding exists for every supported programming language.[3] This part communicates with the Browser driver using a dedicated JSON wire protocol.

The browser driver receives the requests from the language binding and invokes the relevant operations on the browser. Each type of browser has its own browser driver. However, because all drivers "understand" the same JSON wire protocol, the same test can be used with a different driver and corresponding browser.

Note   Even though the language binding communicates with the driver over HTTP, this communication has nothing to do with the communication that goes between the browser and the server of the web application.

Selenium's language binding is not a testing framework but rather a mere code library. Therefore, you can use it from any type of application, even though it is most commonly used from one of the unit testing frameworks.

---

[3]Some languages are compiled into byte-code that is run by a dedicated runtime engine. The Java Virtual Machine (JVM) and .Net Common Langauge Runtime (CLR) are the most known ones. Libraries that are compiled for these engines can be consumed by applications that are written in any language that can also be compiled for the same engine. So, for example, the WebDriver library for Java can be consumed by tests written in Scala and Groovy, and the C# (.Net) binding can be consumed by tests written in VB.Net and F#.

The flexible architecture of Selenium allows other special tools to be integrated with it, including Selenium Grid, which allows on-site cross-browser testing, and also various vendors of cloud-based testing, like BrowserStack and SauceLabs. In addition, Appium also takes advantage of this flexible architecture to allow mobile testing using the familiar Selenium API.

Figure 3-1 demonstrates the typical architecture of a test that uses Selenium.

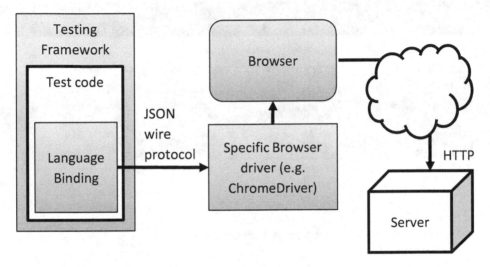

Figure 3-1. *Typical architecture of Selenium-based test automation*

WHAT'S SELENIUM WEBDRIVER?

Without diving into too much detail, Selenium 1.0, also called *Selenium RC* (or *Selenium Remote Control*), was the original technology for automating web UI. In version 2.0 it was merged with another technology called *WebDriver*, and together formed "*Selenium WebDriver*," which is the popular technology that is widely used in recent years. Note that today the terms "Selenium" and "WebDriver" are often used interchangeably.

As mentioned above, UI automation tools usually come with an inspection tool for identifying UI elements and their properties. Selenium does not come with such a tool, as all modern browsers have such a tool built in. All modern browsers have built-in developer tools (usually opened by pressing F12). The developer tools include the DOM[4] explorer, which allows you to identify the elements and their properties. Figure 3-2 shows the DOM explorer in Chrome.

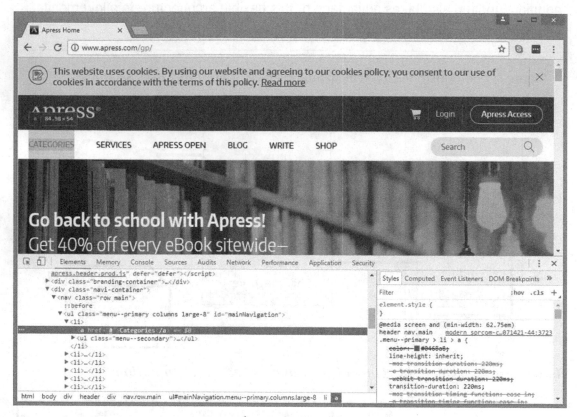

Figure 3-2. *Chrome's DOM Explorer*

Selenium IDE

Selenium also provides a dedicated plug-in for FireFox, called *Selenium-IDE*. This plug-in allows recording test cases, and basic management and editing of these test cases without writing code. It also allows exporting the tests to code in Ruby, Java, or C#, using a variety of popular testing frameworks. While these features are nice, this tool is rarely considered as a viable professional test automation tool. As of August 2017, Selenium

---

[4]DOM is an acronym for *Document Object Model*. The DOM describes the tree of HTML elements and their properties at any given moment. Using JavaScript, the page itself can manipulate its DOM at runtime, making the page dynamic. Note that while the DOM can change, the HTML is the *static* description of the page as the server sent to the browser.

team has announced in their blog[5] that Firefox 55 will no longer support the Selenium IDE, and at least for now, it will no longer be developed or maintained. Figure 3-3 shows the UI of Selenium IDE.

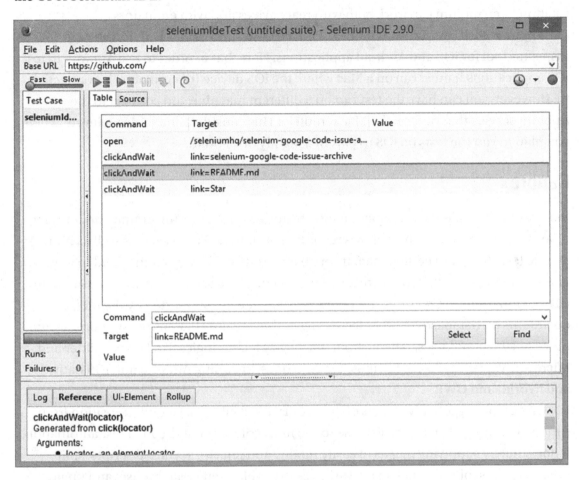

Figure 3-3.   *Selenium IDE*

Appium

Appium is an extension to Selenium WebDriver, which allows UI automation for mobile applications on Android, iOS, and also Windows 10 applications. For the latter, it supports both Universal Windows Platform (UWP) and classic Win32 applications. Like Selenium, Appium is designed to be used directly from code. Appium supports both native mobile apps as well as mobile web apps and hybrid apps. As long as the

---

[5]https://seleniumhq.wordpress.com/2017/08/09/firefox-55-and-selenium-ide/

application is similar on different platforms, the code of Appium tests can be reused for these platforms. Appium can be used through the existing WebDriver APIs, but also extends it with some mobile-specific capabilities, like touch gestures, orientation, and rotation, etc. Appium can work both with real devices and with emulators.

Appium itself can run on Windows, Linux or Mac, and comes with its built-in inspector tool for iOS and Android applications. Note that in order to use Appium to test iOS applications it must run on a Mac where the iOS device (or emulator) is connected to. However, you can have the test run on a different machine and connect to the Appium service that runs on the Mac remotely. This consideration is also relevant when you plan to run the tests on iOS as part of a nightly or CI build.

Ranorex

Ranorex is a complete UI automation tool, featuring an IDE, testing framework, runner, reporting, and more. Ranorex allows recording of complete test cases, as well as more atomic test steps, and editing them through an intuitive UI (without the need to write or edit code). However, it does create C# code behind the scenes, and allows us to write custom functions in C# as well, for operations that are not supported by the tool, like operations on databases or other technologies that are not UI. Ranorex supports a wide range of UI technologies, ranging from old, legacy technologies like PowerBuilder and Microsoft Visual FoxPro, to the most modern ones, including Android and iOS native and hybrid, and UWP.

One of the biggest advantages of Ranorex is that it allows a smooth transition from simple recording of an entire test case to the most complex hand-coded test automation. It does that by supplying means to easily modify and refactor recorded scripts, split them into reusable modules, using variables to enable even greater reuse, and finally also converting small pieces to code as needed. You can even use Ranorex as an API that you can consume from any .Net language (e.g., C#) and combine it with another testing framework of your choice.

Ranorex provides a built-in inspection tool, which also provide a nice abstraction over different UI technologies. This tool works closely with the Object Repository feature that allows you to manage all the UI elements in a hierarchical order. The Object Repository uses a special variant of the XPath[6] syntax, called *RXPath* and allows us to edit it in a smart and interactive way.

---

[6]https://www.w3schools.com/xml/xpath_intro.asp

While Ranorex has supported UI automation for browsers from the very beginning, starting at version 7.0, Ranorex also supports Selenium WebDriver as a separate UI technology, allowing to take advantage of the rich ecosystem of Selenium, including Selenium Grid, and the various cloud testing vendors like SauceLabs and BrowserStack.

Microsoft Coded UI

Microsoft Coded UI is a set of technologies that provide UI automation, mainly for Windows application and the variety of Microsoft's UI technologies, including Win32, Windows Presentation Foundations (WPF), Silverlight, Microsoft Store Apps, Universal Windows Platform (UWP), etc. It also supports Web applications, but I find no significant benefit using Coded UI over Selenium for this case. Probably the biggest advantage of Coded UI is its integration with Visual Studio and Microsoft Team Foundation Server (TFS). In fact, Microsoft Coded UI is part of Visual Studio Enterprise, and not a product on itself.

Similar to Ranorex, Coded UI allows you to work in a variety of styles, ranging from pure recordings to pure code. Unfortunately, unlike Ranorex, it doesn't provide a smooth path between the different styles. The main reason for that is that the means it provides for editing recordings without going into code are pretty limited. However, if you need to automate Windows application in C# or VB.Net, and you're willing to write the automation in code, then this is a very viable alternative. Even though the API that Coded UI provides is not very intuitive and friendly, it does provide pretty good control. For that reason, I created a wrapper to Coded UI with a more convenient API, called TestAutomationEssentials.CodedUI (see Appendix C), which is available on GitHub and as a NuGet package.

Coded UI's test framework is based on MSTest. When you create a new Coded UI project from Visual Studio, it creates a skeleton of a test class, and a **UIMap.uitest** file. The UIMap.uitest file stores the recordings and elements that you identify using the built-in Coded UI Test Builder tool. The UIMap.uitest designer is shown in Figure 3-4. Using the designer, you can edit and make some basic modifications to the recordings and to the way elements are identified. In fact, behind the scenes this file is stored as an XML file, and every edit made to it using the designer also generates a **UIMap.Designer. cs** (C#) file. Because the C# file is regenerated with every change to the designer, it's not safe to edit the C# file yourself. However, the designer lets you move complete recordings to a separate file (UIMap.cs) so that it won't be overridden by the designer. Unfortunately, this operation is only one-way: from this moment on, you don't see the recording in the designer and can only edit it through C# code editor.

Note   You can create multiple UIMap files in a single Coded UI Test project, to make the maintenance of large Coded UI projects easier.

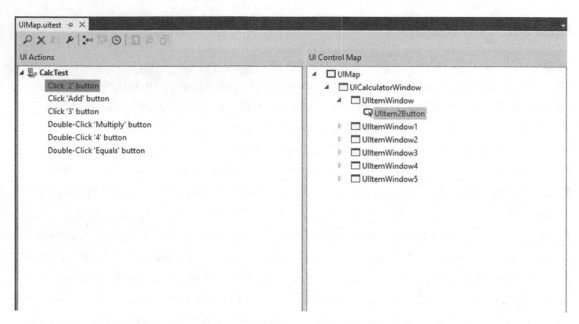

Figure 3-4. *The UIMap.uitest designer*

If you're writing the test in code, then instead of the Coded UI Test Builder, you can use the Inspect.exe tools that ships with the Windows SDK. This tool is a bit more fine-grained and sometimes provides more detailed and accurate information about the properties of UI elements.

Microsoft Visual Studio Test Professional and Coded UI

Another interesting use case that Microsoft provides is to record actions as part of a manual test, using the Microsoft Visual Studio Test Professional (Also known as *Microsoft Test Manager,* or *MTM*). Microsoft Visual Studio Test Professional allows you to record steps of a manual test case, and replay then the next time you execute the test. Then, if you create a Coded UI test project, it allows you to import these recordings into the UIMap file, and continue to edit them from Visual Studio. However, this operation is also unidirectional: while you can overwrite the recording with a new one and use it to regenerate the recording in the UIMap, if you edit the recording thought the UIMap designer, it won't update the recording that Microsoft Visual Studio Test Professional is using. Obviously, because you don't have much control over the recording that Microsoft Visual Studio Test Professional generates, in most cases it doesn't make for a reliable and viable tool for test automation, other than maybe saving some time to manual testers, given that the recordings stays stable without any intervention. This however is a pretty rare situation in most modern and dynamic applications.

Unified Functional Testing (UFT)

UFT, formerly known as QuickTest Professional (QTP), is probably the most veteran UI automation tool in the market. QTP was first released by Mercury Interactive in May 1998, and was acquired by HP in 2006. HP changed its name to UFT in 2012. As it was the first and dominant player in the market until recent years, it was a pretty expensive product, and was mainly used by big companies that could afford it.

UFT allows to record and edit UI operations on many applications and UI technologies including WPF, Java, SAP, Mainframe terminal emulators and many more. It provides a "keyword view" where one can edit the recorded script in a grid-like view, without having to write code. Behind the scenes UFT generates VBScript code, which you can also edit directly in an "Expert view" and the changes are synchronized back to the Keyword view.

In 2015 HP released a new, more modern product called LeanFT, which is more oriented toward developers and professional automation developers, in which it allows the tests to be written also in Java or C# using all of the common testing frameworks. LeanFT also provide better integration with source-control systems, common build systems, and a much more compelling price.

SoapUI

Unlike all the above mentioned tools, SoapUI by SmartBear is not a UI automation tool, but rather a HTTP API automation tools. It supports record, edit and playback of HTTP communications (REST or SOAP). There are two versions of SoapUI: the open-source (free) version and the Pro version, which is also part of the ReadyAPI suite. The Pro version adds many productivity enhancements, refactoring, additional protocols, libraries and more.

SoapUI uses the Groovy programming language which is a dynamic language compatible with Java. In addition to sending and receiving HTTP messages, SoapUI can create mocks for web services (AKA *Simulators*, see Chapter 6 for more details), and is suited also for Load testing (see chapter 18 for more information on Load testing).

Test Management Suites

This category of tools is usually not specific to automated tests, but rather to testing activities and testing processes in general. However, these tools often have some features related to test automation and automated tests can be integrated and managed by them.

These tools typically allow managing suites of tests, scheduling of tests, test results and provide reports, graphs and trends for management. Automated tests can usually be attached or be related to a test case, and their results can be automatically reported to these tools. These tools usually manage or closely integrate with another tools that manages bugs and other Application Lifecycle Management (ALM) artifacts like requirements, versions, milestones, etc. The most popular tools in this category are Microsoft Visual Studio Test Professional (part of Microsoft TFS), and HP's Quality Center.

Build Tools and CI/CD Pipelines

This last category of tools is an entire domain in and on itself, and most of it is beyond the scope of this book. However, these tools play a very important role with regard to test automation. These tools are used to run the tests in a centralized way, usually after compiling and deploying the product. Running the tests in a centralized way (as opposed to running them on any developer machine) ensures that the tests passes on a clean environment without any dependencies or presumptions that might be true only on that specific developer's machine. Typically automated tests run either on a scheduled nightly build, or on a continuous integration (CI) build, which is trigged by every check-in of every developer, possibly preventing broken code from entering the source-control repository

Today, most of these tools allow to define a pipeline of a broader scope, which sometimes include manual steps, in which a build advances in a pipeline through various tests and possibly manual approval processes, until it is published to production. This approach is known as *Continuous Delivery* (CD). The same approach, but without manual approval steps is called *Continuous Deployment*. For more details about CI/CD see Chapters 5 and 15.

The most popular tools today in this category are Jenkins, Microsoft Team Foundation Server (and its online version Team Foundation Services), JetBrain's TeamCity and Atlassian's Bamboo.

Other Considerations for Choosing Tools

Obviously the first consideration for choosing an automation tool, is to ensure that it can interact with our SUT. In addition, we already talked in the beginning of the chapter about the importance of matching the tool to the skillset that you expect the automation developer to have and how you're going to use it in your organization. And finally, you probably want that all of the tools that you choose play well together. Finally, there's one more important aspect that you should consider: *pricing and licensing*.

Allegedly, there's not much to say about pricing, as we all prefer to pay less than more... And I'm not going to tell you that cheap is eventually expensive or other similar clichés, as this is not the point here. In fact, the most significant price you're going to pay for the test automation project derives from the quality of the work that the automation developers will do, and much less from all the other factors. However, there's one important aspect for pricing and licensing that you might not consider at the beginning of a test automation project, but later it can have a significant impact on the way you use it:

When you have only one, or a few people that develop the automation, the price of the tools that they use doesn't play a significant role. But as mentioned in Chapter 1, the automation is best used if you give the developers the ability to run the tests before checking-in their changes. If you want to get to that at some point, you'd want that *all of the developers* will use the automation tool! For that reason, you should seriously consider using *cheap* tools or at least tools whose licenses structure won't restrict you when time comes to use it widely.

CHAPTER 4

Reaching Full Coverage

Before getting into the more concrete and interesting stuff of good practices for building a reliable and maintainable test automation, let me set the stage by discussing the goal that many people aim for: reaching full coverage.

Often, people that don't have any background about test automation think that within a few weeks to a few months, it will be possible to automate all of their manual test cases, covering the entire functionality of their relatively complex product. Obviously, the complexity of each product is different, and in some cases it's possible to reach this goal, but usually, after starting to implement a few test cases, they realize that it takes much longer to build a single automated test case than what they originally thought, and the goal of reaching full coverage looks way farther than they originally thought. There are many reasons that can cause the first tests to take a lot of time, including lack of skills, investing more time in the foundations, but also because like any software, there are many nitty-gritty details that must be flushed out in order to make it work. Clearly, it may be faster if they use recording techniques, but as we've already discussed previously, the price of this saved time will most probably be paid in the form of reliability and maintainability of the tests. However, if the automation is built wisely, then the pace of adding the first tests will probably be pretty slow, and even though after a while it will usually accelerate significantly, the goal of reaching full coverage still looks pretty far away than the original plan. In many projects, reaching full coverage can take years! This gap in expectations can cause a lot of frustration for management, and they can eventually cancel the entire automation project if they run out of budget or can't justify it.

But the gap in expectations is not the only problem. During the long period it takes to reach full coverage, the development team doesn't stand still. They keep adding more and more features, and more and more test cases that needs to be automated to cover these new features too! So now the questions become: Does adding new automatic tests take more time than adding new features to the product, or less? Obviously, this can vary from feature to feature, but we need to look at the overall picture. In many cases, test

© Arnon Axelrod 2018
A. Axelrod, *Complete Guide to Test Automation*, https://doi.org/10.1007/978-1-4842-3832-5_4

automation projects start with very few automation developers compared to the number of product developers, so it looks reasonable that the automation pace will be slower. Also, in many cases when a test automation project starts, the automation developers belong to a different team than the product developers (often the automation developers belong to the QA team, as opposed to the development team). But why does it matter at all to compare their progress pace?

Here's why: if the pace of adding new automatic tests is slower than the pace in which the product developers add new features, it means that the gap just gets bigger and bigger over time. So, if for example, you currently have 10% coverage (regardless of how you measure it), then a year from now, even though the number of tests will increase, their percentage will be *lower than 10%*, and every subsequent year it will go further down. This means that the relative value of the test automation will decrease over time instead of increase. Therefore, if we don't consider closing this gap by putting more people to beef up the automation efforts, then we should reconsider the efforts we put into the test automation in the first place!

This seems like a huge investment that will only show its real fruits in a few years, when that automation will be able to replace all of the manual regressions tests. The good news is that later in this chapter I'll show you how you can gain value from the automation pretty much from the beginning of the project, while gradually and slowly closing the gap. If you focus on providing this value in the beginning, it will be easier and even obvious to justify the investment over time.

How Do You Measure Coverage?

Anyway, if we want to reach 100% coverage, we must ask ourselves first, how do we measure it? 100% of what? The three most common metrics that attempt to answer this question are:

1. Percentage of manual test cases covered by automation

2. Percentage of covered features

3. Percentage of code coverage

Let's analyze the true meaning of each of these metrics:

Percentage of Manual Test Cases Covered by Automation

If you convert the manual tests to automated tests as is, then you may be able to say that you reached 100% when done. However, in this metric, 50% doesn't mean that 50% of the work was done, as some tests may be much simpler and shorter than others. In addition, as discussed in detail in Chapter 2, manual tests rarely fit automation as is and they need to be broken into a few tests, changed, and occasionally merged in order to be converted into properly maintainable and reliable automated tests. And, of course, some tests, like tests that verify that the user experience is appropriate, are not adequate for automation whatsoever, and *should* remain manual.

But besides all of that, there's a big assumption here. In order to use this metric in the first place, we have to assume that the manual test scenarios actually cover 100% of what there is to cover. Especially in legacy applications, this is not always true. This brings us to the second metric.

Percentage of Covered Features

Whether we're talking about manual or automatic tests, how can we measure how much of the functionality of the system, or features, they cover? Well, it depends on how you count "features" and how do you measure a coverage of one feature. Suppose that you have a list of features that were developed (e.g., in TFS, Jira, Excel, or any other way) and a description of these features, and you also have a list of test cases that are related to these features (probably managed using the same tool). In this case it's easy to say that any feature that doesn't have any associated test, is not covered. However, does it mean that those who have at least one associated test *are covered*? Probably not... The case may be that one simple feature may have 10 comprehensive tests, but another very complex feature may have only one minimalistic test...

In addition, these lists of features (however they are managed) rarely reflect the true functionality accurately. They're either written before the functionality was implemented and document the *intent* of the customer or product manager, or they were written a while after the fact in order to document what has been done. In the first situation, it's possible that during the implementation of the feature, decisions were taken to change some things in the original plan due to conflicts or obstacles that were encountered. Unless you're in the medical business or other business with very strict regulations, chances are that these decisions were made verbally and the document wasn't updated accordingly (maybe even the developer took the freedom to take these decisions on his own). The second situation where the documentation is written after the fact usually happens when the development has started without properly managing any documentation, and one day someone decides that it's needed. At that point the documentation is written to explain how the system works. In this case the documentation will probably reflect the real state of the system, but there's no practical way to ensure that it really covers everything that was developed! It's possible that there are some "hidden" features that the person who writes the documentation is not aware of or simply forgot about, while real users may still use it.

So let's look at a much more objective measurement: code coverage.

Percentage of Code Coverage

Almost any programming language or runtime technology today (.Net, JVM, etc.) has tools that allow us to intercept some pieces of executable code (DLLs, JAR, EXE, etc.) to detect at runtime whether each line or segment of code was executed or not. After you instrument the executable code, you can run the tests and get a report about which, and how many lines of code were executed and which weren't. This technique is known as *code coverage* and is a very objective and accurate measurement. Most people think that code coverage is good only for unit tests, as they call the instrumented modules directly. But most code coverage tools can be used for any type of test, even manual! Usually the instrumented module does not care from where it is called and which process hosts it.

Measuring code coverage as a metric is great, but what's more important is the analysis of the uncovered areas. Generally speaking, when you discover a line or an area in the code that is not covered, you should either add new tests to cover it, or delete that code if you come to the conclusion that it's not being used (AKA "dead code"). Getting even close to 100% code coverage builds great confidence that the tested code is pretty close to being bug free! Having a high-code coverage provides a comfortable ground for refactoring and improving the inner code quality.

However, code coverage also has its drawbacks:

1. While this measurement is pretty accurate, and it's easy to see the coverage percentage, it's more difficult to get the true meaning about the uncovered areas. In order to understand what functionality is covered and which isn't, you must dive deeply into the code. This is not something that managers can usually reason about.

2. There are few techniques that code coverage tools use in order to measure code coverage, and each measures slightly different things: some simply detect whether a line of code was executed or not. But sometimes a single line can contain several code segments that each may be executed independently from the others. Here's a simple example for this:

    ```
    if (x > 10) DoOneThing() else DoAnotherThing();
    ```

    So another measurement technique counts control-flow *branches* rather than lines. There are a few other techniques and nuances that some tools use, but the bottom line is that there can be slightly different meanings to the exact "Percentage of code coverage" depending on the technique that the tool uses.

3. Suppose that we've managed to get to 100% code coverage, and all tests pass. It's still doesn't mean that we have no bugs. Don't get me wrong: it's a wonderful place to be in! The chances to find bugs in this situation is wonderfully low, but still it's not zero. The fact that all lines were executed doesn't mean that they were executed in all possible sequences and paths. Listing 4-1 is a simplified example of such case. As you can grasp from this example, Test1 and Test2 cover all lines (and branches) of ClassUnderTest as they exercise both the "then" part of the "if" statement in ClassUnderTest.Foo, and also the "return 1" statement that gets executed if the "if" condition is not met. Also, both of these tests should pass. However, if we'd add a test that calls Foo(1), then a DivideByZeroException will be thrown. If this is not what the user expects, then we have a bug although we have 100% code coverage. Another, even simpler example, is that the tests exercise 100% of the code, but some of them don't verify the right thing, or don't verify anything at all! (i.e., they assert the wrong thing, or have no Assert statement at all).

Listing 4-1. Code with 100% code coverage that still has a bug in it

```
[TestClass]
public class Class1
{
        [TestMethod]
        public void Test1()
        {
                var result = ClassUnderTest.Foo(3);
                Assert.AreEqual(50, result);
        }

        [TestMethod]
        public void Test2()
        {
                var result = ClassUnderTest.Foo(-1);
                Assert.AreEqual(1, result);
        }
}

public class ClassUnderTest
{
        public static int Foo(int x)
        {
                if (x > 0)
                        return 100 / (x - 1);

                return 1;
        }
}
```

4. Sometimes a programmer writes some lines of code that may be
    executed only in extremely rare cases, usually external errors that
    may be very hard to simulate in a lab environment. In addition,
    there are cases (which are rare but do exist) that the code coverage
    tool will consider a line of code as uncovered even though it's not
    reachable, yet cannot be deleted. For example, in Listing 4-2, some

tools will report the closing line in ClassUnderTest.Foo as well as the closing brace of the try block in CheckIfFooThrewException as uncovered. For these reasons it's usually impractical to get to 100% code coverage.

Listing 4-2. Uncovered lines that cannot be deleted

```
[TestClass]
public class CodeCoverageTests
{
    [TestMethod]
    public void FooWithTrueDoesNotThrow()
    {
        bool exceptionThrown = CheckIfFooThrewException();
        Assert.IsTrue(exceptionThrown);
    }

    private bool CheckIfFooThrewException()
    {
        bool exceptionThrown = false;
        try
        {
            ClassUnderTest.Foo();
        } // this line is not covered
        catch
        {
            exceptionThrown = true;
        }
        return exceptionThrown;
    }
}

public class ClassUnderTest
{
    public static void Foo()
    {
        ThrowException();
    } // this line is not covered
```

```
private static void ThrowException()
{
    throw new Exception("Boom!");
}
```
}

CORRECTNESS PROVING

As the famous computer scientist Edsger Dijkstra wrote back in 1970: "Program testing can be used to show the presence of bugs, but never to show their absence!"[1] The reason for that boils down to the notion that testing can only prove that *specific examples* work correctly, and not that the program works correctly *in all cases*.

I recall from my Computer Sciences studies that we've been taught to prove the correctness of algorithms or pieces of code. For example, we learned to prove that the Merge Sort algorithm correctly sorts any array of any length, with any numbers as its elements (given some assumptions). Unlike testing, this proof holds true for *any valid input*! Theoretically you can prove the correctness of the entire code in your system, thus not having to use tests at all! But clearly, for any real-world application, this is way impractical. Moreover, a proof is bound to a specific implementation. Suppose that we've proven the correctness of one version of the application, then any change we make to the code we must prove its correctness again (at least for the module that has been changed), which is again, impractical.

To conclude: there's no one right way to measure the coverage of the tests, and each metric has its drawbacks. But if you add some common sense to any of these metrics, you'll be able to get a rough estimation about your progress in the journey to cover the application with automated tests.

---

[1]Dijkstra (1970). "Notes On Structured Programming" (EWD249), Section 3 ("On the Reliability of Mechanisms").

Gaining Value Before Reaching Full Coverage

So by now we can agree that:

1. It will take long to close the gap and reach full coverage.

2. Even though it may take very long, it's still important that we'll be minimizing the gap between new features and covered features over time, and not increasing it.

In order to minimize this gap, you'd probably need more people writing tests, and that costs money that probably your boss won't be willing to pay. At least not yet. But don't worry: we can get high value from the automation long before closing the gap, and if this value will be visible to your boss, convincing him to put more money on it will be a no brainer. In order to understand what the value that we can gain while having only a partial coverage, let's first understand the full value that we will gain once we actually reach the full coverage goal.

What Do We Do When We Have Full Coverage?

Let's suppose for a moment that we've got 100% coverage and all tests pass! What do we do the morning after opening the champagne to celebrate the event (and after the hangover wore off)?

If at this point we'll declare the automation project "done" and lay off all of the automation developers, then when new features will be added, the coverage percentage will drop again below 100%, not because we have less automation, but because we now have more features! So we're not really done after all. Also, if one or more tests break due to a change in the application, we want to ensure that the tests are immediately fixed. What we really want to make sure the morning after we've reached 100% coverage of passing tests is that we just keep this state. In fact, this is the ideal state that is described in Chapter 2, in the section titled "Getting the Most Out of Test Automation."

Keeping 100% coverage means that:

1. New tests must be developed for each new feature

2. Every change that breaks existing tests must be fixed ASAP

Also, in order to keep all the tests passing, when a test fails due to a real bug, then this bug must also be fixed ASAP. And in this state, it's pretty straightforward to do: after all, this bug was caused by the most recent check-ins. At this stage, the developers have the code fresh in their heads. Also, it will be ridiculous to declare that a user story is done when it just broke something that previously worked. Therefore, it only makes sense to simply fix it immediately.

Anyway, in terms of throughput, after we've reached 100% coverage, we must be able to add tests *faster* than we're adding new features in order to keep having 100% coverage. If we should be able to add tests faster than adding features *after* we've reached 100% coverage, let alone we must be able to do that long before!

How Do We Get to 100% Coverage?

Let's take one step backwards in time. Suppose that we started the automation project a year ago, and at that time we had 100 test cases to cover (however we measure it). Now, a year later, we've covered all of these 100 tests and all of them pass. Does it mean that we now have 100% coverage? Only if 90% of the developers went on a year-long vacation… (Sounds fun!), and the rest 10% stayed just to fix bugs (not fair!). What's more likely happened is that new features were added to the product throughout this year, so now we have X more test cases to cover. If X is greater than 100 (let's say 150), then it will take us an additional 1.5 years to cover them too, but by the time we'll do it, we'll have additional 225 uncovered tests… This is when the gap just gets bigger and bigger. Figure 4-1 demonstrates this situation. If X is exactly 100 (i.e., exactly the number of test cases that we've managed to automate last year), then next year we'll finish covering those new 100, having a total of 200 automated test cases, but then we'll probably have an additional 100, meaning that the gap remains constant. In this case we can keep forever, like a pipeline, but we'll never really get to 100% coverage. Figure 4-2 demonstrates this situation. So once again, if we want to get to 100% coverage, we must develop and stabilize automated tests faster than new features are added, as shown in Figure 4-3.

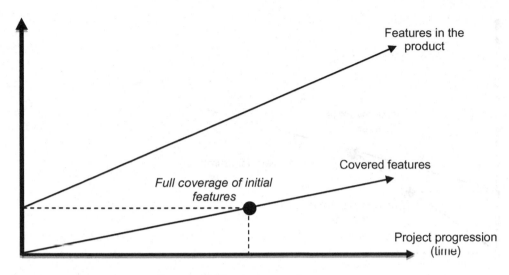

Figure 4-1. *Growing gap between features and coverage*

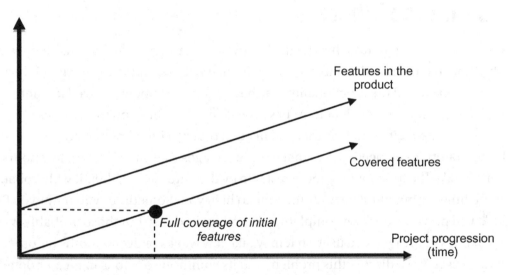

Figure 4-2. *Constant gap between features and coverage*

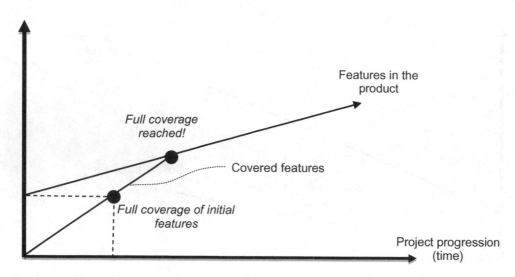

Figure 4-3. *Closing the gap between features and coverage*

Reversing the Wheel

One important thing to note is that the further the development of the automated tests from the time that the functionality was developed, the harder and less efficient it is. The person who developed the functionality may have left the company, moved to another job, or just forgot most of the details. At best, he's simply too busy on the next task to help you with some "negligible" details that you need in order to implement your automated test. If, for example, you need him to make some changes that should take a few hours, in order to make the functionality more testable by the automation, then it will probably take some time for him until he finds the time to help you. Sometimes you may even find bugs that will prevent you from completing the automated test, but those probably won't be critical bugs in the eyes of a user, so it may take few weeks or even months before someone fixes it. We'll discuss this problem and its common solutions in greater detail in the next chapter.

By contrast, when an automated test is developed hand in hand with the development of the functionality that it tests, then the collaboration between the application developer and the automated developer will be much better, yielding a better automation in much less time! But this also have other, even more important benefits:

1. Because it's much easier to test smaller and simpler components, than monolithic, "spaghetti" code, designing for testability implies design for modularity, extensibility, and reuse. Developing the tests and the functionality together forces these design traits, which eventually benefits the overall design of the system

2. Having to design and implement an automated test requires that all of the relevant details will be well-defined and clear. This often raises questions and issues about the expected behavior of the feature and may find bugs even before the feature was implemented!

3. Most bugs in the implementation of the new feature will be caught and fixed by the application developer before he even checked-in his code! While it is highly recommended that the manual tester will still verify that the functionality behaves correctly at least once (providing one more safety net to verify that the automated test is correct!), the chances that he'll find trivial bugs are very low, which saves precious time and headache of the common ritual of finding the bugs, reporting, investigating, triaging, fixing and reverifying them. In fact, the manual tester can focus more on exploratory testing that will probably find the less obvious bugs

---

Note   Obviously, developing the automated test together with the tested functionality may be even easier if the same developer implements the functionality and its automated test together. This makes the process even more efficient! Of course, in this case there's less control and feedback about the work of the developer, but this concern can be addressed by other techniques like pair-programming, code reviews, having the manual tester review the test case before the implementation of the automated test, etc. In general, the effectiveness of doing so depends mainly on the specific person/s involved and the organizational culture. See the previous chapter for a more detailed discussion about the pros and cons of the different organizational patterns.

So if it's so much more efficient and valuable to develop the automated tests together with the tested functionality, or at least close to it, why wait for full coverage to start doing it?! Let's get back for a moment to the case where the pace of developing a new feature is exactly the same as the pace of adding new automated test cases (the case depicted in Figure 4-2). Because we'll always have a gap of 100 test cases, we can decide at any point to skip the remaining 100 test cases and jump directly to the ones that are now being developed. At this point on we'll act exactly as we would act if we've reached full coverage, except that we'll always have 100 unautomated test cases that we'll need to test manually. But if the gap was constantly 100 test cases, then this would be the case anyway! It's just that instead of manually testing the *last* 100 test cases, now we're always testing the same 100 test cases manually and keep automating the new ones. But this is better, because as explained above, developing the automated tests in conjunction with the feature is much more efficient.

Note   Developing and running tests prior, or in conjunction with the tested functionality is called *progression testing*, as opposed to *regression testing*, which is what we normally do when we develop and run the tests after the tested functionality is completed. Sometimes also referred to as *acceptance tests*, after these tests pass against the latest build, they join the suite of regression tests in the next builds and versions of the product.

If developing new automated test cases is faster than functionality anyway (like depicted in Figure 4-3), then we can decide at any moment to start developing progression tests, and complete the remaining regression tests later, in between the development of the progression tests. Because we know we develop tests faster than we develop product functionality, we can be assured that we'll have enough time to close the gap of the regression tests in between the development of the progression ones. Theoretically, we should get to the point of full coverage in exactly the same time as if we developed all the tests in a regression fashion, because we're just *changing the order* that we develop the tests! Moreover, because developing progression tests is more efficient than regression, then we'll probably even reach this point sooner! Figures 4-4 and 4-5 together demonstrate that the order of which the tests are being developed does not change the actual time it takes to reach full coverage

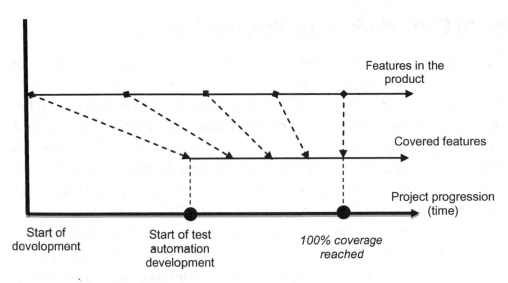

Figure 4-4. *Developing regression tests first*

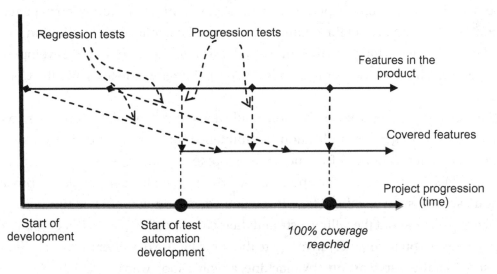

Figure 4-5. *Developing progression tests first*

My Road Map to Successful Automation Project

So if you're following me up to this point, then we can conclude that it makes more sense to start working on progression test automation before reaching full coverage on regression. But now two questions arise:

1. What's the right time to start working on progression tests?

2. How to prioritize the work on regression tests?

When to Start Working on Progression

From what I told you so far, you'd probably think that I encourage you to start working on progression from day one, before even starting developing regression tests. Well, it may be possible, but in practice that's not what I usually do, or recommend. At the beginning of a new test automation project, the investment is higher than the return. You need to build a lot of infrastructure in order to make the first tests work, which would probably take more time than it would take to implement the functionality of the user story. This is true especially if the user story is only a small improvement over an existing feature. In this case you would still need to build most of the infrastructure needed to test the entire scenario, even though the user story is only about that small improvement. Therefore, my recommendation is to start with a *sanity* suite of tests, which verifies the basic functionality of the system and its main features. Building this suite will help you build and stabilize the infrastructure of the main features in the application. During that period, you'll also gain some experience and insights about test automation in general and about test automation in the context of your specific application. In addition, you should use this time to integrate the automated tests into the CI tools and development processes. See Chapter 15 for more details on how to integrate the tests into the CI process.

While developing the sanity suite, constantly make sure that all the tests pass, (as long as there's no bug in the application that influence your tests). If needed, make changes to your tests and/or infrastructure to adopt to any changes to the product. In case a test fails due to a bug in the application, strive to get it fixed as quickly as possible and don't settle just on opening a bug. If you don't get a buy-in for that at this point, just send daily reports about the failing tests and their corresponding bugs, but emphasize the time it takes you to routinely investigate the same failure day after day. In addition, make sure that the tests work on any machine, as you'd soon want to give the developers the option to run the tests on their machines. You should ensure that it's easy to diagnose failures and of course strive to keep your tests easy to maintain. See Part II on writing maintainable tests and infrastructure, Chapter 13 on diagnosing failures, and Chapter 15 for some tips on stabilizing the tests.

The moment the sanity suite is ready, is part of the CI, and is stable, you're ready to start working on progression. If there are still tests that fail due to known product bugs, then these bugs should be fixed first. Obviously, you need the buy-in for that move from relevant stakeholders in the organization (especially dev leads and dev manager), and it has to be done in appropriate timing and not arbitrarily. Especially if the release cycle is still only every few months, it's important to find the right timing, to avoid stressful periods in which managers are less tolerant to experiments and failures. If you're the development manager then it's simply your call. If not, you'd probably need to do some groundwork before getting the consent of the development team leaders. One simpler sell can be to start by developing test for every bug that is being fixed, and only later proceed to actual progression tests. See Chapter 15 on how to gradually change the culture to support developing tests in conjunction with development.

Once you start developing tests for new user stories, the development of the tests should be done very closely with the developers who implement the user story, and the user story should only be considered as "done" only when all the tests (including the new ones) pass. See Chapter 16 on the ATDD methodology which emphasizes implementing the tests even before the tested functionality.

Prioritizing the Work to Fill the Regression Gap

From that point on, it's pretty easy to keep the tests stable. The sanity suite ensures that if a developer broke something critical, then it is fixed ASAP, before manual testers takes the version for a spin. The progression tests (which gradually become regression) ensures that the newly developed features continue to work.

Now you need to continue thinking about the rest of the regression tests. And there's a lot… So how do we decide which ones to automated first? My general advice here is to prioritize according to their value and the risk from not testing them often. Here are some guidelines:

1. First and foremost, you should focus on the features that bring the most value to the business and to the customers. Finding and preventing bugs in these features directly affects the revenue of the product! However, this guideline alone is not enough. You should weigh it against the next guidelines in order to decide on the priority of covering this feature.

2. If a component or a feature is planned to be replaced soon, having its entire behavior changed, then it's not worth to create tests for it at this point. Just wait until the new behavior will be developed, and then develop the new tests along with it.

3. If a feature is very stable and there are no plans to touch it soon, then it's also not very cost effective to cover it with automation. There's a very small risk that something *will* somehow affect it. This is especially true for legacy components, which even though may be very critical in the system, no one dares to touch their code. Looking for something with a higher risk will yield a higher value sooner.

4. If a feature is completed and works correctly, but there's a plan to replace its underlying technology, or to do a massive refactoring to its internal structure, then this is a great candidate for covering with test automation. The tests should not be changed when the underlying technology or internal structure change, and should continue to pass afterward, ensuring that the exiting behavior was preserved.

5. Similar to the above, *improving the performance* of a feature usually involves a change to the internal structure while preserving the external functionality. Similarly, in this case, the tests should continue to pass after the changes just like they were passing before.

6. Consider to prefer covering a feature that breaks a lot. However, note that a feature that breaks a lot is a sign for a problematic design. For this reason, this feature has a high potential to be a candidate either for refactoring (in which case the automation will be very valuable), or for a complete rewrite (in which the automation will probably need to be rewritten too...).

In addition to covering existing features, for every bug found *not by the automation*, before this bug is being fixed, an automated test should be written to reproduce it. Only when an automatic test successfully reproduces the bug, the bug should be fixed. This way we ensure that no bug will ever hit us twice.

If you follow these guidelines, you manage the risk and your progress in an efficient way. You can easily keep your automation results green and catch most of the trivial bugs very early. On top of that, you gradually cover more and more areas of regression tests. As discussed in Chapter 2, test automation won't replace the manual testers completely, but the first condition to stop performing the tedious manual regression tests on a feature is that the test automation of that feature can be trusted! As long as the automation is not reliable, it cannot replace the manual tests whatsoever. If you try to get to 100% regression before putting it in CI, you'd probably have a very hard time stabilizing the tests and gain trust in them. The described road map makes it easy to keep the tests stable from the start, and therefore make them much more trustworthy. Because of this, you can gradually reduce the manual regression testing efforts of covered features, freeing the manual testers to perform more valuable exploratory testing.

CHAPTER 5

Business Processes

As you probably realized from the previous chapters, a test automation project can't stand on its own. Its life cycle is tightly related to the life cycle of the application that it tests. Like any software project, its existence is only relevant if someone uses it; otherwise it's worthless. In the case of test automation, the "user" is actually the entire development team. It may seem like the main user is the QA manager or Dev manager, but in fact, they're not using it themselves for their own good. They may require the fancy reports and tell you what they want you to do (and sometimes even how...), but as we discussed in Chapter 1, one of the principle advantages of test automation is that it helps the *team* detect and fix the bugs more quickly. But for this to happen, the team needs to learn how to use it effectively, which usually requires some sort of work processes. The processes can be less strict if the team is small and everyone simply understands the value behind such processes. But whether these processes are strictly enforced by management or the team understands their value, these processes need to be followed in order to allow proper collaboration and to get the maximal value from the automation.

Running the Tests on a Regular Basis

As mentioned before, if you only run the tests rarely on a code base that developers work on, many tests will likely fail due to simple changes in the product. In this case, it will take a long time to investigate the failures to determine which faults are bugs in the application, and which are caused by valid changes. Moreover, when many tests fail due to valid changes, it creates the impression that the results, and the test automation as a whole, are unreliable.

Therefore, the first thing that you should care about is that the tests will run regularly, and failures that occur as a result of legitimate changes are handled ASAP.

© Arnon Axelrod 2018
A. Axelrod, *Complete Guide to Test Automation*, https://doi.org/10.1007/978-1-4842-3832-5_5

The Simplest Approach

Even before setting up a formal build process that runs the tests automatically and reports the results, as soon as you have a few tests that are ready, you should run all of the completed tests at least once a day to ensure that they're stable. If you get a new build from developers more rarely than once a day, then you should expect less failures between those builds. However, tests can still fail due to the following:

- A bug in the test;

- An environmental issue, like issues related to network, hardware, the operating system, and other infrastructure.

- A bug in the product that does not reproduce consistently.

Whatever the fault is, you should investigate and handle it quickly and thoroughly to ensure that the automation is stable and reliable (See Chapter 13 for more details on investigating failure tests). If fixing the issues is beyond your reach (i.e., a bug in the product or an environmental issue) and you cannot push to fix these issues quickly and/or thoroughly, then at least report this issue and emphasize its importance to the automation stability. See later in this chapter more specific guidelines and practices to handle these cases from a process perspective.

However, if you get a build more often than once a day (or in case you still don't have an automatic build process, you can get the developers' changes by syncing and building it locally on your machine), then in addition to the above-mentioned reasons for failures, failures can also occur due to:

- A regression bug in the product: that is, a developer checked-in code that has a bug in a flow that worked before and should not have changed.

- A legit change in the product that changed the behavior that one or more tests expect: i.e., the tests became outdated due to this change.

Once again, these failures should be investigated and handled ASAP. In case of a legit change, you must update your tests to reflect the change.

Nightly Runs

Running the tests yourself on your local machine once a day is nice, but it is more error prone:

- You need to remember to run the tests every day.

- You may be in the middle of some changes or developing a new test, and your code may not compile or work correctly.

- You may have specific conditions in your local machine that may not be the same on others.

Therefore, we should automate the process of running the tests daily too. A very common approach is to run the tests every night automatically using an automated build process. The main reason to run it at night is to maximize the time for investigating the failures before the next run, especially if the total length of the run is a few hours. Similar to the previous approach, someone has to investigate the failures the next morning and handle them appropriately. Fixing any issues that are caused by the automation and any issues caused by valid changes to the product should be done by the automation developer ASAP. For product bugs, at the minimum you have to open a bug report in your bug tracking system (e.g., TFS, Jira).

QA or Dev managers often request getting an automatic report of the nightly tests results. While this is pretty common, these managers rarely have something meaningful and useful to do with them, because failure information tends to be too technical, and only after some investigation one can get an idea of the fault, its severity, and the means to fix it. By contrast, a *manual* report, created after investigating the results and reaching some more meaningful conclusions is much more valuable for them. See Chapter 15 for more information about this topic.

Instead of running the tests only once every night, given that the entire test run doesn't take too long, you can make the automated tests run on every check-in, which makes the CI build much more valuable. Even though it seems like a very small change from a nightly run (and technically speaking, that's true), in order for it to be effective, it also requires some important changes to the work processes. I'll explain the required changes to the work processes later in this chapter, after building the ground for it with some more common concerns and approaches.

Handling Bugs That Are Found by the Automation

Traditionally, when a tester encounters a bug, he reports it in the team's bug tracking system (e.g., TFS or Jira) and leaves it there until someone decides that its priority is high enough in order to fix it. After it's fixed, he only has to verify that it's fixed. Due to the differences between manual tests and test automation (which were discussed in Chapter 2), this is fine for tests that are found in manual tests, but not as much for automated ones. I'll explain why.

One of the major problems of test automation that is mostly overlooked is that of the **medium severity bugs**. It is so overlooked that most people don't see it as a problem at all. But in my opinion, it impairs building trust in the automation, wastes precious time, and overall hurts the value of the automation. Why am I clinging just to *medium* severity bugs? Aren't high severity bugs more severe? The thing is that high severity bugs are usually fixed very quickly. By the following nightly run, they'll probably be fixed. However, when medium severity bugs cause automated tests to fail, it may take weeks, months, and sometimes forever until they'll be fixed. During this time there are three common approaches to deal with in regard to the automated tests. Each one of them has its drawbacks though...

Keep the Failing Tests

The first option, which is the most common one, is to keep the tests that fail due to the known bugs failing until they're fixed. The upside of doing so is that the test results seem to reflect the true picture about the quality of the software. However, there are a few downsides to it as well:

- It forces that someone (usually the automation developer) will reinvestigate the same failure again and again every morning. The fact that a particular test failed both yesterday and today doesn't necessarily mean that it fails for the same cause. If a test has five steps in it, and yesterday it failed on step 3, it could be that today there's another bug (or even a legitimate change) that causes step 1 or 2 to fail. If you don't investigate each failure over and over again each morning, then you might miss a bug! When such bugs add up, the time it takes to investigate all the failures each morning can become a trouble and can erode from the time supposed to be dedicated for writing more tests.

Note   If the time it takes to investigate all the failures exceeds one working day, then there's no point running the next nightly run, as you become the bottleneck of the process! However, if this situation happens frequently, it can hint to many other significant problems, like bad reports, unstable environments, inadequate design, bad time management, and more…

- Unless all of those bugs are fixed, which is pretty unlikely, the overall result of each test run will always be "failed." In most cases, there's more than one bug that cause tests to fail, and for quite some people I talked to, having around 10%–20% failing tests was considered a normal state. In this case, it's very difficult to notice a new bug from the old ones. The difference between 11 failing tests and 10 failing tests is much less noticeable than the difference between 1 failing test and 0 failing tests!

- Often, the bug causes the test to fail not on its final verification (assertion), which is the main purpose of that test, but rather in one of the prior steps. This means that the test doesn't even test what it's supposed to, but nevertheless you can't use this test until the bug is fixed. If a manual tester would perform the test, he'd probably be able to bypass the bug and continue to check the main thing, but the automated tests simply can't do that automatically. This means that the automation can miss additional bugs this way, which you won't be able to find until the first one was fixed.

- When the original bug is finally fixed, the test may still fail on legitimate changes that took place while the bug was active. Because it may have been a long period of time, it may be difficult to analyze the failure and find how to fix it, rather than it would have been if those changes were identified as soon as they were done. For this reason, often it's said that a code that doesn't get executed for a long time "rots."

- On top of the previous problems, often the same bug causes more than one tests to fail. On one hand, if it causes too many tests to fail, then you'd probably manage to get its priority high enough to be fixed quickly. On the other hand, if it causes only a few tests to fail, then it might still be ignored for a long period. This means that all of the above drawbacks should be multiplied not only for every bug, but for every test that this bug affects, which may be a few times more.

Exclude the Failing Tests

The second approach is to exclude tests that fail due to known bugs from the regular test runs until these bugs are fixed. This will allow you to notice new bugs more easily and relieve the need to reinvestigate all the results each day. Anyway, the bugs are managed in the bug tracking system so you don't have to worry about it every day. However, this approach still suffers from some of the drawbacks of the previous approach, plus a few of its own:

- Similar to the first approach, if the bug causes the test to fail at one of the middle steps, as opposed to the final verification of the test, you may be missing bugs.

- Also similar to the first approach, if the bug hits more than one test, then you're actually giving up on all of these tests.

- While in the first approach it was hard to notice if the reason of the failure changed between yesterday and today (e.g., yesterday it failed on step 3 and today on step 2), in this approach you can't even see it because the test doesn't run at all, which means that you can miss even more bugs!

- While in the first approach the steps that follow the failing step could rot, in this approach the entire test can rot.

- On the practical side, it's difficult to track which tests are excluded and due to which bug, and to remember to include them back after the bug is fixed. Automating this process may be possible, but because the test can "rot," returning it automatically to the test run without first ensuring that the test passes is not recommended. In addition, I don't know of any commercial bug tracking tool that does this out of the box.

Creating Work-Arounds in the Test

The third approach is relevant mainly when a bug affects an intermediate step in the test, and not the entire essence of the test. It is usually used only if a single low-priority bug affects many tests. In this approach a work-around is performed in the test in order to allow it to continue its execution and verify the main essence of the test.

This approach resolves many of the previous issues:

- The overall result is passed so it's easy to notice and investigate new failures.

- It maintains the main essence of each test and lowers the chances to miss bugs.

- If the problem affects many tests, and the automation is designed properly, then the work-around should be in one place.

- It prevents any of the code from rotting.

But obviously, it has its own downsides as well:

- It hides the fact that there's a problem! There's probably at least one test (or there should be) whose essence is to verify the problematic step. If the work-around is applied globally, then this test will pass only due to the work-around without actually testing what it's supposed to.

- Work-arounds typically make the code of the automation more complicated and more difficult to maintain.

- If managing excluded tests and remembering to return them to the cycle is difficult, then tracking the work-arounds and remembering to remove them when the bug is fixed is nearly impossible!

- Tests that fail due to bugs in the functionality that they directly verify, are normally considered valuable. But usually tests that fail due to medium- or low-severity bugs in a step that only sets up the preconditions for the test, is perceived as a false positive. In this case the most natural solution would be to create a work-around instead of "wasting" the time involved in opening and managing bugs that do not affect the sheer essence of the tests. This causes many bugs to be completely ignored.

AN OPTIMAL APPROACH?

I once tried to come up with an optimal approach that addresses *most* of the downsides of the three approaches described above, which are supposed to work like this:

- When opening a bug that affects automated tests, it should be associated with the failing tests, together with a substring of the failure message or stack-trace, which serves as a "differential diagnosis" for this particular failure. In subsequent runs, this substring will be used to automatically identify whether the test failed on the same problem and on a different one. For example, if the failure manifests itself with a message such as: "Error: the file Temp\152243423\Data.Info cannot be found", (where 152243423 is a number that can change at each run), then the substring "Data.Info cannot be found" would probably be a valid differential diagnosis for the failure, while "Error", "152243423" or the complete message won't serve that purpose well because they are either too generic or too specific to the particular occurrence.

- At the end of each run a report is automatically generated. The report generator queries the bugs tracking system and also the substrings that are associated with those bugs. If it identifies the corresponding substring in the error message, then it marks this test in yellow instead of in red to indicate that it's a known bug. This way it's easy to different regressions (red) from known bugs (yellow).

- In addition, if a test that is associated with a bug, passes, then it is marked in a different color (blue) to indicate that the bug should probably be closed.

Note: this technique can even be improved by using regular expressions instead of substrings, though it also makes it more difficult to use.

Anyway, I'm not aware of any commercial product that help you do that. I once managed to implement something similar (tailor made for the customer), but unfortunately most people didn't understand how to use it properly. Maybe it was only a matter of training…

Anyway, I still believe that treating any automation bug as a critical bug would be a better approach, as I'll describe shortly.

Treating All Automation Failures as Critical Bugs

While each of the above approaches has its benefits and for each of them there are cases where it's most appropriate, due to the mentioned drawbacks, I generally recommend on a fourth approach. This fourth approach is to treat each bug that cause automated tests to fail as a critical bug, even if the effect on the final user is only medium or low. This means that each such bug must be fixed until the next test cycle (e.g., next nightly run). **This is the only way to keep the automation suite clearly and promptly alert us when new regression bugs are introduced (without compromising the coverage).** At first, it may look like a very extreme and expensive approach, but if we'll look at it from a different angle, you'll see that it's very realistic:

- Given that all tests passed on the few previous runs, a new failure can only be related to a recent change. Because there should only be a limited set of changes between each run, it should be very easy to identify which change caused it.

- It's much easier and quicker to fix changes that were made recently than it is to fix bugs related to old changes. If they're going to be fixed at some point anyway, it's much cheaper to fix them soon.

- The time wasted by investigating the same failures again and again, or to filter the known failures from the new ones, is also costly.

- In the worst case, reverting only the latest changes will surely fix the problem. Most users would probably be more annoyed if an existing feature that they know and love suddenly stops working as they expect, than if the delivery of a new feature would be slightly delayed. But frankly, this should very rarely happen – in most cases the developers will be able to fix the bug quickly.

Running the tests every night and engaging the developers and management to keep all the tests green by fixing every issue at the same day is great. This really allows us to improve the quality of the product, increase the coverage, and encourage refactoring to allow the system to be maintainable over a long period of time.

But running it only every 24 hours is also not the best option. 24 hours can mean many check-ins, especially if it's a large team. In addition, 24 hours after a developer checked in a change, he's usually already immersed on a completely different task. Doing the context switch back to the previous change can be time consuming and

91

confusing, especially over weekends, where "24 hours" are actually 72 hours... And this is before we mention what happens when the developer who is responsible for the broken test is just went on a week-long vacation...

Continuous Integration

Most developers are familiar with the term "Continuous Integration" (or CI in short). As already mentioned in Chapter 2, this term means that before every check-in the code is automatically being built and that the automatic tests verify it. Only if everything passes, then the changes are being checked in. The process that builds the code and runs the tests typically runs on one or more dedicated build servers, and not on the developer's machine. This allows a centralized control over this process, and also frees up the developer's machine to do other stuff while the process runs.

SMALL VARIATIONS ON CI

While nowadays the above description of a CI is the most typical one, there are other variations to this. These variations were more common in the past, though they are still pretty common these days too. As they are also simpler, sometimes they are used in smaller teams.

1. Instead of having the build and tests run *before* the changes enter the main source control repository, they are being run *after*. Because this way it's not possible to prevent the check-in, the build process (which includes the build and the tests together) only reports whether the process passed or failed. Often these results are also being sent automatically to the relevant people via email, especially the developer who performed the check-in. The recommended practice is that whenever a build fails, that developer should fix the failure as fast as possible before anyone else is allowed to check in other changes.

2. The second variation is usually used when the team is very small, or when no one has the skills to install and configure a build server. While this variation is generally less preferred as it relies more on self-discipline rather than on tools, it still holds the essence and the idea behind CI. In this variation, every developer is responsible for getting the latest sources, builds and runs the tests *locally*, and only if everything passes he proceeds to check in.

Moving from a nightly run to CI may be somewhat challenging. But eventually the benefits outcomes those challenges. See Chapter 15 for more information about how to make this transition properly.

Acceptance Test Driven Development (ATDD)

While CI answers the questions about who, when and how should *run* the tests, it doesn't answer the questions about who, when, and how should *write* the tests. In Chapter 3 we already covered the question "*who* should implement the tests." Also, in Chapters 2 and 4 we discussed why it's better to write the tests alongside the development and not later. Finally, in Chapter 16 we'll discuss this topic in much greater depth. But as this topic is related to business processes, I must at least give you an overview about it here.

Acceptance Test Driven Development (ATDD), which has a few small variations known as *Behavior Driven Development* (BDD) and *Specification by Example* (SbE) is a methodology that is based on the following concepts:

1. For each User Story, the team defines together with the product owner one or few scenarios that will demonstrate its intended use after it will be implemented. These scenarios become both the *acceptance criteria* of the user story, as well as the flows of the tests that will verify the implementation.

2. The tests are implemented before the product code. Implementing the tests may surface additional questions and gaps in the definition of the user story. It also forces the team to start planning the product code in a testable manner. Obviously, the tests cannot pass at this stage (if they do, it indicates a problem in the test!).

3. The developers implement the code in order to make the tests pass. They shouldn't develop any functionality that is beyond the scope of the tests. They must run all of the existing tests also to make sure that they didn't break anything.

4. Only when the tests pass, the user story is considered "done," and it can be demonstrated to the product owner, customer, or even pushed to production.

Among the benefits of this technique is that it ensures that testers and automation developers are involved at the earliest stage possible, allowing them to really influence the quality of the product. In addition, if this process is followed since the beginning of the project, then it means that the tests cover all the defined functionality (that is relevant to be tested by automation), and all of them pass! As mentioned before, it allows the developers to refactor the product code as often and as much as they feel like, as they can easily ensure that they didn't break anything. As a result, it increases the inner quality of the code and allows adding new features faster and safely.

When introducing this approach in the middle of a project, many of its benefits are less obvious, but it's still valuable at least in the long run. See Chapter 16 for guidelines that will help you introduce it in the middle of a project.

Continuous Delivery and Continuous Deployment

The subject of Continuous Integration that was discussed earlier is not complete without expanding the subject to continuous delivery and continuous deployment.

Until about 10 years ago, delivering a new version of most commercial software was a huge effort. It involved manufacturing of physical CD ROM discs, with an elegant case and printed graphics, and often a printed user manual. Adding a new feature in the last moment before shipment could mean that all of the printed material and CDs themselves had to be reprinted. Not to mention the supply chain management overhead…

Today, most commercial software can be downloaded from the Internet, with the user manual being a bunch of HTML pages or another downloadable PDF file. This, together with automated tests, removes most of the obstacles of shipping new changes very rapidly. Naturally, web applications are even easier to update. Most internal software projects are also web applications or are updatable via a centralized deployment and distribution system.

However, in order to really make the deployment process seamless, it needs to be automated as well. Having manual steps in the deployment process both increases the risk for mistakes and takes longer to complete. If you plan your test automation to be run in isolated environments, as you should probably do also for CI, then it also forces you to automate the deployment process, which can then be used to more easily automate the process of deploying new versions to production. See Chapter 7 for more information about isolation, and Chapter 15 for integrating the tests into the CI. Automating the entire deployment process is called *Continuous Deployment*.

While technically it's possible to automate the entire process, many companies prefer to keep the final decision about what goes into production and when, as a manual business decision. In this case they usually want the new version to first be deployed to a production-like environment in order to perform additional manual tests and validations. So, in this case, the entire process is automated, but the final step requires a manual intervention. This is called *Continuous Delivery*.

Continuous Deployment is more suitable for companies that provide SaaS[1] and other Web applications that are not mission critical (like Facebook, for example). These companies can accommodate having small glitches here and there for a small portion of their users, as long as these can be fixed very fast. But mission-critical applications, like medical applications, which cannot bare even the smallest glitch, or domains in which applying a fix can take a long time, like in avionic embedded systems, are most likely to choose a Continues Delivery approach.

Another approach that has started in the largest web companies, but gradually make its way to the mainstream, is that individual features are validated in production. Each feature is first deployed only in a small scale, and gradually as it proves to be valuable and reliable, it is delivered to all the customers. This approach is called *Canary Release* or *Gradual Rollout*.

Canary Releases

Highly scalable and highly available web applications (e.g., Facebook, Twitter, Google, etc., but even smaller companies) are distributed by nature and cannot be deployed all at once in the first place. Because there are many servers (often referred to as Nodes) running the same application behind a load balancer, each of them must be updatable independently of the others. If the application is not mission critical, it can be deployed first only to one node, and route only a small portion of the traffic to it, even before it's thoroughly tested. This newly updated node should be highly monitored to see if there are any problems or anomalies that can indicate that there's some problem. If something does go wrong, then this node can be taken down until the bug is fixed. If everything goes well, then it's possible to continue to gradually deploy the new version to more and more nodes. In fact, as this approach is normally applied when the nodes are virtual machines (VM) or containers (which are, in essence, super lightweight and modular

---

[1]SaaS stands for *Software as a Service*. These are applications (typically Web or mobile applications) that their operators charge for their usage.

VMs), then instead of updating existing VMs, new VMs are gradually created and connected to the load balancer, and old ones are gradually destroyed.

In addition, instead of using just the load balancer to randomly choose the clients that will get the new version, it's possible to provide one URL to regular public clients, another URL to beta customers, and yet another URL for internal users. Each URL is directed to a different load balancer. When a new version is first deployed to a new VM, this new VM is first added to the load balancer of the internal users. When confidence is built around these changes (may be after running some manual tests as well), it is removed from the first load balancer and added to the second one that serves the beta customers. If after some beta period no special problems are revealed, then it can be moved further on to the load balancer that serves the public customers.

In order to be able to deploy individual features separately, the architecture of the application should be made of many, very small components that interact with one another, usually asynchronously. This kind of architecture is called *Micro-Services architecture*.[2] See the next chapter about the relationships between test automation and the architecture of the SUT.

A/B Testing

Another related concept that is often used in large-scale web application providers is called *A/B Testing*. "A/B Testing" is a term borrowed from marketing and business intelligence, where you give a group of potential customers one variant of a product (variant "A"), and another group a variant of the same product that only differs in one property (variant "B"). Then the marketing data is analyzed to determine whether this property increases the sales of the product or not.

A similar idea can be applied to web applications: In order to validate whether one variant of a feature is better than another, the two variants are being developed, and deployed to different sets of nodes. These two variants are monitored and compared in order to analyze which one of them the users use more often, and whether it have a positive impact on some business KPIs. In case of ecommerce or SaaS sites, this is usually translated directly to increased revenue!

---

[2]For an in-depth description of micro-services architecture, I recommend to read Martin Fowler's article at: https://martinfowler.com/articles/microservices.html

Summary

As you can see, test automation does not stand on its own. Its value comes from the way it is being used. If it only supports testing in the traditional way, then its value is pretty limited. But if is used as part of the entire development and the overall business processes, then it can even directly impact revenue. Remember that A/B testing cannot be achieved without Continuous Delivery or at least Continuous Deployment, Continuous Delivery cannot be achieved without Continuous Integration, and Continuous Integration cannot be achieved without Test Automation.

CHAPTER 6

Test Automation and Architecture

Because the vast majority of manual tests is done through the UI, and on a complete system that attempts to mimic the production environment as much as possible, it is often assumed that this is also the right approach for automated tests. However, as we already discussed in Chapter 2, there are different considerations for manual tests and for automated ones. In this chapter we'll discuss some strategic considerations about the architecture of the test automation. As we'll see, the considerations about the architecture of the test automation are tightly related to the architecture of the SUT.

Test Architecture Considerations

Like any other software project, test automation should also have some kind of architecture. The architecture of a software system typically conveys the high-level decisions that affect the entire system and are more difficult to change down the road. For a test automation system, these decisions usually affect how tests are written, how they are being run, what they can and cannot do, etc. However, the architecture of the test automation should also take into account the architecture of the SUT. These architectural decisions also affect the isolation of the tests as will be described in the next chapter, which in turn have a very high impact on their reliability. Here are some high-level considerations that you may want to take into account when architecting the test automation solution:

1. Who should *write* the test and what skills do they have?

2. Who should *run* the tests and when?

© Arnon Axelrod 2018
A. Axelrod, *Complete Guide to Test Automation*, https://doi.org/10.1007/978-1-4842-3832-5_6

3. Which parts of the SUT we want to test? (Or – which parts of the tests are more important for us to test?)

4. Which parts of the SUT *can* we test *reliably*?

5. How long the tests would run?

6. How easy it will be to write new tests?

7. How easy it will be to maintain existing tests?

8. How easy it will to investigate failing tests?

We already discussed the first two considerations in previous chapters. In this chapter we'll focus mainly on considerations 3–5, and the rest will be covered by later chapters.

Understanding the SUT Architecture

Most people facing the question "which components of the SUT you want to be tested," simply answer "everything." But, in most cases, testing the entire system end to end may cause the tests to be unreliable, hard to maintain, and sometimes not even feasible. Therefore, we must first understand the architecture of the SUT in order to make the appropriate decision.

Back to Basics: What's a Computer System?

In order to understand the architecture of the SUT and its impact on test automation, let's first get back to the first lesson in computer sciences, and answer the question: "What's a computer system?" The answer is typically described as a system that gets some kind of inputs, processes them, and spits out output, as shown in Figure 6-1.

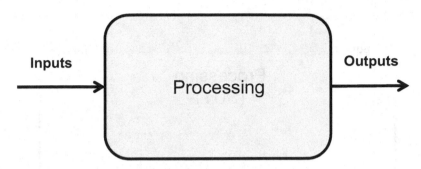

Figure 6-1. *A generic explanation of a computer system*

One important attribute that this description implies and is true for every given computer system, is that the outputs yielded from the system depend only on the sequence of inputs provided to it. Even when the computer yields random numbers, these numbers are only *pseudo-random* and the computer uses the system's clock, which is an input device, to compute them.

Note   Some people think that machine learning (ML) and other "Artificial Intelligence" (AI) technologies, which have become more popular lately, does not adhere to the above claim as they mimic the human way of thinking that is non-deterministic. Well, the truth is there's no magic behind any of these technologies. The main thing that differentiates them is that they depend on **high volumes of inputs**, and a complex processing of those inputs, but the principle is the same. As mentioned, algorithms that use random numbers actually use pseudo-random sequences that depend on the system's clock, which is also an input.

What's an Automated Test?

While in Chapter 1 we gave a generic definition of an automated test, considering the above definition of a computer system, we can define an automated (functional) test as a computer program that sends inputs to another computer system (the SUT); compares the output sequence, or part of it, to some predefined expected result; and outputs the result of that comparison. Figure 6-2 shows that description of an automated test.

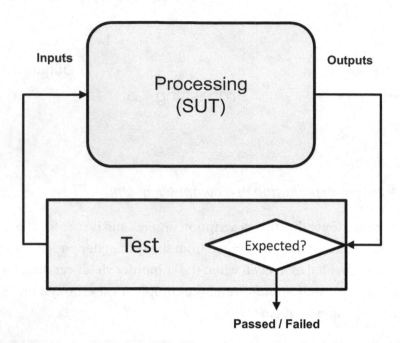

Figure 6-2. *Description of an automated test*

Real-World Computer Systems

While the above description of a computer system is theoretically true, most computer systems are themselves composed of smaller systems (often called *Services*), communicate with external systems, get inputs from many sources, and yield many kinds and high volume of outputs. Diagrams of real software looks more like Figure 6-3.

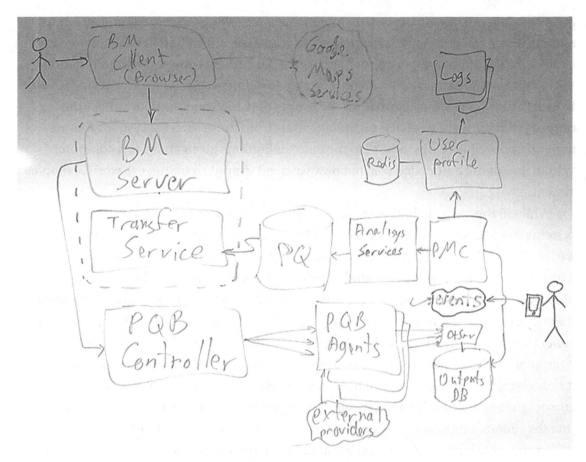

Figure 6-3. *Typical software arcitecture diagram*

Moreover, very few systems today are really "stand-alone," or "black box," having no dependency on any other system. Rather most systems depend on some external services or component that we don't have full control over their development and/or behavior. This imposes a real challenge: on one hand, our customers shouldn't care that we depend on third-party services; but on the other hand, problems in these services are not under the control of our development team. Therefore, it's difficult to draw a clear line between where our system ends and other's start, and to our concern: What components or services we care to test?

For manual testers this is a lesser concern. Manual testers interact with the system through the UI, like the end users, and validate that what they see *makes sense*. If the manual testers encounter a clear warning that some external service is not available and that he should try again later, he can verify that this service is indeed unavailable right now and he won't report a bug for it. Furthermore, even if the service is up, often the outputs of our system depend on inputs that it receives from that external service, and the tester can determine whether they're correct or not, although he can't predict in advance what these outputs should be. But as we already know, for test automation, *make sense* is not an option, as we must be able to define a *deterministic* expected result. In order to do so, **we must control all the inputs of the system that may affect the outputs that we want to verify**, including inputs from those external systems that we depend upon! This brings us back to the basic definitions given above of a computer system and of the automated test, but now we need to apply it to the real-world, complex system.

While in the basic definition we talked about a single sequence of inputs, in real systems this sequence is composed of many different independent input sources that we usually think of as different sequences, or streams. The same goes for the output: a typical system generates many kinds and sequences of outputs for different targets. Moreover, the inputs and outputs are often so tightly related that it's hard to think about them as distinguishable from each other. For example, when you move the mouse, you generate inputs, but as a result, in a complete synchronization with your moves, the computer moves the cursor on the screen – which is the output it generates (in fact, it only changes the color values of individual pixels, which gives the illusion that the cursor "moves"). A similar thing happens when you type text in a textbox: your key presses generate inputs, and as an immediate result, the system outputs the glyph of the appropriate letter to the correct location on the screen! But keyboard, mouse, and screen are not the only sources of inputs and outputs (I/O) that a computer system has. Most system uses disk storage (in the form of files or database records), network communication, etc. Some systems interact with a specific hardware and perform additional, unique I/Os for that. Another important input that many systems depend upon is the system's clock.

While looking at the I/O in that low-level form helped us understand how the theoretical view of a computer system applies to a real-world system, it's still not very helpful in order to reason about the architecture of the SUT and to plan our automation accordingly. But if we'll look at a block diagram like the one in Figure 6-3 and draw a line between the components that compose our system, and systems, services, and sources that we consider as external to our SUT, we can reason about which inputs to the SUT can affect which of its outputs. Figure 6-4 shows an example of how we can draw such a line. Lacking a standard term for that, I like to call the selection of components that we consider part of the SUT, the "Test Scope."

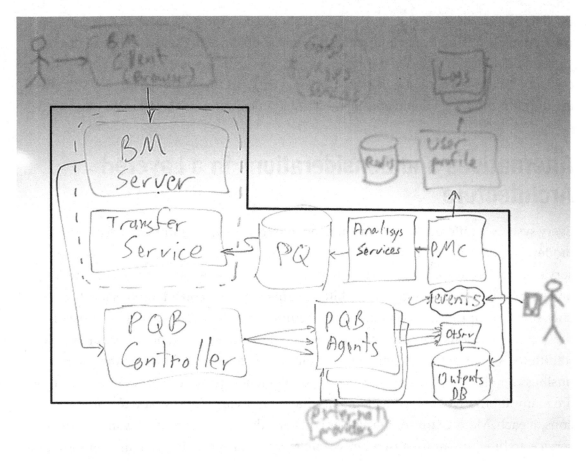

Figure 6-4. *Drawing a line between the SUT and external sources defines our "Test Scope"*

If we would have control over all of these input sources, then we can define tests with deterministic expected results. Controlling inputs received from external systems may not look feasible to you right now, but later in this chapter I'll explain how we can at least mimic those inputs. Of course, that input source may also include files, external devices, and user interactions. The bottom line is that the test must control whatever we consider as inputs to the SUT and that may affect the output that we want to verify.

Note that storage means, like files and databases, are usually something that systems use internally for their own use, but some systems use them as means to communicate with other systems. For example, if your application writes data to a database that can be later used by another system to create reports, then you can consider this database as an output target. Vice versa, if your system is the reporting service, it should create reports according to data that an external system writes to the database, then you should treat the database as an input source that the test should control. In general, if your system uses a database or files only internally, then you should not bother with that at all, and you should consider it part of the Test Scope. However, because it's usually not feasible to start with a clean database in every test (or at all!) and the existing data may still affect the outputs, then you should consider the isolation techniques described in Chapter 7.

Alternatives and Considerations in a Layered Architecture

Every system is different and has a different architecture. As mentioned before, most modern systems are composed of services that communicate between them (micro-services architecture), but even so, it may be helpful to talk about a more traditional and simpler layered client/server architecture first, and the considerations for choosing the appropriate components to include in the Test Scope. After all, most of these considerations also apply to the more modern systems, and hey, there are many traditional systems still out there. In this example we're talking about a stand-alone business application, without any relevant dependencies on external systems. Still, there are many alternatives and considerations that we'll discuss shortly, and the pros and cons of each. Many of these alternatives and considerations are still relevant in a micro-service architecture or to most other system architectures out there. Figure 6-5 shows the typical layered architecture that we're about to discuss.

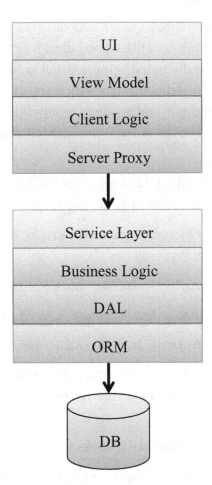

Figure 6-5. *A typical layered architecture*

The Relationships Between the Scope and the Test

Before I'll describe the purpose of each layer and the alternatives of choosing the test scope, I want to clarify the relationships between the test scope and the tested scenarios. In fact, in most cases, the test scope, which defines the tested components included in the SUT, can be independent of the scenario, which defines the purpose and the steps of a particular test. In other words, you can implement almost any scenario (test) with any test scope. This is true as long as the component that implements the core logic that is verified by the test is included in the test scope, which is usually the Business Logic layer. In addition, in order to be able to use any test scope with any scenario, the scenario should be planned and described in high-level business terms, instead of using full and precise technical details, like exactly which buttons to click to complete some business activity. Note that even though describing test scenarios for automation with as much details as possible may sound like a good idea, it actually leads to tests that are harder to maintain (this will be discussed in more detail in Part II). So, test scenarios that are described in the level of detail that lends themselves best for test automation makes them both easier to maintain and be scope independent. Here's an example of a scenario for an e-commence bookstore website, which is described using high-level business terms:

1. As the administrator, add the following books to the catalog and assign them to the "Test Automation" category:

   - *Growing Object-Oriented Software Guided by Tests*, by Steve Freeman and Nat Pryce: $54.99

   - *xUnit Test Patterns*, by Gerard Meszaros: $74.99

   - *The Complete Guide to Test Automation*, by Arnon Axelrod: $39.99

   - *Specification by Example*, by Gojko Adzic: $49.99

2. As the administrator, define a promotion that states if the customer buys 3 books from the "Test Automation" category, he gets a $10 discount

3. As the end user, add the following books to the cart:

   - *Growing Object-Oriented Software Guided by Tests*

   - *xUnit Test Patterns*

   - *The Complete Guide to Test Automation*

4. Verify that a $10 discount is given and that the total amount to pay is $154.97 (74.99 + 49.99 + 39.99 -10)

Note that this description does not specify all of the clicks and keyboard entries needed to add the book to the catalog, create the promotion, or add the books to the shopping cart. Therefore, now I can implement this test using an end-to-end test scope, for example, using Selenium, to exercise the relevant actions on the browser (which is connected to the entire back end and database) and verify the expected result also on the browser, or I can choose a smaller test scope like sending requests directly to the server to complete these business activities, and even up to a unit test that tests a single class that contains the promotion's logic. There are more options in between, of course, each with its pros and cons as we'll discuss shortly. In addition, we'll discuss how you can mix and match different test scopes to take advantage of more than one option, and also the price of doing that too.

While in the above typical example, the scenario can be implemented using different scopes, sometimes you want a test to verify details that are specific to one layer. For example, if you want to verify that a certain button is *disabled* after the user completed a transaction, you must include the UI layer in the test. Similarly, if you want to verify that data that the user enters is persisted after the system is restarted, then you must include both the UI and the database in the test scope. But some tests really require only one layer, like when you want to verify that a Save button is disabled if the user didn't fill in some mandatory field, which requires *only* the View Model layer.

Overview of the Layers

Our stereotypical application is a classic three-tier architecture: the top tier is a rich client application (i.e., Windows application), which communicates with the server via some proprietary HTTP-based protocol. The middle tier is the "heart" of the system where the main business logic resides. The bottom tier is a relational (SQL) database that mainly stores and retrieve the data, but also contains some stored procedures that perform complex queries in order to improve performance. Each tier is a separate process and can potentially be deployed on a different machine. However, each tier by itself is composed from its own internal components (e.g., DLLs, JARs, etc,. according to the technology used) as the following.

The Client Tier

The client tier is composed of the following layers:

1. UI Layer – this layer is responsible for the graphical layout and appearance of the UI. It's mainly produced either with a WYSIWYG[1] editor or kind of a declarative markup, like HTML, XML, or XAML. If it contains code, it should be very simple and only handle the UI layout and appearance.

---

[1]WYSIWYG stands for *What you see is what you get*. This means that when you edit something you see the result immediately. MS-Word is a great example: as you type you see how the document will look like when printed.

2. View Model – this layer is responsible for providing the data that should be displayed in the UI layer and dispatch user events (e.g., clicking a button) to the relevant objects in the Client Logic layer.

3. Client logic – this layer is responsible for the logic and the flow of the client application. Unlike the "Business Logic" layer in the server, this layer doesn't handle the business logic per se, but rather the logic of transitioning between screens, and ties together the communication with the server with the UI behavior. For example, when a button is clicked in the UI and the View Model passes it to the Client Logic layer, the Client Logic layer can switch to a view that lets the user specify more details. On that view, when the user clicks "OK," the Client Logic asks the Server Proxy to send the information to the server. According to the response from the server, this layer can decide which view to show.

4. Server Proxy – this layer is a technical layer that provide a convenient API that the Client Logic can consume (in the form of objects and methods) and simply packs the parameters of these methods as a request message to the server. The data in the response is then translated back to objects that those methods return. Some technologies provide this layer as an "out-of-the-box" component, with only some configuration or very little code.

The Server (Middle) Tier

The server, middle tier is composed of:

1. Service layer – this is the counterpart of the Server Proxy layer in the client. It transforms the messages that the client sends into events that call methods in code.

2. Business Logic layer – this is the "brain" of the system. All of the hard-core logic and calculations are done in this layer. When this layer needs to retrieve or store some data in the database, it uses the Data Access Layer (DAL) to do it.

3. Data Access Layer (DAL) – this layer provides the business logic layer with a convenient API to access the database. While the Object Relational Mapping (ORM) layer underneath it handles all of the heavy lifting automatically, sometimes there's a need to provide an API that is more natural, simple, and abstract (i.e., technology agnostic) for the BL tier to consume.

4. Object Relational Mapping layer – this is usually a third-party technology that translates from objects and properties to SQL statements that read and write data to/from relational tables. Usually it's based mostly on configuration and doesn't involve custom code.

The Database Tier

The database tier in our example does not contain a lot of logic, except of a few stored procedures to increase performance. But even besides the stored procedures, and even though the database engine itself is a commercial product, it still contains some artifacts that the development team produces: the schema (structure) of the tables, indexes, views, constraints, etc.

The Alternative Test Scopes

OK. Now that we understand the architecture, let's see what options we have for the test scope for the automation and what are the consequences of each of these options.

End-to-End Test Scope

The first and most obvious option for a test scope in a system that doesn't have external dependencies, is end to end. Figure 6-6 shows this option. The biggest advantage of this option is that it's most similar to what the users do, and it does not compromise the testing of any component or integration between components. However, these tests are naturally slower, harder to stabilize, and maintain due to frequent changes in the SUT and make failure investigation harder.

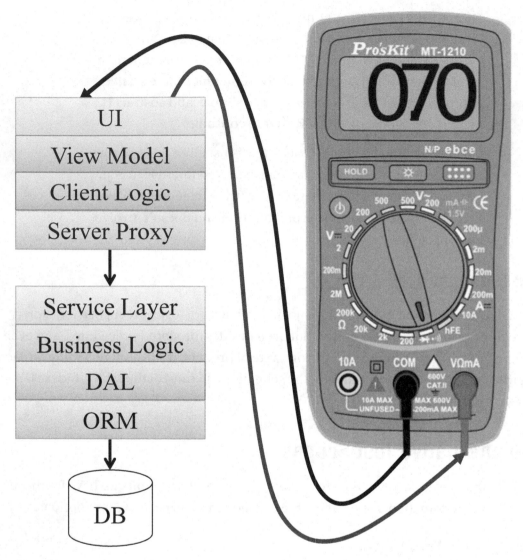

Figure 6-6. *End-to-end test scope*

In this approach the tests interact only with the UI, but the tests usually perform actions that exercise all of the tiers and layers.

CLARIFYING THE "END-TO-END" AMBIGUITY

When some people say "end-to-end" tests, they mean very long-winding scenarios, usually mimicking a complex real-world user scenario. For example, such a test for an e-commerce site could start from user registration, searching for different items in the catalog, adding many items to the shopping cart, removing some of them, changing the quantity of some products in the cart, going to the checkout process, splitting the payment to two different payment methods, using a coupon, finishing the transaction, etc. While these scenarios have some value of validating that such scenarios are working correctly, they lend themselves poorly for test automation because their maintenance usually becomes arduous. If the program is evolving (and as discussed In Chapter 2 – if it doesn't, then there's probably not a lot of value in test automation anyway), then these scenarios would need to change constantly and they will often fail on legitimate changes. The investigation of these failures will take pretty long because the scenario is complex. There may be some value in having a few of these that run only after all the other tests have passed, but relying mostly on this kind of tests is not recommended.

By contrast, when other people, including me, say "end-to-end" tests, or "end-to-end test scope" to be more precise, we mean that the tests interact with the complete system as a whole "black box" and not with only part of it. In other words, the test scope includes all of the layers and components of the system. However, it doesn't mean that the scenarios should be long and winding. For example, the scenario can be as simple as a user adding only one item to the shopping cart, but it's still done on a complete system.

One-Way End to End (UI to DB or DB to UI)

In this approach, shown in Figure 6-7, the test scope is also the entire system and technically it's the same as the previous option. But unlike the previous option, here the test interacts both with the UI and the database, and not only the UI. It has more or less the same advantages and disadvantages of the end-to-end option, but there are a few important differences. First, when you manipulate or check data through the database, you're not testing the system as the use would use it. This has two caveats: first you can miss bugs that the user may encounter; and second, your tests may fail due to problems that are not real bugs. However, it is often faster and simpler to use the database rather than to mimic all of the user actions that are required to create or verify the data.

Note that the chances for failing due to problems that are not real bugs are not necessarily higher than if you do everything from the UI, but there's still a significant difference between these cases: if the UI changes it's probably directly related to a change in requirements. But the database is an implementation detail that the developers can change on their own will. Entering or retrieving the data directly to or from the database often bypasses validations and business rules that the server should enforce, which may bring the system to states that it was not designed for and that would never happen in production.

Another risk that you want to consider when relying on the database is that you take a dependency on one more technology that may change as a whole. When your tests interact with the SUT through the UI, if the UI technology is replaced at some point (e.g., from Windows Forms to WPF), you'll have a tremendous amount of work refitting the tests to the new UI technology. When your tests interact with the SUT both through the UI and through the database, you double the risk, as both the UI technology as well as the database's technology may be replaced one day. Even though these occasions are rare, if you plan the test automation to be long lived, then it can definitely happen in a range of few years. For example, these days many teams replace their database engines from a relational (SQL) database like MS-SQL Server or Oracle, to some "noSQL" alternatives, like MongoDB, or other, more scalable solutions.

However, there are some cases in which this approach is clearly advantageous over end to end:

- Some systems are designed such that customers can interact with the DB directly and/or write applications that interact with the DB directly. In this case it's important to validate that what the customers can do works the way it should.

- Other systems *use* an existing database that another application manages. This other application can be considered "third party" even if it's developed by another team within the same company, as long as their development efforts of the two teams are independent from one another and their release schedules are not synchronized. In this case it may make sense to interact with the database directly instead of with the third-party application

- Speed: it may be much faster to create data directly in the database rather than through the UI. If the purpose of most tests is to work with existing data that already exist in the database, rather than to test the ability to create it, but you still prefer not to rely on shared data (see the next chapter about isolation), then it will probably be much faster to create it in the database directly. Note that you also have a choice to create the data by calling into the server (through the Server Proxy layer or by sending a HTTP request, or using any other layer) instead of using the database directly.

- Reliability and maintainability: despite what I wrote above about the database schema being an implementation detail, in cases where the schema is not likely to change anytime soon, but the UI does, then using the database may be more reliable and easy to maintain, especially if the schema of the database, or at least the parts that we need to interact with, is simple enough.

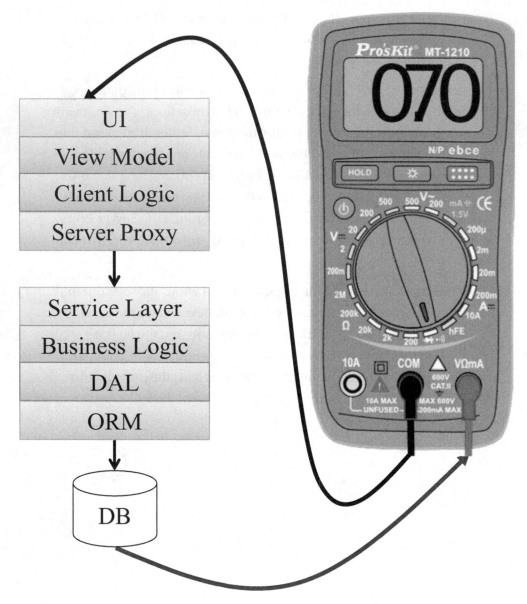

Figure 6-7. *One-way end-to-end test scope*

Server Only (Round-Trip)

This approach, shown in Figure 6-8, is also very common and has some great advantages over an end-to-end test scope. Among its advantages are improved speed and reliability. It is especially appropriate in the following situations:

- The client is only a thin layer over the server.

- The client is changing much more often than the API or protocol in which the client and server communicates.

- The server exposes a public API that customers can use directly (see sidebar titled "API, Backward Compatibility, and Test Automation Maintenance").

- The system has many types of client applications (e.g., for different operating systems, web, mobile, etc.), and there's no point in choosing one over the other. In this case server tests can be combined with separate client only tests (see below) for each client and also few simple end-to-end tests for each client.

In this approach, instead of manipulating and verifying results on the client, the test communicates directly with the server using the same protocol that the client applications use to communicate with the server (most commonly http/https). The fact that the test does not manipulate the UI does not mean that each test should verify just one request/response pair, and in fact mostly all scenarios can describe actual user scenarios, as already mentioned above.

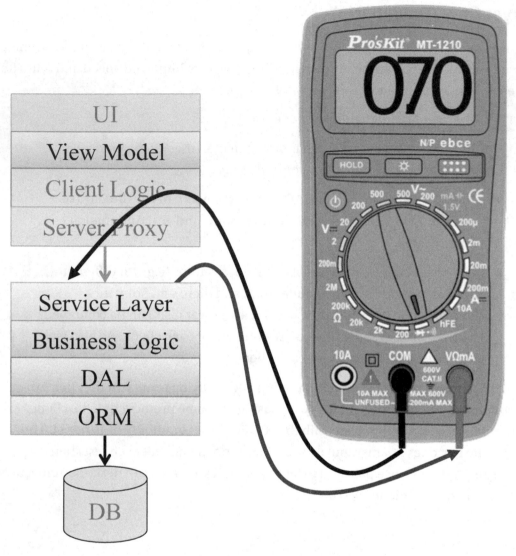

Figure 6-8. *Server-only test scope*

API, BACKWARD COMPATIBILITY, AND TEST AUTOMATION MAINTENANCE

When the application under test exposes a public API, which is exposed to customers or third-party vendors, it makes the lives of the automation developers much easier than usual, as they need to care less about maintainability. If customers or third-party vendors are using the public API of your application, they probably expect your company to maintain and provide backward compatibility of that API between versions. That ensures that every test that passed in one version of the software continues to work exactly the same in newer versions;

otherwise it's a compatibility breaking bug. In other words, the test code of a previously working test should rarely need to change.

For example, suppose that your team develops a blogs engine website. In addition to allowing users to publish new blog posts through the website's UI, it allows developers to write applications that communicate with the website and publish new posts using a REST API. So, for example, a customer may develop his own tool that reads the weather from several other websites, calculates its own average forecast, and uses the API of your blogs engine to publish that forecast automatically. Another customer may use the API to be notified of new posts and to send them automatically by email to relevant recipients according to categories and tags associated with each post.

Maintaining backward compatibility means that those applications that the customer wrote and that use the API of the first version must continue to work seamlessly and exactly the same in newer versions of the blog's engine website, without having to change anything in these applications. New features and functionality could be added to the blog's engine website, but nothing should be removed, and there should be no breaking changes. Note that just keeping the structure of the messages (or public interfaces of classes and methods) intact, is not enough for keeping compatibility. It also requires that the *external behavior* remains the same.

For example, suppose that at some point the product manager requires that each new blogpost has a short abstract that describes what the post is about in order to show in the list of blogposts, and in order to attract the readers to look into the posts that interest them. He also wants to enforce that the abstracts are at least 100 characters long in order to make the writers fill in something relevant. As long as it applies only to blogposts that are created manually through the website, there's no problem with that requirement. However, if we enforce this new constraint also in the API, then our customers that use these APIs will be very annoyed, because now the software that they wrote (e.g., the weather forecast publisher) will no longer work! Clearly, changing their software is not a simple thing, it takes time and money, and if the developer that wrote it left the company then the problem may be even worse… A possible solution for this example is either not to enforce this rule for API-generated blogposts, or to automatically create a placeholder for the abstract that states that this is an automatic blogpost.

Continuing our example, another requirement that the product manager requested is that automatic posts that are generated by API will have the prefix "AUTO:" appended to their title. On the surface, it seems that the API should not be affected by this new feature and there's no problem of backward compatibility. The client will still be able to use the same API message for creating a new blogpost. It can also use the same API message for retrieving all the blogposts filtered by date as it did before. However, if a client application creates a new blogpost, and then searches for the blogposts it created by exact matching of their titles, then now the client's application may fail to find these blogposts because their titles are now prefixed with "AUTO" and no longer match exactly what the application has created. That's why it's important (and much trickier!) to ensure that we keep backward compatibility for the *behavior* and not only the structure of the API messages. But if we have to do it for our customers, then the automation developers can enjoy it too.

Breaking Changes

While in theory 100% of the tests that passed in one version should continue to work in newer versions, reality is always more complicated. If you're working for one of the big companies that has millions of customers that use the API, then breaking backward compatibility is a big deal, and sometimes even bugs are intentionally kept in newer versions just for the chance that fixing it will break existing client's software (this is especially true for vendors of compilers and related technologies that are used as the foundation technology for many applications). But if your team's product has only a handful of customers that use the API, then it may be acceptable to break compatibility here and there in order to fix bugs or make some improvements that the clients may appreciate.

One area that bugs are usually treated in higher priority than backward compatibility is security. This means that if your application had a security breach, and the only feasible fix requires to break the backward compatibility of the API, then it's normally worth paying that price. But then again, creative solutions appropriate for the specific problem at hand may be found to solve the bug without breaking compatibility or at least minimizes the risk for old clients and solving it completely for clients that are willing to update their code.

Server-Only Test Scope (One Way)

This is simply an intersection between the one-way end-to-end approach and the round-trip server-only approach. Like the server-only approach, the test interacts with the server through its API, but like the one-way end-to-end approach, it also interacts directly with the database to enter data as input to the SUT, or check the data written by the SUT. The considerations for this approach are basically the same as of the one-way approach and the server-only approach combined. For example, this approach can be useful to test that the server writes the relevant data to the database on an "update" request, or to inject prerequisite data for a scenario that is implemented though the public server's API. Figure 6-9 shows the architecture of this approach.

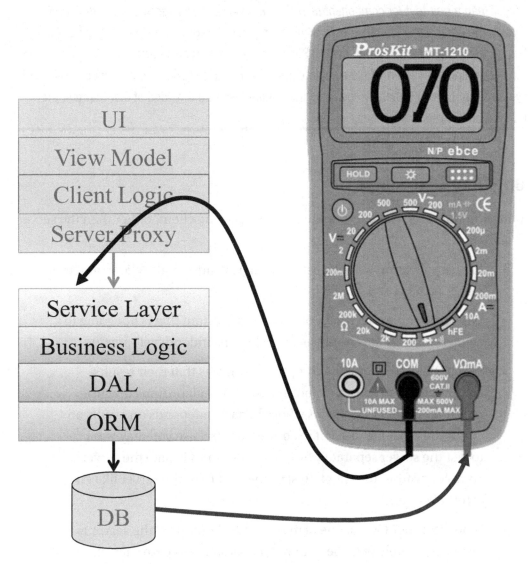

Figure 6-9. *Server-only one way*

WHAT EXACTLY ARE INTEGRATION TESTS?

Even though the term "Integration Tests" is used very broadly, there's no one concise definition for this term. The closest thing I can think of is something like: *every test scope which is bigger than a unit test (or component test) on one hand, and smaller than an end-to-end test on the other hand*. In many cases when people say "integration tests," they refer to the "server-only" approach, but not always. Some even use this term to describe tests that cover the integration between multiple complete systems (like a few end-to-end scopes of different systems combined!) Generally speaking, integration tests are any kind of test that test the integration between two or more components.

Client-Only Test Scope

In some situations, the more important part to test is the client, rather than the server. For example:

- In an application where most of the logic resides in the client, and the server is only used sparingly.

- When the server is a legacy or third-party system that is not going to change, while a new, sophisticated client is under development.

- When the server contains complex algorithms that their results are difficult to predict and control: especially algorithms that use random numbers, or servers whose behavior depends on events and conditions that are difficult to control. In this case you may want to test the server separately from the client, and isolate the server's complexity from the client's test scope (i.e., treat the server like an external system).

- When the client is just one of many other clients, and the server is tested separately (see "Server only" above). In this case each client will be tested separately as well as the server, and only few simple end-to-end tests for each client should be written to validate the integration.

In these cases, it may be beneficial to isolate the server completely from the tests, in order to make the tests faster, more reliable, and easier to deploy. However, in order to do that, we must create a simulator for the server. The simulator should mimic the protocol that the server uses, but the test infrastructure should control the exact content that is emits to the client. In addition, the test can verify what the client sends to it. Simulators are explained and covered later in this chapter. Figure 6-10 shows this option.

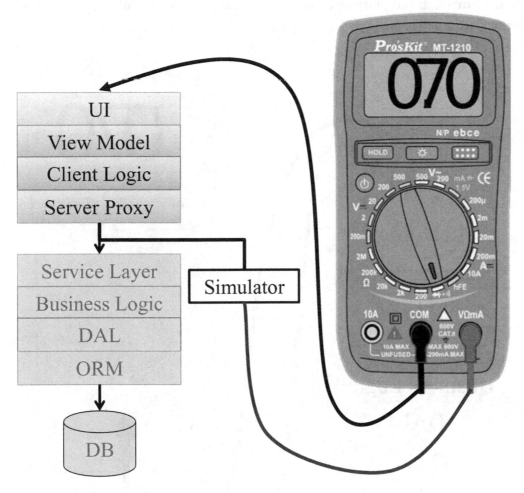

Figure 6-10. *Client-only test scope*

Under-the-Skin Test Scope

Sometimes testing through the UI is not feasible, because the UI's technology doesn't provide a good automation interface or is simply not reliable enough for automation. If you still want to have a test scope that is closest to end to end as possible, you can test the application "under the skin," as shown in Figure 6-11. This approach is very similar to the end-to-end approach, but instead of really mimicking the mouse movements and keyboard strokes, the automation detours the actual UI layer and talks directly to code underneath it, namely the View Model layer.

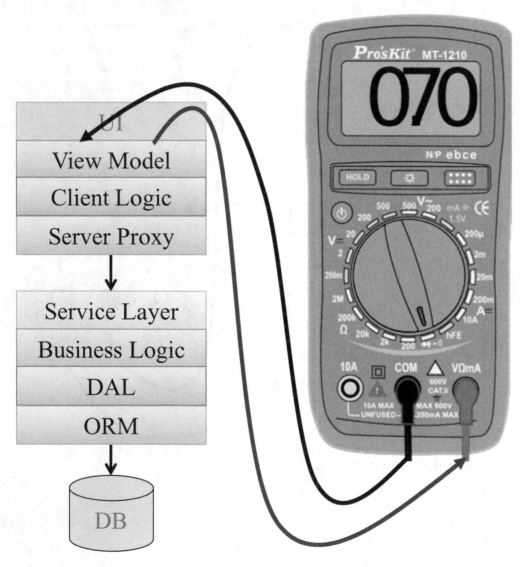

Figure 6-11. *"Under-the-skin" test scope*

While this approach may seem very logical, it poses some series challenges. If these challenges can be addressed, then it can be a valid approach, but you'd better try to tackle these challenges at the very beginning to assess the feasibility and the associated costs of potential solutions, as these challenges may become showstoppers for using this test scope. Note that in most cases these challenges involve some refactoring of the client application. These challenges are:

1.   First and foremost, the view layer should be easily separable from the other layers. If one of the MV* patterns[2] is applied properly, then this should be pretty easy. But often the actual architecture drifts a bit (or more...) from the planned architecture. In this case you should first assess whether it's feasible to refactor the code back to the planned MV* architecture.

2.   Initialization – Each program that starts executes a method called "main." This method typically loads all the resources that the application needs, and eventually opens the main window. At this point, the process stays idle waiting for input (mainly mouse and keyboard events), and as these occur, the application invokes the relevant code to handle the relevant event. After the event is handled, the application returns to its idle state, waiting for further events. Only when the user closes the application window, or chooses to exit in some other way, then the application returns to the end of the "main" method and exits. However, tests behave somewhat differently. The testing framework (e.g., JUnit, NUnit, MSTest, etc.) implements the "main" method for you and lets you define different tests, each of which is like its own little program. In addition, these frameworks allow you to run code before all the tests and after all of the tests. If we'd simply call the SUT's "main" method from the framework's initialization code or from one of the tests, then it will show the UI and wait for user input. Until a real user won't close the window, the call to the main method won't return, and the test won't be able to continue! (Most frameworks will raise a timeout error after some period of time,

---

[2]MV* refer to any of the following design patterns: MVC (Model-View-Controller), MVP (Model-View-Presenter) or MVVM (Model-View-View Model).

failing the test.) Therefore, we must create our own initialization code that from one hand initializes all the relevant resources (e.g., opens a connection to the server), but on the other hand doesn't actually show the UI, or at least doesn't enter the loop that waits for user input. Writing that initialization method and separating the initialization of the view from the initialization of the other component may require a massive refactoring, depending on the actual design and complexity of the system. Here too, if the actual architecture follows a well-structured MV* pattern, then this should be easier.

3. Dialogs and popup messages – Yet again, if the separation of concerns of the MV* architecture is strictly kept, then this should be much easier. But dialogs and popup messages often make it more complicated to implement the pattern correctly, and therefore provide a significant challenge for the automation. If at some situation the application needs to display a message to the user or needs to ask the user for additional input, then it might open a message box or a modal dialog box. If this code is called from the test, then the dialog will actually appear while the test runs (!) and will never continue past the line that opens the dialog unless a real user will close it. If the pattern is implemented correctly, then the event handler should not open the dialog directly. Instead it should use an abstract factory object to do that. If the test can replace this factory with a different factory that will return fake dialog objects, then this problem is solved. These fake dialog objects will not be real dialogs with UI, but rather just pure

objects that implement the same interface as the dialog, and will return immediately with the "input" that the test provides to the application in place of the user.

Note that this approach means that most of the client code is loaded into the memory space of the test process.

Pure Logic Test Scope

While this is not a very popular approach, I think that it's interesting to mention, at least in order to encourage you to think "out of the box." If the business logic is spread over both the client and the server (or other components) and you want to test them together, but you also want the tests to be fast and be able to run without any special deployment and configuration, then this approach may be relevant to you.

In this approach, we take only the components that contain the business logic, and glue them together, bypassing and mocking all of the more technical layers, as shown in Figure 6-12. Mocking[3] is conceptually very similar to simulating, but instead of communicating with the SUT over a communication channel, it communicates with it using direct method calls, usually by implementing an interface. Mocking is used mainly in unit testing, but it is useful in this approach too.

---

[3]Some purists would say (according to Gerard Meszaros book "xUnit Test Patterns", and mentioned in Martin Fowler's blog at `https://martinfowler.com/bliki/TestDouble.html`) that this is not the correct definition of *Mocking*, but rather the definition of a *Test Double* or more specifically of *Fake*. Test Double is a generic term, which includes *Dummies*, *Fakes*, *Stubs*, *Spies* and *Mocks*. However, even though according to this terminology, "mock" is a very specific use of Test Double, it is the most widely used term, even in its more generic meaning.

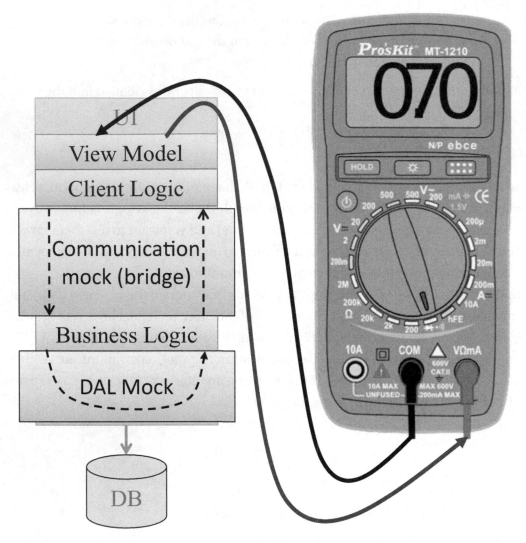

Figure 6-12. *Pure Logic test scope*

In this option, the test communicates directly with the View Model layer, similarly to the "under-the-skin" approach. However, instead of having the client and the server communicate over a real communication channel, through the Server Proxy in the client and the Service Layer in the server, we connect the two together using a mock that behaves like a simple bridge: it directs any call from the client directly to a method call in the server and returns the results accordingly, on the same process and thread. Finally, we mock the Data Access Layer (DAL) to simulate any communication with the database. Usually we'll mimic the database behavior by storing and retrieving the data in and from memory instead of the real database.

Component Tests

Component tests are tests that test a single component (e.g., the Business Logic component, or the DAL component) separated from the rest of the system. A component is usually a single DLL or jar file. It may have external dependencies, like files, database, etc. But in most cases if the component under test depends on another component that is part of the developed application, then the test will provide mock objects that simulate the dependent component.

Note that if you create separate tests for each component in a layered architecture, then except for the Business Logic layer, most tests won't reflect scenarios from a user perspective, but rather a more technical usage of its API. While this may not be the most interesting thing to verify from the end-user perspective, it may be very interesting from an architectural and design perspective. Besides verifying the correctness of the code, a Component test also ensures that the tested functionality is indeed implemented in the intended component, and it helps ensure that the intended design is kept. If component tests are implemented in an early stage of the development, the act of designing the tests also helps shape the design of the components and the APIs to be easier to use and maintain.

This is especially beneficial for components that should be reusable in different applications. This is true for reusable components that are used in multiple applications developed by the same company, for internal optimization purposes, but it is even more important and beneficial for components that the company develops and should be reused by its customers. For example, an application that is used to control some electronic device that the company manufactures may contain a component that communicates with that device. This component, besides being used by the application itself, can be exposed to customers that want to interact with the device from their own applications. As writing the tests against the component is similar to using it from another client, writing these tests in an early stage of development helps shape the API of the component to be easy to use.

Unit Tests

While Component tests test a single component, unit tests test an even smaller piece, which is usually a single class or even a method. Unit tests are considered to test the smallest testable functionality. Because these tests are so tightly coupled to the implementation, typically the developers who write the product code also write the unit test that verifies the code that they've written. In Chapter 17 we'll talk in more detail about unit tests as well as about the test-driven development (TDD) methodology that helps writing these tests effectively.

Real-World Architecture

While the above-mentioned layered architecture is still pretty common in many traditional business applications, every application is different and today most systems are more complicated than this. After we'll discuss few patterns I'll present a few real-world examples of application architectures and the chosen automation architecture.

Intended Architecture vs. the Actual One

Most projects start with a pretty looking architecture diagram (e.g., like the above-mentioned layered architecture), but very often after some mileage, the *actual* architecture becomes less clear and pretty as the diagrams, and some components begin to "grab" responsibilities that should have been of another component, making the actual architecture messier. In these situations, some of the above alternatives may not be very relevant or may be more difficult to implement. It is very common that when starting to develop automated tests late in the process of a software project, to hit obstacles that are caused by such differences. Trying to overcome these obstacles usually makes the test code more complicated, difficult to maintain, and less reliable. However, compromises often have to be made between these drawbacks and the price of refactoring the code to eliminate them. Because you usually hit these obstacles when you implement the tests, then it means that you still probably don't have enough coverage to refactor the code safely...

Common Variations

Before we'll talk about more complex architectures, let's talk about some common variations to the described layered architecture:

1. Today most business applications are web based, possibly with a mobile (smartphone) client rather than a classical Windows application. The technologies for the web-based clients also vary, mainly on how much of the logic is done on the client (the

browser) and how much on the server. With mobile applications, there are a few common variations in the technologies and concepts of the UI: whether the app uses the UI of the OS directly ("native"); a web UI (adopted to the mobile user); or hybrid, which is a mainly a web browser embedded inside a native app.

2.   Many applications support more than one type of client. They may have a desktop application, a website, and a mobile app, which mostly do the same things, but each one of them is more suited to the technology and form factor of the machine that they run on. This brings an interesting challenge to test automation: Do we want to implement each scenario using each technology? Later in this chapter we'll discuss this situation.

3.   Because browsers can handle the rendering of the UI, and also the communication with the web server for us, it's pretty common for traditional web applications that the web server serves mostly static HTML pages to the browser and handles most of the "client logic" and the "business logic" at the same tier, and maybe even in the same component (as one monolithic layer). For example, if the user clicks a column header in a grid to sort by that column, the browser sends a request to the server, which serves a new page with the new sort order. Many traditional but more complex systems split the web server and put the "UI logic" in a Web Server tier that communicates with a different tier (server or "service") that contains the business logic and/or the access to the database. In most modern web applications, however, the client side contains complex JavaScript code that contains the client's logic. Usually this JavaScript code itself is componentized and uses one of the many JavaScript frameworks or libraries, with Angular and React being the most notable ones these days. From the test automation perspective, this can be useful for client-side unit or component tests, but it can also be used by invoking JavaScript functions from Selenium in broader test scopes.

4. Sometimes the application has two or more different types of clients for different personas. For example, a main client application for the end user and another website client application for the administrator and/or executives.

5. Many modern applications take a *service-oriented architecture* (SOA) or even a micro-service approach, in which almost every component is a separate service that resides in a separate process and can be deployed to different machines to allow for better scalability.

6. On the other side of the spectrum, many older systems contain most of the business logic as stored procedures inside the database layer instead of with a separate tier.

7. Some (mostly modern) applications have two separate databases: one for fast handling of transactions, and another one that is more optimized for querying. After the data is written to the transactional DB, it's also transferred via some asynchronous queue mechanism to a service that transforms the data to the structure, which is more suitable for querying, and saves it there. This architectural pattern is called "Command and Query Responsibility Segregation" or CQRS for short. Some applications may have even more databases for different purposes, and even use different database technologies to best match the needs of each of them (e.g., relational "SQL" database, document database, graph database, etc.).

Combining Tests

Even though you can choose only one test scope and use if for all of your tests, there are at least two ways in which you can combine more than one approach.

Mix and Match

Because each option for a test scope has its own pros and cons, often the most efficient strategy is to create a mixture. It can be decided which portion of the tests should be implemented using which scope, or what are the criteria for choosing one scope over another for each test. For example, it can be decided that one representative scenario from each feature will be implemented as end to end, while all other tests will be server only. In addition, we can decide that developers should write unit tests to cover the business logic for every new functionality that they write. Mike Cohn's Test Pyramid[4] is a classic example of such a mixture, though there are many other valid approaches, and I suggest that you consider for yourself what makes sense and working best for you. In fact, while I believe that under some optimal conditions the end result should be similar to the Test Pyramid, I discourage aiming for it by deciding on percentages for each test scope. Just choose the most appropriate scope for each test according to the pros and cons of each scope, and let the percentages be whatever they be, even if it doesn't form a "pyramid."

A better approach, in my opinion, is to let the team choose the right scope for each test. While it's certainly not confined to it, I find it especially appropriate when using the ATDD methodology (see Chapter 16), as it also encourages the team to collaborate on the tests and define them according to their business value. While I strongly recommend this approach, it has its drawback backs too: using too many kinds of test scopes can become difficult to manage and maintain. In addition, there's no one clear rule to decide which test scope is best suited for each test, so there can be disputes. See the summary of considerations below for some guidelines that will help you decide on the right scope for each test.

Abstract Test Scopes

Because test scopes are independent of the scenarios, sometimes it's desirable to reuse the test scenarios and be able to run those using different scopes. For example, a smaller scope for fast feedback, and a larger scope to verify the integration with all layers. The main idea is that relevant business actions that the test performs are implemented in a layer that can be injected to the test class or overridden by derived classes. In this case, this business layer serves as an adapter between the test and the SUT. This way the test itself remains the same, but we can provide different implementations of the relevant actions to support the desired test scopes. Figure 6-13 shows how the test can use different adapters to interact with the application using different test scopes. Listing 6-1 shows a pseudo-code for such a test. In this listing, the InitializeSut method instantiates the chosen adapter, which is then used throughout the test (using the _sut member) to perform different actions through that adapter.

---

[4]Mike Cohn, *Succeeding with Agile: Software Development Using Scrum* (Boston, Massachusetts, United States: Addison-Wesley Professional, 2009)

Listing 6-1. Abstract Test Scope

```
[TestClass]
public class PromotionTests
{
  private IApplication _sut;

  [TestInitialize]

  public void TestInitialize()
  {
    /* The following line reads a value from the configuration file
    determines whether it should return an object that uses Selenium to
    implement an end-to-end test scope, or another object that uses
    HTTP do talk directly to the server. */
    _sut = InitializeSUT("Configuration.xml");
  }

  [TestMethod]
  public void DiscountIsGivenForCategoryPromotion()
  {
    var category = _sut.Admin.CreateCategory("Test Automation");
    var book1 = category.Add(
    "Growing Object-Oriented Software Guided by Tests", 54.99);
    var book2 = category.Add("xUnit Test Patterns", 74.99);
    var book3 = category.Add(
    "The Complete Guide to Test Automation", 99.99);
    var book4 = category.Add("Specification by Example", 49.99);

    _sut.Admin.CreateCategoryPromotion(category, 10);

    var shoppingCart = _sut.User.ShoppingCart;
    shoppingCart.Add(book1);
    shoppingCart.Add(book2);
    shoppingCart.Add(book3);
    Assert.AreEqual(10, shoppingCart.Discount);
```

```
Assert.AreEqual(book1.Price + book2.Price + book3.Price - 10,
shoppingCart.Total);
    }
}
```

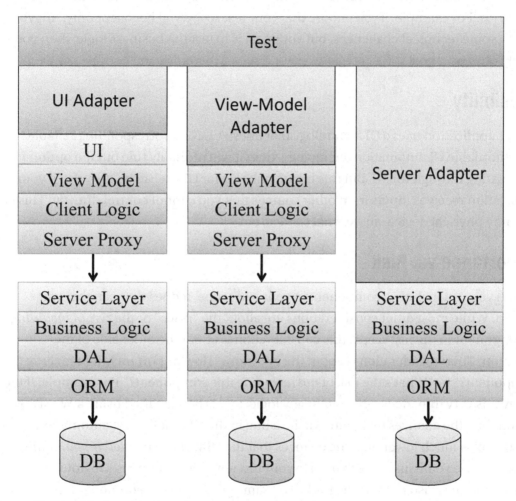

Figure 6-13. *Abstract test scope*

Summary of the Considerations

Now we covered many alternatives and how we can combine them, but when you'd need to really choose the right one for you, you may still be perplexed. In order to help you choose, here's a summary of the considerations.

Goal

Before we start designing our test automation we must have a clear picture of our goal: What are the most important scenarios that we plan to cover, and why? According to this goal, we must ensure to include all of the important components that participate in these scenarios. For example, if you choose that your test scope will be "client only," maybe due to some technical challenges, but your goal is to test the business logic, then you'll surely miss your goal.

Feasibility

If your application uses a UI technology that doesn't have a corresponding reliable and affordable UI automation technology, then it will probably rule out the option for automating through the UI. But this is true not only for UI – it can be true also if your application receives inputs from other sources that you cannot control directly. This can be some physical device, an external service, etc.

Importance vs. Risk

Even if you can include a component in your test scope, it doesn't mean that you should. While most other considerations are about the "price" or the risk of *including* a component in the test scope, this consideration is about the other side of the equation. This consideration is about the question: "How important is it to include this component?" or "What's the risk of *not including* this component?" For example, if the UI layer is very thin, does not contain any logic, and is being edited using a WYSIWYG editor, then the chances that there will be a bug in the UI that the test automation will detect is much lower than the chances that the UI will be changed *intentionally*, in which case you'll just have to update your test anytime it happens. Obviously, this consideration is also not specific to UI. The same goes for every component that doesn't have much logic in it or is already tested and is not being changed anymore.

Speed

If the tests are planned to run only at night, then this may not be a significant factor, unless the entire run starts to slip from the night hours to the morning. However, if you plan to run the test in CI or expect the developers to run the tests before they check in their changes, then you can't expect them to wait a few hours for the tests to complete.

In addition to the feedback cycle that the automation provides to application developers, the tests speeds directly impact the feedback cycle of the automation developers, which translates to their productivity and the quality of their work. While you develop, debug, fix, or refactor a particular test, the time it takes to run that particular test can make a huge difference because it can easily become the most significant portion of the time that you spend doing these things. While developing, debugging, and fixing are usually necessary, and you'll do them one way or another, if running a single test takes too long, it may be so frustrating that you'd avoid refactoring the test code – which will eventually make it unmaintainable.

There are many techniques that can make your tests runs faster, and they are detailed in Chapter 15. As a general rule – UI automation, communications between machines, and accessing large amounts of data can have a big impact on the speed of your tests. Pure unit tests are almost always many folds faster than end-to-end tests (though they have their drawbacks and limitations too, of course).

While the test speed is important, don't overrate its importance. Other considerations may be more significant than this. In addition, don't assume anything about the speed of the tests before measuring! Sometime a properly designed end-to-end or integration tests can be pretty fast if you don't rely on large amounts of data, and maybe the server also resides on the same machine.

What's Likely to Change?

Any change in the interface between the test and the SUT means that you need to update the tests – whether this interface is the UI, API, DB schema, etc. Some of these interfaces change more often than other, creating more maintenance costs for the tests. In fact, there are two types of such changes: gradual, constant changes; or one-time replacement. If the interface changes gradually and constantly, then you need to update your tests constantly as well. However, if the entire interface is being replaced, then in this case you'll need to re-create large portions of the test automation from scratch, or maybe even rewrite everything! For example, in many cases the UI may change often. This is a gradual, constant change. However, if it some point the entire UI technology is replaced completely, then you need to rewrite all the code of the automation that interact directly with the UI. The same can happen to the API, though it's much less likely if this is a public API in which the company is obligated to maintain for backward compatibility.

While this is a very important consideration, the unfortunate thing is that often you cannot predict the future. Maybe today an internal API changes more often than the UI, but at one point the entire UI technology will be completely replaced. Likewise, the opposite can happen just as well, and you usually can't predict what the future holds.

However, even though you can't predict the future, sticking the test scenarios to business functionality, and creating a modular infrastructure that abstracts all of the technology-specific details inside replaceable modules, is the best bet (See the first few chapters in Part II for more details). Finally, you can often make pretty good bets about what's likely to be replaced and what's not, and also what changes gradually more often.

Limited Resources

If you design your test automation to use some expensive or limited resource, then this may limit your ability to expand the usage of your tests. Such a resource may be hardware equipment, software licenses, or some paid service. If for example, in order to run the tests, you need expensive software to be installed on that machine, then probably you'll have a hard time justifying to management that all developers should run the tests before check-in. If the license is required only in order to develop the test, then you'll be able to ask the developers to run the tests before check-in, but they won't be able to fix or create new tests – which of course relates to the discussion in Chapter 3 about people and tools.

Extensibility and Customizability

If your application is customizable, it means that regular users can change its default behavior without having to know how to write code. These changes are usually pretty limited related to what the user can achieve using extensibility, but still adds a level of complexity to your test matrix. In most cases the application comes preset to a default configuration that the user can change (customize). Note that these customizations, including the default configuration are in fact *inputs* of the system. Therefore, you probably don't want to use the default configuration in your tests, but rather have the tests take advantage of the customizability to make things easier to test. For example, if the user can customize a form by adding fields to it, or remove some of the default fields, then you may want the test to customize the application to include only a small subset of the fields in most tests, but create fields of different kinds in other tests that are dedicated to testing the customizability feature itself.

If your application is designed to be extensible, this means that customers can develop their own extensions that will either replace or add to the default behavior of the application. In this case too, the application is likely provided with some default extensions, but you should not rely on their existence for your tests. You should separate testing the code functionality from the extensions, as these default extensions may or may not be used by the customer. In addition, it can be useful to create a special extension for the needs of the test for various purposes, but mainly to test that the extensibility entry points are called when they should.

Beyond the Layered Architecture

The discussion about the different alternatives of testing a layered architecture should have helped you get the idea of the possibilities to architect the tests for that classic architecture. However, as mentioned in the beginning of the chapter (and depicted by Figure 6-3), many systems are more complicated than this, or simply, different. While the number of possible architectures is infinite, the basic ingredients of the layered architecture exists in virtually all architectures: big systems are made out of smaller subsystems that communicate with one another. These subsystems often store and retrieve data and are typically built from smaller components. Lastly, most systems have some form of a user interface. Because we've already encountered all of those ingredients in the layered architecture, you should be able to apply most of the ideas and considerations to the architecture of any system that you need to plan your test automation for.

You may want to take a look at Appendix A to get some ideas for how to apply these ideas in real-world applications, but before you do that, there's one more concept that we only mentioned above briefly and we still need to cover in more detail – **simulators**. As the layered architecture described above was of a stand-alone application that don't have dependencies on any other systems, we didn't need simulators, but in most real-world systems, as you can see in the appendix, simulators are an essential pattern that you likely need to use too.

Simulators

In the context of test automation, a *simulator* is a component that is developed specifically for the purposes of the tests to simulate another component that the SUT depends upon and interacts with it, but we don't want to test that component. Simulators have several benefits:

- Because the test controls it, it can simulate situations that may be very difficult to produce in other ways.

- It helps us make our tests more reliable, because we avoid many unexpected situations that we can't anticipate. Usually, we would prefer to simulate third-party services that we can't control.

- It can be used also to verify that the SUT sends the correct messages to the simulated component.

- In case that the service we want to simulate is a limited resource, the simulator helps us test earlier and more often (which shortens the feedback cycle). Examples for such limited resources can be a legacy Mainframe system, a paid service or some kind of physical device.

For example, suppose our system communicates with a third party or a legacy service that predicts the weather by communicating with some sensors, and our system makes some decisions upon the predicted weather. If we'd try to test the system end to end, it will be very difficult to verify that our system makes the appropriate decisions if we can't control the predicted weather. We can try to control the predicted weather by physically controlling the heat, moisture, and wind in the sensors' area, but that would be very difficult and expensive to do, especially if we need many test environments. In addition, it will be difficult to assess how the physical parameters that we control should affect the predicted weather. But if we simulate the weather prediction service altogether, we can have the test *tell it* directly to predict a stormy weather or calm weather so that's what our system will see, and then we can easily test our system to see if it made the appropriate decision according to the kind of weather that we told the simulated service to report.

This means that a simulator generally has two interfaces: The first one communicates with the SUT just as if it was the real service. The second one is the interface that allows the test to control what the simulator reports to the SUT and/ or to retrieve information about the messages that the SUT sends to the service. Note that when you develop such a simulator, while you can design the interface with the test any way you like, you must keep the interface with the SUT exactly like of the real service. However, you can and should sterilize what the simulator sends to the SUT to the necessary minimum in order to make it easier to control and maintain. Also, you should consider whether you want the simulator to reside inside the process of the tests or in a separate process. If you decide to implement it as part of the test process, then the test can interact with the simulator by directly accessing shared data in memory (e.g., a static list of objects) If you decide to go for a separate process, you need to have another communication channel between the tests and the simulator to allow the tests to control the simulator. Continuing the previous example, the test should use this channel to tell the simulator to "predict" stormy weather. Whether you implement the simulator in the same process as the test or a separate one, you may have to take care to synchronize access to data (whether it's in the test process's memory or in that of the separate simulator process) to avoid race conditions[5] if the SUT interacts with the simulator asynchronously from the test.

There are two common misconceptions about simulators. The first one is that they should replay real-world data. For some people it sounds easier to record the communication traffic and let the simulator replay it. However, replaying messages "as is" usually isn't going to work, as some parts of the message either depend on date and time, on order, on data received in the request (which the simulated service responds to), on uniqueness, etc. Attempting to make the simulator manipulate the messages accordingly will just complicate it, make it less reliable and more difficult to maintain. It also makes it much more difficult to specify the expected result deterministically and also prevents you from testing rare edge cases that the recording didn't capture simply because they're rare and may be missing from the recording.

The second misconception is that the simulator should be stand-alone. A stand-alone simulator is one which always replies with the same response, or has some internal logic to always reply with an "appropriate" response, but cannot be controlled by the test. While there are some uses for this, the main caveat of a stand-alone simulator is that you don't really have control over the inputs that the simulator provides to the SUT and cannot simulate all the cases you need. In addition, over time it leads the code of the simulator to be complicated and possibly buggy because its internal logic will just get more and more complicated, while actually trying to duplicate the behavior of the

---

[5]A Race-condition is a case where the state of a system is dependent on the sequence or timing of asynchronous events. It becomes a bug if it brings the system to a state that the programmer did not anticipate or handle correctly.

original service in order to reply with the "correct" response to all possible permutations of the request.

The preferred approach I usually recommend is to make the simulator as thin as possible and allow the test to control it directly. In addition, if you also want to verify the messages that the SUT sends to the simulator, then you should also add a feature to the simulator to retrieve the data that was sent to it, so you can investigate it in the test.

OVERCOMING THE PSYCHOLOGICAL BARIER

For some reason, in most of the cases that I suggested to a customer to implement a simulator, the initial response was that even though it's a cool idea, it's not realistic, at least not in the near future. This answer usually came from test managers, but sometimes also from dev managers. I guess that this reaction comes because it's a big mind-shift from manual testing, and it seems much more complicated and risky because of that. However, in most cases when I persistently asked what it would take to build the simulator, explained its benefits and the risks of instability in case we won't have it, it turned out to be much simpler than everyone would have initially thought. In most of these cases there was one relevant developer who had either written the service or the component that talks to it, which once I found and talked to him, he gave me all the technical details that I needed in order to build the simulator.

In some cases, though, I had to reverse engineer the protocol, which was more time consuming, but still certainly doable. Note that when you follow the procedure of writing one test at a time, as will be described in Part 2, then you don't need to reverse engineer and implement the entire protocol at once, but rather only the minimum that is necessary for the particular test. Once you write one test with the simulator and everyone can see that it's working, no one will stop you!

Simulating Date and Time

Many systems execute batch jobs or raise some events on particular date or time intervals or at particular dates and times. In these cases, many scenarios are often not feasible to test effectively without some kinds of work-arounds. Tampering with the system's clock is not recommended because it affect all processes on the machine (especially if you run Outlook). Sometimes it's possible to tamper with the data in the database to cause the event we want sooner, but that's not always an option and may cause data integrity issues.

As the date and time are inputs to the system like any other inputs, if we want to control it in the test we need to simulate it. However, the date and time are usually not provided from a "service" but rather directly from the operating system. While it's not feasible to mock the operating system itself, the trick is to create an abstraction layer between the operating system's clock and the application. If the system employs a dependency injection (DI) mechanism, then it may already have such an abstraction layer. If not, then the code of the application should be refactored to introduce this layer. If there are many places in the code that access the system's clock, then it can be a risky refactoring, but if not, then it's not that hard. Then you can implement two classes that implement this abstraction: one uses the real system's clock – this is the class that is used in production; and another one is the simulator (or mock) that the test can control. You should either create a special build target (in addition to the standard "debug" and "release") that uses the date/time simulator or have some kind of mechanism to inject that class at runtime.

Note that no system is designed to handle a case where the time moves backward, so the simulator should only allow the test to jump the simulated time forward. It's also important to mention that if a few subsystems or services rely on the system's clock, then it's important that all of them will use same simulator in order to be synchronized with one another. See the third example in Appendix A for a real-world application of this solution.

Summary: Making Your Own Choice

Now that you're familiar with the main techniques and approaches for architecting how the test automation can interact with the SUT, and the considerations for each of them, you may want to take a look at Appendix A to see some real-world examples. With or without reading Appendix A, you should have all the tools you need in order to plan the architecture for the test automation of *your* system. Note, however, that when you'll try to apply this knowledge for the first time, you may still be confused. This is because there's usually more than just one right way. Few alternatives may be valid, even though each has different pros and cons. Eventually, after considering all the options, you should choose what you believe to be the best for you and for your organization and go with it! Over time, you'll learn and adjust, or maybe even decide to change direction, but at least you've gained valuable experience.

CHAPTER 7

Isolation and Test Environments

In the previous chapter about architecture, we mentioned that for every computer system, the outputs yielded from the system depend only on the sequence of inputs provided to it. According to this claim, we said that we must control all the inputs in order to determine what the output should be in a particular test. However, this claim also implies that we need to re-initialize the system before each test!

In order to understand what it means, let's start from a very simple example: if we test the Calculator application on Windows and press "1", "+", "1", and "=" we expect to see an output of "2" in the result window, right? However, this is true only if the initial state is just after starting the application or after pressing the "C" button, which clears the current calculation. If we already pressed some keys before we started our tests, for example, already pressed "1", then the result will be "12" (the first "1" we press in the test will join the initial "1" that was there before the test to form an "11", and then the "+", "1", and "=" will change it to "12").

State

While Calculator is a simple application and we can pretty quickly restart it before each test, this is not always practical for other applications. But fortunately, the above-mentioned claim is too strict, and the following softened version of it is still true: "*the outputs yielded from the system depend on the sequence of inputs provided to it, **and its initial state**.*" *Another, more common way to phrase it is that "The output of a computer system is completely determined by its inputs and its current state."* This means that in order for the tests to be reliable, we must have full control, not only on the inputs, but also on the state of the application. Even though the internal state of an application is

© Arnon Axelrod 2018
A. Axelrod, *Complete Guide to Test Automation*, https://doi.org/10.1007/978-1-4842-3832-5_7

mostly controlled directly by the application itself and not by the test, the test can bring it to most desired states by starting from an earlier state and applying the necessary inputs. In our calculator example, instead of having to restart the calculator before each test, it suffices that we press the "C" button in order for the test to be correct in all cases.

Note that **state** is anything that the system remembers, in any kind of memory. This includes (though not limited to):

1. The CPU registers. Among others, this includes the Instruction Pointer register that tells the CPU the address of the next command to execute.

2. The RAM. Normally the variables and data that a program stores at runtime, which are not saved to disk is stored in this memory.

3. Local hard drives. The data stored in hard drives is typically either in the form of files and folder (the file system), or in the form of a database (which typically uses the file system underneath). The Windows Registry is another form of data that is stored on the hard drive.

4. In case of a virtual machine (VM), both the host and the guest machines have their own CPU registers, RAM, and local hard drives. Obviously, the guest machine only uses the resources provided by its host, but to most purposes these look and behave like two distinct machines.

5. Remote hard drives. Similar to the local hard drives, but these drives are connected to another computer on the network. These drives are typically accessed either through a network file system or through a database service over the network.

6. The state of remote machines and services, including cloud services. These days most computer systems consume cloud services or services from remote machines. If we treat these services as part of our system, then the state of these systems should also be considered as part of the state of our application. For example, if our application uses a cloud-based indexing service, then the state of this service can affect the outputs of our system.

7. The browser's cache and cookies. While these are in fact stored in RAM and/or local hard drives, in web applications these have a special significance, as the web application accesses them, and is affected by them, in a different fashion than regular RAM and hard drives.

Hypothetically, any external change to any piece of information stored in these locations can affect the state of the application and interfere with the results of the tests. Luckily, most of these storage forms are controlled and managed by pieces of software that limit the access that a program has to these storage, to only the portions assigned to it or specifically permitted. In addition, the more the application is modular, the more we can consider the state of each module separately and guarantee that a certain output can only be affected by the state of certain subsystems. We can even take advantage of these limits and guarantees to make our test automation system more reliable and predictable by having better control over the state of the system. Harnessing these guarantees to our needs is called *isolation*.

In contrast, when these guarantees are not harnessed appropriately, then this can often cause serious problems to the test automation and hurt its reliability. I like to say that these problems are caused by *lack of isolation*.

Isolation Problems and Solutions

Let's first consider some common problems that are caused by lack of isolation and then we'll talk about relevant isolation techniques that can solve these problems. After that, we'll discuss some other advantageous "side effects" that we can gain from using proper isolation.

Problem 1 – Manual Tests and Automated Test Running in Different Times

Consider an e-commerce application that sells audio equipment. Kathy is one of the most veteran automation developers in the team. One of the first tests that she has written was a sanity test that tries to add the product "earphones," which is known to cost $100, to the shopping cart; and the "Microphone" product, which is known to cost $50, and verifies that the total price of the cart is $150. This test was very stable and was running as part of the nightly sanity suite in the QA environment for a long time, and only failed when there was a major problem or bug.

One morning, the QA manager asked John, a manual tester, to verify that when the administrator changes the price of products, existing invoices keep showing the original price. John performed the test and happily reported to his boss that the application worked correctly (or maybe he wasn't so happy, because he feels more satisfied when he finds bugs?).

Anyway, the next morning when Kathy examined the results of the automated nightly sanity suite, she was surprised to see that this old and reliable test failed. Further investigation showed that the actual total of the cart was $170 instead of the expected $150. A deeper investigation revealed that someone changed the price of "Earphones" to $120. You probably realize by now who is this someone...

Such stories are pretty common. Usually when the automation project is young and there are not so many tests, the frequency of such events is pretty low and can be fixed very specifically when they occur. However, when the automation grows and there are many tests that rely on a large variety of existing data from a shared database, the frequency of such events goes up and can adversely affect the reliability of the automation results.

Problem 2 – Manual Tests and Automated Tests Running Simultaneously

One other test that Kathy wrote verifies that when a customer completes an order with three earphones, the inventory is updated accordingly. More specifically, when the test starts, it first reads the number of earphones in the inventory; then it performs the transaction of buying three earphones, and eventually it reads the inventory level once again and verifies that it was reduced by three relatively to the original read.

This test worked perfectly fine at nightly runs, but occasionally when this test ran during the day, and especially in pressured times before releases, this test failed. The reason is that John (and other manual testers) performed additional transactions during the day and occasionally bought earphones exactly between the time the test started and the time it ended. The automatic test fails because it expects the updated inventory to be exactly three below what it was at the beginning, but because of the other transactions that the manual testers did in parallel, it drops even more.

Problem 3 – Order Matters

As the result of the previous experiences, Kathy implemented some isolation mechanism: instead of using existing products from the database (like "earphones" and "microphone"), the test automation infrastructure has created special products ("test1," "test2," etc.) before any test was run, and delete it after the last test completes. The tests now only use these products instead of the real ones.

One day a new automation developer named Bob has joined Kathy's automation team. The first task that the QA manager assigned to him was to automate the test that John used to perform, which verifies that when the administrator changes the price of products, existing invoices keep showing the original price (the same test that was mentioned in problem #1).

Bob successfully implemented this test and ran it few times to make sure that it's stable. In addition, the QA manager warned him that there could be a conflict with the sanity test as was mentioned in problem #1, so he ran this test a few times, too, and made sure that it also continued to work properly.

For some nights both of these tests were running without any problem. One day, Kathy noticed that the name of the test that Bob wrote was not very descriptive so she changed it. To everyone's surprise, the next night the sanity test failed. Like in the previous case, the test failed because the actual result was $170 instead of $120. When Kathy ran the test again separately, it still passed. All manual tests looked fine too. Kathy was baffled, and finally decided that it was probably a one-time thing (maybe a bug that was already fixed this morning?) and that the failure couldn't be reproduced.

To her even bigger surprise, the next night the test failed again! Feeling more baffled, she decided to investigate more thoroughly. Eventually she found out that changing the name of the test caused the order of the tests to change and make Bob's test run before the sanity test, while before the name was changed it ran after the sanity test, and that Bob's test was modifying the price of "test1," which the sanity test also used, similarly to what happened when John ran this test manually.

However, Bob still didn't understand why it didn't fail when he ran the two tests just after he wrote them. So, he turned to Kathy to help him understand what he did wrong then. After he explained to her how he ran the tests, she told him that the isolation mechanism that she implemented re-creates the test data whenever a suite of test starts to run. Bob indeed ran his test before the sanity test, but he ran them *separately* (as opposed to running them together as one suite), which caused the infrastructure to re-create the data between them and therefore "hide" the problem.

Problem 4 – Automated Tests Running Simultaneously

After the automated test suite grew, and the time it took to run all them was too long, Kathy decided to split the tests into four groups and run each group on a different machine in parallel. The runtime indeed decreased significantly, but occasionally tests that used to be very stable before were failing with an unclear reason. Running the test again separately didn't reproduce the failure. Especially the inventory test that was mentioned previously was failing from time to time, even though the tests were running at night when no one interacted with the system manually.

Obviously, the reason for the failures is very similar to the reason of problem #2, but instead of manual testers interfering with the automation, this time different automated tests that ran in parallel interfere with each other.

Isolation Techniques

Theoretically speaking, the best isolation will be achieved if for each test case we'll start from a "virgin" environment, on which the application was never installed. The initialization of the test will install all the relevant components of the application, start them, and only then execute the test. In real life, however, this is very rarely feasible. So, let's examine some techniques that are more feasible. Some of these techniques are complementary to each other and can be used together.

Use Separate Accounts

If the application provides a service to individual users or customers and has a notion of "accounts" that should not see one another's data, then this is a "low hanging fruit" when it comes to isolation. First, you can create one account that is dedicated to the test automation system so manual testers won't intervene. Then you can (and should) even assign a *different* account for each automation developer and test execution environment (e.g., the where the nightly tests are run) to eliminate collisions between tests running by different developers simultaneously.

Separate Between Manual Testing and Test Automation Databases

Many teams have a limited number of environments that serve different phases of the development cycle. Typically, these are called Dev, Test (or QA), Pre-prod (AKA Staging or Acceptance), and Prod (for production), though different teams have some slight variations in the number, names, and purposes of the environment. Each of these environments typically includes its own copy of the database.

If your team uses such environments, the next recommended isolation technique after using separate accounts is to create just one new environment with its own copy of the database, just for the automation. This technique becomes most valuable when creating an automated build that runs the tests. The build should first create or update the automation environment, and then run all the tests on it. This also requires us to automate the deployment of the environment (if we still haven't). The good news is that once you cracked all the intricacies of creating this automatic deployment script, then you can use it to create or update any other environment (e.g., Test, Prod) on demand, much more easily and safely than when the deployment was manual! See Chapter 15 for more information about it.

If this environment is only used for running centralized test cycles and its usage is managed and synchronized by the build system (or even manually if the number of people using it is very small), then this isolation technique ensures that the automation has full control over the environment. and it eliminates almost all excuses for unexplained failures.

Having Separate Environments for Each Team Member

The assumption of the previous technique that only one user can use the environment at a time may be appropriate if the number of people having to use it simultaneously (e.g., automation team members) is small and the time it takes to run a cycle is also short. But that assumption may very quickly become incorrect, and that environment that we've created becomes a bottleneck. While automation developers add new tests or change existing ones, they need to run them in order to verify and sometimes debug them in order to test the tests themselves. If there's only a single test automation environment, then they'll probably test and debug them in another, non-sterile environment. But first, the environments may differ, which means that what they test won't necessarily reflect what will happen in the "formal," centralized cycle; and second, they may dismiss any nonobvious failure as caused by the non-sterile nature of the environment.

For these reasons, the next logical step is to create multiple automation environments, and even have a separate environment for each automation developer. But what about application developers? If we want to encourage (or enforce) them to run some tests before check-in, then they also need a separated environment.

Usually the largest obstacle for doing that is that the system is too big to put on every developer's machine (and clearly, it's too expensive to have another dedicated machine for each developer). But in most cases, even if in production the system uses several dedicated servers, it's not that big of a deal to put them all on one machine. The only thing that is usually really big is the database. But as a matter of fact, in most cases the automation does not need all the data in there. You can keep only a bare minimum portion of the data that the automated tests actually use (see the next technique that complements this approach).

Some people are concerned that such minimized environments don't reflect the load and the scale of the real system. Well, that's true, but that's not the sweet spot of functional automated tests anyway. Load tests, which are covered in Chapter 18, require their own dedicated environment that may have a lot of data, and should be more similar to actual topology of the production environment. However, the load environment, as well as the load tests themselves, should be completely separate and different from the regular functional tests and their environments.

Another concern that is often raised is that each environment we add adds more maintenance and management costs. This is indeed the case when some of the deployment steps are done manually. Updating the database schema is often performed as a manual step, which is very risky. If you skipped the previous technique, then now you'll be required to fully automate the deployment process too! Once the process is completely automated, it takes very minimal effort to spin up a new environment, especially if you're using VMs or containers (see below).

Running Tests in Parallel

It you overcame the challenges of creating many separated environments, you can leverage this to create few environments for the main test cycles (e.g., CI or nightly builds) and split the tests among these environments. Each portion of the tests will run on a different environment in parallel with the others, and therefore the total time of the test run will be reduced significantly. Just make sure that the total time of each portion is close enough to the total time of all the rest, and the total time of the entire test cycle will be divided by the number of environments.

Resetting the Environment Before Each Test Cycle

While usually the theoretic approach mentioned above of starting from a clean environment for every test case is not feasible, it *is* often feasible to do it once before each test *cycle* (e.g., before the nightly or CI runs). The true meaning of "clean the environment" may vary, but in general it means somehow reverting the state of the environment to some well-known initial state.

This can be achieved in several ways, depending on the architecture and the technologies used by the application. Here are a few examples:

- Restoring the database from a known "baseline" backup;

- Deleting any files that the application creates during its run, or replacing them with their original versions;

- Given that the application has an install/uninstall program, use this program to uninstall and reinstall the application.

One question that often arises when thinking about these solutions is whether resetting the state should be done *before* the tests or *after*? In most cases the preferred answer is *before*. This ensures that the environment will start fresh even if the previous cycle was aborted in some way before reaching the cleanup phase. In addition, if tests fail and you need to investigate, keeping the environment intact may help you get more information (e.g., log files, DB entries, etc.) about the cause of the failure.

Another common and very powerful technique for resetting the environment before each test cycle is to use Virtual Machines or Containers, possibly using a cloud service.

Database Backup and Restore

Given that the application is using a single database, and that you already have a separate environment for the automation, or even multiple separate environments, you might want to consider starting each test cycle, or even each test suite from a clean slate, by restoring the database from a backup that was prepared in advance. Each time that a test cycle runs, it first restores the database from this backup.

In case you need to update the schema or the data in the backup file due to changes to the product and/or to the tests, you must re-create that backup. In order to do so, restore the previous backup, apply the needed changes, and then re-create the backup. It would be valuable to keep these backups in the source-control system so that they'd be synchronized with the changes of the SUT. However, one disadvantage of storing backup files in source control is that backup files are typically binary and source-control tools typically can't store deltas for binary files, so they need to keep the full file for each and every change. It also means that you can't compare different versions of the file. Therefore, a better approach you should consider is to store scripts that re-create the database instead of a database backup per se. Accordingly, instead of restoring the database from the backup file, the tests infrastructure will run that script in order to create the clean environment.

Transaction Rollback

Another isolation technique that involves a database and falls into the category of resetting the environment is to start each test by starting a new database transaction and ending it (whether successfully or not) with rolling back the transaction. This ensures that every change that was made by the test to the database is undone.

This approach is more suitable for component tests than for end-to-end tests, because it requires that the SUT will use the same transaction that the test started. In addition, it is typically more adequate as a technique to isolate between individual tests rather than between test cycles, as the rollback time is pretty short.

If you're using it for a component test, the component under test should be able to take an existing database connection through which it communicates with the database, typically through its constructor, so the test should open the connection, begin a new transaction, and give the connection to the component. When the test completes, it rolls back the transaction or simply closes the connection without committing the transaction, which abandons it and practically rolls it back.

With an end-to-end test this is generally only possible if the application provides some kind of a hook or "back door" to start a new transaction and to roll back it, only to solve this particular problem, which might introduce a significant security hole. Other disadvantages of this approach in end-to-end tests is that it implies a high degree of coupling and presumptions between the test and implementation details of the SUT. For example, the type, name, etc., of the database are implementation details and not some specified requirements. Even though the type or instance of the database is not something that changes often, sometimes a re-architecture of a feature still involves such a change (e.g., taking a few tables out from a relational database into a "NoSQL" database), in which case the changes to the tests would be huge. Moreover, the intervention of the test in the database transactions might cause the SUT to behave differently under test than it would be in production, which makes it less reliable. This can happen if the SUT assumes that a transaction was committed, which is true in production, but the test rolled it back.

Use Virtual Machines (VMs), Containers, and the Cloud

In case you're not familiar with VMs, here's a quick recap: A VM is like a computer hosted within another computer. To be more precise, it's an operating system (OS) that is hosted inside another OS. The host OS allocates some of its resources, like CPU time, memory, disk space, network bandwidth, etc., to the VM, while the VM is not "aware" that's it's being hosted and it behaves like a complete, normal OS. As a user, you can interact with the VM either through a special application in the host or via remote desktop. But in many cases VMs are used to run services that only other applications interact with, or that can be accessed through a browser. One host can host multiple VMs, and there are often dedicated, powerful machines whose sole purpose is to host multiple VMs.

Containers are like a very lightweight VM. A typical VM takes quite a lot of resources, and the time to turn it on is similar to the time it takes to any normal OS to load (which is typically a few minutes on most Windows versions). With containers however, the host typically *shares* parts of itself and its resources with the container (as opposed to *allocate* the resources) and therefore uses less of them. This imposes some restrictions and limitations on the container, which cannot be any arbitrary OS as in the case of VMs. Therefore, a container is much more limited and does not have a GUI, but it loads almost instantly and uses much less resources like memory, disk space, etc.; provides greater flexibility and manageability; and still provides similar isolation to those of VMs.

There are two main features that make VMs and containers interesting for our isolation needs:

- Snapshots: because the "hard disk" of the VM is not a real hard disk and merely a file on the host, it's possible to save special backups (which are called snapshots) of the VM and restore them later. In fact, a snapshot can even contain the state of the memory of the VM and not only its hard disk so it can be taken while the VM is "powered

155

on" and be restored exactly to the same state. Also, the virtualization technology usually allows us to save only the differences from the base image of the VM so it doesn't take so much space and takes less time to create and restore. The test automation can use this feature to restore the system to a snapshot that was taken in advance and contains the predefined initial state for our tests.

- Templates: similarly, an image of a VM can be cloned to create multiple instances of the same VM. It's a bit more complicated than just copying the image, because in order to prevent network collisions and ambiguities, each VM must have a different name, IP address, MAC address, etc. But luckily the host can take care of managing these differences and therefore it's still possible. The ability to create multiple instances of VMs from the same image makes it easy to *scale out* applications (see the next sidebar). Similarly, for test automation purposes, it can be used to create multiple similar environments that can test in parallel with proper isolation.

Some of the major Internet players, like Google, Microsoft, and Amazon maintain some huge datacenters around the world and rent compute resources from them, mainly in the form of VMs and containers, to anyone who wants them. This type of service is known as the *cloud*. Its main benefit over using your own VMs is the flexibility to increase or decrease the resources you consume, while you just pay for what you use. They also free you from the responsibility for maintaining the expensive hardware. There are many other benefits and options for using the cloud, but that's beyond the scope of our discussion.

The bottom line is that snapshots and templates of VMs and containers are a great way to achieve isolation, parallelism, and help you create and manage large numbers of environments.

SCALING UP VS. SCALING OUT

Traditionally, the hardware that was used to run a heavy-loaded server application was a single "heavy-duty" computer. Mission critical servers often used a pair of adjacent machines called a cluster, one denoted to be the primary and the other secondary, so that if the primary had a failure, the secondary would take over instantly to continue serving requests seamlessly, while the primary could be fixed. If the load on the server increased over time, usually adding more memory or a faster CPU would be the solution applied to the problem. This is known as *scaling up* the hardware. The problem was that the hardware for these high-end heavy-duty machines were very expensive and therefore it was a big deal to upgrade such a machine. In addition, even though the failover provided some redundancy, it's still very limited, as the two machines were physically close to each other and any physical disaster would probably hit both of them. There were solutions to this problem but they were also very expensive and complicated.

In the "dot com boom" era, companies started to leverage a large number of normal PCs to provide redundancy and scalability. The application should be architected properly to support it, but if it does it allows these companies to add more compute resources by simply deploying the application on yet another machine. This is known as *scaling out*. This allows us to add more computers much quicker than it takes to order and install expensive specialized hardware. In recent years, with the advances in the area of VMs and the cloud, it has become even more popular and today it is mostly considered bad practice to design a "monolithic" system that does not support scaling out.

Create Unique Data for Each Test

Most of the isolation techniques we've mentioned so far deal with isolation between environments and between test cycles. But what about isolation between tests in the same cycle and environment? Recall problem #3 discussed earlier in this chapter.

As it's usually not feasible to create a complete isolation between individual tests in the same cycle and in the same environment (except for unit tests), it's possible to reduce the chances of collisions by applying some relevant design techniques. The common to all of these techniques is that they avoid or prevent sharing mutable data between tests.

One such technique to avoid sharing data between tests is simply to create a unique set of data for each test. If each test creates and uses the data it needs to change or access, one test cannot affect other test's data. Note that when I say that the test creates data, I don't mean that it accesses and inserts data directly into the database, but rather that the test invokes operations on the SUT that creates the data. For example, if the test has to change a price of a product, then it should first create the product *through the application* and not directly through the database. This ensures that the data is consistent and valid.

For optimization reasons it's not always appropriate to create everything through the UI though. If the application exposes an API to create this data, then you should probably use that anyway. If not, then consider reusing the DAL components of the SUT to create the data. Only inject the data directly to the database as a last resort, both to avoid possible inconsistencies, and also to reduce the coupling between the tests and the database schema, which is usually an implementation detail of the SUT.

The catch in the concept of creating the data you need in the test is to determine which data *can* be shared and which *shouldn't*. It's pretty obvious that transient data that only the test changes should be created. But consider the following case (continuing the problematic scenarios of Kathy, John, and Bob): A new feature was developed that allows the manager to define promotions that gives a discount for any product out of a group of products that participate in the promotion. For example: buying either a speaker, earphone, or microphone gives a 10% discount. Bob writes a test that *creates* such a promotion, and associates it with the existing "earphone," "speakers," and "microphone" products in the test DB. The data related to the product themselves is not changed, only referred to by the new promotion that he created. When Bob runs his new test it passes, but at the nightly build Kathy's famous sanity test fails because the expected total was now 10% lower than expected. Note that superficially, Bob followed the guideline and created a new promotion, which is the only entity he actually changed. But even though the product entities themselves didn't change, they were affected by the new promotion entity.

So, it's not enough for each test to create only the data it *changes*. It should also create any data that it *uses*. However, beware not to take this rule too far either: most applications use a set of data that very rarely change, often called *reference data*. For example: the list of countries and currencies. In the mentioned example, the prices of the products use some default currency that is defined somewhere in the database. Creating a separate currency for each individual test is probably an overkill. There's some gray area between such reference data and data that rarely change. The list of products also changes pretty rarely, but as we saw, we better create a new product for each test nonetheless.

There are a couple of rules of thumb that can help you decide whether a piece of information should be created by each test or can be seen as reference data:

- Do many of the tests use this type of data directly? In our example, on the one hand, the notion of which products the customer buys is key to many tests; therefore it should probably be created for each test. On the other hand, if the entity is mostly used indirectly, like the currency in the above example, then it can probably be shared among most tests. However, tests that use or verify certain characteristics that are closely related to the notion of a currency should probably add their own currency entity for their particular use.

- Can most of the tests work correctly if there was only one default instance of the type of entity in the database? Even though the real database would probably define 196 countries or so, the vast majority of our tests can work with a single, default country. So, we can keep that single record in the reference database and use it for any purpose that does not specifically need a special property of a country. Here again, if the test needs to interact more closely with the country entity, then it should probably create a new one. However, it's probably not adequate to refer to one specific product in the tests DB as a "default product" because each product is unique and many tests need more than one.

The outcome of these rules is that you should probably have a very thin database, containing only one entity of the reference data tables, and no data at all in all other tables. This also has the advantage that creating a new environment is much faster and leaner (i.e., requires less storage space, and therefore faster to copy or re-create).

I also prefer to use *dummy* reference data, which is intentionally different from the real data (e.g., "Dummy country1", "Dummy country2", instead of the real list of countries). This way I discover whether there are other assumptions in the system about the actual values. If everything works correctly with the dummy data, I leave it as is. But if I encounter a dependency on real values, I question whether it is really necessary or not. If it is, I replace the dummy data with the real one, but if not, I'll open a bug and push to remove the unnecessary dependency. While the value of removing such dependencies is not immediately apparent, it makes the code of the SUT more reusable and maintainable in the long run.

Defining this minimal set of data can be a big challenge, as often the database schema and the necessary data that the application requires in order to function properly are poorly documented, and often no one really knows all the details. The solution may take some time but is not very complicated. If you'll do it, then in the process you'll gain back the invaluable knowledge about the real prerequisites and structure of your application – a knowledge that was lost along the way of developing the application and will probably be valuable again in the future. This knowledge will be very valuable once some relevant parts of the system need to be refactored or rewritten. In addition, using a minimal set of data rather than a full-blown database often has a nice side effect that makes the system, and correspondingly the tests, run faster.

Essentially the solution is to reverse engineer and debug the system. Simply start with one sanity test that does not rely on existing data (that you aware of), and try to run it against an environment with an empty database. The test would probably fail. At first, chances are that the failure would be that the system won't even start! Whatever the failure is, you should find the missing data that caused the failure, fix it, and then try to run the test again. To find the missing data, try invoking or even debugging the operation that failed both against a full database and against the new thin one, and compare the results. Continue this process until all of the failures in the test have been fixed, and the test passes. After you've done it for the first test, the next one would probably go much faster.

The details, however, may be somewhat different according to the type of application:

- If the application is a shelve product, and assuming that you create the data either through the UI or through a public API, then in any failure the application should provide a clear error message to the user. If it does, add the missing data as part of the code of the test. If it doesn't, you should debug the system until you find the root cause. Then, either fix the error message yourself, or if you're not allowed to change the source code, ask a developer to do so or open a bug. If you can fix the code yourself, it's best, because you can verify that the error message is clear before you add the missing data.

- If the application is a Software as a Service (SaaS) and you're using a separate account for the tests as suggested in the first technique, then every account should be considered the same as a shelve product. However, there's probably some reference data that is common to all accounts (e.g., countries, currency, etc.) that only administrators, marketing people, or any internal personnel can modify. In case that such data is missing, giving a nice error message is only nice to have, but not critical, as the end user should never encounter this error. However, it's still recommended to provide a clear error message in the log at least. Anyway, because the missing reference data is common to most of the tests, then instead of creating it as part of each test, either create it at the beginning of the test suite, or add it directly to a snapshot database (as described above in the technique "Resetting the Environment for Each Test Cycle").

- If the application is a website (either public or internal application), but does not use accounts and does not require registration, then all of the data and configuration are probably common to all users. This is probably the hardest case. In this case you have to decide what data is true reference data that should never change, and which data should be considered as input. In some cases, it's not that difficult because anything that is editable by any user (including an admin) is something that the test should create, and data that can only be changed by someone in the development team should be included in the snapshot of the database that the automation uses as a starting point. However, in other cases the distinction is not that clear. In today's DevOps approach (and also in some less mature organizations), there's no clear distinction between the development team, administrators, and businesspeople. Accordingly, internal tools are developed to aid the relevant people to add or update different parts of the data. For some parts of the data, a corresponding tool is created at the beginning of the project as a one-time thing to enter the data into the database. As internal tools, they're often quite "hacky" and it's unclear whether this data should really be editable. In addition, some parts of the data may not come from a user, but rather from external systems. Similarly, the data could have been imported from the external system once at the beginning of the project, and it's not expected to change any time in the future. In these vague cases, just choose what data to treat as a reference data and which to not, according to your own judgment, but try to write the tests in a way that will be easy to maintain if one day you decide to change that decision.

- In complex, monolithic, and poorly documented systems, the approach of starting from an empty database and find what's missing may not pay off. If this is the case, try to do it on a test-by-test basis or at least feature by feature. Instead of starting with an empty database, start with the existing (full) one, but identify what relevant data your tests rely on. Make sure that your test creates that data that it needs instead of relying on existing ones. Over time, review which data is probably not needed and delete it (after creating a backup). If the tests keep working correctly, it means that this data was indeed no longer relevant. However, if tests fail due to this missing data, either fix the failing tests to stop relying on that data, restore the old database from the backup, or add the missing data that the tests or the system need. Gradually, you can delete irrelevant data from specific tables and make your test database smaller and leaner.

Each Test Cleans Everything It Creates

Having each test create the data it needs resolves most of the conflicts. However, there are cases where a test needs to change some global state, or that an entity that one test creates might affect other tests even though they don't use it directly. For example, one test can create a promotion that gives a 10% discount for every sale above $100, or a different promotion that gives a discount for every sale that occurs on Fridays between 5:00 and 6:00 p.m. (Happy Hour), while another test can create a sale with total of more than $100 or that coincidentally occur on Friday 5:24 p.m. without being aware of the existence of the promotions that the first test has created. Therefore, it's also recommended that each test will delete or roll back the changes it made.

Most common unit testing frameworks (e.g., JUnit, NUnit, MSTest, etc.) provide a way to define special methods that run *before* each test in a test class, and methods that run *after* each test method. For example, JUnit uses the `@Before` and `@After` annotations to identify these methods. (See Chapter 3 for a description of unit testing frameworks). In different frameworks these have different names, like `SetUp`/`TearDown`, `TestInitialize`/`TestCleanup` etc. For the matter of clarity, I'll refer to them as Initialize and Cleanup methods. The main purpose of these cleanup methods is to provide a common way to perform the cleanup of the tests. However, it turns out that the way they work does not lends itself very well for many cases and writing really robust cleanup code is very difficult.

There are several reasons for that:

1. A test class can contain more than one test. Even though the tests in the same class should be related, it's not always true that they all require the exact same cleanup.

2. Generally, these Cleanup methods run only if the corresponding Initialize method succeeded (didn't throw an exception), but regardless of whether the test passed or not. In most cases it makes sense because if you failed to initialize something, there's no need to clean it up. On the other hand, if the test failed, then you still need to clean up. However, often the Initialize method creates more than one entity that needs to be cleaned up, and it's probable that the creation of the first entity succeeds and the second one would fail. In this case, the cleanup method won't be called and the first entity will remain and won't be cleaned up properly.

3. Often the test itself creates an entity. Seemingly there's no problem with that as the cleanup code can still delete it. However, the test may fail before or while creating the entity, which can cause the Cleanup method to fail too when it tries to delete the entity that wasn't created.

4. A test (or the Initialize method) may create two entities that one depends on the other. For example, a test can create a new customer and create an order from that customer. If in the Cleanup method we'll try to delete the Customer before cancelling and deleting the Order we'll get an exception.

5. Combining 3 and 4 together (i.e., the test creates multiple entities with relationships between them), makes writing a cleanup code that works correctly in all failure situations very difficult. In addition, it's very difficult to simulate such failures, which makes *testing* the Cleanup code almost impossible!

The solution is to keep a list of commands to be executed on cleanup. Whenever the tests perform an action that requires some cleanup, it also adds the appropriate cleanup command to the list. Adding the command to the list does not invoke it at this point. Only when the test completes, either passing or failing, all of these commands are executed in reverse order (to address issue #4). Naturally, when a test fails, it jumps directly to the cleanup code, skipping the rest of the test. This ensures that only the actions that were actually performed are cleaned up (issue #3). Appendix B contains detailed implementation and explanation on how to implement such mechanism. In addition, Test Automation Essentials (See Appendix C) have a full implementation of this mechanism too.

Read-Only Shared Data

Lastly, it's worth mentioning that if the application is using a database but uses it only to read data that was produced by another system, then this data is not to be treated as state, but rather as input. Therefore, you don't really need to isolate instances that use the same data!

In many cases, though, it implies that the SUT is not really the entire system, and that you should probably test the integration between the system that produces the data together and the system that consumes it. However, you may choose to have few system tests that exercise the subsystem that produces the data as well the one that consumes it, but keep most tests separated for each subsystem, which is totally fine. See Chapter 6 for the options and considerations of fitting the tests to the architecture of the SUT.

In many of these cases, people tend to use a copy of an existing production database and use it for the tests. But before you're going down that route, you should consider the following questions:

- Is the data you're using diverse enough and represent all the cases that you want to test? If for example, the data is taken from a single customer while different customers may use the system a bit differently, then you may not be able to cover all the cases you need for the other customers.

- Is it possible that the schema or the meaning of some data will change in future versions? If that's possible, then when it happens, you'll need to take a different copy of the database, which would most probably have different data in it. This will make all of the expected results, and many other assumptions of your tests no longer valid! In some cases, that may be a disaster for the test automation, as you'll need to write almost everything from scratch...

- Is it easy to understand the relationship between what a test does and its expected results? In other words, if you're writing a new test, can you tell the expected results without looking at the actual output of the system? If not, how can you tell that what the system does today is correct? You'd probably say that what's there today has been so for many years and no one complained so far, and therefore it can be considered as correct. I totally agree with that, but if any of the logic that relies on this data will intentionally change in the future, it will be very difficult to say whether the new logic is correct or not either (and if this logic is not to be touched, then there's a low value testing it anyway).

The alternative to using a copy of production data would be to create a synthetic instance of the database, which contains data you specifically put in it for the tests. In fact, the process of creating this synthetic data is identical to the process of reverse engineering and debugging described earlier under the topic "Create Unique Data for Each Test" for creating the minimal set of reference data.

Summary

In order to ensure reliability and consistency, the architecture of the test automation should control not only the inputs of the chosen test scope, but also its state. In this chapter we discussed various *isolation techniques* for controlling the state of the SUT and to avoid inconsistent results in the tests. Besides making the tests more reliable, some of these techniques have the nice side effect of allowing us to run the tests in parallel, gain a better understanding of the true behavior of the system, and make the tests run faster.

CHAPTER 8

The Big Picture

In Chapter 5 we've talked about the relationships between test automation and business processes. In Chapter 6 we've talked about the relationships between test automation and the software architecture. In this chapter we'll look at the bigger picture and discuss the strong correlation between business structure and architecture, and between business processes and culture. And of course, we'll also discuss how test automation is connected to all of these as well and how everything is related.

The Relationships Between Software Architecture and Business Structure

Back in 1967 the computer scientist Melvin Conway published a paper titled "How Do Committees Invent?"[1] In the third-to-last paragraph of this paper he stated an adage that later became famously known as Conway's law.

Conway's Law

Conway's law states that *"organizations which design systems [...] are constrained to produce designs which are copies of the communication structures of these organizations."* While this law isn't restricted to software, it is the most obvious and well known in this field.

This observation implies that the business structure, culture, and also informal communication patters are reflected in the architecture of the system and vice versa. People in the same team usually communicate more frequently, and the pieces of their work (e.g., lines of code) are more intertwined with one another, producing a well-defined module. When the module they produce should interface with a module

---

[1] http://www.melconway.com/research/committees.html

© Arnon Axelrod 2018
A. Axelrod, *Complete Guide to Test Automation*, https://doi.org/10.1007/978-1-4842-3832-5_8

that another team produces, people from the two teams must communicate with each other in order to define this interface. But this is not restricted to formal structure: if two people in the same team or in different teams don't communicate well with each other, the integration between their pieces of code will very likely be clunky; solitary developers may create code that only they understand; close friends in different teams may create "hacky" interfaces that only they understand, etc.

Conway's law works both ways: on one hand, if an architect comes up with the desired architecture, but a manager decides to organize the teams in a way that does not correspond to that architecture, the software that will be built eventually will more likely have an actual architecture that corresponds to the actual business structure rather than the architecture that the architect first envisioned. On the other hand, if a major restructuring of the software is planned, a smart manager can harness Conway's law to that goal and reorganize the teams accordingly.

Horizontal Teams vs. Vertical Teams

Traditionally, most business systems were designed in a layered architecture. Typically, the highest layer is the UI, below that the business logic, below that is a data-access layer (DAL) that communicates with the database, and below all is the database itself. Accordingly, each of these layers was usually developed by a separate team. The benefit of that approach is that any of these layers typically requires a different set of skills and tools and so it made sense to put all developers with similar skills alongside one another in the same team to promote sharing of knowledge and practices.

The downside of this approach is that almost every feature depends on all of these layers. As long as everything is well designed upfront, it's not a big issue. But if the customer requests to make the smallest change, add the simplest feature, or if a bug is found, it almost always requires that *all* of the teams will participate in the implementation of the change. In addition, because the chain of dependencies, usually higher-layer teams would not be able to start working until the lower layer team completes their work. This makes such rigid architecture and business structure very resistant to change requests, bug fixes, and new features...

This notion brought many large projects to adopt an architecture and business structure that correspond to "vertical" features rather than on technical layers. In this approach, each team consists of people with different skills and expertise (i.e., UI, database, business logic, etc.), but all are dedicated to the same feature or business domain. Furthermore, some teams consist mainly of people with versatile skills, commonly known as "full stack developers." In addition to different developer expertise, in most cases this organizational structure also includes dedicated testers and product managers as part of each team. Probably the most influential book that advocates this approach is Eric Evan's *Domain Driven Design – Tackling Complexity in the Heart of Software.*[2]The downside of this approach is exactly the upside of the layered approach (knowledge sharing between people with the same expertise) but in most cases its upside, which makes the software more maintainable and accommodating for changes, clearly outweighs its downside. Figure 8-1 shows the vertical vs. horizontal division.

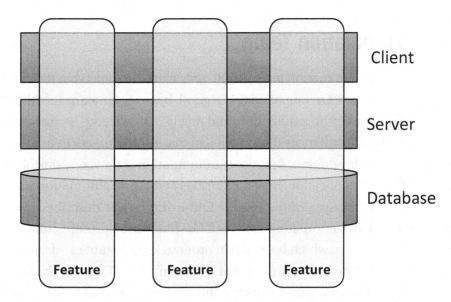

Figure 8-1. *Vertical vs. Horizontal division*

In practice, many complex projects have their own unique architecture and team structure, but you can pretty clearly identify the correlation between the organizational structure and the system's architecture and identify where the lines that divide the responsibilities between teams are vertical and where they are horizontal. For example, in one of the largest projects I've worked on, the organization was divided unto one client team (it was supposed to be a "thin client," hence only one team) and many server teams, dedicated to different business domains. The testing team was a horizontal one, covering the cross-feature scenarios.

---

[2]Evans, Eric (2004). *Domain-Driven Design: Tackling Complexity in the Heart of Software.* Addison-Wesley. ISBN 978-032-112521-7. Retrieved August 12, 2012.

The Relationships Between Software Architecture and Organizational Structure with Test Automation

Naturally, team members communicate more often and freely with their teammates than with members of other teams. But composing, implementing, and maintaining automated tests also require a great deal of communication with developers on various teams. This also has some implications on the relationships between the organizational structure and the structure of the test automation.

Dedicated Automation Team

If there is one dedicated automation team, it will most likely be somewhat disconnected from the development team. On one hand this is good, because it means that they'll have complete responsibility over the automation, and that like in a layered architecture and organizational structure, it enhances the knowledge sharing and practices among the automation developers. In addition, because the automation team is responsible for the automation of the entire application, they'll more likely create an automation suite that covers the entire application as a whole, like the End-to-End scope described in Chapter 6.

On the other hand, the automation team will less likely get a prompt collaboration from the development team, which is critical in order to keep a stable and robust automation (See the section in Chapter 5 titled "Handling Bugs That Are Found by the Automation"). In this structure, it will probably be pretty difficult to integrate the automated tests into the continuous integration process (see Chapter 15), as it will be difficult to convince both the application developers and the automation developers that the application developers should fix failures that happen in the automation.

Automation Developers Inside Horizontal Teams

Typically, if automation developers are members of horizontal teams, or the members of the horizontal teams develop the automation, they will lean toward implementing automated tests that cover only their own layer. They don't want to be bothered by failures that are not their fault. Clearly, this will only ingrain the effects of Conway's law, and will likely cause more integration problems between the teams. These problems can manifest themselves as bugs, as delays in the project schedule, as personal or inter-team conflicts, etc.

Blame vs. Collaboration Culture

This phenomenon is not limited to horizontal teams, as it might apply to any teams that depend on one another and which the communication between them is lacking, but because horizontal teams are inherently dependent on the teams that develop the lower layers, this is very common in this situation. The essence of this phenomenon is that when something goes wrong, the teams start to blame each other for the failure. I was once asked by one such team (let's call them team "A") to develop tests for the components developed by another team (team "B") so that when something doesn't work, team A will be able to prove that the faults are of team B... I politely refused, explaining that it's not effective to write tests for another team, because automated tests require constant maintenance. Instead I suggested that they'd write integration tests that cover both the code of team A and of team B together. That way they'll get much higher value out of it. Instead of being "right," they'll be able to ensure that the software that they give *their* customers is working correctly. In case it doesn't, they should be able to investigate and analyze the root-cause quickly enough (see Chapter 13 for techniques to investigate and analyze failing tests) and if the blame is indeed in team B, then they should be able to prove it using the evidence that they collect in their tests anyway. In addition, this will encourage team A to cooperate with team B in order to make the tests work, and will foster trust between the teams, as they'll be able to communicate about facts and proofs rather than on assumptions and subjective terms.

In general, any technique, tool, and practice that provide transparency and encourage collaboration can have an impact, usually positive, on the culture of the organization. Source-control systems, CI builds, automated testing, and production monitoring are all tools and techniques that provide this kind of transparency and have some impact on the culture. I say that the impact is "usually positive," because unfortunately every such tool can also be abused or used in an incorrect fashion that achieves the opposite results. Chapter 15 contains some tips for leveraging the test automation to gradually change the culture to the more collaborative direction.

Automation Developers Inside Vertical Teams

Generally speaking, given the trade-offs mentioned above, the most effective organizational structure in most cases with regard to test automation is probably when the automation developers are members of vertical development teams, or the developers in vertical teams write the tests themselves. Pay attention though: even when the teams and architecture are divided vertically, there are still dependencies and interactions between the vertical modules/teams, and many scenarios should involve more than one module.

Another potential problems in this structure is that there tends to be more duplication between infrastructure pieces of each module, as they're being developed separately by each team. This is true both for the application code as well as for the automation's code.

But despite these problems, tests that such teams produce typically cover complete scenarios, and because each team is responsible for its tests, it also makes them more reliable. In addition, because the automation developers and the application developers work together, their collaboration is better, and the application developers are much more likely get the most value out of the automation.

Flexible Organizational Structure

Some large teams adopt a flexible approach in which smaller teams are formed dynamically to adopt to the needs of the user stories at hand. Dan North gave a fascinating talk[3] in the "Scaling Agile for the Enterprise 2016" congress in Brussels, Belgium, about a method he calls *Delivery mapping*, which helps form these teams efficiently. Using this or other similar techniques, the structure of the teams constantly changes to reflect and adjust to the user stories and goals that the bigger team works toward. Each feature or user story is assigned to an ad hoc team, sometimes called a *feature crew* or a *squad*.

This approach is very challenging in and on itself but helps focus each such feature crew on the task in hand, and if automation is developed by each such feature crew for the functionality it develops, it encourages each automated test to be written in a way that involves the relevant modules that need to be changed for that feature. This is again, pretty challenging, but if done successfully, the automated tests that will be developed for each feature are most likely use the most appropriate test scope for that particular feature. The ATDD methodology described in Chapter 16 lends itself very well to this approach.

---

[3]https://www.youtube.com/watch?v=EzWmqlBENMM

Having an Automation Expert

Regardless of the structure of the teams and modules, people tend to make choices (often unconsciously) regarding the structure of the automated tests that they design and implement, based on what's easy and what incurs the least friction in the process. Many times, these choices are suboptimal with regard to the ROI of the test (how much value it will give vs. how maintainable and reliable it will be). But if you have someone whose automated tests are his passion, and he has a broad perspective and experience about this subject, then he'd be likely to make better decisions for the test automation. If this person is really enthusiastic about this subject, he naturally becomes the "go-to" person that people come to in order to get advice. In large teams, it worth it that this person has his own role of "test automation expert" and not be part of any particular team. This way this person can keep the overall view of the test automation and lead it to be successful. Day to day, this person can improve the infrastructure of the tests, review others' tests, perform trainings, and advise each team how to build the automation that best suits their needs.

Summary

Different organizations have different structures, different cultures, different constraints, and different strengths. These attributes are reflected in the architecture of the system and also are highly correlated to the business processes.

Test automation is tightly related to all of these in both directions: it is affected by these attributes, but it also affects them back! If you look at the big picture through the lens of test automation, you'll probably succeed not only in creating the best test automation for your current organization, but also to leverage it to improve your organization as well!

Creating a stable, reliable, and valuable test automation requires collaboration of people from different teams and disciplines, and in return, provides clarity and transparency about defects and breaking changes. The improved collaboration is a hidden "side effect" of test automation but is also one of its biggest advantages!

A person who facilitates communications is a leader. Naturally, managers are more equipped for that, but an automation expert or any enthusiast automation developer that envisions how to leverage test automation for that purpose can leave a significant mark on his organization and become a leader. See Chapter 15 for more information on how to gradually change the culture of your organization even without authority and how to become that leader.

PART II

The "How"

In Part I we discussed a lot of theory and gave a broad overview of the world of test automation, explaining what it is and what it isn't. We covered its important aspects from a pretty high-level point of view, giving you the tools to make strategic decisions about the test automation for your project.

In this part, we'll talk more technically about how to design and implement the test automation infrastructure as well as individual tests, and how to leverage it as part of the overall software development life cycle. In the next few chapters, I'll walk you through a hands-on tutorial in which we'll build a test automation project for a real application.

CHAPTER 9

Preparing for the Tutorial

You probably noticed that that the concern of maintainability was raised over and over again in Part I, but I still haven't really explained how to achieve it. We also haven't discussed how to start planning and building a new test automation solution from scratch. The following few chapters act as a tutorial in which we'll start building a test automation solution for a real application. This chapter serves a few purposes:

1. Provides an overview of the process and approach we're about to take in the next chapters. This process is good not only for this tutorial but for any test automation project.

2. Provides a short overview of the application that we're about to write tests for.

3. Provides a step-by-step guide for installing the prerequisites needed for the rest of this tutorial

Prerequisites and Presumptions

In Chapter 3 we discussed the relationships between the skills of the automation developer and the tools that match those skills. We concluded that writing the automation using a general-purpose, object-oriented programming language will give us the most flexibility and if we'll use it wisely, we're less likely to hit maintenance problems over the long run.

For these reasons, in this tutorial we'll create the automation in code. More specifically, we'll use C# as the programming language. Note that if you're more familiar with Java, or even Python, I believe that you'll be able to follow along even if you won't understand every nuance of the language, as most of the principles are the same no matter what object-oriented language you use. If you don't have any

© Arnon Axelrod 2018
A. Axelrod, *Complete Guide to Test Automation*, https://doi.org/10.1007/978-1-4842-3832-5_9

object-oriented programming background and you plan to build your automation using one of the tools that don't require programming at all, then I still encourage you to read and try to get as much as you can from the tutorial, as many of the concepts I describe can be applied also to many tools that don't require you to code. Note that in the tutorial I'll do my best to provide step-by-step instructions, starting from how to set up the development environment, so you can follow along even without any prior knowledge. In case a step is not clear enough, you'll most likely be able to find the missing information on the web, or ask a question in the book's forum at `http://www.` `TheCompleteGuideToTestAutomation.com`.

In addition to choosing C# as the programming language, we'll use Selenium WebDriver as the underlying UI automation technology, since the SUT is a web application, and Selenium is the most popular and straightforward choice for implementing web-based, UI automation in code. As the system does not have any tests, and was not written with testability in mind, we'll start from few system tests that will comprise the sanity suite. In fact, in this tutorial we won't go beyond these few sanity system tests, but the main ideas remain very much the same for other test scopes. Once again, don't worry if you're not familiar with Selenium or if your project is not a web application. As mentioned, most of the ideas and concepts remain the same even for tests that don't interact with the UI whatsoever.

Applicability of the Process for Existing Test Automation Systems

The process I'll use in this tutorial, and which I'll describe shortly, guides how to write maintainable automated tests and their infrastructure. While it works best and assumes you start from a clean test automation project, you can apply most of its ideas in an existing project as well. Applying these ideas to an existing test automation system may lead you to make some compromises and trade-offs, and you may not get all the benefits of that approach at first, but if you'll choose to, you'll be able to gradually shift your existing automation to follow the ideas and techniques described in the tutorial in order to enjoy the benefits of improved maintainability and reliability that the process provides. Obviously, if at some point you'll have to write a new automation system, then you'll be able to apply all the ideas from the very beginning.

Overview of the Process

The tutorial is based on a practical process that I've been following myself for many years and have also trained many people to do the same. In the next few chapters I'll walk you through this process hand in hand so you'll get a clear picture of how to do it. However, before I'll lead you through this journey, I want to "show you the map" of this journey by giving you an overview of the process. But even before that, I need to give some little background about two general approaches in software development, to set the stage for the overview.

Bottom Up vs. Top Down

Maintainable test automation projects contain, besides the test methods themselves, a lot of infrastructure code. This infrastructure code contains common code that you don't want to repeat. Some people refer to it as "helper" classes and methods or "plumbing" code, but in fact, this part of the code often becomes much larger than the test methods themselves.

A common practice in a traditional, more "waterfall-ish" approach is to design and implement the entire infrastructure of a software system, that is, the lower layers, before starting to implement the upper layers. This approach is called *bottom up*. Just like any other software project, this approach can be applied to test automation too: design and implement the infrastructure and only then start implementing test cases. This is especially common when different people implement the infrastructure and others implement the test cases. However, as described in Chapter 3, this approach has its drawbacks when it comes to maintainability. For those reasons I mostly prefer that the entire automation code will be developed and maintained by the same people.

When the same people write the tests and the infrastructure code, I prefer to take the opposite, *top-down* approach. It may be counterintuitive at first, but I prefer to design and implement one test case before implementing the infrastructure that it needs. Not only do I implement the infrastructure after I implement the test, but I also implement only the infrastructure that the first test needs, and nothing more! After I do that with the first test, I continue doing the same with all other test cases: I design and implement the next test case first and then add the missing infrastructure that the new test needs. This process ensures a few things:

- Because the code of the test is written first, it allows me to write it in a way that is most readable and easy to understand.

- Because it is developed according to true needs and not according to speculations, the infrastructure is useful and easy to use.

- Anytime that the entire test suite runs, the entire infrastructure is exercised and tested too. If there's a bug in the infrastructure code, it's revealed very early, and it's easy to fix.

The Process

Now that I explained why I prefer to take a top-down approach, here's a more detailed description of the process that we're going to go through in this tutorial, and which I recommend to follow also regardless of the tutorial itself. In the next few chapters I'll go even deeper to explain and detail additional guidelines for each of these steps.

1. Design the first test case.

2. Write a skeleton of the first test case in "pseudo-code." That is, write the code in your actual programming language, but assume that you have all the infrastructure code that you need, even though you don't. Obviously, the code won't even compile...

3. Create the minimal necessary infrastructure code to make the first test compile, and then also implement it until it runs correctly and the test passes (assuming it *should* pass).

4. Design another test case.

5. Write the skeleton of the new test case in pseudo-code. This time, if you need an infrastructure code that already exists and you can use as is, simply use it. There can be two possible situations here:

    a.   If all the infrastructure that you need to support this test already exists, then this test should compile and run correctly. If this is the case, then you're done with that test case and you can continue to the next one. This, however, should happen pretty rarely, especially in the first tests.

    b.   If you need additional infrastructure code that doesn't exist yet (or it doesn't fit as is), assume it exists. The code won't compile.

6.   Add the necessary infrastructure to the make the new test and all the existing tests, compile, and run correctly. Either while doing so, or after all the tests run correctly, refactor the code to remove any duplication and to improve the structure of your code. **Remember: your test automation code has nearly 100% code coverage, so if you run all the tests, you can be sure that the refactoring didn't break anything!**

7.   Go back to step 4.

In addition, when you encounter any technical obstacles or frictions that hinder the flow of your work, change the infrastructure code to remove these obstacles and friction points. Here are a few examples:

- While you investigate failing tests, make sure that you have all the necessary information to aid you investigating it faster.

- When you encounter unexpected results due to isolation issues, improve the isolation.

- If you want to give other people your tests to run, make it as easy as possible for them to get started.

Getting to Know the SUT

The tutorial will use the **MVCForum** open source project. MVCForum is a fully featured responsive and themable discussion board/forum with features similar to StackOverflow, written in C# using the ASP.NET MVC 5 framework. The home page of the project can be found at http://www.mvcforum.com and its latest source code at https://github.com/YodasMyDad/mvcforum. However, because the project may evolve from the time of writing this book, I cloned the GitHub repository so that the tutorial should always be usable.

Overview on MVCForum

The application is pretty feature rich. Here are just some of the most important ones:

- Theme Engine

- Community Badge System

- Multi Lingual

- Private Messaging

- Likes, Mark as Solution, Favorites

On the main GitHub page[1] of the project you can find the full list.

Anyway, the easiest way to get an idea about this application is to go to the support forum at https://support.mvcforum.com/ that is managed using the application itself (note that this site is not under my control, and the version it uses might be more advanced, or the site might even be down). Assuming that the site hasn't changed much, you should see a website similar to the one shown in Figure 9-1.

---

[1]The version that we use in the tutorial is at https://github.com/arnonax/mvcforum. The most up-to-date version is at https://github.com/YodasMyDad/mvcforum, but pay attention as I cannot guarantee that it will stay compatible with the book.

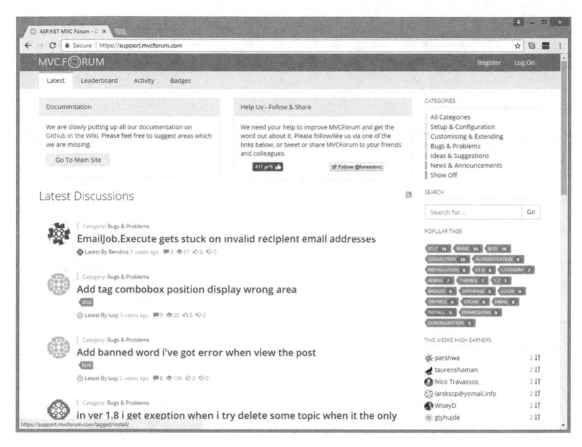

Figure 9-1. *Main page of MVC Forum's support site*

As you can see, the site displays a list of the recent discussions. You can read all discussions without registration or sign-in. By registering (which if free), people can post new discussions and comment on each other's discussions. Discussions are assigned to one category and can also have tags to facilitate filtering and finding the discussions that you're interested in.

Apart from this basic functionality, the forum lets registered users to like or dislike others' discussions and comments, and also allows the initiator of a discussion to mark one comment as an answer. Users can earn points and badges according to various rules and configurations that the site's administrator can configure. The users with the highest points of the week and of all times are displayed in the Leaderboard page (Figure 9-2).

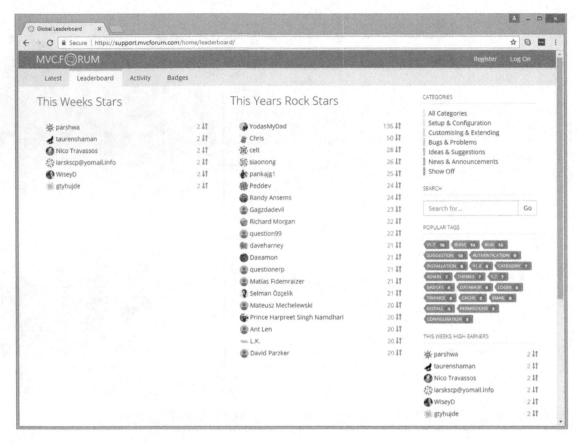

Figure 9-2. *The Leaderboard page*

Most of the features of the site are highly customizable by the administrator, which is a special user with additional rights. When the administrator logs in, a special menu item leads him to the Admin page, where he can see and change all of the customizations and configurations of the site, as shown in Figure 9-3.

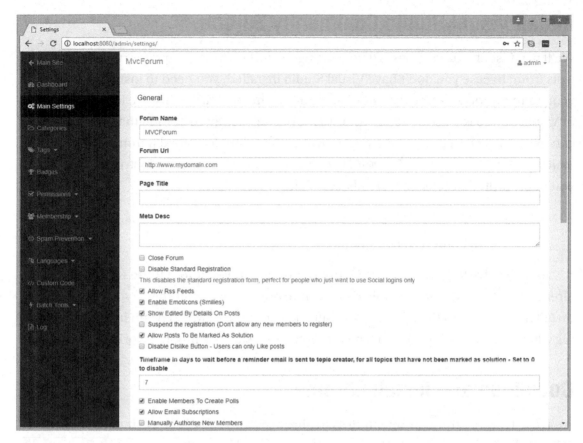

Figure 9-3. *Admin configuration page*

Preparing the Environment for the Tutorial

Before we can start the tutorial, we have a few administrative tasks to care about, namely to install and prepare our working environment. The installation procedure was tested on Windows 10 Professional but should probably work the same for any version of Windows from 7 and on. If you're using a fresh installation of Windows 10, you'll need at least 25GB of free disk space for all of the installations. This includes installing Visual Studio and SQL Server Express edition and more. Note that the mentioned versions of some of the applications may become obsolete and unavailable in the future. In this case, try to use the newer versions. If things don't go well, search the web for a solution or visit https://www.TheCompleteGuideToTestAutomation.com where a solution may already be posted. If not, post a question on the website and I'll do my best to help you.

Install Visual Studio Community Edition

We'll use Visual Studio as our IDE for writing the test code in C# and for running test tests from. In case you don't have Visual Studio installed, you need to install it if you want to really follow along this tutorial. As of the time of writing this, the latest version of Visual Studio is 2017. Visual Studio 2017 has a fully featured edition that individuals can use free of charge.[2] As of the time of writing, you can download it from `https://www.visualstudio.com/vs/community/`, and follow the installation instructions. When you're prompted to select workloads, select the following:

- .Net Desktop Development

- ASP.Net and Web Development

And click **Install**. Note that if you install Visual Studio without these workloads, or already have Visual Studio installed and you're not sure whether these workloads are installed or not, then the first time you open the solution of MVCForum in Visual Studio (as will be described soon), you'll be prompted to install the missing workloads.

Download and Install Chrome

We'll use Chrome through Selenium as the browser through which we interact with the SUT. We'll also use Chrome's Developer Tools to identify the elements we need when we implement the test cases. If Chrome is not already installed, download and install it from `https://www.google.com/chrome/`. Follow the instructions on the screen to complete the installation.

Download and Install SQL Server Express

SQL Server is required by the application to store its information. If you don't have any edition of SQL Server installed, download and install SQL Server Express. As of writing these lines, SQL Server Express 2017 is available from `https://www.microsoft.com/en-us/sql-server/sql-server-editions-express`.

---

[2]For definitive legal information, please consult Microsoft's Visual Studio website.

Important   The installation wizard may fail if it is not being run with administrator privileges. Therefore, after downloading, don't run the installation directly! Instead, open the file location, right-click the file, and select "**Run as Administrator.**"

1. When the installation wizard starts, select **Basic** as the installation type.

2. Follow the further instructions in the wizard to complete the installation.

3. Click "**Install SSMS**" to install SQL Server Management Studio. This will redirect you to download another installation wizard from Microsoft's website. Download and run the file, then follow its own installation wizard.

4. Click **Close** to close the main installation wizard, and approve that you want to exit.

Download and Build the Application

While the GitHub page of the application mentions several options to install the application, we're going to download the Git repository and compile the code though Visual Studio. In order to do that:

1. Go to `https://github.com/arnonax/mvcforum`, click on the "Clone or Download" button, and select "Open Visual Studio," as shown in Figure 9-4.

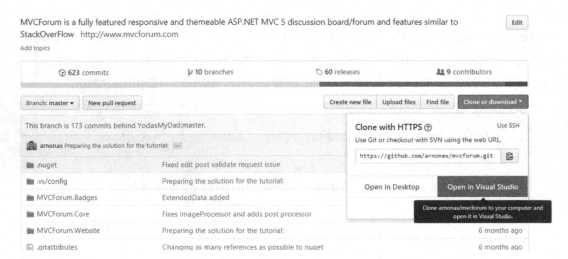

Figure 9-4. *Downloading the repository*

2. Visual Studio should be opened (if it wasn't already), showing the
    Team Explorer pane as shown in Figure 9-5. (If for some reason
    it doesn't, you can open the **Team Explorer** pane from the menu
    View ➤ Team Explorer.) The URL for the GitHub repository
    should be filled in automatically. You can also leave the default
    path for your local repository, or choose a different location, for
    example: `C:\TheCompleteGuideToTestAutomation\MVCForum` as
    shown in the figure. Click **Clone** to complete the operation.

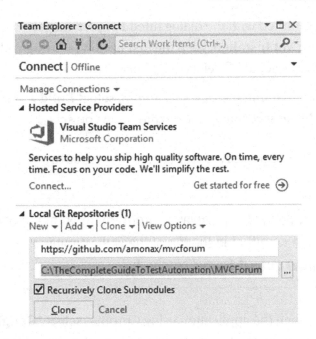

Figure 9-5. Cloning the GitHub repository to your local machine

3. From the **Solution Explorer** pane (**View ➤ Solution Explorer** if it does not appear), double-click on the **MVCForum.sln** file to open the solution and its contained projects.

4. If you haven't installed the necessary workloads yet, you'll be prompted with a dialog titled "**Install Missing Features**." If this is the case, click **Install**.

    a. When the Workloads window appears, select the **.Net Desktop Development** and **ASP.Net and Web Development** workloads, and click **Modify** in order to install them. Note that you'll be prompted to close Visual Studio to continue.

    b. When the update is done, open **MVCForum.sln** again.

5. If you're prompted with the dialog titled **Project Target Framework Not Installed**, keep the first option (starting with "Change the target to...") selected and click **OK**.

6. From the main menu bar of Visual Studio, select **Build ➤ Build Solution.** Make sure that in the **output** pane you see:

```
========= Build: 19 succeeded, 0 failed, 0 up-to-date, 0 skipped =========
```

Note   If the **Output** pane is not displayed, from the main menu bar select **View ➤ Output**. Also make sure that in the top of the Output pane, the item "**Build**" is selected in the "**Show output from:**" combo-box.

---

7. In order to open the application using Chrome, select "**Google Chrome**" from the toolbar as shown in Figure 9-6. Then Press F5 to run the application.

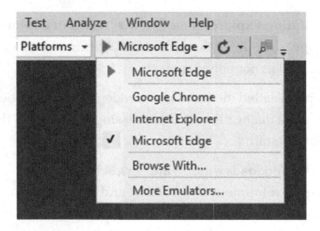

Figure 9-6. *Run using Google Chrome*

8. If a warning titled "**Just My Code Warning**" appears, select the last option "**Continue Debugging (Don't Ask Again).**"

9. The first time you run the application it may take a moment, and then you'll see the application open up in Chrome as shown in Figure 9-7.

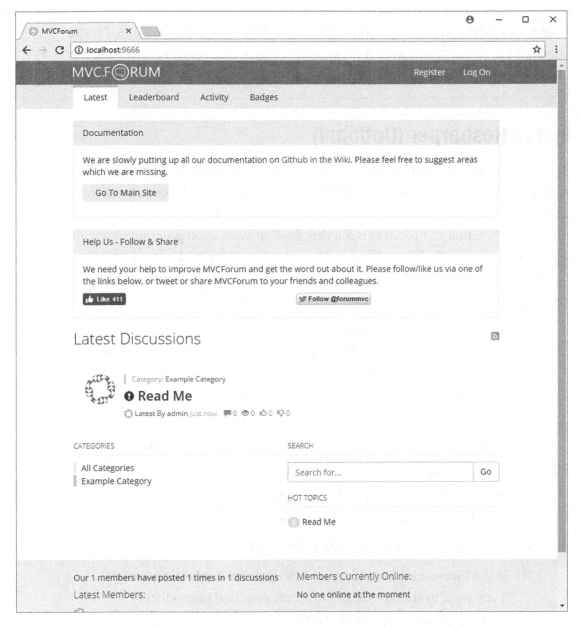

Figure 9-7. *MVCForum as seen when run locally for the first time*

Congratulations! You now have a complete working environment to start the tutorial.

Note   In case you got any trouble completing one of the above steps, please consult the documentation of the relevant product, and search the web or the book's website for help.

Install Resharper (Optional)

Resharper is a third-party commercial productivity add-on to Visual Studio, delivered by **JetBrains**. Personally. I use this add-on every day and I can't live without it... In the tutorial I'll show you how I use it, but also tell you how you can achieve the same things without it. Note that this product has a very flexible evaluation program: it is a 30-day trial, but you can easily freeze the countdown in days that you don't use it!

You can download Resharper from `https://www.jetbrains.com/resharper/download/`. After downloading, run the installation application:

1. In the first page you'll be able to choose additional JetBrains' products to install. In addition, if you have more than one version of Visual Studio installed, you can choose the versions you want to install Resharper on.

2. Accept the License Agreement and then click **Install.** After the installation completes, click **Exit** to close the installation wizard.

3. The next time you'll open Visual Studio, you'll be prompted to accept **JetBrain's Privacy Policy**. Scroll all the way down to enable the "**I Accept**" button, and click it.

4. Click **OK** on the next page (**Data Sharing Options**).

5. In the **License Summary** page, click the **Start Evaluation** button if you want to start the 30-day evaluation period immediately. Then click **OK** to close the Wizard.

Note   If you don't start the evaluation period when prompted after the installation, you can start it by choosing **Resharper ➤ Why Resharper is Disabled** from the main menu bar of Visual Studio, click the **Start Evaluation** button, and **OK** to close the dialog.

You can also pause the evaluation period by going to **Resharper ➤ Help ➤ License Information**, click the **Pause Evaluation** button and **OK** to close the dialog. Note that Resharper counts partial days as whole days. Also, if you keep another instance of Visual Studio open, then the evaluation period continues.

1.   After starting the evaluation you'll be prompted to **Select Resharper Ultimate Shortcuts Scheme**. I suggest that you select the first option (Visual Studio), unless you're more used to using **IntelliJ IDEA**.

Tip   In my opinion the most efficient way to use Resharper is using keyboard shortcuts rather than the mouse. For this reason, I recommend downloading and printing the Default Keymap poster and keeping it beside your keyboard, or hang it on the wall in front of you. I highly recommend that you practice working with the keyboard rather than with the mouse as much as possible. See Appendix D for more tips for working effectively with the keyboard.

Using Git Through Visual Studio

While the tutorial guides you step by step and shows you most of the code that you need to write, in some cases it won't be practical to show everything. In addition, you may want to look at my code and compare to yours in case something went wrong. For these reasons I tried to keep a clean and ordered revision history of all the steps of the tutorial inside the Git repository. I also put tags on any code listing and important milestones so you can find them more easily. Because Git is a distributed source-control system, once you cloned the repo (Git repository) to your machine (as explained previously in this chapter), you have your own copy of the entire history right on your local machine.

If you're familiar with Git you can work with it using your preferred tool (e.g., Git bash, Git Extensions, SourceTree, etc.). But if you don't, here's a brief explanation of how to use Git directly from within Visual Studio.

Most Git operations in Visual Studio are done through the **Team Explorer** pane, which as mentioned before, can be opened from **View ➤ Team Explorer.** The **Team Explorer** has several views in it. Figure 9-8 shows the **Home** view in the **Team Explorer** pane.

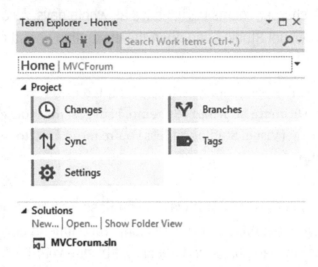

Figure 9-8. *The Home view in the Team Explorer pane*

From the **Home view** you can easily navigate to the other views (**Changes**, **Branches**, **Sync**, **Tags**, and **Settings**). While these buttons appear only on the Home view, you can also switch between the views from any other view using the combo-box right beneath the toolbar of the pane (where it reads "Home | MvcForum" in the figure).

Switching Between Branches

The GitHub repository contains several branches, and most of them are inherited from the original repository. However, the **Tutorial** branch is the one I created myself, which contains all of the revisions shown in the tutorial. You can refer to the revisions in this branch if you want to see more details and better understand the changes described in the tutorial.

By default, the local repository contains only the **master** branch, which reflects the starting point of the tutorial. To switch to the **Tutorial** branch for the first time, do the following:

1. In the **Team Explorer** pane, switch to the **Branches** view.

2. Expand the **remotes/origin** folder to see the list of branches in the remote repository. The view should look like Figure 9-9.

Figure 9-9. *List the remote repositories*

3. Right-click on the **Tutorial** (remote) branch, and select **Checkout**. The **Tutorial** branch should be added to the main list of (local) branches, near the **master** branch.

To switch between the local branches, double-click the branch that you want to switch to (e.g., **master** or **Tutorial**). Note that switching to the **Tutorial** branch will bring you to the *final* state of the tutorial. In addition, if you've made changes to one of the files in the solution, then you won't be able to switch to another branch unless you either commit or undo your changes. Obviously if you want to retain your changes you should commit them, and if not, then you should undo. Also note that when you switch to another branch, it always checks out the *latest* revision in that branch. I advise that you create your own branch and commit your changes to it (by selecting **New Branch** from the **Branches** view), though you can feel free to commit your changes to the **master** branch. Remember that this is your local copy of the repository (and you can't push your changes back to GitHub because you don't have the proper permissions) so don't be afraid to commit your changes.

In order to view your changes and either commit or undo them, switch to the **Changes** view. Figure 9-10 shows the Changes view.

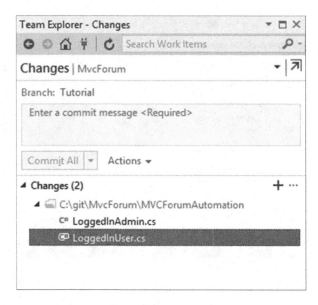

Figure 9-10. *Team Explorer, Changes view*

Before you decide whether you want to commit or revert your changes, you can compare each changed file with its original state. To do that, right-click on the relevant file and select **Compare with Unmodified...** or just double-click it. To commit your changes, you must enter a commit message in the yellow textbox, and click the **Commit All** button. If instead you want to revert one or more files, you can select them or their common containing folder, right-click. and select **Undo Changes...**

To view the revision history of a branch, from the Branches view. right-click on the desired branch and select **View History...** The history view is usually opened in the main documents area and looks like in Figure 9-11.

Figure 9-11. *The History window*

In this image you can see the tags (at the right side of some of the revisions) that can help you find the relevant revision more easily. Hovering with the mouse over a tag also shows the description associated with it. Double-click a revision to display its changed files in **Team Explorer**. From there you can compare each file with its previous revision or open it, to see how it looked in that revision. Unfortunately, you cannot check out the entire revision directly from Visual Studio in order to debug or investigate the entire code structure, but you can do it from the command line as follows:

1. From the **Team Explorer** pane, either from the **Changes** or the **Branches** view, select **Actions ➤ Open Command Prompt**.

2. In the command prompt that opens, type: `git checkout ID`, where ID is the value displayed in the ID column of the history window. For example, type: `git checkout ca2a6f05` to check out the revision titled "Added TestEnvironment configuration file". Alternatively, in order to check out a tagged revision, type `git checkout tags/tag-name`, where *tag-name* is the name of the tag, for example, type `git checkout tag/Listing 14-16` to check out the revision titled "Support Firefox and Edge".

3. Switch back to Visual Studio and you'll see a dialog titled "**File Modification Detected**." Click on the **Reload Solution** button. Now you should be able to see and debug the code on the revision you checked out.

Summary

In this chapter I explained the course of action that we're about to take in the next chapters for writing the first tests and building the infrastructure code to support them, and guided you on how to prepare the environment so you can follow along the tutorial. I strongly encourage you to really follow and *actually do* everything in the tutorial on your machine, and not just read through it. Actually doing it, tackling the real problems, and experiencing the workflow is the best way to really understand the power of this process. So, let's get started!

CHAPTER 10

Designing the First Test Case

In this chapter I'll explain how to approach designing the first test case, which is the first step in our process. Most of the technique is also relevant for any subsequent test case, but first we should consider how to choose the first test case.

Choosing the First Test to Automate

The question "which test to start from" may be stunning. You probably have tens, if not hundreds or even thousands of test cases that you would like to automate. They're probably divided into features, screens, subsystems, or whatever your company used to categorize all of them. If the system is complex and compound from several distinct and mostly independent subsystems, then this question is even more challenging.

However, sometimes when I come to a customer who asks me to help them start to build test automation, they already have ideas as to what the first tests should be, or even chose the first test cases to automate beforehand. The obvious choice, which is correct in most cases, is to start from the sanity tests. Most customers have a well-known and established set of tests that are considered "sanity," which they execute (manually) pretty often. But the criteria of how these tests were chosen to comprise the sanity suite are not always so clear, and the definition of what a sanity suite should contain can vary from one company or team to another. Unfortunately, from my experience, in many cases, a substantial part of these sanity tests is not suited for automation at all.

© Arnon Axelrod 2018
A. Axelrod, *Complete Guide to Test Automation*, https://doi.org/10.1007/978-1-4842-3832-5_10

Therefore, in most cases, after I look at the description of the manual test cases in the customer's sanity suite, I put those aside, and ask a few questions that help me choose the most important tests to start with. The questions I ask are along these lines:

- Who are the main customers and users of the system?

- What's the main value that the system provides to these customers/users?

- What are the *outputs* that provide this value?

- What are the necessary *inputs* that are needed to produce these outputs?

Sometimes it helps to refine those questions by asking the following leading questions too:

- What harm will be done if the system stops working?

- How does this system help the organization earn more money or save money?

- Among the *outputs* of the system, if one of them stops working for a while in production without anyone from the dev or support noticing it (hypothetically), which one will cause the most harm? Which user will likely to notice it first, when and how?

- What was the first and most important feature that was the incentive for starting developing the system at the first place? What did the users do before this system existed?

The purpose of all of these questions is to answer the one important question, which is:

"What's the most important thing that the application is doing?"

Or in words that are more relevant to our discussion:

"What's the most important thing that we should test?"

Note that the answer to these questions always encompasses an output, which is a result of some important and unique functionality and that can be verified.

Unfortunately, many tests that people consider as "sanity" do not answer these questions. Here are some examples of tests that are **not** very appropriate as first tests, or even as automated tests whatsoever:

- Tests that does not specify a concrete and specific expected result. For example: "Pressing the 'Submit order' button should succeed." Even if this button does the most important thing in the application, if we can't specify what the expected outcome should be, there' no point in testing it.

- Relying on a "success" message as a proof that an operation succeeded. For example: "Perform a purchase and verify that a 'success' message appears." Even though the expected result is specified very clearly, it does not really prove that the system did the important thing it should have. In other words, it doesn't prove that the system *provides the value* that it should. Displaying a success message is important for the user's experience, but it's much less important than some other outcome, which is the essence of the functionality. Ask yourself: If the system will display the message even though it won't do anything else, does it have any value? In the above example, verifying that a purchase succeeded may involve navigating into "my purchases" page and verifying that the purchase, along with all of its details, are there. Of even better, verify that the seller sees the order!

- Tests that verify that a user can log in. Login is never the real purpose of a system. It's just something that the user has to do in order to be identified when doing other important stuff using the system. No one would build a system just for the sake of allowing users to log in, just as no user will ever want to use a system whose most important feature is that it allows him to log in. The fact that this is the first *step* in many tests doesn't make it appropriate as the first *test*! Later in the automation project, you may want to test some security or user management features. Only in this context it will be appropriate to write tests that cover the login process as the tested feature itself, and not just as a step to reach another goal.

- Tests that verify the layout of windows or pages. Problems in the layout of pages, like cropped text, unaligned controls, bad colors, etc., are pretty easy to detect by a human tester. However, besides the fact that this is rarely the most important feature of a system, machines cannot easily detect such problems. Even using tools that help detecting these, every small change to the layout will require maintenance.

- Test that verify that when a page appears, certain buttons and fields are disabled, and others are enabled. This is a little better than just testing layout, but it's still not the purpose that systems are built for. Also, each button or field that can be disabled must also be enabled in some other case, which means that the more important thing to verify is that the field becomes enabled or disabled according to the relevant conditions. Testing all buttons and fields on a page for their enabled/disabled state doesn't tell us much and may easily break if any of the relevant condition changes.

- Tests that verify that the user can fill in all the details in a form. Like in the other cases, there's no value in a system that allows the user to enter data if this data is not being used anywhere. The data should either affect other features, be transferred to another system that uses it, or at the very minimum be stored and retrieved again by the user at a later time. Most probably, the highest value from this data is obtained when it's used by the system to affect some other automatic operation. Storing and retrieving data is nothing special to a specific application (unless you're part of a team that develops a database engine, which you probably aren't). Therefore, it's often worth having a separate test for each value in a form, only to verify that it affects the appropriate functionality in the way that it should.

DOES IT ALWAYS PAY OFF TESTING THE MOST IMPORTANT FEATURE?

It could be that the most important functionality of a system is so stable that the priority of testing it is not so high anymore. If that's the case, there could be two options:

1.   We haven't chosen the right system to test. If the components of the system that implement the critical scenario are not going to be touched anytime soon, then we probably don't test the relevant components, and we need to think again about what system (or subsystem) we want to test.

2.   The main scenario is pretty stable, but the components that it uses are being touched in order to add or change other features. In this case, even though that the chances for regressions may be pretty low, I still think that it's worth starting from that scenario for two reasons:

     a.   Even though the chances may be low, it's still possible that this highly important scenario would break. It's better to catch this case sooner (by the automation) than later (by manual testers or in production).

     b.   Probably most other features and scenarios are a variation, or somehow related to that critical scenario. Starting from this test will help us build the infrastructure that will be reusable by most other tests.

Once we've identified what's the most important output that we want to test, we need to plan how we're going to test it. For that, we need to answer a very simple question (though the answer is not always that trivial...), which is:

"What are the necessary inputs that affect the output that we want to test?"

Note the word "necessary." Many inputs can probably affect the output in one way or another, but we want to start from the simplest scenario that shows the value of the system. Other tests that we'll write later may verify the affect that other inputs have on the same output, or also other outputs. The default way to answer this question should be to ask the product owner. However, because the product owner usually thinks about how the product is actually being used in production, often the answer she'll give you is that everything is necessary and that it's impossible to isolate only few inputs in order to get the result you need. Therefore, often I find that the best way to answer this question is simply by experimenting or by looking at the code of the SUT. The developers can often guide you where to look and shorten the process.

From those two important questions we can start building a scenario, which may raise other questions about *how* to perform certain operations, or how to implement them as part of the automation. In general, the scenario should involve controlling the inputs of the SUT in a way that will affect the important output and verify that the output that we want to verify was indeed affected in the way that we expect. You may want to refer back to Chapter 6 at this point to consider the most appropriate architecture for the test, and how the test should interact with the SUT. Note that if you don't have control over the relevant inputs because they're being received from an external system, or if the important outputs are only visible through an external system, then you may want to consider creating a simulator for these external systems.

Choosing the First Test Case for MVCForum

Back to our hands-on tutorial, as our SUT is a forum application, its main value comes from its ability to publish questions to a wide audience and allow other people to respond. Note that the scoring and badging rules are an important differentiating feature (as it motivates the users to use the site to the benefit of all) and therefore should also be considered as one of the first tests, but they still only support the main purpose, which is to allow public discussions, and they have no value of their own sake without it.

So, what's the most important output of the system then? In order to provide the value that we identified above, the most important output of the system is the messages that other people post. Note that if each user can only see his own messages, then the system doesn't provide the basic value we expect it to. Therefore, we should verify that any user (even an unregistered, anonymous one) can see messages that other users post. We should also verify that one user can answer or comment on another user's discussion; otherwise this would just be a bulletin board, and not a discussion forum. However, in order to keep the tests small and easy to maintain, we should create a separate test for each of these verifications.

And what about the inputs? In our example the answer is trivial. These are also the messages and comments that users write. However, when we'll design the test case in more detail, you'll see that we'll need to provide more inputs in order to complete the scenario.

The Scientific Method for Designing a Test Case

Scientific facts do not become "scientific facts" only because scientists decided so. In fact, never is any scientific claim really proven! On the contrary: the scientific method motivates scientists to refute other's theories. In order to do that, they need to perform an empirical test that shows an example that is not consistent with the claims of that theory. It is sufficient to find one such counterexample in order to refute one's theory! However, as more scientists perform such empirical tests but still no one finds a counterexample, this theory becomes more established and accepted as being "true."

Likewise, when you come to design a test case, you should think about this test case as a scientific claim. The claim is a sentence that can be either true or false. This claim is what we'll try to refute in the test, so the first thing that you have to do when designing a test case is to phrase that claim. At this point, I open my favorite text editor and write down this phrase. I usually add a line of "="s below it to mark it as the title of the test. Note that this method is useful for all test cases, not only automated, but it's especially important for automated tests because the expected must not be subject to interpretation.

For our MVCForum application, we can phrase the claim for our first scenario as shown in Listing 10-1.

Listing 10-1. The claim of the first test

```
When a registered user starts a discussion, other, anonymous users can see
it
==============================================================================
```

Now, after we defined *what* is it that we want to test, we have to define *how* we're going to test it, such that if the test fails, it will refute the claim.

Designing the Steps of the Test

Continuing our scientific method analogy, we design the steps of the test as the steps of a scientific experiment. For a scientific experiment, we want to isolate any irrelevant parameters and "noise" that may affect the outcome, which is not relevant to the claim that we want to try and refute.

We also want to make the experiment as simple and as short as possible, so it is clear to everyone reading it how they can reproduce it.

There's one small difference between a scientific experiment and an automated test though. A scientific experiment doesn't need any maintenance as the laws of physics won't change anytime soon... However, we write automated tests for systems that continuously evolve, and therefore we must ensure that our tests are maintainable. This difference is reflected in the level of detail in which we describe the scenario. While eventually when we'll write the code, we'll have to fill in all of the details to make the scenario work, when we're designing the test as an experiment, we leave only the minimal necessary details that aid in understanding the flow of the test. We'll leave all other fine-grained details to be implementation details that are of less importance to the essence of the experiment. In the code, we'll put these details in lower-level reusable components that we'll create or use default values for things that we may need to change in other tests or in the future.

Continuing our MVCForum example, the complete test case can be written as an experiment as shown in Listing 10-2.

Listing 10-2. Adding the steps to the first test

```
When a registered user starts a discussion, other, anonymous users can see
it
==============================================================================
Login as a registered user
Start a discussion titled "Hi!" and body "dummy body"
Enter the site as an anonymous user (from another browser)
Verify that a discussion titled "Hi!" appears
Open that discussion
Verify that the body of the discussion is "dummy body"
```

Notes:

- You may have noticed that in the first line we have a presumption here, which is that we have a well-known registered user. While in reality, or in a standard testing environment this is always almost the case, we can't just use any arbitrary user, due to isolation concerns. So now we need start thinking about the isolation technique regarding the registered users (see Chapter 7 for more information).

If in the vast majority of tests we would need only one registered user, I'd say that we should create one such user as a prerequisite in the automation environment. However, because the application is a discussion board, I assume that there will be many tests that need more than one registered user. So maybe we should create two then? But what if we'll need more? Also, any activity of a registered user may be seen by other users, so our environment may become dirty and some tests may have unpredictable results... There's no one right way here, but at least for now, my choice is to encapsulate the registration of a user inside the "Login as a registered user" activity itself. This means, that each time the test will run, a new user will be registered. Moreover, if we'll reuse this step in other tests, each time this step will be performed a new user will be registered. While the description of the operation may be a bit misleading as it hides the fact that it also registers a new user, it makes this operation completely atomic and autonomic, and therefore reusable, and it still fulfills its promise: it logs in using some registered user. You may also worry about the amount of users that we'll create during a test run, but I don't suppose that it's a real issue because the system should support it. We'll probably start from a new empty database every run to improve isolation anyway, so it's really not that big of a deal.

- I used hard-coded texts "Hi!" and "Dummy body." However, when implement it, I'll probably replace "Hi!" with some random string because we'll need to identify the message by its title, and even if we'll run the test multiple times (or different tests that all use the same string), we'll always be able to identify the one we created. Regarding the body though, we can keep "Dummy body" because we don't have to search by this value.

- You may think that it's better to use longer and more sophisticated message bodies, for example, ones that contain bold and underlined text, and to see that they appear correctly. However, this is not the purpose of this test and should be verified in different tests, as we don't want this basic test to fail on that kind of issue.

- If you'd try to perform this scenario manually right after installing the application, you'll see that the newly registered user can't create a new discussion. This is because by default there's only one category called "Example Category," which only the administrator has permissions to create new discussions in. In addition, when creating a new discussion, the user must assign the discussion to a category. Therefore, we can either add the required permissions for the "Example Category" or add another category that will be used as the default category for all tests that don't need a specific category, and give all registered users the necessary permissions to create new discussions in this category. While the second option is cleaner, the first option is simpler, so let's start with it. We'll write the code in such a way that it will be easy to change this decision later on. Anyway, this should be a prerequisite of the test and not part of the test itself. Later we'll have to decide how we're going to implement it: by performing these changes through the UI (using the administrator user) before the first test runs, by making changes to the database, using a backup file, etc.

Thinking in Terms of Objects and Entities

In principle, the next step in our workflow should be to translate these steps into code. But in order to translate it to code that is easy to maintain, and enhance reusability, we want that code to adhere to proper *object-oriented* design principles. And in order to make it easier for you to translate these steps to object-oriented code, I recommend doing one extra thing before jumping into the code: near each line, write a *noun* that constitutes the "object" or an "entity" that makes the *context* for the operation described by that line. This context is better described in business, or real-world terms rather than technical ones, because these terms make sense to more people and will also be more likely to remain correct for a longer period of time, after the system may undergo serious architectural or technical changes. Note that there's no deterministic formula for coming up with these contexts (or objects), and even when I demonstrate writing the same test twice to different people, I often end up with different ways to describe the steps and their corresponding objects. It takes some experience in order to sense what are the right abstractions that make more sense and will lead to a better designed code.

In many cases, including in our example, the context for the first operation will be simply the application itself (the SUT). The context for other operations are often the result of a previous one. Later when we'll translate this to code, it will mean that one method returns an object, and the next line invokes another method on that object. Also, sometimes the best way to describe the context of a line is using a few nouns (two or three, not more!) the first is the broader context, and next are more specific ones. This translates into entities containing other entities, or objects referring to other objects in the code.

For our example, we can write these contexts as shown in Listing 10-3.

Listing 10-3. Adding the context of each step

```
When a registered user starts a discussion, other, anonymous users can see
it
===============================================================================
Login as a registered user
                // MVCForum (the application)
Start a discussion titled "Hi!" and body "dummy body"
                // Logged-in user
Enter the site as an anonymous user (from another browser)
                // MVCForum (new instance)
Verify that a discussion titled "Hi!" appears
                // MVCForum.LatestDisucssions.Top (*)
Open that discussion
                // Discussion header
Verify that the body of the discussion is "dummy body"
                // Discussion
```

Notes (*)   When we first designed the test, we didn't say where exactly we should look for the discussion to appear. Technically we can look either at the list of latest discussions (that appear on the main page), or go to the category of the discussion and list all discussions in it. Theoretically, both of these are unique features that may change independently of the main functionality that we verify in the test. In order to resolve this, instead of specifying MVCForum.LatestDiscussions, we could specify MVCForum.AllDisucussions. We can implement this list using lazy loading (i.e., only fetch an item when we try to access it, going through all the pages if there's more than one page), in order to avoid fetching all of the data into memory at once. However, being pragmatic, it's reasonable to assume that there will always be a way to get the list of all discussions ordered from the latest to the oldest, so in case this feature will change, we'll just replace the implementation.

In addition, we can only be certain that the discussion will be the latest (top) one if there's no one else but us to use the same environment. We'll take care of it later as part of our isolation solution. (See Chapter 7 about isolation techniques.)

Notice how the "Logged-in user" context of the second operation is the result of the first "Login as a registered user," the "Discussion header" is of the discussion we identified in the previous step, and the "Discussion" itself is the result of opening the discussion from the "Discussion header."

Modeling the Application

We often say that these objects and the relationships between them *model* the application and the real-world world entities that are represented by it. We also say that these objects and relationships constitute a *model* (as a noun, rather than a verb) that represent that application and the real-world entities. For example, we can model the sentence "a customer adds a product to an order," using Customer, Product, and Order classes. These classes will likely have the methods shown in Listing 10-4.

Listing 10-4. Modeling example

```
class Customer
{
        public IList<Order> Orders { get { /*...*/ } }

        public Order CreateOrder()
        {
                //...
        }
```

```
        //...
}

class Order
{
        public IList<Product> Products { get { /*...*/ } }

        public void AddProduct(Product product)
        {
                //...
        }

        public void Submit()
        {
                //...
        }
        //...
}

class Product
{
        public string Description { get { /*...*/ } }
        public decimal Price { get { /*...*/ } }
        //...
}
```

The Page Object Pattern

One common and much-known pattern for modeling the SUT in an object-oriented way is the *Page Object Pattern*. This pattern applies only to user interface test automation and describes either complete or parts of a web page or window, exposing methods that reflect the operations that the user can perform on that UI area.

I find the Page Object pattern very compelling for people because it's very easy to understand, easy to implement, and frees the automation developer from thinking too creatively about modeling his business domain. I use this pattern too, but I don't stick to it very religiously, as I see it as only one of many options to model an application. Here are some drawbacks that you should be aware of when you model the application *primarily* using page objects:

- Because it's only relevant to UI, it can't model features that are not UI centric.

- If the UI changes drastically, even if the business logic remains pretty much unchanged, then very large portions of the automation should be rewritten.

- If you'll want to change some operations later to be performed through a lower layer (e.g., through API), then not only your implementation will have to change but also your model. In other words, if you'll use abstractions that represent business operations and entities rather than UI pages, it's more likely that such changes will be local to the *internal details* of a specific class or method, while if you only use page objects, then you'll probably need to replace a whole bunch of them together.

If you still decide to use the Page Object pattern as your primary abstraction, here are some tips and recommended practices to make your code easier to maintain:

- Hide Selenium details inside the page object class. For example, if you have a Submit button on the page, instead of having a public property (or a getter method) that returns `IWebElement` for that button, put a `void Submit()` method on the object that finds the button and clicks it internally.

- Moreover, *avoid* exposing all fields as public properties (i.e., getters and setters for the *value* of the field), and a method for each button. Instead I prefer to expose methods that perform higher-level, more conceptual business operations. For example, for a `LoginPage` class, instead of exposing getters and setters for `UserName` and `Password`, and method to click the Submit button, I prefer to have one method `Login`, which takes the username and password as arguments, fills those in, and click the Submit button altogether. Using higher-level methods will make your test more readable and easier to maintain. Even if the elements on the page change, only the code *inside the method* will have to change, and not any code that calls it.

- When an operation leads the user to a different page, or displays a new view, the method that performs the operation should return the page object that represents that new view. This makes the code more streamlined and easier to reuse. This is especially beneficial due to auto-completion that most IDEs feature. For example, if after the Login the user is directed to the main page, the `Login` method from the previous example should return the `MainPage` object. So eventually the method's signature should look like this:

```
MainPage Login(string username, string password)
```

- Despite its name, "Page Object" should not correspond only to whole pages. Instead, it's recommended to decompose a page into subpages or views, according to the logical layout of the page. For example, a typical email application can have a `MainPage` object containing properties for the toolbar, the folders tree, the list of headers, and the preview pane. Each of these views should have its own Page Object. This idea can even be repeated in a nested manner, so that these views hold yet their own inner views. For example, the preview pane can hold the header of the message (which is fixed), and the body (which is scrollable). Figure 10-1 and code Listing 10-5 shows how this looks in the UI and in the code.

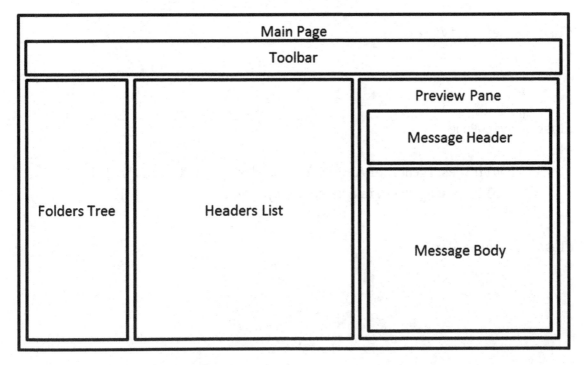

Figure 10-1. *Nested PageObjects*

Listing 10-5. Page Objects for a typical main application

```
class MainPage
{
        // ...
        public ToolbarView ToolBar { get { /*...*/ } }
        public FoldersTreeView FoldersTree { get { /*...*/ } }
        public HeadersListView HeadersList { get { /*...*/ } }
        public PreviewPane PreviewPane { get { /*...*/ } }
}

class ToolbarView
{
        //...
}

class FoldersTreeView
{
        //...
}

class HeadersListView
{
        //...
}

class PreviewPane
{
        public MessageHeaderView MessageHeader { get { /*...*/ } }
        public MessageBodyView MessageBody { get { /*...*/ } }
}

class MessageHeaderView
{
        //...
}
```

```
class MessageBodyView
{
        //...
}
```

- For views that appear in multiple places in the application, you should use different instances of the same Page Object class. For example, MVCForum features a rich text editor in various places in the application: when creating a new discussion, when replying on a discussion, and also in the admin console to enter a description for a category. Another typical case is when you have tables, which support sorting, grouping, and filtering, but appear in different places with different columns and rows. In some cases, the rows themselves can be much richer than just a line of values and can be seen like having their own subview, in which case these rows can have their own page object, and the table should expose a property that returns a collection of these page objects that represent these row subviews. The list of discussions in the MVCForum application is an example of this, as each discussion header is a view that contains an icon, the title, category, author, etc. In all of these cases you should use different instances of the same Page Object class. **This means that you should avoid using static members on these classes.** Also, I don't recommend using singletons as even if you don't think that you'll ever need more than one instance, you'll be surprised how often these assumptions turn to be wrong. And when you reach the moment when this assumption is wrong, you'll have a very hard time changing it. Even for the main page, you may create two instances to simulate two concurrent users!

- Sometimes there are views that appear in different places in the application, but with slight differences. Or there are similar views that part of them is fixed and other parts changes according to their type. In these cases, consider using abstract classes containing the fixed parts of regular properties, and the different parts as abstract properties. Then create derived classes for each type. For example, in the mail application, regular messages and meeting invitations have a lot in common but are also different in some aspects, and therefore their preview pane may look somewhat different. In the above example, `MessageBodyView` may be an abstract base class, having `MailMessageBodyView` and `MeetingMessageBodyView` as derived classes.

Beyond the Page Object Pattern

As I already mentioned, I don't stick to the Page Object pattern very religiously. Instead, I use whatever abstraction I can find that best represents the business concepts and operations that I want. I'm trying to think about reusability, clarity, and lack of duplication when I model the application. As you'll see in the next chapters, the act of removing duplication, which I emphasize a lot, plays a big role in continuously improving and sharpening the model over time, as I add more and more tests. Designing and sharpening the model often raise important questions and misalignments between the actual functionality and the desired one (in other words, bugs), and lead you to better understand the product.

When you use more conceptual business entities rather than UI pages, in case you'd want to change the scope of your tests from UI to API or some other scope someday in the future, it will be much easier, as you won't have to change the model – only the implementation. The same is true even for enlarging the scope. That is, if right now you're using API testing and may want to allow UI testing in the future, then you'll also only need to change the implementation but not the model.

If the application is very well architected, then probably all of the important functionality that we want to test in our first test or tests is encapsulated in the Business Logic layer, which already models the business entities and their relevant operations. In this case, my advice is to write these tests directly on the Business Logic layer as unit or integration tests. However, in reality often the separation is not as strict as we'd like it to be, and therefore we may prefer to write the tests as system tests. (See Chapter 6 for more information about choosing the appropriate test scope.)

Often when I model the application using higher-level business entities, I still use the Page Object model under the hood. That is, the tests use objects that represent business entities, but these objects use Page Objects internally to interact with the application through the UI and usually not used directly by the test methods.

As you can see, and will see even more clearly soon, the process of defining the context for each operation leads us from the textual description of the test to an object-oriented design that we can implement in the code. In the following chapter we'll continue the tutorial and finally start writing code!

Summary

In this chapter we went from choosing the first sanity test to automate, through the "scientific method" of defining the test case, to modeling the SUT in an object-oriented approach, which will soon serve us as a design guideline for our test code. While we haven't written a single line of code yet, and although we only planned one single test, we did some very important design work. Skipping this design or doing it carelessly will later cause costly maintainability issues. Note though that doing it properly also requires some practice and experience, so be patient, and try to learn from your experience.

CHAPTER 11

Start Coding the First Test

Finally! After 10 chapters, we're ready to write some code...

In this chapter we'll build the skeleton for the first test that we designed in the previous chapter, writing the code of the test itself and empty classes and methods that it should use. We'll end this chapter when the code compiles but does nothing. In the next chapter we'll continue to implement all the methods and won't rest until the test passes. Many parts of the code that we'll write will also serve as an infrastructure that we'll be able to use in the next tests. As also mentioned in Chapter 9, we'll use Visual Studio and C#, and Selenium of course. So, let's start!

Creating the Project

In order to write a test, we first need to create a new test project. In Visual Studio, a project is always part of a solution. So technically we can create a new solution for the test automation or add our project to the solution of the SUT. This question is relevant also to the real world, and both ways are fine. If possible, I prefer to add the tests to the solution of the SUT, so that developers can run the tests more easily. It also allows us to reuse certain parts of the SUT in the tests. I know that it may sound awkward or even a bad idea to use parts of the SUT for testing the SUT, but I rarely use the logic of the app, but reusing things like constants and sometimes interfaces may be very handy and ensure that the test uses the same values as the application itself. Testing that the values themselves are correct is not very meaningful for automation, because anytime someone has to change a constant, he would anyway need to change the same constant in the tests too...

So, let's start by adding a new test project to the MVCForum solution:

1. Start Visual Studio, and open the MVCForum solution (MVCForum. sln) from the location of the Git repository you downloaded in Chapter 9. If you followed Chapter 9 step by step, then you'd probably see MVCForum at the recently opened solutions.

© Arnon Axelrod 2018
A. Axelrod, *Complete Guide to Test Automation*, https://doi.org/10.1007/978-1-4842-3832-5_11

2. Open Solution Explorer (**View ➤ Solution Explorer**), right-click on the root element (**Solution 'MVCForum'**), and select **Add ➤ New Project...**

3. Inside the **Add New Project** dialog, shown in Figure 11-1, on the left pane, select **Visual C# ➤ Test** (1), then select **Unit Test Project (.Net Framework)** in the middle pane (2). Type "MVCForumAutomation" in the **Name** field at the bottom (3), and click **OK** (4).

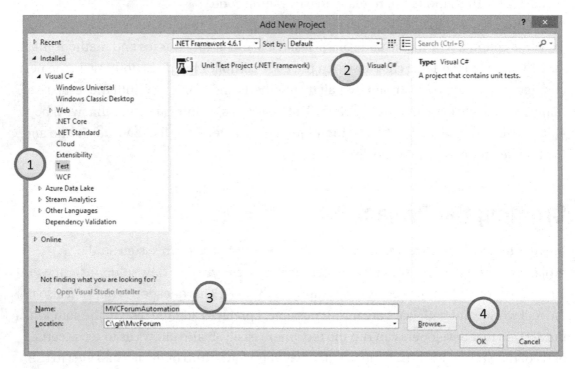

Figure 11-1. *Adding a new Test Project*

Note   The "Unit Test Project (.Net Framework)" project type creates a test project that uses the MSTest unit-testing framework.

---

4. If you scroll down the **Solution Explorer** pane, you should see the new project **MVCForumAutomation** added to the solution, containing a **UnitTest1.cs** file. Double-click on this file to open in the code editor. Figure 11-2 shows the new file as how it looks in the text editor.

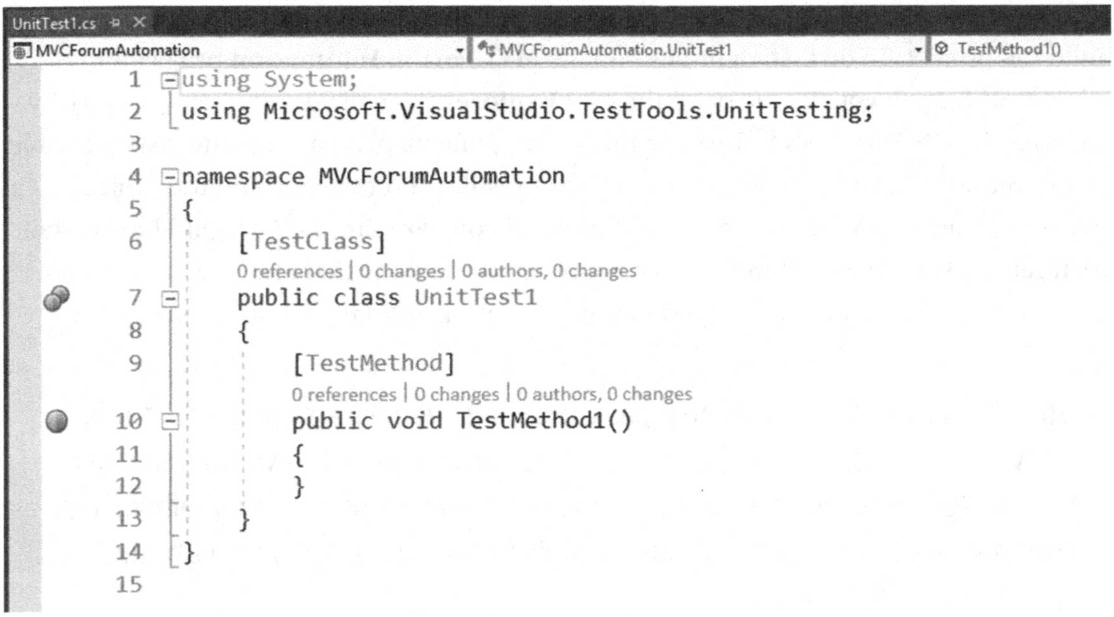

```
UnitTest1.cs  ↗ ✕
📄 MVCForumAutomation                    ▾ ⁂ MVCForumAutomation.UnitTest1           ▾ ⊙ TestMethod1()
         1   ⊟using System;
         2    using Microsoft.VisualStudio.TestTools.UnitTesting;
         3
         4   ⊟namespace MVCForumAutomation
         5    {
         6         [TestClass]
                   0 references | 0 changes | 0 authors, 0 changes
    🔘   7   ⊟    public class UnitTest1
         8         {
         9             [TestMethod]
                       0 references | 0 changes | 0 authors, 0 changes
    🔘  10   ⊟        public void TestMethod1()
        11             {
        12             }
        13         }
        14    }
        15
```

Figure 11-2. UnitTest1.cs

Note   If you're using Visual Studio Community Edition, you may not see the small gray text that appears above the class and method declarations ("0 references…"), as it's a feature available only in Visual Studio Professional edition and up. Also, if you're not using Resharper, you won't see those green circles near lines 7 and 10.

This is an example file that Visual Studio adds to the project. We'll change it very soon, but let's first look and try to understand the content of this file.

In an MSTest project, tests are methods decorated with the [TestMethod] attribute. However, in order for MSTest to look for these attributes inside a class, the class must also be decorated with a [TestClass] attribute. An MSTest project can contain many test classes, and each test class can contain many test methods. Every test method can be run independently from the others, but you can also choose to run all the tests in a class or all the tests in the project. There are other filtering abilities, but that's beyond our scope of this book. There's more to MSTest than that, but that's all we need to know for now.

In order to see how the test can run (even though it's still empty), you should first build the project. To do that, right-click on the **MVCForumAutomation** project and select **Build**. Then you have to open the **Test Explorer** pane (if it's not already open), by selecting **Test ➤ Windows ➤ Test Explorer**. This pane displays a list of the tests available in the solution, lets you run them, and see their results. After you've built the project, you should see **TestMethod1** appear in the **Test Explorer** pane. If you right-click on that **TestMethod1**, and select **Run Selected Tests**, you should see that after few seconds its icon near the test name has changed to a green V mark, marking that the test passed.

Note   If you wonder why the test passed even though it's empty, then the rule is very simple: a test always passes unless an exception is thrown from the test method. MSTest provides a class called `Assert` that exposes a few methods that perform verifications. Each of these methods throws an exception in case the appropriate verification fails.

Tip   In Visual Studio you have many ways to perform every action, like running a test method. I show you just one way, but you're welcome to explore and find other ways.

Renaming the Class, Filename, and Test Method

It's not a good idea to keep the name UnitTest1, as this name tells us nothing. We need to change both the name of the class and the name of the file. We'll call the new test class `SanityTests`, as we plan to put the sanity tests in it. When you rename the class, Visual Studio allows you to change the filename to match the name of the class:

1. In the code editor, double-click on the class name (`UnitTest1`) to select it.

2. Type `SanityTests` to replace the name of the class.

3. Press **Ctrl+.** (**Ctrl** and the period key together) to open Visual Studio quick-actions menu and select **Rename file to match type name**.

Tip   There are many naming conventions for test classes and test methods, but there's no one standard. For the name of the test method itself, my rule is that it should be similar to the claim we defined in the previous chapter (even though it may be a pretty long name). Regarding the class names, I tend to have one file for all tests of a feature and name the class after the feature. However, because the first tests are usually very generic, and not specific to one feature, I simply call the first class **SanityTests**. It's usually pretty easy to change these names later anyway.

Renaming the test method is straightforward. Simply edit it to be the name of the test you want. The naming convention that I promote is to use the claim that we defined when we planned the test, remove the spaces, and start new words in capital (AKA PascalCase[1]). In our example, the name of the test method would be: WhenARegisteredUserStartsADiscussionOtherAnonymousUsersCanSeeIt

So now, our test class, whose file name is now SanityTests.cs is as shown in Listing 11-1.

Listing 11-1. SanityTest.cs

```
using System;
using Microsoft.VisualStudio.TestTools.UnitTesting;

namespace MVCForumAutomation
{
    [TestClass]
    public class SanityTests
    {
        [TestMethod]
        public void
        WhenARegisteredUserStartsADiscussionOtherAnonymousUsersCanSeeIt()
        {
        }
    }
}
```

---

[1]https://blogs.msdn.microsoft.com/brada/2004/02/03/
history-around-pascal-casing-and-camel-casing/

Note   The line break before the name of the test method is only due to the limited space in the book. In the code editor, it should be on the same line as the `public void` keywords preceding it.

Write the Pseudo-code

In this step, we're going to translate the text that we wrote in the previous chapter to a valid C# syntax inside the code editor. Without going too deep into compilers theory here, a valid syntax does not mean that the code compiles. In loose words, it only means that the code "looks like" a valid C# syntax, even though some required definitions and identifiers are missing. For this reason, I call it "Pseudo-code" at this stage, even though I try not to change this code later on, but only add the missing declarations and implementations. So eventually the pseudo-code will become the real code.

To make it easier to write the pseudo-code, instead of switching back and forth between the text editor (where we wrote the textual description of the test) and Visual Studio, I like to copy that text as a comment, write the code. and then delete the comment. Note that the code should be self-describing, looking very similar to the original text, so there's no use in keeping this comment. Figure 11-3 shows what the code looks like after writing the code but before removing the comment.

```
/*
Login as a registered user                               // MVCForum (the application)
Start a discussion titled "Hi!" and body "dummy body"    // Logged-in user
Enter the site as an anonymous user (from another browser)  // MVCForum (new instance)
Verify that a discussion titled "Hi!" appears            // MVCForum.LatestDiscussions.Top
Open that discussion                                     // Discussion header
Verify that the body of the discussion is "dummy body"   // Discussion
    */
[TestMethod]
0 references | arnonax, Less than 5 minutes ago | 1 author, 2 changes
public void WhenARegisteredUserStartsADiscussionOtherAnonymousUsersCanSeeIt()
{
    const string body = "dummy body";
    LoggedInUser userA = MVCForum.RegisterNewUserAndLogin();
    Discussion createdDiscussion = userA.CreateDiscussion(Discussion.With.Body(body));

    MVCForumClient anonymousUser = new MVCForumClient();
    DiscussionHeader latestHeader = anonymousUser.LatestDiscussions.Top;
    Assert.AreEqual(createdDiscussion.Title, latestHeader.Title,
        "The title of the latest discussion should match the one we created");
    Discussion viewedDiscussion = latestHeader.OpenDiscussion();
    Assert.AreEqual(body, viewedDiscussion.Body,
        "The body of the latest discussion should match the one we created");
}
```

Figure 11-3. *Writing the pseudo-code*

Note   I recommend you to look at Figure 11-3 in the e-book version of this book in order to see the syntax highlighting and the red color that Resharper uses to indicate the missing definitions

---

Remarks About the Pseudo-code

As you can see, the pseudo-code that we created is a valid C# syntax, even though it still cannot compile because many definitions are missing. You can also see that the pseudo-code reflects pretty well the text in the comment, employing the contexts that we defined in the text as the objects in the code.

While writing the code, I had to make some additional design decisions. Some of them are apparent from the code you see in Figure 11-3, but some are more implied. Here are some of them:

- While in the textual steps I wrote "Login as a registered user," in the code I called it `RegisterNewUserAndLogin` to better reflect what it does. If you try to register a new user in the application, you'll notice that when the registration succeeds, the user becomes logged in automatically. Therefore, the `RegisterNewUserAndLogin` method is actually one operation despite the 'and' in its name. Note that if this behavior will change at some point, we will be able to change only the internal implementation of this method and perform the same thing as two distinct operations internally (register and log in), but without having to change any test that calls it.

- When creating a discussion in the application, there are various parameters that the user can specify. The most trivial way to model this is by making each one of them a parameter of the `CreateDiscussion` method. However, there are currently four parameters excluding the body of the message, and most of them are optional. In addition, as systems evolve, more and more parameters are added to entities that the user can create. Having overloads with so many parameters makes the method cumbersome and hard to maintain. Therefore, I prefer to use the *Test Data Builder*[2] pattern. The `With` static property of the `Discussion` class will instantiate and return a `DiscussionBuilder` object, with a method for each parameter. The `CreateDiscussion` method should use this builder in order to fill in the values in the form.

- The sentence "Enter the site as an anonymous user" is actually not an operation that the user performs after navigating to the site, but rather this is the state right after navigating to the site. Therefore, we only need to create a new instance of a browser and navigate it to the site. I decided to name this class `MVCForumClient`, as this is what it actually represents. Note that the `MVCForum` identifier is not a name

---

[2]Steve Freeman and Nat Pryce, *Growing Object-Oriented Software Guided by Tests* (Menlo Park, CA: Addison-Wesley Professional, 2009), p. 258.

of a class but rather a property name in the test class. The `MVCForum` property is actually also of type `MVCForumClient`, even though you cannot see it yet from the pseudo-code.

- I considered using the Factory Method pattern[3] to create the new `MVCForumClient` instance for the anonymous user. I may still revise this decision in the future, but for now I didn't see any benefit from doing it, without making the code more cumbersome.

- I declared two variables of type `Discussion`: `createdDiscussion` and `viewedDiscussion`. The first one represents the discussion as the registered user created it, and the second one represents what the anonymous user sees. Even though they should actually be the same, we cannot assume this in the test as this is what we want to verify, by comparing their title and body.

- The `Assert.AreEqual` method is the most common method to perform the verifications in tests. A similar class exists in virtually all unit tests frameworks, but there can be slight differences between them. In MSTest, the first argument is the expected result, the second is the actual result, and the third is an optional message to display when the assertion fails. Note that replacing between the first and the second arguments won't change the outcome of the verification, but regardless of the third parameter, the error message always mentions the expected and actual results using these arguments, so if you replace them this message can be confusing.

THE VAR KEYWORD IN C#

In C#, the compiler can infer the type of a local variable according to the expression that you use to initialize that variable (assuming you initialize it in the same line), which saves you from specifying the type explicitly. In order to use it, you can replace the type to the left of the variable name with the keyword `var`. For example, the following two lines are equivalent and generate exactly the same runtime bytecode:

---

[3]Erich Gamma, Richard Helm, Ralph Johnson, and John Vlissides, *Design Patterns: Elements of Reusable Object-Oriented Software* (Menlo Park, CA: Addison-Wesley Professional, 1994), p. 107.

```
int i = 3;     // explicit type declaration
var i = 3;     // compiler inferred type declaration
```

Note that this does not make the variable dynamic, as the compiler determines the type at compile time and it cannot change it later at runtime. This means that the variable is still strongly-typed (AKA statically typed), and if you'll try to call methods or access properties that do not exist on this type, you'll get compile-time errors and not only runtime errors as you would if it was a dynamic type.

The use of this keyword is controversial, but it's mostly a matter of taste. When this keyword was first introduced in C# 3.0, I didn't like it at first, but over time I got more and more used to it, and today when I look at code that doesn't use it, it looks very cumbersome to me.

When I write the pseudo-code of a test myself, I usually use the var keyword. But for the sake of clarifying my intentions, in the above example I specified the types explicitly. But don't worry; I'll change it back to var when we'll be done.

Getting the Code to Compile

Ok, so we wrote the pseudo-code, but now what? It doesn't even compile! And where's Selenium?! Ok, we need a bit more patience until we use Selenium, but let's get the code to compile first.

The important thing to keep in mind at this step is not to go and try to implement everything. We should only focus on making the code compile and about creating the model, which is the structure of the classes and method signatures, but **without writing any code inside methods**. Completing the model before starting to implement the methods helps us validate that our model is complete (as far as our first test needs), and that we didn't forget anything important along the way. Also, as long as our code doesn't compile, we won't be able to run our test and check if it actually works as we expect, and we're likely to write more code than we'll need or be able to test quickly. We want to take baby steps here to validate that every few lines of our test automation code does exactly what we expect it to. **Remember: if the quality of the test automation code will be poor, its reliability will be poor too!** S,o let's stick to the current step: only make the code compile.

Tip   I find that using the keyboard rather than the mouse wherever possible significantly improves the productivity when writing, editing, or even just reading code, though it can take some time to get used to. Appendix D contains useful tips for working effectively with the keyboard. Accordingly, the following instructions use keyboard shortcuts wherever possible.

The methods and properties that we'll create in order to make the code to compile will all have a single statement: `throw new NotImplementedException();`. As you'll see later in the tutorial, these exceptions will guide us through the process and will ensure that we don't forget to implement anything.

If you're using Resharper, you can use **Alt+PgUp/Alt+PgDn** to navigate between the compilation errors and warning. You can also use **Alt+Shift+PgUp/Alt+Shift+Pg Dn** to navigate only between the errors. If you're not using Resharper, simply traverse the red squiggly lines, or open the Errors pane (**View ➤ Error List**) and use **F8/Shift+F8** to navigate between the errors.

Once the cursor is on an unrecognized class or method name, press **Alt+Enter** (Reshaper) or **Ctrl+.** (without Resharper) to open the quick-actions menu, and select (using the arrow keys and **Enter**) the option to create that class or method. Note that Resharper gives you much more control when creating classes and methods. Especially important is that when you create a method using Resharper, it brings your cursor to edit the types and names of the method parameters and return values, while Visual Studio without Resharper gives some default names and the types it can infer, and leave it like that, which is not what you always want. In this case, you have to explicitly go to the declaration of the method (using **F12**) and edit those manually. Both Resharper and plain Visual Studio adds the `throw new NotImplementedException();` statement to methods that you create this way, but unfortunately they don't do it by default for properties, leaving them to return `null`, so we'll have to do that manually.

Tip   Resharper allows you to change its default behavior to create a body with `throw new NotImplementedException();` statements also for properties, through its Options dialog. To do that, go to **Resharper ➤ Options**, choose **Code Editing ➤ Members Generation** from the left side navigation bar, and under the **Generate property body style** section select **Accessor with default body**.

Whether you use Resharper or Visual Studio's native quick-actions menu, when you create a class you have an option to create it in its own file, or inside the current file. Even though eventually every class should be in its own file, I find it more convenient to create all the classes in the same file, at least until it compiles, or until the first test passes, and only later move each class to its own file. Resharper allows you to do it for all classes in the file in one shot, while using Visual Studio itself you have to do it one by one.

Declaring the LoggedInUser Class

The first compilation error we see is that the type LoggedInUser is not defined. Put the cursor on this identifier and press **Alt+Enter** (or **Ctrl+.**), and select **Create type 'LoggedInUser'** (or **Create class 'LoggedInUser'** without Resharper), as shown in Figure 11-4.

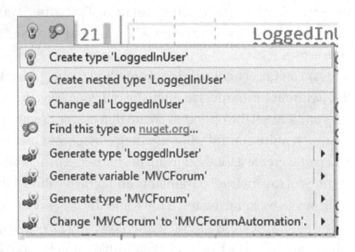

Figure 11-4.   *Creating the LoggedInUser type using the context menu*

Declaring the MVCForum Property

The next undeclared identifier is MVCForum. While the LoggedInUser identifier could only mean a type (class) name due to its location in the syntax, there are few options that can satisfy the compiler regarding the MVCForum identifier. The most obvious one is also a class name, but then the method RegisterNewUserAndLogin must be static, and that wasn't my intent. My intent was that MVCForum will be a read-only property or type MVCForumClient. If you're using Resharper, select **Create read-only property 'MVCForum'** from the quick-actions menu; otherwise select **Create property**

'**SanityTests.MVCForum**'. Either way, because neither Visual Studio nor Reshaper knows which type the property should be, they'll use `object`. But Resharper also puts the cursor on the `object` keyword and lets you change it right away, which without it you'll need to manually select it. So now change the property type from `object` to `MVCForumClient`, which of course is still not declared either. We also want to change its getter to throw `NotImplementedException` and delete the redundant private setter (you don't have to do that if you followed the tip above). Then we can go ahead and create the `MVCForumClient` class, just like we did for the `User` class. The code up until now should look like Listing 11-2.

Listing 11-2. After adding MVCForum property and MVCForumClient class

```
using System;
using Microsoft.VisualStudio.TestTools.UnitTesting;

namespace MVCForumAutomation
{
    [TestClass]
    public class SanityTests
    {
        [TestMethod]
        public void
        WhenARegisteredUserStartsADiscussionOtherAnonymousUsersCanSeeIt()
        {
            const string body = "dummy body";
            LoggedInUser userA = MVCForum.RegisterNewUserAndLogin();
            Discussion createdDiscussion = userA.
            CreateDiscussion(Discussion.With.Body(body));

            MVCForumClient anonymousUser = new MVCForumClient();
            DiscussionHeader latestHeader = anonymousUser.
            LatestDiscussions.Top;
            Assert.AreEqual(createdDiscussion.Title, latestHeader.Title,
                "The title of the latest discussion should match the one we
                created");
            Discussion viewedDiscussion = latestHeader.OpenDiscussion();
            Assert.AreEqual(body, viewedDiscussion.Body,
```

```
            "The body of the latest discussion should match the one we
            created");
    }

    public MVCForumClient MVCForum
    {
        get { throw new NotImplementedException(); }
    }
}

public class MVCForumClient
{
}

public class LoggedInUser
{
}
}
```

Note   While there's no apparent reason to restrict the MVCForum property to be read-only, it's this kind of things that makes your code more reliable and less error-prone, especially in the long run. The Poka-Yoke topic in Appendix D explains this idea of preventing potential mistakes in more detail

---

Declaring the RegisterNewUserAndLogin Method

While the caret (the keyboard cursor) is on the RegisterNewUserAndLogin method reference, select **Create Method 'MVCForumClient.RegisterNewUserAndLogin'** from the quick-actions menu. Note that because we already declared the LoggedInUser class, Visual Studio knows to use LoggedInUser as the return type of the method. If we were using the var keyword instead, and were not using Resharper, Visual Studio would use object as the return type. We would then have to explicitly go to the declaration of the method and change it. If we were using Resharper, then when we created the new method the caret would move to the new declaration allowing us to specify the return type we want. If we would then write a name of a nonexistent class (e.g. LoggedInUser), it would then let us select **Create type 'LoggedInUser'** to create that class.

In addition, pay attention that the body of the new method contains the statement "throw new NotImplementedException();". We'll leave it like that for now because all we want is the code to compile. Later you'll see how we go about replacing it with the actual implementation. Note that IDEs for other languages sometimes just leave an empty body (or a return null; statement), which is unfortunate, because it will make it harder for us later to find all the places that we need to implement. If you're using one of these IDEs, I suggest that you make yourself a habit to add a statement similar to throw new NotImplementedException(); whenever you add a new method.

Declaring the Rest of the Classes and Methods

Continue going over the undeclared identifiers one by one, and create the classes and methods as we did before. Here are some notes:

- The CreateDiscussion method has a complex expression as its argument, which is still not defined either. For that reason, if we'll try to create the CreateDiscussion method first, the suggested argument type will be object. However, if we define the identifiers in the argument expression first, then CreateDiscussion will already be created using the proper argument type. In general, it's better to define expressions inside parentheses before declaring the outer expressions. In our case, we should do it in the following order:

    a. Create the Discussion class

    b. Create With as a read-only property and make it of type DiscussionBuilder (as explained in the remarks about the pseudo-code above), which is still not defined

    c. Create the DiscussionBuilder class as a nested class inside Discussion

    d. Create the DiscussionBuilder.Body method (you should do it from the original line). Change its return type to DiscussionBuilder and the parameter's name to body. Note that in the Test Data Builder pattern, all methods return the same instance (this) in order to make it easier to chain a few calls together. This is why we return DiscussionBuilder from a method declared inside the DiscussionBuilder class

e. Finally, create the CreateDiscussion method. The suggested argument type should already be DiscussionBuilder and the returned type Discussion. You should only change the name of the argument from the suggested name body to builder.

- LatestDiscussions property should be of a new class, which will also be called LatestDiscussions.

- The properties Discussion.Title and DiscussionHeader.Title should both be of type string.

When your code looks like Listing 11-3 the code should finally compile, and the model of the application as far as our first test needs is complete! In order to compile the code, select **Build ➤ Build Solution**. If the code actually compiles, you should see a small message "**Build Succeeded**" at the status bar at the bottom of the screen. If the compilation fails, then the **Error List** pane should appear (if not, select **View ➤ Error List**) showing you the compilation errors. Fix these and try again.

Note   In the listing, some lines are broken due to lack of space. If you copy the code as is and put a line break inside a string value as it appears in the listing, you'll get a compilation error **Newline in constant**, followed by some other syntax errors. Rejoin the string to a single line to fix this.

Listing 11-3. SanityTests.cs when it compiles

```
using System;
using Microsoft.VisualStudio.TestTools.UnitTesting;

namespace MVCForumAutomation
{
    [TestClass]
    public class SanityTests
    {
        [TestMethod]
        public void
        WhenARegisteredUserStartsADiscussionOtherAnonymousUsersCanSeeIt()
        {
```

```
        const string body = "dummy body";
        LoggedInUser userA = MVCForum.RegisterNewUserAndLogin();
        Discussion createdDiscussion = userA.
        CreateDiscussion(Discussion.With.Body(body));

        MVCForumClient anonymousUser = new MVCForumClient();
        DiscussionHeader latestHeader = anonymousUser.
        LatestDiscussions.Top;
        Assert.AreEqual(createdDiscussion.Title, latestHeader.Title,
            "The title of the latest discussion should match the one we
            created");
        Discussion viewedDiscussion = latestHeader.OpenDiscussion();
        Assert.AreEqual(body, viewedDiscussion.Body,
            "The body of the latest discussion should match the one we
            created");
    }

    public MVCForumClient MVCForum
    {
        get { throw new NotImplementedException(); }
    }
}

public class DiscussionHeader
{
    public string Title
    {
        get { throw new NotImplementedException(); }
    }

    public Discussion OpenDiscussion()
    {
        throw new NotImplementedException();
    }
}

public class Discussion
{
```

```
    public static DiscussionBuilder With
    {
        get { throw new NotImplementedException(); }
    }

    public string Title
    {
        get { throw new NotImplementedException(); }
    }

    public string Body
    {
        get { throw new NotImplementedException(); }
    }

    public class DiscussionBuilder
    {
        public DiscussionBuilder Body(string body)
        {
            throw new NotImplementedException();
        }
    }
}

public class MVCForumClient
{
    public LoggedInUser RegisterNewUserAndLogin()
    {
        throw new NotImplementedException();
    }

    public LatestDiscussions LatestDiscussions
    {
        get { throw new NotImplementedException(); }
    }
}
```

```
public class LatestDiscussions
{
    public DiscussionHeader Top
    {
        get { throw new NotImplementedException(); }
    }
}

public class LoggedInUser
{
    public Discussion CreateDiscussion(Discussion.DiscussionBuilder
    builder)
    {
        throw new NotImplementedException();
    }
}
}
```

Now it's also a great time to split the file into separate files: one for each class, using the quick-actions menu. If you're using Resharper, you can right-click on the file **SanityTests.cs** in the **Solution Explorer** pane, select **Refactor ➤ Move Types Into Matching Files...** and click **Next** in the dialog that pops up. Now you should have one class per file. Make sure that the code still compiles after that change.

I'll also use this opportunity to replace all explicit type names with the var keyword.

Model Code Review

When more than one automation developer work on the project, after one has created all the classes and methods that make a test compile, this is a great time for a code review. Even though nothing was really implemented, the reviewer can examine:

1. Is the code of the test clear and readable?

2. Does the code of the test reflect the steps that prove or refute the claim which is the name of the test?

3. Does the model (the classes and methods) represent reality and the application correctly?

4.   If this is not the first test, are similar methods or classes already exist, and should they be reused?

If the reviewer has important comments, it's much easier to fix those at this stage rather than after the entire test was implemented!

Summary

In this chapter we wrote the code of the test method according to the way we've planned it verbally in the previous chapter. While we've written a lot of code that actually does nothing, we essentially created the skeleton (or the design) for the test and its infrastructure code, in a way that is modular and reusable. In addition, because we tried to stick to the way we've described the test verbally, the code of the test method came up very readable. In the next chapter we'll finally implement the methods so the test will actually do what it's supposed to do.

CHAPTER 12

Completing the First Test

OK, so now that our code compiles, what do you think will be the next thing we should do?

(Buzzer sound goes here) WRONG answer! I bet that you said, "start implementing the methods" (at least this is what 99% of the people I ask this question say). What we're about to do now will probably sound very silly to you at first: We're going to run the test!

But wait, we can't! It can't possibly work! The computer will blow up! Well, you're right, it won't work. But it won't blow up the computer either (I know you didn't really mean it…). So, what *will* happen? The test will fail of course, because every exception causes the test to fail and we have many `throw new NotImplementedException();` statements. The point is that when we run the test and it will fail, we'll know exactly what's the first method that it tries to run, and this is the first method that we need to implement.

If we'll stick to this process of implementing one method at a time and running the test to see where it fails next, we'll be able to test every new method that we write and verify that it works correctly and reliably. If it doesn't, the test will fail on something that we have already implemented and we should go back and fix it. This way we are constantly improving and fortifying the reliability of our code. In addition, it's also a great way to make sure that out tests are repeatable without having to reset test data, environments, etc. This is of great importance when we'll later want to make them part of a CI/CD process (see Chapter 15).

Running the Test to Find What to Implement First

So. as we said, we'll first run the test in order to see what the first failure is. Continuing where we left off in the previous chapter, in order to run the test, open the Test Explorer pane (if not already open), by selecting **Test ➤ Windows ➤ Test Explorer**. Then right-click on the test's name and select **Run Selected Tests**. You should see that the test failed

© Arnon Axelrod 2018
A. Axelrod, *Complete Guide to Test Automation*, https://doi.org/10.1007/978-1-4842-3832-5_12

by the red X near the test name. At the bottom of the **Test Explorer** pane. you should see the details of the failure, including the error message and the stack-trace that shows the chain of method calls in which the exception was thrown. By default. this lower part is pretty small, but you can enlarge it by dragging the splitter. After the failure the Test Explorer should look like Figure 12-1.

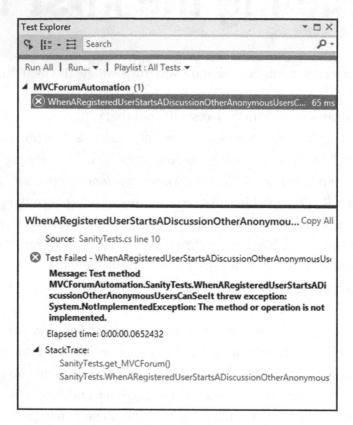

Figure 12-1. *Test Explorer showing the first failure*

The error message says: "**Message: Test method MVCForumAutomation. SanityTests.WhenARegisteredUserStartsADiscussionOtherAnonymousUsersCanSeeIt threw exception:**

System.NotImplementedException: The method or operation is not implemented."

Note   According to your operating system's locale, parts of the message may be phrased in your system's language.

While the error message may look a bit daunting, it's actually not that complicated. Because the name of the test, which is long by itself, is also shown in its full form that includes the namespace and the class name, this takes up most of the error message... So in order to understand the message we can simplify it as: "**Message: Test method** *<test method name>* **threw exception: System.NotImplementedException: The method or operation is not implemented.**" Oh, this makes much more sense now! The good thing about `NotImplementedException` is that the top line on the stack-trace tells you exactly where the unimplemented method is. If you hover over the link in the stack-trace, you should see a tooltip stating the exact file path and line number. If you click the link, you'll be taken to that exact place, which is the body of the `MVCForum` property getter. Implementing the property getter is very straight-forward. Simply initialize the property to a new instance of `MVCForumClient` as follows:

```
public MVCForumClient MVCForum { get; } = new MVCForumClient();
```

And now what do we do? This time I hope you had it correct: run the test again! Note that when we run the test again, Visual Studio automatically saves our changes and re-compiles our code, so when the test runs it includes our recent changes. Now the `NotImplementedException` is thrown from the `MVCForumClient.RegisterNewUserAndLogin` method. However, we have to go back a little bit first, because the website should be opened in the constructor of `MVCForumClient` and only then we should implement `RegisterNewUserAndLogin`.

Adding Selenium to the Project

In order to implement the constructor of `MVCForumClient` to open the MVCForum website, we should start using Selenium WebDriver. We'll then use it for all of the following methods that should interact with the website, of course.

Note   While Selenium is a very popular test automation tool, teaching Selenium is not the focus of this book. I'll explain only the bare minimum so that you understand the tutorial. There are tons of other resources about Selenium WebDriver on the web, or you can read **Selenium WebDriver Recipes in C#** (second edition) by Zhimin Zhan.[1]

Adding Selenium to a project in Visual Studio is very easy:

1. In **Test Explorer**, right-click on the **MVCForumAutomation** project and select **Manage NuGet Packages...** The NuGet Package Manager window will be opened.

2. Click on **Browse** (at the top of the window).

3. Type "Selenium" inside the **Search** box, and press **Enter**. Note that for some reason Visual Studio won't show any results until you've typed in the entire word. You should see results similar to those shown in Figure 12-2.

---

[1]Zhimin Zhan, *Selenium WebDriver Recipes in C#: Second Edition* (New York: Apress, 2015).

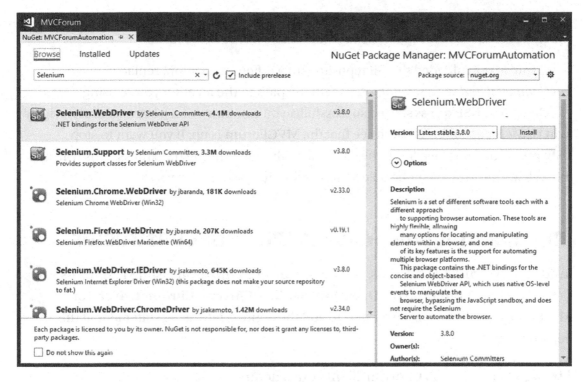

Figure 12-2. *NuGet Package Manager showing Selenium results*

For now, we'll choose each one of the first three (**Selenium.WebDriver**, **Selenium.Support**, and **Selenium.Chrome.WebDriver**) and click the **Install** button on the right. That's it! We've added Selenium to our test project.

Running IISExpress

In fact, before we can open the MVCForum website through the browser (and accordingly through Selenium), we need to make sure that the website itself is running. While in a true CI environment we'll probably want to deploy the application to some web server, container, the cloud, or what have you and run the tests against this deployment, we'll use **IISExpress.exe** to run the website locally. For now, we'll do it manually, but it will be a good idea to have an option, based on a configuration file for example, to run it automatically whenever the test suite starts.

To run the website using IISExpress, open a command prompt window and type the following on one line.

```
"%ProgramFiles(x86)%\IIS Express\iisexpress.exe" /path:C:\
TheCompleteGuideToTestAutomation\MVCForum\MVCForum.Website\
```

If you've downloaded the Git repository to a different location, replace *TheCompleteGuideToTestAutomation* with the path to the location you're using.

Given that IISExpress started successfully, you can now open a browser and navigate to `http://localhost:8080` and see that the MVCForum is up. If you want to stop IISExpress you can press 'Q' at the command window running IISExpress. This will stop the website and you won't be able to access the site from the browser.

Implementing the MVCForumClient Constructor

Inside the `MVCForumClient` class, add a constructor as shown in Listing 12-1. Press **Ctrl+.** and select **Import type 'OpenQA.Selenium.Chrome.ChromeDriver'** (or **Alt+Enter** if you're using Resharper) to add the appropriate using statement at the beginning of the file.

Listing 12-1. The MVCForumClient constructor

```
public MVCForumClient()
{
    var webDriver = new ChromeDriver();
}
```

The line inside the constructor only tells Selenium to open a Chrome browser. Let's run the test again and see if it's working.

Obviously, the test still fails on the same `NotImplementedException` in `MVCForumClient.RegisterNewUserAndLogin` because we haven't implemented it yet. But what *has* changed, is that now a new, empty Chrome browser window gets opened when we run the test. However, this window isn't closed when the test ends, which is pretty annoying, especially when you run the test multiple times. So, let's now fix this before we continue further.

In order to close the browser when the test ends, we can use the object's finalizer method, which the .Net Garbage Collector calls whenever the object is not needed anymore.

Note   The Garbage Collector calls the finalizer method asynchronously, which means that the browser may be left open for a few extra seconds more than what we need. One way to tackle it is to use the `AddCleanupAction` method from the **Test Automation Essentials** library. See Appendix B for more information about this library. But for now, I won't use it so that I keep things simple for the tutorial.

In order to close the browser, we need to call the `Quit` method on the `ChromeDriver` object we've created. But because we want to call it from the finalizer, we must first convert the local `webDriver` variable into a member. Because I'd like to adhere to the default naming convention that Resharper suggests, I'll add an underscore to the name of the field, making it `_webDriver`.

Note that if you're using Resharper, you can change the local variable to a field automatically. Put the caret on the name of the local variable, press **Ctrl+Shift+R** to open the **Refactor This** context menu, and select **Introduce Field...** In the dialog that comes up, change the name to `_webDriver`, check **Make field readonly** and click **Next.**

Eventually, after adding the field and the finalizer, the constructor we've created in Listing 12-1 should be replaced with the code in Listing 12-2.

Listing 12-2. MVCForumClient constructor and finalizer

```
private readonly ChromeDriver _webDriver;

public MVCForumClient()
{
    _webDriver = new ChromeDriver();
}

~MVCForumClient()
{
    _webDriver.Quit();
}
```

If you'll rerun the test, you'll notice that now the browser opens and then closes automatically.

There's one more thing that we need to do in the constructor though: navigate to the website of the MVCForum application. Because we're currently running it locally using IISExpress, we need to navigate to `http://localhost:8080`. We do this by setting the `Url` property as shown in Listing 12-3.

Listing 12-3. Navigating to the local MVCForum website

```
public MVCForumClient()
{
    _webDriver = new ChromeDriver();
    _webDriver.Url = "http://localhost:8080";
}
```

Note that this constructor currently encapsulates two important hard-coded details: the type of the browser that we use (Chrome) and the URL of the website. We'll probably want to allow running the tests on different browsers and against different environments (URLs) so we should extract these details to an external configuration file. However, because of the way I write the code, which ensures that I don't duplicate such details, I prefer to defer implementing the mechanism that reads from a configuration file to a later time when I'll really need it. When I'll really need it, it will be pretty easy to change (because it's only in one place), and then I'll also be able and motivated to test that it actually works in all the relevant environments. For the meantime, I'll change the type of `_webDriver` to the `IWebDriver` interface, which is common to all browsers, so I won't accidentally rely on Chrome specific features (see the Poka-Yoke topic in Appendix D). Don't forget to add the appropriate `using` statement to use the `OpenQA.Selenium` namespace. I'll also add a comment to remind me and others that I intend to change this in the future, and we'll actually change this in Chapter 14.

If you run the test now, it will still fail on the same thing, but you'll be able to see that the browser now navigates to our website before it gets closed.

Implementing RegisterNewUserAndLogin

So now we're ready to focus on and implement the `RegisterNewUserAndLogin` method. Typically registering a new user is a pretty long process. While here there's one page with very few details that the user must fill in, it's still not exactly an atomic operation. Therefore, we won't implement the entire process of registering a user in a single method. Instead, we'll use the same top-down technique that we used to write the test, but now for implementing the `RegisterNewUserAndLogin` method. So first we'll replace the throw new NotImplementedException(); statement with the code in Listing 12-4, which make our code non-compilable again.

Listing 12-4. Implementing MVCForumClient.RegisterNewUserAndLogin

```
public LoggedInUser RegisterNewUserAndLogin()
{
    var username = Guid.NewGuid().ToString();
    const string password = "123456";
    const string email = "abc@def.com";

    var registrationPage = GoToRegistrationPage();
    registrationPage.UserName = username;
    registrationPage.Password = password;
    registrationPage.ConfirmPassword = password;
    registrationPage.Email = email;

    registrationPage.Register();

    return new LoggedInUser();
}
```

Remarks:

- Because we want the username to be unique, we initialize the username variable to a new GUID. Note that sometimes it worth creating a special class for generating random strings and values according to various constraints, like length, allowed characters, etc., but right now we can do without it.

- The password and email addresses don't have to be unique, and they don't even have to be realistic. As long as it satisfies the requirements for the registration we're good to go.

- The `GotoRegistrationPage` method that we yet to define will click the Register link and return an actual Page Object representing the registration page. We'll name this Page Object class `RegistrationPage` (See Chapter 10 for more details about the Page Object pattern).

- All of the property setters of RegistrationPage will enter text into the corresponding fields. The Register method will click the Register button.

- Currently we return a new LoggedInUser object, without providing anything in its constructor. We'll probably have to initialize it with the username in the pretty near future, but we'll do it only after the process we're following will force us to do so.

As you probably guessed, now we have to make our code compile again by creating the missing methods, properties, and classes, similar to how we created the classes and methods in the previous chapter, though now we should choose to create new classes already in new files. Specifically, we need to create the GoToRegistrationPage method whose return type is RegistrationPage, and the RegistrationPage class itself with all the members that we call. Listing 12-5 shows the RegistrationPage class definition (we'll add it in a new file). Note that we still don't implement the body of any of the new methods, and keep the throw new NotImplementedException(); statement.

Listing 12-5. The RegistrationPage class definition

```
namespace MVCForumAutomation
{
    internal class RegistrationPage
    {
        public string Username
        {
            get { throw new System.NotImplementedException(); }
            set { throw new System.NotImplementedException(); }
        }

        public string Password
        {
            get { throw new System.NotImplementedException(); }
            set { throw new System.NotImplementedException(); }
        }
```

```
    public string ConfirmPassword
    {
        get { throw new System.NotImplementedException(); }
        set { throw new System.NotImplementedException(); }
    }

    public string Email
    {
        get { throw new System.NotImplementedException(); }
        set { throw new System.NotImplementedException(); }
    }

    public void Register()
    {
        throw new System.NotImplementedException();
    }
  }
}
```

Now let's run the test again. Unsurprisingly the test now fails on the NotImplementedException inside MVCForumClient.GoToRegistrationPage. So, let's implement it.

In order to get to the registration page, we need to click on the **Register** link at the top right part of the page (near the **Log On** link). Figure 12-3 shows the main page containing the **Register** link.

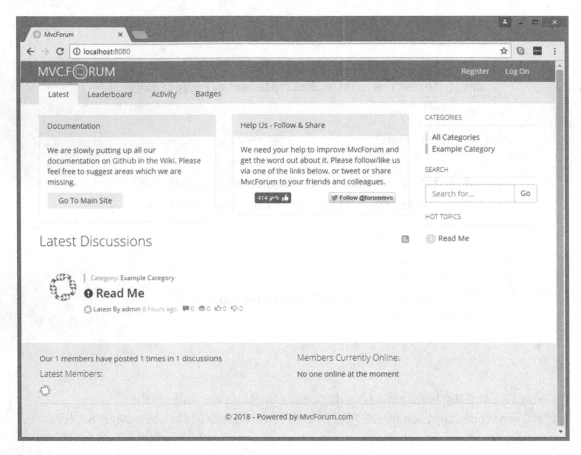

Figure 12-3.   *The MainPage containing the Register link*

In order to click it, we first need to tell Selenium how to find it. Selenium can identify elements using different characteristics of the element, called *locators* in Selenium's jargon. There are various types of locators (see following note box), but the most important rule is that the locator should match only the element (or elements) we're looking for, and not others. The sidebar contains more tips for choosing the best locator. All of the locators are matched against the DOM[2] of the page.

In order to see the DOM of the page and find the best locator for the **Register**, first open Chrome and navigate to the website (`http://localhost:8080`), then *right-click* on the **Register** link and select **Inspect** from the context menu. This will open the **Developer Tools** pane (which you can also open and close by pressing **F12**), which shows you the

---

[2]DOM stands for *Document Object Model* and is the tree data-structure that represents the HTML elements on the web page. Unlike the source HTML of a page, the DOM can be manipulated and changed at runtime using JavaScript.

tree of elements in the DOM and highlights the element of the **Register** link. This is shown in Figure 12-4.

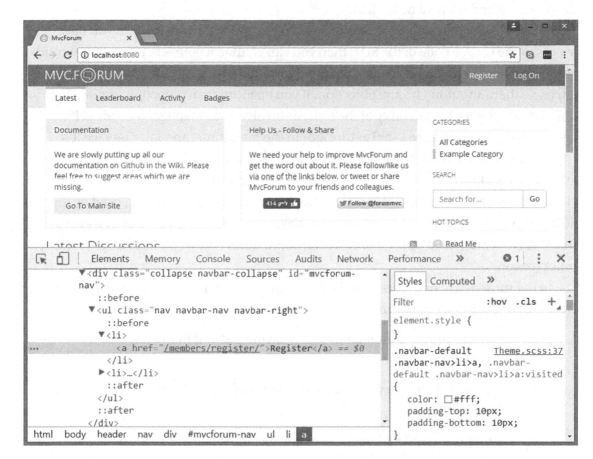

Figure 12-4. *Inspecting the Register element using the Developer Tool*

Tip   Appendix D contains an explanation on the various Selenium locators and tips for how to choose the most appropriate one.

Asking the Developer to Add a Unique Automation Identifier

While we can identify the **Register** link using its link text ("Register") it's not recommended, especially because the site is multi-lingual, and the same element may appear with a text in another language. Even if it wasn't a multi-lingual site, we prefer not to rely on a specific spelling and wording, because if it will change, then our test will fail until we change our code too. However, there's no other locator that uniquely identifies that element and is also a better fit.

In such cases, the recommended approach is to add the id attribute. If you have access to the source code of the SUT, then you can change it yourself. If not, you should ask a developer to add it for you. It's really a one-minute task that should have no side effect, so there shouldn't be any objection. If you encounter an objection, explain the importance of it to the reliability of the tests, or involve your manager if needed. If it takes time, you can use the LinkText locator in the meantime, and later replace it to Id.

Another variation on this approach is instead of adding an id attribute, you can add a unique class name, just for the sake of the test automation. You can prefix this class name with "auto-" for, example, to clearly emphasize that it's being used by the automation. As elements can have multiple classes, this approach is safer as it ensures that this class name will be used only for the automation and won't be changed for any other reason.

In the tutorial, we have access to the full source code of the SUT, so we'll add the class "auto-register" ourselves:

1. In the Solution Explorer pane, type **_Layout.cshtml** in the search box.

2. Double-click the **_Layout.cshtml** file in Solution Explorer to open it in the editor.

3. Go to line 86, and add the class name declaration in the **<a>** tag, as follows:

```
<li><a class="auto-register" href="@Url.Action("Register", "Members")">
@Html.LanguageString("Layout.Nav.Register")</a></li>
```

4. Save the file and build the solution.

5. Go to the Chrome browser, and press **F5** to refresh the page. You should now see the new class name in the Developer Tools.

Now we're ready to implement MVCForumClient.GoToRegistrationPage as shown in Listing 12-6.

Listing 12-6. GoToRegistrationPage implemented

```
private RegistrationPage GoToRegistrationPage()
{
    var registerLink = _webDriver.FindElement(By.ClassName("auto-
    register"));
    registerLink.Click();

    return new RegistrationPage(_webDriver);
}
```

Also create the RegisterPage constructor that accepts the webDriver argument. You can use Resharper or Visual Studio quick-fix menu to create the constructor for you, but make sure to declare the _webDriver field as readonly, as shows in Listing 12-7.

Listing 12-7. RegistrationPage constructor and the _webDriver field

```
internal class RegistrationPage
{
    private readonly IWebDriver _webDriver;

    public RegistrationPage(IWebDriver webDriver)
    {
        _webDriver = webDriver;
    }

    ...
}
```

> **Note** Strictly following our process, I had to write the simplest thing that passes our current exception, and therefore I had no reason to pass webDriver to the constructor of RegistrationPage at this stage. However, because the RegistrationPage class is a Page Object, which will surely need the webDriver object in order to access the elements on that page, then I allowed myself to take this little shortcut here and create the webDriver parameter right now.

Implementing the Property Setters

After implementing the GoToRegistrationPage method, we fail on the setter of RegistrationPage.Username. If we'll identify this element using the Developer Tools, we'll see that it has an id attribute with the value UserName. So, we can implement this setter as shown in Listing 12-8.

Listing 12-8. RegistrationPage.Username

```
public string Username
{
    get { throw new System.NotImplementedException(); }
    set
    {
        var usernameInput = _webDriver.FindElement(By.Id("UserName"));
        usernameInput.SendKeys(value);
    }
}
```

Continuing the process, we'll fail on the Password, ConfirmPassword, and Email property setters and implement them accordingly, similar to the way we implemented the Username property, one at a time. At this point **RegistrationPage.cs** should look like Listing 12-9.

Listing 12-9. RegistrationPage.cs after implementing all properties

```
using OpenQA.Selenium;

namespace MVCForumAutomation
{
    internal class RegistrationPage
    {
        private readonly IWebDriver _webDriver;

        public RegistrationPage(IWebDriver webDriver)
        {
            _webDriver = webDriver;
        }

        public string Username
        {
            get { throw new System.NotImplementedException(); }
            set
            {
                var usernameInput = _webDriver.FindElement(By.
                Id("UserName"));
                usernameInput.SendKeys(value);
            }
        }

        public string Password
        {
            get { throw new System.NotImplementedException(); }
            set
            {
                var passwordInput = _webDriver.FindElement(By.
                Id("Password"));
                passwordInput.SendKeys(value);
            }
        }
```

```
public string ConfirmPassword
{
    get { throw new System.NotImplementedException(); }
    set
    {
        var confirmPasswordInput = _webDriver.FindElement(By.
        Id("ConfirmPassword"));
        confirmPasswordInput.SendKeys(value);
    }
}

public string Email
{
    get { throw new System.NotImplementedException(); }
    set
    {
        var emailInput = _webDriver.FindElement(By.Id("Email"));
        emailInput.SendKeys(value);
    }
}

public void Register()
{
    throw new System.NotImplementedException();
}
    }
}
```

Note   If you wonder whether it's a good practice or not to put the string literals of the locators directly in the body of the properties, please refer to the topic about hard-coded strings in Appendix D for a comprehensive discussion about it.

Removing Duplication from the Property Setters

Now our test fails on the unimplemented `Register` method. But before we'll implement it, notice how similar all the property setters we've just implemented! This is a clear example of duplicated code. It's true that these are pretty small methods, there are only four of them and they're all in the same class, but still – it's a duplication that can be eliminated by refactoring. As we go along and remove such duplications, we make our code more generic, extensible, and overall – easier to maintain. While it's reasonable that this duplication will repeat itself in other page objects too, I'm cautious from over-generalizing, and therefore I'll only remove the duplication in this class for now. If later we'll see that other classes need this behavior too, then we'll remove that duplication and make our code even more generic. But now, let's stay focused on removing the duplication between the setters inside the `RegistrationPage` class. We'll do it by introducing a new private method `FillInputElement` that will contain the common code and receive the id of the element and the value to enter. We'll use this method in all of the property setters instead of their current bodies.

Tip   Using Resharper, you can take the `Username` setter, for example, and apply the following refactorings: **Extract Method**, **Introduce Parameter** on the `"Username"` string literal, Change signature to replace the order of the parameters, and **Rename** to change the name of the `usernameInput` variable to just `input` (because now our method is not specific to the username input element). Then you can replace the implementations of all other setters with calls to the newly created method. Resharper can also help you reorder the properties and methods inside the class easily and safely. Note that doing this sequence of small manipulations to the code reduces the chance that we'll do something wrong dramatically.

After this refactoring, RegistrationPage.cs should look like Listing 12-10.

Listing 12-10. RegistrationPage.cs after removing the duplication

```csharp
using OpenQA.Selenium;

namespace MVCForumAutomation
{
    internal class RegistrationPage
    {
        private readonly IWebDriver _webDriver;

        public RegistrationPage(IWebDriver webDriver)
        {
            _webDriver = webDriver;
        }

        public string Username
        {
            get { throw new System.NotImplementedException(); }
            set { FillInputElement("UserName", value); }
        }

        public string Password
        {
            get { throw new System.NotImplementedException(); }
            set
            {
                FillInputElement("Password", value);
            }
        }

        public string ConfirmPassword
        {
            get { throw new System.NotImplementedException(); }
            set
            {
                FillInputElement("ConfirmPassword", value);
            }
        }
```

```
    public string Email
    {
        get { throw new System.NotImplementedException(); }
        set
        {
            FillInputElement("Email", value);
        }
    }

    public void Register()
    {
        throw new System.NotImplementedException();
    }

    private void FillInputElement(string id, string value)
    {
        var input = _webDriver.FindElement(By.Id(id));
        input.SendKeys(value);
    }
  }
}
```

Let's run the test once more to verify that our refactoring didn't break anything. The test still fails on the Register method, so apparently, we're OK. So now we can implement the Register method as shown in Listing 12-11.

Listing 12-11. RegistrationPage.Register

```
public void Register()
{
    var form = _webDriver.FindElement(By.ClassName(
"form-register"));
    form.Submit();
}
```

Note   Clicking a `button` element that has a `style="submit"` attribute, inside a `form` element, has exactly the same effect as calling `Submit` on the `form` element. In this case it was a bit easier to locate the `form` element than the `button`, therefore I chose this way.

After we run the test again, it will fail on the line in the test following the call to `RegisterNewUserAndLogin`, which means that we've completed this method for now. We may need to get back to it to pass something into the constructor of the `LoggedInUser` object that it returns, but for now we'll continue to follow the failure messages.

Hitting the Isolation Problem

When we continue the process, we'll need to implement the getter of `Discussion. With` and `Discussion.DiscussionBuilder.Body`. After that we'll fail on `LoggedInUser. CreateDiscussion`. However, if you haven't changes anything through the admin page, then when you'll open the application and manually register a new user, you'll notice that the user doesn't see a **Create Discussion** button at all. In fact, we already noticed it in Chapter 10 when we planned the test scenario, and decided that our first attempt would be to add permission to everyone to create new discussions (topics) in the "Example Category." Figure 12-5 shows the admin page for editing the permissions, with the **Create Topics** permission checked for the "Example Category."

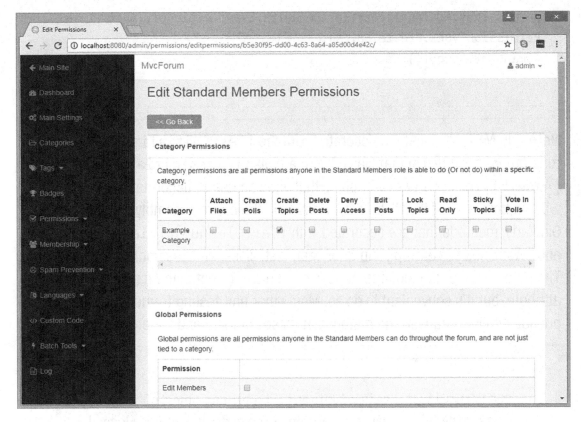

Figure 12-5. *Admin page for changing permissions*

Performing the actions to change this permission is not part of the test itself, so we'll do in the test initialization method. Once again, we'll write the initialization method top down: starting from pseudo-code, creating the methods and classes, and then implementing the methods one at a time when we see where we fail next. Listing 12-12 shows the TestInitialize method in the SanityTests test class.

Listing 12-12. SanityTests.TestInitialize

```
[TestInitialize]
public void TestInitialize()
{
    var adminUser = MVCForum.LoginAsAdmin();
    var adminPage = adminUser.GoToAdminPage();
    var permissions = adminPage.GetPermissionsFor(TestDefaults.
    StandardMembersRole);
```

```
    permissions.AddToCategory(TestDefaults.ExampleCategory,
    PermissionTypes.CreateTopics);
    adminUser.Logout();
}
```

Note   In MSTest, a method decorated with the [TestInitialize] attribute runs *before each test* in that class. There are also [ClassInitialize] and [AssemblyInitialize] attributes that you can use to decorate methods that will run before *all* of the tests in the class or in the entire assembly, respectively. Similarly, methods that are decorated with [TestCleanup], [ClassCleanup] and [AssemblyCleanup] run *after* each test, class, and assembly respectively. The names of the methods themselves don't have to match the name of the attribute, but it's convenient to do so. Most other unit testing frameworks also provide similar means to run methods at these "before" and "after" occasions.

Notes:

- MVCForumClient.LoginAsAdmin should return an object of type LoggedInAdmin. Because the admin user can do everything a logged-in user can do, we'll make LoggedInAdmin derive from LoggedInUser. Note that the Logout method should be at the base class, as every logged-in user can log out from the system.

- While the "Standard Members" role exists by default, the admin user can add or remove such roles. Therefore, I want to leave the flexibility of specifying different roles in the GetPermissionsFor method.

- I could simply pass "Standard Members" as the parameter to GetPermissionsFor to identify the role, but that would be a bad model. A "role" in MVCForum is not just a string – it's a complete entity. The rule of thumb is: **if the user can type whatever he wants, use a string; if he can only choose between strings, then it should be a strongly typed object**. If we use a string where the user can only choose an existing item, then make our code more error prone (read the Poka-Yoke topic in Appendix D). If someone will need to use this method later on and he'll be able to pass any arbitrary string, there's a bigger chance that the method will fail at runtime than if he has to pass a strongly typed object.

- Because we still want to rely on some default entities that exist in the system, but we don't want to create a tight coupling to them, I defined a `TestDefaults` property of a class with the same name to hold those default entities. If at some point the defaults in the application will change, or I'll want to use different defaults for the tests, this class should be the only place I should change. If I won't use such a class, then when such a change occurs, I will have to change in many places in the code-base of the tests.

- Everything I said about the "Standard Members" role is also true for the "Example Category" category.

- The list of permission types is a fixed (i.e., it's predefined in the system and the admin user can't change this list). Therefore, I chose to model `PermissionTypes` as an `enum`, in order to restrict ourselves only to members of that list and avoid potential mistakes.

Continuing our process, we first create the classes and methods that make our code compile, then, as usual, run the test to see where it fails and implement that method.

Skipping most of the details (as I hope you get the idea by now), when I implement `MVCForumClient.LoginAsAdmin`, I noticed a duplication between the `RegistrationPage` and the `LoginPage` classes where both need the `FillInputElement` method that we've implemented in the `RegistrationPage` class. In order to remove this duplication, I extracted a base class called `FormPage` that contains this method, and changed the `LoginPage` class to also derive from it. Note that both `RegistrationPage` and `LoginPage` classes has `Username` and `Password` properties, which correspond to **Username** and **Password** input fields. However, in my opinion even though these properties and their implementations are completely identical, this is not a true duplication! That's because there's no direct relationships between these fields. On each of these forms they serve a different purpose: on the Registration form, their purpose is to let the user *choose* his username and password, while in the LogIn form, their purpose is to let the user *specify* what he has previously chosen.

Another important change that is worth mentioning, is that I added the default admin username and password to `TestDefaults`, and had to pass it to `MVCForumClient` in the constructor, so it can use it on the `LoginAsAdmin` method. Consequently, I had to pass it also to the instance that we create inside the test (change the line "`var anonymousUser = new MVCForumClient();`" to "`var anonymousUser = new MVCForumClient(`**`TestDefaults`**`);`"). But because this litters the test code with implementation details, I extracted the instantiation to a separate method called `OpenNewMVCForumClient`, so eventually the line became: "`var anonymousUser = OpenNewMVCForumClient();`", which conveys the essence of this line more clearly.

Note   When you run the application for the first time, you'll see a single discussion titled "**Read me**". If you open it, you can see that the default admin user name and password appear there and that they are "admin" and "password" respectively. The administrator is encouraged to change the username and password before going live. Because we only use this site locally and don't have real and important information in the application's database, then we can keep these credentials for now.

You can see the complete source code where `TestInitialize` is complete by checking out the Git revision tagged **TestInitializeCompleted**, or online at `https://github.com/arnonax/mvcforum/tree/TestInitializeCompleted/MVCForumAutomation`.

Implementing CreateDiscussion and Analyzing the Failure

Now that `TestInitialize` is working as expected, let's implement `LoggedInUser.CreateDiscussion`. The implementation is shown in Listing 12-13.

Listing 12-13. LoggedInUser.CreateDiscussion

```
public Discussion CreateDiscussion(Discussion.DiscussionBuilder builder)
{
    var newDiscussionButton = WebDriver.FindElement(By.ClassName("createtop
    icbutton"));
    newDiscussionButton.Click();

    var createDisucssionPage = new CreateDiscussionPage(WebDriver);
    builder.Fill(createDisucssionPage);
    createDisucssionPage.CreateDiscussion();

    return new Discussion(WebDriver);
}
```

Notice how we use the Test Data Builder pattern here: we simply call the Fill method of the builder, which should do all the work of filling in all the relevant values. The CreateDiscussion method itself should not change to support additional parameters.

When we run the test though, we get a failure: **Message: Test method MVCForumAutomation.SanityTests. WhenARegisteredUserStartsADiscussionOtherAnonymousUsersCanSeeIt threw exception: OpenQA.Selenium.NoSuchElementException: no such element: Unable to locate element: {"method":"class name","selector":"createtopicbutton"}** , and the stack-trace is pointing as expected at the FindElement call in the method we've just implemented. Reverifying the class name of the button assures that it's the correct one.

In order to analyze what's going on, we have two options:

1. Put a breakpoint on the relevant line and debug the test.

2. Add relevant diagnostic information to the test result.

While the tendency of most people is for the first option, I generally prefer to try the second option first, and only if it doesn't help fall back to debugging. The reason I prefer the second option is that diagnostic information that I add to the test can serve me to investigate future failures as well. In particular, when a test fails during a CI or nightly build and cannot be reproduced on the environment of the automation developer, then debugging won't help, while diagnostic information would. See the next chapter for more information about investigating failures.

So, the most basic diagnostic information that can help us identify this problem is a screenshot of the page at the moment of the failure. On the one hand, if we see the button in the screenshot, then it means that there's a problem in the way we try to find it. If, on the other hand, we won't see the button, then we'll have to continue investigating further, but the screenshot will probably provide us with more hints regarding the problem. Listings 12-14 and 12-15 show the code we add to SantiyTests.cs and MVCForumClient.cs respectively in order to take the screenshot. Note that most of the code we add to SanityTests.cs is specific to MSTest, but you can do similar things in other unit testing frameworks too.

Listing 12-14. SanityTests.cs – adding screenshot on failure

```
public TestContext TestContext { get; set; }

[TestCleanup]
public void TestCleanup()
{
    if (TestContext.CurrentTestOutcome != UnitTestOutcome.Passed)
    {
        var screenshotFilename = $"Screenshot.{TestContext.TestName}.jpg";
        MVCForum.TakeScreenshot(screenshotFilename);
        TestContext.AddResultFile(screenshotFilename);
    }
}
```

Listing 12-15. MVCForumClient.cs – adding screenshot on failure

```
public void TakeScreenshot(string screenshotFilename)
{
    _webDriver.TakeScreenshot().SaveAsFile(screenshotFilename);
}
```

Now let's run the test again and see what happens. Obviously, the test till fails with the same error message, but now Test Explorer shows us another link named **Output** as shown in Figure 12-6.

WhenARegisteredUserStartsADiscussionOtherAnonymousUsersCanSeeIt Copy All

   Source: SanityTests.cs line 38

❌ Test Failed - WhenARegisteredUserStartsADiscussionOtherAnonymousUsersCanSeeIt

   **Message: Test method
MVCForumAutomation.SanityTests.WhenARegisteredUserStartsADiscussionOther
AnonymousUsersCanSeeIt threw exception:
OpenQA.Selenium.NoSuchElementException: no such element: Unable to locate
element: {"method":"class name","selector":"createtopicbutton"}**
    (Session info: chrome=63.0.3239.84)
    (Driver info: chromedriver=2.33.506120
(e3e53437346286c0bc2d2dc9aa4915ba81d9023f),platform=Windows NT 6.3.9600
x86_64)

   Elapsed time: 0:00:09.4216038

   Output

▲ StackTrace:

    RemoteWebDriver.UnpackAndThrowOnError(Response errorResponse)
    RemoteWebDriver.Execute(String driverCommandToExecute, Dictionary`2 parameters)
    RemoteWebDriver.FindElement(String mechanism, String value)
    RemoteWebDriver.FindElementByClassName(String className)
    <>c__DisplayClass20_0.<ClassName>b__0(ISearchContext context)
    By.FindElement(ISearchContext context)
    RemoteWebDriver.FindElement(By by)
    LoggedInUser.CreateDiscussion(DiscussionBuilder builder)
    SanityTests.WhenARegisteredUserStartsADiscussionOtherAnonymousUsersCanSeeIt()

Figure 12-6. *Test Explorer shows the Output link*

Clicking on the **Output** link opens a special document window in Visual Studio, containing pretty much the same information as the lower pane of Test Explorer, but with an additional section titled **Attachments**, containing the link to our screenshot. Clicking on the link open the screenshot shown in Figure 12-7, which tells the whole story...

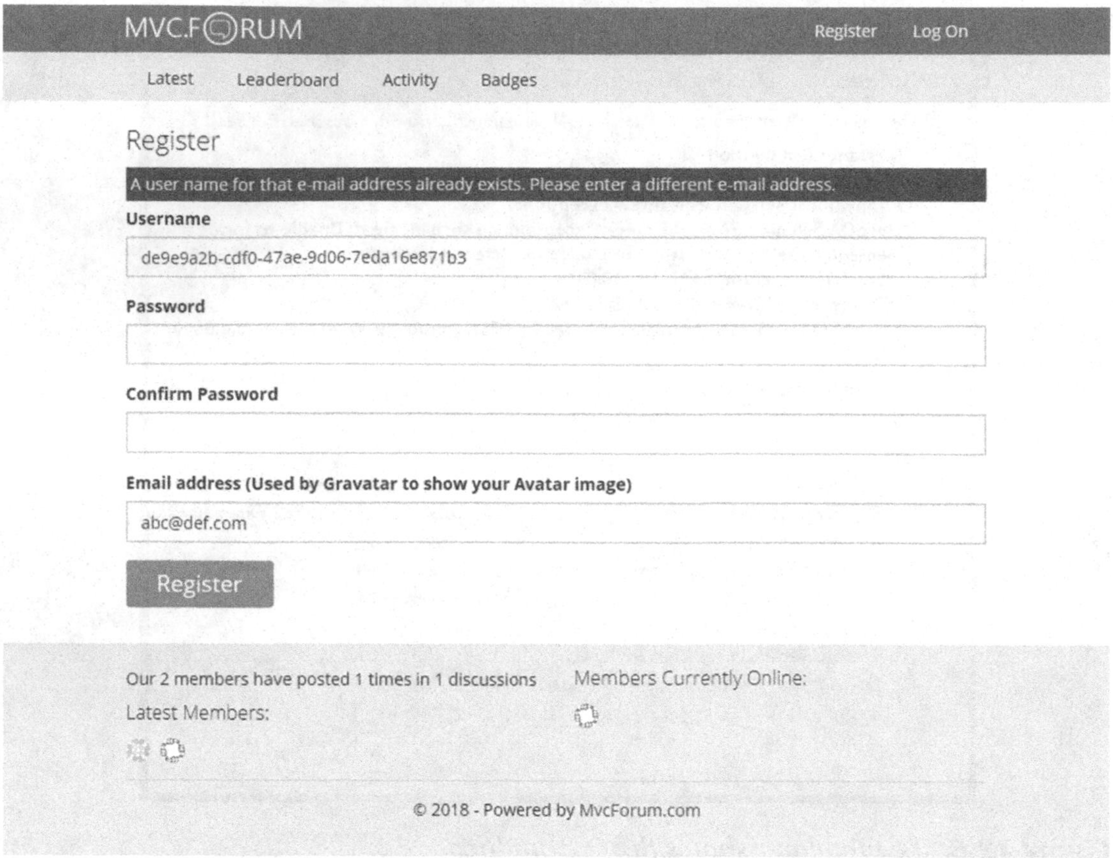

Figure 12-7. *The failure screenshot*

Apparently, the problem was that we were stuck in the **Registration** page after clicking **Register** and didn't even get to the main page where the **New Discussion** button should appear. As the screenshot tells us, the reason we failed to complete the registration is because not only the username should be unique, but also the email address.

In order to fix this, we'll create a random email address on each run too, replacing the line in MVCForumClient.RegisterNewUserAndLogin:const string email = "abc@ def.com";

with:

```
var email = $"abc@{Guid.NewGuid()}.com";
```

Completing the Test

Now this issue is behind us, and we also have a simple mechanism that will take a screenshot on every failure. So now we can continue our cycle of running – fixing – refactoring until the test passes. After about nine additional cycles like this, the test suddenly passes! Figure 12-8 shows what success looks like.

Figure 12-8. *The first test passes*

To see the final code of the test check-out the Git revision tagged **FirstTestCompleted** or online at `https://github.com/arnonax/mvcforum/tree/` `FirstTestCompleted`. You can also see the individual steps that lead us here by looking at the revisions history at `https://github.com/arnonax/mvcforum/commits/` `FirstTestCompleted` or through Visual Studio (see Chapter 9 for details).

Summary

During the process we've created many classes and many more methods. It may seem a lot for just one test, but all of these classes and methods were written in a way that is reusable, so we're likely be able to use them in other tests too. Also, all of the code that we wrote was executed and tested and proven to work repeatedly and reliably. There is still some work that we need to do in order to support running the tests on different machines or environments, support multiple browsers, and add more logging to help us investigate failures, but most of what we've done so far can stay with us for long, and be very easy to maintain. In the next chapter we'll improve the code to help us investigate failures more easily, and in Chapter 14, we'll add more tests and improve some of the things that we've postponed.

CHAPTER 13

Investigating Failures

Here's a true story: In the previous chapter we completed our first test, and it passed consistently. My original intent was to continue showing you more tests, then write a chapter about investigating failures. However, reality struck and changed my plans.

After I completed writing the previous chapter, I wanted to send the author of MVCForum, Lee Messenger, a pull-request[1] with the tests I created, as the project didn't have any tests before. But before I could send the pull-request, I had to first pull his latest changes and merge them into my repository. However, after I did that, the test stopped working.

Note that this situation happens all the time in the real world. Whenever a developer makes changes to the application, there's a chance that some tests will stop working. For that reason, integrating and running the tests often ensures that those changes between every run are small and it's easy to find out what has changed. Naturally, good maintainability, both of the application, but more so of the tests, ensures that fixing these issues is as easy as possible.

This experience inspired me to focus this chapter on this concrete example rather than on explaining about failure investigation only theoretically.

Integrating with Latest Version of MVCForum

When I ran our single test after integrating with the latest version of MVCForum, I saw the failure shown in Figure 13-1.

---

[1]A *pull-request* is an operation in GitHub that is used to send source code contributions to an open source project owned by another user. It is called "pull-request" because the contribution isn't automatically pushed to the owner's repository, but rather a message is sent to him asking him to pull the changes from the contributor's repository. This way the owner has control over the contributions and can accept or reject them.

© Arnon Axelrod 2018
A. Axelrod, *Complete Guide to Test Automation*, https://doi.org/10.1007/978-1-4842-3832-5_13

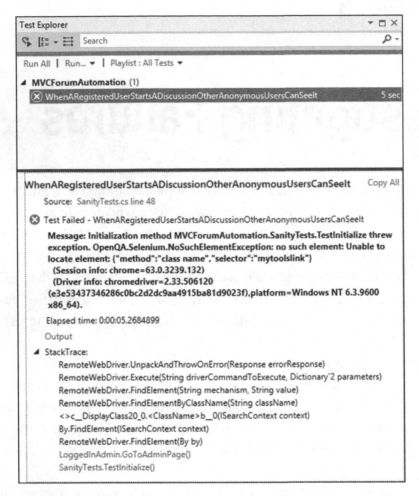

Figure 13-1. *The first failure after integrating the latest version of MVCForum*

As mentioned briefly in Chapter 10, in order to ensure isolation and consistency, I intend to clean the database before each test run. As this should be done only per run and not per test, I prefer to do it using a batch file or some other kind of script, external to the test code. In the meantime, in order to ensure that everything indeed works consistently, I occasionally re-created the database manually before running the test. The mentioned failure that happened after integrating the latest changes only happened after re-creating the database. To re-create the database, stop **IISExpress**, delete the **MVCForum** database from **Microsoft SQL Server Management Studio**, create a new database named **MVCForum**, and restart **IISExpress**. The next time you browse to the website, all of the tables and default data will be created automatically.

As we can understand from this failure message and stack-trace, we failed to find the "My Tools" menu in order to navigate to the Admin page. Let's click the Output link and look at the screenshot to see whether this menu appears or not. The screenshot is shown in Figure 13-2.

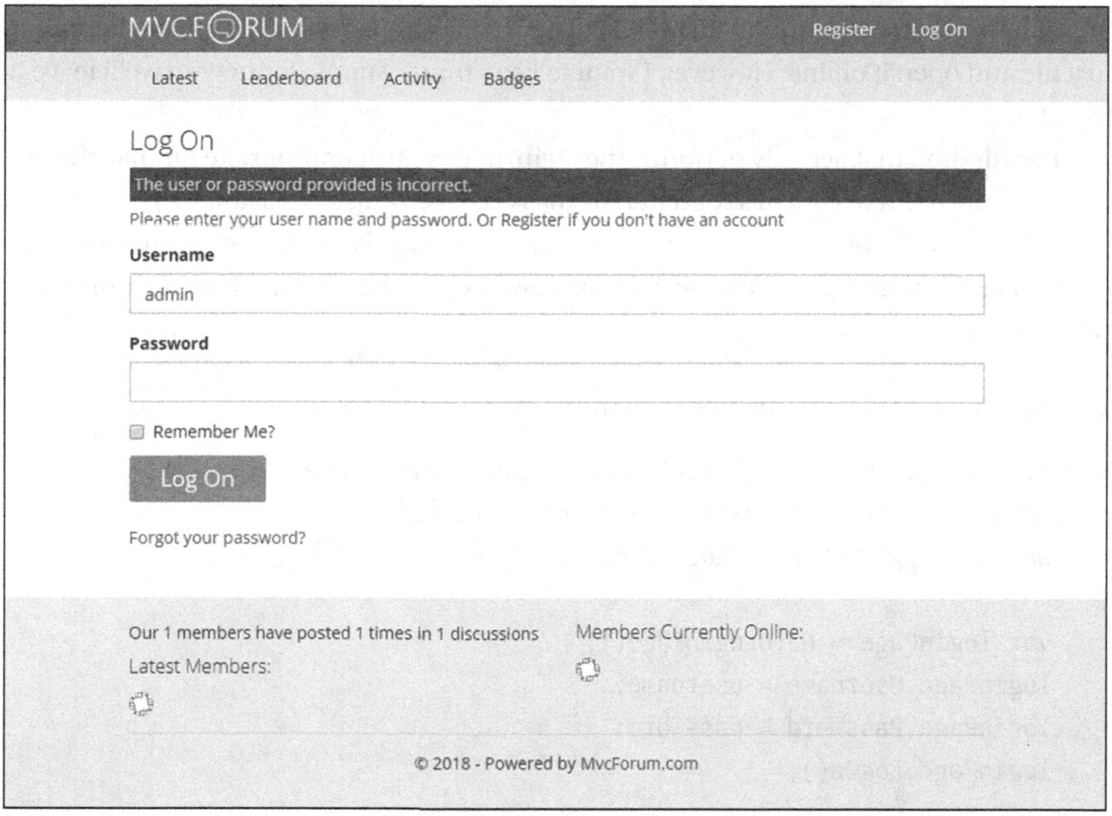

Figure 13-2. *The screenshot of the failure*

From the screenshot we can understand that we actually failed to log in.

Improving the Error Reporting

Seeing the problem from the screenshot is cool, but the first indication that we got was that the **My Tools** menu is not found which wasn't very indicative of the real problem. So before we'll fix and even investigate the root cause any further, let's fix the error message to be more indicative if a similar problem will happen again in the future.

In order to do that, after clicking the **Log On** button, we'll check that there's no red error message, and if there is, we'll fail the test immediately and provide all the relevant information at the failure message.

In order to identify the error message bar, we can either try to reproduce the problem manually or run the test through the debugger and break after clicking the **Log On** button. There's another option that I'll use later in this chapter, which is to save the page to a file and open it offline. However, I want to keep things simple for now so we'll leave it for later.

The method that actually performs the login, and is most appropriate for that check is the private method MVCForumClient.LoginAs<TLoggedInUser>. Listings 13-1 and 13-2 show the changes we made to this method and to the LoginPage class respectively in order to improve the error message. Of course, we implement one method at a time as we did before.

Listing 13-1. MVCForumClient.LoginAs improved validation

```
private TLoggedInUser LoginAs<TLoggedInUser>(string username, string
password, Func<TLoggedInUser> createLoggedInUser)
    where TLoggedInUser : LoggedInUser
{
    var loginPage = GoToLoginPage();
    loginPage.Username = username;
    loginPage.Password = password;
    loginPage.LogOn();

    var loginErrorMessage = loginPage.GetErrorMessageIfExists();
    Assert.IsNull(loginErrorMessage, $"Login failed for user:{username} and
    password:{password}. Error message: {loginErrorMessage}");

    return createLoggedInUser();
}
```

Listing 13-2. LoginPage.GetErrorMessageIfExists

```
/// <returns>
/// The error message displayed on the Login Page, or null if no error is
    displayed
/// </returns>
public string GetErrorMessageIfExists()
{
    var errorMessageElement = WebDriver.TryFindElement(
    By.ClassName("validation-summary-errors"));
    return errorMessageElement?.Text;
}
```

Notes:

1. Because I generally tend to avoid `null` as valid values (see Appendix D for more details), I added the XML comment that clearly states that it can return `null` if no error appears. Visual Studio displays these XML comments as tooltips whenever you hover over the name of the method.

2. The `TryFindElement` method is not yet declared. I'll declare it as an extension method[2] to make the code more readable, and the idea is that it will return an element if found, or `null` if not.

Listing 13-3 shows the implementation of `TryFindElement`.

---

[2]Extension methods are a C# language feature, which allow us to associate methods to existing classes or interfaces, as if they were instance members of these classes or of all classes implementing those interfaces. These methods are in fact simple `static` methods, but they make the code more elegant. The idea is that the object on which the extension method acts upon (in our case, `WebDriver`), is passed to the first parameter, which is specifically annotated with the keyword `this` in the method declaration (as you can see in Listing 13-3). You can read more about C# extension methods at `https://docs.microsoft.com/en-us/dotnet/csharp/programming-guide/classes-and-structs/extension-methods` or simply search the web for "C# extension methods."

Listing 13-3. SeleniumExtensions.cs containing the TryFindElement extension method

```
using System.Linq;
using OpenQA.Selenium;

namespace MVCForumAutomation
{
    public static class SeleniumExtensions
    {
        /// <summary>
        /// Tries to find the element using the specified locator
        /// </summary>
        /// <param name="context">The context in which to find the
            element. This is typically an object implementing <see
            cref="IWebDriver"/> or <see cref="IWebElement"/></param>
        /// <param name="locator">The locator (<see cref="By"/>) to use for
            finding the element</param>
        /// <returns>An <see cref="IWebElement"/> representing the element
            if found, or null if the element could not be found</returns>
        public static IWebElement TryFindElement(
            this ISearchContext context, By locator)
        {
            var matchineElements = context.FindElements(locator);
            return matchineElements.FirstOrDefault();
        }
    }
}
```

Note   The first parameter of the method, context, which is annotated with the this keyword, is the object to which this extension method is applied. I declared its type as ISearchContext, which both IWebDriver and IWebElement derive from, so that it will be applicable for all objects that implement any of them.

Now when we run the test, we see the error message: **Assert.IsNull failed. LogOn fail for user:admin and password:password. Error message: The user or password provided is incorrect.**

As you can see, this error message is much more accurate than the one we got originally, and we can also see the username and password that we attempted to use. So we know that we failed to log in using the default admin username and password... but why?

Avoid Debugging

The instinct of many developers (be it product developers or automation developers) when they encounter a bug is to start debugging. Indeed, today's IDEs provide very rich debugging experience, and it can give you very deep insights about what's going on. However, there are a couple of drawbacks to debugging:

1. You can only debug a failure that reproduces consistently in your environment. Debugging other environments is possible but usually much more cumbersome, and debugging through a scenario that fails inconsistently is a total waste of time. In the context of test automation, it means that failures that happen only on the build environment will be difficult to debug, and flickering tests (tests that fail inconsistently) will be much harder to diagnose.

2. After you end a debugging session, most of the information and knowledge that you gained during the session is lost. If you or someone else will have to debug a similar problem in the future, he'll need to go over the entire debug session all over again, trying to understand what you've just learned.

For these reasons, I prefer to avoid debugging in most cases. Instead, I constantly improve my error reporting, logging, and other diagnostic data collection, so gradually it becomes easier and easier to investigate failures. At first, the investment may be a bit higher than debugging, but in the long run it pays off big time.

Investigating the Root Cause

As you recall from the previous chapter, we found that the default administrator's username and password are "**admin**" and "**password**," from the **Read Me** topic (that is created automatically on the first run). So let's look at the **Read Me** topic again and see if something has changed. Figure 13-3 shows the new **Read Me** topic.

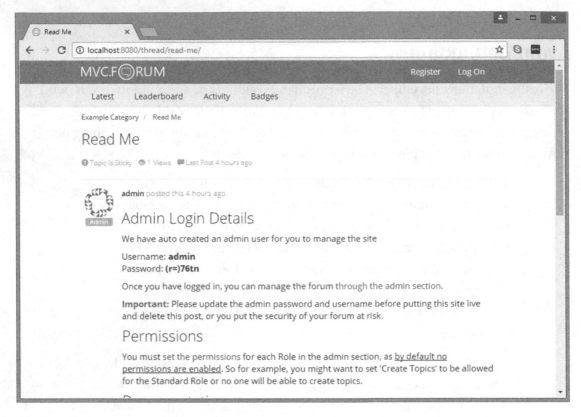

Figure 13-3. *The updated Read Me topic*

As you can see, the password is now **(r=)76tn** and not **password** as it was. Apparently this is not just a new default password as before, but rather a generated one (if you'll try it yourself you should see a different password). Digging in the code of MVCForum and talking to the developer, it turns out that in order to improve the security when people deploy the real application in production, the default password has changed to some randomly generated one rather than "**password**." The new password is generated when the database is created.

Resolving the Problem

Of course that we don't want to use **(r=)76tn** as it will change the next time we'll re-create the database. So, in order to make our test future proof, we must somehow know the generated default administrator password. Obviously, the password is not stored in the database as plain text, so the only way to get it is exactly as a real administrator user would get it: by reading it from the **Read Me** topic!

Now the question is how to find and open the **Read Me** topic in a consistent manner. There are a few alternatives, each with its own potential problems, but we'll stick to the simplest one now. We may change it later, if we'll have a good reason. We already know how to get the top topic from the Latest Discussions list. But because tests will add more topics on top of it, we need to get the bottommost one instead. Taking the bottommost one can be tricky if there's more than one page, but we'll ignore it for now. Later we'll decide whether to enhance its implementation to go to the last page or move this initialization to [AssemblyInitialize] so it always run on a clean environment and avoid this complexity altogether. We may even decide to start the tests by restoring the database from a backup in which these permissions arc already given.

In addition, we'll need to find the password itself within the entire message body, but that's pretty easy as we can use Selenium to find the second bold element within the body of the message. Listing 13-4 shows the updated TestInitialize method and the new GetAdminPassword method that it calls.

Listing 13-4. Take admin password from the Read Me discussion

```
[TestInitialize]
public void TestInitialize()
{
    var adminPassword = GetAdminPassword();
    var adminUser = MVCForum.LoginAsAdmin(adminPassword);
    var adminPage = adminUser.GoToAdminPage();
    var permissions = adminPage.GetPermissionsFor(TestDefaults.
    StandardMembers);
    permissions.AddToCategory(TestDefaults.ExampleCategory,
    PermissionTypes.CreateTopics);
    adminUser.Logout();
}
```

```
private string GetAdminPassword()
{
    var readMeHeader = MVCForum.LatestDiscussions.Bottom;
    var readmeTopic = readMeHeader.OpenDiscussion();
    var body = readmeTopic.BodyElement;
    var password = body.FindElement(By.XPath(".//strong[2]"));
    return password.Text;
}
```

Note   In Chapter 10, the first tip I gave for using the Page Object pattern correctly was not to expose the elements of the page as public properties. The `Discussion.BodyElement` property seemingly breaks this rule. But this case is special because the body can contain almost any arbitrary HTML, which IWebElement represents most naturally. Therefore this can be considered as an exception to that rule.

More Issues...

After implementing the missing methods and properties and removing duplication with existing ones, we still fail but with a different message:

> **Message: Initialization method MVCForumAutomation.SanityTests.TestInitialize threw exception. OpenQA.Selenium.NoSuchElementException: no such element: Unable to locate element: {"method":"class name","selector":"postcontent"}**

From the screenshot, stack-trace, and the code, we can conclude that the **Read Me** discussion didn't open. This should have happened in `DiscussionHeader.OpenDiscussion`, but unfortunately the root cause wasn't very apparent. So let's fix that too.

We should change `DiscussionHeader.OpenDiscussion` to fail if it couldn't complete its task successfully. In fact, we should even fail the constructor of `Discussion` (which is called by `DiscussionHeader.OpenDiscussion`) if a discussion is not displayed. Moreover, as the Discussion class is practically a page object, if we can identify an element that is the *container* of the discussion view (i.e., it contains everything related to the discussion, but not the menus and all surrounding elements), we should use it as the root element for the page object. This root should be used as the context for all

FindElement calls instead of IWebDriver. We can then fail the construction if we can't find that container. Listing 13-5 shows part of the Discussion class after the changes.

Listing 13-5. Fail the constructor of Discussion if a discussion is not open

```
public class Discussion
{
    private readonly IWebElement _container;

    public Discussion(IWebDriver webDriver)
    {
        _container = webDriver.TryFindElement(By.ClassName("topicshow"));
        Assert.IsNotNull(_container, "Failed to open discussion");
    }

    public string Title
    {
        get
        {
            var titleElement = _container.FindElement(By.CssSelector(
            ".topicheading h1"));
            return titleElement.Text;
        }
    }

    ...
}
```

Note that before the change we had IWebDriver _webDriver member and we now replaced it with IWebElement _container.

Note   I don't consider the use of Assert in this class as an assertion of the test, but rather simply as a convenient way to throw an exception. Some frameworks however, for example, JUnit, report failures due to asserts differently than failures due to exceptions, in which case it is not recommended to mix between the two.

Acting Like Detectives

Now the failure message is indeed better: **Assert.IsNotNull failed. Failed to open discussion**, but why?

From the screenshot we can see that indeed the discussion wasn't opened, so the message does not lie. So we need to investigate further. If we'll examine the stack-trace, we shall see that DiscussionHeader.OpenDiscussion is the method that called the constructor of Discussion, which threw the exception. This method is shown in Listing 13-6.

Listing 13-6. DiscussionHeader.OpenDiscussion

```
public Discussion OpenDiscussion()
{
    var link = _topicRow.FindElement(By.TagName("h3"));
    link.Click();

    var driver = ((IWrapsDriver) _topicRow).WrappedDriver;
    return new Discussion(driver);
}
```

Because the call to the Discussion constructor happens after link.Click(); we can assure that the click was executed before the failure, and returned successfully (otherwise we wouldn't have got to the last line of the method where the failure occurred). While looking at the stack-trace and at the code isn't the most trivial or fast way to diagnose a problem, it's a very accurate and reliable one. To really investigate failures reliably, we should act like detectives: collect evidence, make speculations about the suspects, try to prove or disprove each of them, narrowing the possibilities, until the root cause is crystal clear. Elementary, my dear Watson!

So let's conclude what we know so far:

1. The line link.Click(); was called and returned without throwing an exception.

2. The discussion wasn't open when the constructor of Discussion was called, which is right after the click was performed.

Because Selenium is pretty reliable, we can safely assume that Selenium performed the click action on the element referenced by the link variable. So who are the suspects, then?

1. There's a real bug in the SUT, and when clicking the link the discussion isn't opened.

2. It's a timing issue. That is, the discussion page didn't open fast enough, and if we had waited a little longer, it would succeed.

3. We clicked on the wrong element.

Manually performing the operation pretty much denies the first option. The second option is the usual suspect of many test automation developers. While in many cases it is indeed guilty, it's also too often an innocent suspect as I'll explained later in the chapter, but we can easily deny it by adding a delay of, let's say 10 seconds (by adding a Thread. Sleep(10000); statement), after the link.Click(); line. After we denied that suspicion, it's important that we delete the delay!

So our only remaining suspect is that we clicked the wrong element. From the code we see that we identify the link using its tag name h3 inside the element referred to by _topicRow. If we inspect the code (by using **Find All References** from the context menu, or **Inspect ➤ Value Origin** if you have Resharper) we can also see that the _topicRow member is identified using the class-name topicrow. Using the Developer Tool in the browser, we can search for the element using the selector ".topicrow h3" (which is a CSS selector expression meaning an h3 tag inside an element with class topicrow. See Appendix D for a deeper discussion about the different locators, including CSS Selector), as shown in Figure 13-4.

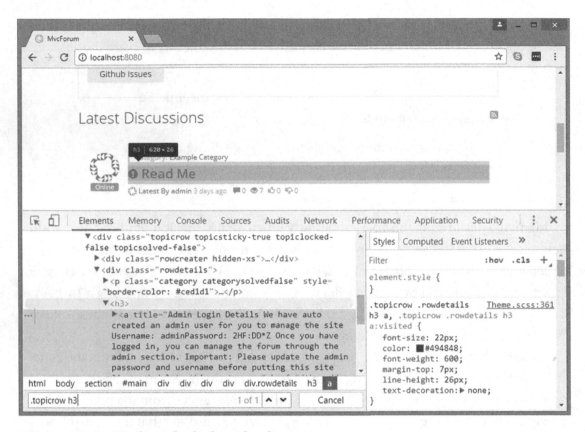

Figure 13-4. *Finding the link to the discussion*

Note   You have to press **Ctrl+F** in order to open the search box inside the Developer Tools in Chrome.

As we can see, this element is found and is unique (as you can see from the "1 of 1" indication at the right of the search box), but we can see that it also contains an "a" element, which is the link itself and that takes only a small part of its parent. Closing the Developer Tools and trying to click on the area highlighted in Figure 13-4 (which is no longer highlighted when you close the Developer Tools), but not on the **Read Me** title itself, does not open the discussion.

One thing still looks strange though. This method hasn't changed since we used it in the first test and before we integrated the latest changes of MVCForum. So why it didn't fail before? If you'll take the time to revert to the previous version and investigate, you'll find out that the titles of the topics that we clicked in the tests were GUIDs, which are longer than the **Read Me** title. These long links crossed the center of the h3 element area, and therefore clicking the h3 element did actually click the link. But because the **Read Me** title is short, clicking on the middle of the h3 element doesn't click the link.

Now that we convicted the criminal (which is me, as the author of this code...), we can fix it very easily. Simply replace the locator of link from By.TagName("h3") to By.CssSelector("h3 a").

Taking More Screenshots

After fixing the locator, the story doesn't end... Now the test fails on **OpenQA. Selenium.NoSuchElementException: no such element: Unable to locate element: {"method":"class name","selector":"createtopicbutton"}**. Looking at the screenshot (Figure 13-5) and the stack-trace, we can conclude that the registration processes completed successfully this time. So we made some progress after all.

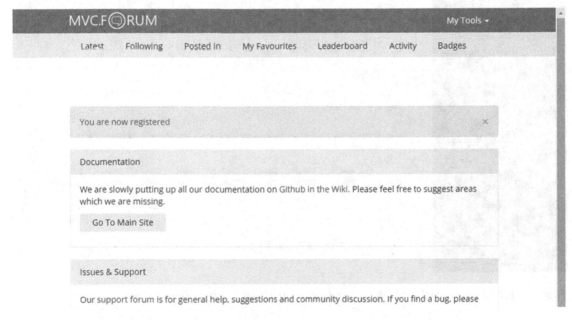

Figure 13-5. *Registration completed successfully*

But also apparent from the error message and the screenshot is that the **Create Discussion** button is not there. As you recall, we had a similar problem in the previous chapter, which was solved by adding the **Create Topic** permission to the **Standard Members** group. So maybe we have a problem with that permission again.

In order to investigate whether we've added the permissions successfully or not, it would be great if we had a screenshot for every click, with the clicked element clearly marked. Developing such a mechanism can take some time, so let's write this idea to ourselves on a sticky note and get back to it after we'll fix the test. For now, we can take two more screenshots: one before adding the permission and one after. We can use the `TakeScreenshot` method that we already added to `MVCForumClient`, and call it before and after the call to `RolePermissionsPage.AddToCategory` from the `TestInitialize` method. As always, we refactor to remove duplication of adding the screenshot to the test results. We do that by adding on event `MVCForumClient.OnScreenshotTaken` and handling it in `SanityTests` to add the file to the test results. You can find the code at tag **AddingScreenshot** in the history of the Git repository.

When we run the test, the two screenshots are added to the output of the test. Both of the screenshots are identical and look like Figure 13-6.

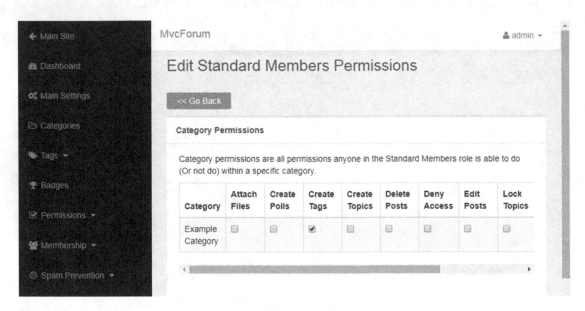

Figure 13-6. *Screenshot before and after adding Create Topic permission*

We see that the third permission is checked, but hey! The third permission is no longer the **Create Topics** permission, but rather a new **Create Tags** permission that didn't exist before... Apparently this is a new permission that the developer added before we pulled the latest changes, and the code at `AddToCategory` relied on the index of the permission (casted to `int` from the `PermissionTypes` enum) because there was no other way to identify the correct checkbox. Adding an Id attribute or `auto-*` class, like we did in the previous chapter, was also not practical because the list of permissions is created dynamically at runtime.

We can fix it by adding the new `CreateTags` permission to the `PermissionTypes` enum in the right position. This is not an ideal solution, but consulting with the developer we concluded that this is the best we can do for now. For a better solution. the developer will need to make significant changes that are not expected to be completed in the near future.

Finally the test passes again!

Logging and Other Evidence Collection

While we could investigate most things using screenshots, error messages, and the code, other problems require more information in order to be identified quickly.

Screen Capture

Capturing and recording the screen video is very helpful at times. You can see exactly what happened during the test. You can see all the flow of the test; go back and forth; and most importantly, you can spot things like error messages, even from other applications or from the OS, that you didn't expect.

Like everything in test automation and in life in general, screen capturing has its drawbacks too. First, it takes quite a lot of disk space, which also depends on the quality of the video that you need. For most cases you don't need a very high video quality, unless your application is rich in animations and graphics. You can also delete the recording if the test passed to preserve disk space. However, it still takes much more space than text and screenshots.

In addition, because the test typically go pretty fast, it can be hard to track what exactly the automation tries to do at any given moment in the video. This is especially true with Selenium and UI automation technologies that don't actually move the mouse cursor. If you don't see the mouse move, you can hardly know which button was clicked. So it can be pretty difficult to understand from the video alone what's happening.

In order to capture video, typically we need to use an external application that does that. The test's infrastructure should start it whenever a test starts and stops it when it ends, possibly deleting the file if the test passed. Obviously, other than that, neither the tests themselves nor any other code in the test project should be changed in order to take advantage of screen capturing.

In Visual Studio Enterprise you can easily turn on video recording for test runs through a *.**runsettings** or *.**testsettings** file. You can find more details at `https://docs.microsoft.com/en-us/visualstudio/test/configure-unit-tests-by-using-a-dot-runsettings-file`.

Logging

Another technique to track what happens during a test is logging. Logging can be as simple as writing text to the standard console output, but it can be much more sophisticated than that as we'll discuss shortly. Unlike screen capturing, logging requires adding dedicated lines of code wherever you want something to be written to the log.

There are many logging libraries out there for pretty much all relevant programming languages, and most of them are open source. These libraries typically allow you to configure one or more destinations to which the log entries will be written. Such destinations can be console output, files, database, etc. They also let you specify the desired format for each entry, which can automatically include the date/time, thread Id, method name, and more with each log entry. Also, typically, these libraries support several severity levels (like Debug, Info, Warning, Error, etc.), which you have to specify when writing each log entry. By changing the configuration, these levels can be used to filter the types of log entries you're interested in.

Nested Logging

One of the challenges with logs is how to decide what to write to the log, and using which severity. On one hand, if you'll write too few entries, you may miss important information when you come to diagnose a problem. On the other hand, if you write too much, it becomes very difficult to see the forest for the trees, and find what you're looking for. There are several remedies to that, but one that I found to works for me the best, and which I used for a very long time now, is to create the log in a nested manner. That is, the logger uses indentation to write lower-level details nested inside higher-level ones. Listing 13-7 shows an example of a nested log.

Listing 13-7. Example of a nested log.

```
Adding a Category
    Opening Admin page
        Clicking on 'My Tools'
        Clicking on 'Admin'
    [Done: Opening Admin Page]
    Opening Categories page
        Clicking on 'Categories'
    [Done: Opening Categories page]
    Creating new category
        Clicking 'Create New'
        Typing 'Test category' in 'Category Name'
        Clicking 'Create'
    [Done: Creating new category]
    Click 'Main Site'
[Done: Adding a Category]
```

The logger keeps track of the indentation level based on special StartSection and EndSection methods that you can call. In C# the using statement and IDisposable pattern can be used to automatically end a section when exiting a block of code, so you don't have to call EndSection explicitly. Any log entry that is written between a StartSection and an EndSection is written with higher indentation than entries outside of this section. This way, when you read the log you always have all the details, but you can easily distinguish the high level entries from the lower-level ones, while easily correlate those low-level entries with the higher level one that initiated them.

Note   The using statement in C# is a compiler feature (AKA "syntactic sugar"), which is equivalent to the try/finally construct, though instead of defining the content of the finally clause directly, it takes an expression of type IDisposable at the beginning and calls its IDisposable.Dispose method in the implicit finally clause. Java 8 have a similar feature called *try-with-resource*, which uses the AutoClosable interface. You can read more on the using statement at https://docs.microsoft.com/en-us/dotnet/csharp/language-reference/keywords/using-statement

---

TestAutomationEssentials.Common (see Appendix B for more details) provides such a mechanism. By default, Test Automation Essentials writes the logs to the console output, but you can easily redirect it to any other destination.

Visual Logging

While regular loggers only support text, some loggers also support images, usually by writing the entries to an HTML file. When doing UI automation, a log that also contains screenshots is much easier to analyze than one that only contains text. **ExtentsReport** is a popular tool that allows you write test logs that include images. It has an open source, "community" edition, and a more feature-rich "professional" payed version.

Some UI automation tools, like Coded UI for example, automatically takes screenshots on every click and keyboard entry, and also highlights the relevant element. This makes it even better for analysis and easier to use from the coding side. As ExtentReport is a separate technology from Selenium, it does not have this capability built in. However, it's possible to combine them together, using the EventFiringWebDriver class (in the **Selenium.Support** library), and a few other little tricks, and make it work for Selenium tests too! Obviously, combining the nested logging concept with the visual logging one, makes the best of all worlds. Later on, we'll build this logger and add it to the project.

Additional Logging and Diagnostics Options

Aside from the logging options mentioned above, there are other possible things that you can use to ease the analysis of failures. Some of these are specific to Selenium, some are more appropriate for API testing, and some are generic. Use whatever fits your application and what helps you investigate failures. You can incorporate many of these things into the more generic logging options too.

Here are some Selenium specific things that you can use:

- `IWebDriver.PageSource` – this property returns the HTML of the current page as a string. For drivers of some browsers, this property returns the original HTML as it was when the page was first loaded, but others, including Chrome, return the HTML that represents the current state of the DOM (which could be different that the original HTML due to manipulations that were done to it using

JavaScript). If you save this string to a file with an **.html** extension, then you can open this file in the browser after the test has finished and see more or less how the page looked like when you saved the file. Unfortunately, because it saves only the HTML without external CSS and JavaScript files, usually the page doesn't look right. However you can usually still get the important information out of the page, and also examine it with the Developer Tools in the browser, which can help a lot in case an element was not found (`NoSuchElementException` is thrown). Even if opening it in the browser doesn't work well, you can always open it in a text editor (preferably one that can color-code HTML elements, jump to the closing tags, etc. like Notepad++ for example).

- `IWebDriver.Manage().Logs` – this property can be used to get the logs from various sources related to Selenium. The most relevant one in my experience is the `Browser` log type, where you can see a message that the application's JavaScript code writes to the browser's console (by calling `console.log(…)`), and other errors that the browser itself writes when exceptions or communication problems happen.

- Using the `EventFiringWebDriver` class you can intercept all of the important method calls to `IWebDriver` and `IWebElement`, including `Click`, `SendKeys`, `GoToUrl`, and more. This class fires events whenever each of these methods is being called, and you can subscribe to these events to automatically log all of these operations automatically. This saves you from remembering to add a log entry on every click, makes your code cleaner, and the log more consistent.

Here are a few other ideas that are not specific to Selenium:

- Log HTTP traffic – while this can be used also for Selenium tests, it's especially relevant to API testing. You can either use an external tool like Fiddler or even log all the requests just before they're being sent to the server, and the responses just as they arrive. You can often also get similar logs from the side of the web server that hosts the application like Microsoft Internet Information Services (IIS).

- Application Log – the logs of the application itself can also be very valuable for investigating test failures. You can either intercept the logs by redirecting them to the test, or simply copy the log files when the test run completes to the test results directory. When you use the logs to investigate failures, make sure to correlate the exact time of every entry in the test's log with the time of the corresponding entries from the application's log. This way you can reason about the root cause of the failure much more accurately than just skimming the log for errors and anomalies. Note that there can be a slight gap between clocks of different computers, but this gap should be pretty constant over the course of a test run, so if you find related entries in both logs, you can have a pretty accurate notion of this gap, and then correlate all other entries very accurately.

- System and middleware log – the Windows Event Viewer and similar mechanisms in other operating systems as well as middleware infrastructure can also be used to explain some global failures. These failures usually don't indicate a bug in the SUT but rather some kind of an "environmental" problem. While in most cases these logs don't provide much information that is related to the failures in your tests, the few cases where they do can save you a lot of time looking for the problem in the wrong place. My advice is to include these logs only if you suspect an environmental problem that you cannot identify in other means. Examples of such issues can be low disk space, network disconnections, security issues, etc. When you do find and identify such a problem, I encourage you to either implement some specific work-around in the infrastructure code of the tests, or add some code to automatically identify the situation and report it clearly in the test failure. It is advisable to write this code before you actually solve the problem (e.g., free up some disk space), so you can test this specific code. Only after you see that the failure message is clear or that the work-around works, solve the real problem and verify that the message doesn't appear anymore.

Adding Nested Visual Logger to MVCForum Tests

As our test already passes, we can get back to implement the visual logger we wrote on the sticky note sooner, and let's make it nested too. You can find the complete solution at the **VisualLogger** tag in the Git repository, but here are some highlights and remarks:

- We use the **ExtentReports** NuGet library as the basis of our visual logger.

- We use the **TestAutomationEssentials.Common** NuGet library for the nesting feature, but we also override its default behavior, which is to write to the standard output, with our own behavior that writes to the ExtentsReport log. We encapsulate this behavior in the new VisualLogger class. We then use only the Logger class of Test Automation Essentials for writing log entries from everywhere we need, and its StartSection method to start a new nesting level. As mentioned above, StartSection implements IDisposable so it can be used in conjunction with the using statement, which automatically calls Dispose when it completes, consequently ends the last nesting level. Listing 13-8 shows the use of Logger. StartSection and Logger.WriteLine in the SanityTests. GetAdminPassword method.

Listing 13-8. Use of Logger in SanityTests.GetAdminPassword

```
private string GetAdminPassword()
{
    using (Logger.StartSection(
        "Getting Admin password from 'Read Me' topic"))
    {
        var readMeHeader = MVCForum.LatestDiscussions.Bottom;
        var readmeTopic = readMeHeader.OpenDiscussion();
        var body = readmeTopic.BodyElement;
        var password = body.FindElement(By.XPath(".//strong[2]"));
        var adminPassword = password.Text;
```

```
Logger.WriteLine($"Admin password='{adminPassword}'");
        return adminPassword;
    }
}
```

- We overrode ExtentReport's default rendering of messages in order for the indented nested log entries to appear correctly.

- We use the `EventFiringWebDriver` class (from the **Selenium. Support** library) for intercepting all calls to `IWebDriver.Click`, `IWebDriver.SendKeys`, and setting the `IWebDriver.URL` property, in order to automatically write these events to the log and also to take a screenshot at each of these events

- On the screenshots we take for the click events, we add a red rectangle that highlights the element we're about to click (using the `IWebElement.Location` and `IWebElement.Size` properties). When you look at the look, it makes it obvious what element was clicked. Pretty cool, isn't it?

Figure 13-7 shows part of the output of the nested visual logger. You can see that the **Opening Admin Page** entry and its **[Done:...]** counterpart are less indented than the entries between them. You can also see the automatic logging of every click event. On the screen you will see a red rectangle around the **My Tools** menu in the first screenshot and another red rectangle around the **Admin** menu item in the second. Note that in the real report, you can click the minified screenshot to open them in their full size.

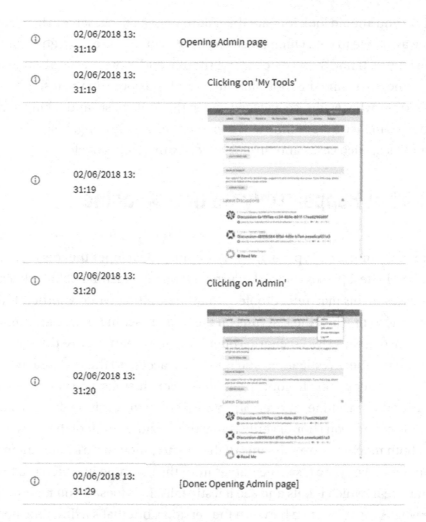

	02/06/2018 13:31:19	Opening Admin page
	02/06/2018 13:31:19	Clicking on 'My Tools'
	02/06/2018 13:31:19	
	02/06/2018 13:31:20	Clicking on 'Admin'
	02/06/2018 13:31:20	
	02/06/2018 13:31:29	[Done: Opening Admin page]

Figure 13-7. *Output of the nested visual logger*

I encourage you to look at the VisualLogger class in order to see how it's implemented. You may also find it useful to look at individual commits in the revision history (preceding the **VisualLogger** tag) in order to understand each feature separately.

Investigating Challenging Failures

The failures we encountered so far were failures that happened consistently on our machine. Such failures are usually fairly easy to investigate. However, there are cases where failures are inconsistent and therefore harder to investigate. In all of these cases the first things you should look into are the failure message, log, screenshots and all of the evidence available to you. Often these pieces of evidence are enough to conclude the cause of the failure. If not, then you can, and should, add more pieces of evidence (e.g., log entries) to help you find the root cause the next time your run the test. However, you can't always know what evidence will lead you to the root cause, and taking a trial-and-error approach can take a lot of time and become pretty frustrating. Following are some typical examples of such cases and tips for handling them effectively.

Failures That Happen Only On One Machine

Sometimes a test passes on one machine but consistently fails on one or few other machines or environments. Typically, the automation developer that developed the test made sure that the test passes (or works correctly) on his machine before checking in his code, so it passes on his machine. Problems may arise either when another developer tries to run the test, or when the test runs on the build machine. These are some differences between these two scenarios but for the most part they're the same. At least in the beginning of the investigation, you must have access to the machine where the test fails. Usually after getting to some preliminary conclusions, you can reproduce the problem on another machine, or even on your machine to continue the investigation.

The first thing that you should verify is that the versions, both of the tests and of the SUT, on both machines are the same. If they're not, then there's no point in the comparison. Try to copy the test executables from the machine in which the test passes to the one in which it fails and see if it still fails. If it doesn't you may still want to investigate what's the difference between the versions, but that's a different story. If it still fails, the difference might be the versions of the SUT.

If the SUT is a locally installed application, then either copy the application from the machine where the test passes to the one where it fails, or reinstall the same version that is installed where the test passes. If the test accesses the SUT remotely (e.g., through the browser or over HTTP), then it suffices to redirect the failing machine to the SUT that the passing machine uses.

If both versions match, our strategy for continuing to investigate the failure should be based on the "lion in the desert" search algorithm (a generalization of the binary search algorithm). Hey, don't panic, I'm not asking you to implement the algorithm, just to act according to its course of action. The idea is to break every problem into two smaller ones, find which one is relevant, and continue to break it down into smaller and smaller problems until you find the root cause. To be more specific: identify one difference between the environments that you suspect to affect the difference in the results, then try to eliminate this difference, by changing one side to match the other. If the results are still different (and the failure message is still the same), look for another key difference and repeat. If the side that you changed now yields the same result as the other one, then it means that the difference that we eliminated is significant to the problem. However, even if we could solve the immediate issue this way, we shouldn't stop here! We must understand the root cause and take actions to prevent this situation from reoccurring, or at least alerting and providing guidelines to overcome the problem.

For example, we might suspect a difference between the databases of the two environments. So first we can try to change the connection string of our environment (where the test passed) to the database of the failed environment. If the test still passes on our machine, using the other database, it means that the problem is not related to the database, and we need to look for another difference. If it fails, it means that the problem is in the database indeed, but we still don't know exactly what. It could be a difference in the data, in the schema, or even in the version of the database engine. Let's say that you noticed that the schema version of the failed environment is newer than the one in our environment. So we can update the schema of our environment (after backing up the database and after restoring the connection string to its original one) and examine the result. If it fails, then we can conclude that the new schema version causes the test to fail, though we still need to find exactly why. If it passes, then it's not a schema problem, and we can continue to compare and match the other differences. We continue this process until we nail down the root cause. Figure 13-8 outlines the decision tree of this example.

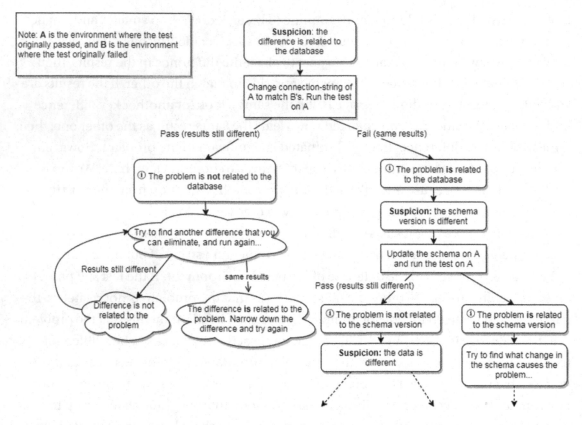

Figure 13-8. *Decision tree for diagnosing a failure that occurs only on one machine*

One important thing to note when going through this process is that the error message and the relevant symptoms are the same. If at some point you get a different error, you should first try to understand if the new error happens before or after the point of the original failure. If the new failure happens *after* the point at which it has originally failed, it means that the original failure didn't happen this time! You may still have to narrow the problem further down as explained above, but in the meantime you should treat the new failure as if the test passed. After you've completed narrowing down the original problem and resolve it, start over the entire investigation, this time with the new failure.

However, if the new failure happens *before* the point at which it has originally failed, or at the same point, but with a different error message, then it probably means that there's more than one difference in the environments that affects the outcome. In this case, try focusing on the new failure first, and then get back to the original one. When things start to get too complex, I found that writing down a manual log file (using a text editor or word processor), of the things that you try and their results, gives me an a better feeling of orientation around the problem than just performing random trial and error. This log especially helps you if you continue to work on the problem the day after. It also helps if you need to explain to other people what the problem that you're trying to solve is, and what are your intermediate conclusions. As with the nested logger, I tend to write this manual log also in a nested manner. For example, if I want to try out some experiment in order to diagnose the original problem, and while I try I encounter another problem that is related only to the experiment itself, then I try to solve the inner problem first, and then continue with the original experiment I had in mind. In this case I log the stuff related to the problems in the experiment itself nested within the other stuff that is related to the original problem and other stuff that I tried.

Running from the IDE vs. Running from Command Line

One common difference between running the tests on your development machine and running them on the build server is that in your development machine you might be running the tests from within the IDE while on the build server it runs from the command line.

Sometimes there are slight differences between the runner that is used by the IDE and the command-line runner. In order to investigate it, look at the logs of the build and try to find the exact command line that was invoked during the build. If you'll try to run the exact command on your local machine you may encounter differences in paths or other environmental differences that won't allow you to run the tests. So you have to find and eliminate those differences first. If you succeed running the test on your machine and it fails with the same error as in the build, then the problem is probably related to the difference between the command-line runner and the IDE runner. You should continue to investigate and nail down the cause for the different behavior between the IDE and the command-line runners, but at least you can now do this investigation all on your local machine.

If you can't reproduce it through the command line on your machine, then the problem is probably not related to this difference. You can try to run an IDE on the build machine if possible just to verify that this is indeed the case. Then try to find another suspicious difference.

Narrow Down the Code

When you try to narrow down the problem, it's often useful to narrow down the code that's related to the problem. You can comment-out lines of code that does not seem to be related to the problem or perform temporary shortcuts to bypass long or complex operations. This will make each experiment run faster, and also narrow down the scope of the problem. Obviously, you should not check-in these changes, but rather just copy the test executables (DLL, JAR ...) to the other machine. Sometimes it's even worth creating a completely new test project and copying to it only the minimal code that reproduces the problem. This way you eliminate a lot of "noise" and help you focus on investigating the root cause. At the end of the process you'd most probably find the exact line of code that behaves differently on the two environments, and it would be pretty easy to understand what's going on.

Investigating Influencing Tests

Sometimes tests pass consistently when run on their own, or as part of a small group of tests, but also consistently fail when run as part of a complete test suite. In most cases it means that there's an inadvertent influence of one test on another. It also implies a problem in the isolation strategy. Look back at Chapter 7 for concrete isolation techniques that can help you solve the problem.

But before you run and apply any of those techniques, you should first have a clear picture of the root cause. As always, first try to look at the log and the evidences and try to understand from them what could be the problem. If you suspect something, try to create a simpler reproduction of the problem and check if you get the same result. If you do, it should usually be easy to come up with a solution.

However, if you don't have an idea what could be the problem, then you can play the "Lion in the Desert" game again, but in a slightly different fashion this time: Suppose that when we run the entire suite, test #28 always fails, even though it passes if run alone. In this case, you should create a new test suite that contains only tests 1–14 and also test #28. If test #28 now passes it means that the influencing test is between 15 and 27. After you verify that it's true, split the remaining test cases to two again, and now take only tests 15–21 (half of 15–27) and test #28. Continue this process until you remain with exactly one test that when run together with test #28 reproduces the error. Let's say that we remained with tests #16 and #28. Now we can continue to narrow down the root cause by removing unrelated stuff from tests #16 until we find the exact operation in it that affect test #28.

While it may sound a very long course to take, it's not as much as you'd think. Because we cut the number of tests in half at each cycle, then if we sum up the number of tests that we run during this search, we'll get exactly the number of tests preceding the one that failed (28 tests in our example). In reality you would usually also have an idea of which tests might be related to the problem and which aren't, so you can minimize the scope even further.

Investigating Flickering Tests

Flickering tests are tests that sometimes fail and sometimes pass, even if run on the same build and on the same environment, with no immediately apparent reason. Whether the failures happen pretty often or pretty rarely, this phenomenon is one of the most disturbing situations for anyone who cares about the results of the test automation, as it destabilizes their reliability. Sometimes the flickering is not bound to one or few specific tests, but each time a different test may fail. Investigating these cases is usually also very frustrating because it's almost impossible to know if you really fixed the problem or you were just lucky this time. Thankfully, there are a few useful techniques to handle these cases. Before we'll get to these techniques, let's first examine a few common anti-patterns[3] and understand their drawbacks.

Anti-patterns for Handling Flickering Tests

The following techniques are applied quite often in attempt to handle flickering tests. However, even though they're pretty common, I consider them as anti-patterns, and they have significant drawbacks. I'm listing those here in order for you to be aware and beware of their consequences.

Retry All of the Failed Tests

One common anti-pattern when flickering tests becomes a big issue is to run all of the failed tests gain, usually two or three times, and only if a test fails all of the times, then it is reported as failed, and even if it passed only once, consider it as passed.

---

[3]An *Anti-Pattern* is a common solution to a problem, that albeit being common, its effectiveness is questionable and often counterproductive.

There are a few drawbacks to this approach:

- It assumes that the failures are mainly the fault of the automation and not real bugs. While this is sometimes true, many times it's not. If it is the fault of the automation, then you're just hiding and deferring the problem rather than trying to investigate and resolve it. If the fault is in the SUT, it means that there's a bug that you don't report. Note that "environmental" problems are usually isolation problems that *are* the fault of the automation. Like any other faults, they should be identified and fixed rather than being swept under the rug.

- When an automation developer develops a new test or maintains an existing one, he should normally run the test a few times in order to debug, diagnose, and eventually to ensure that it works correctly. If a test that passes only once out of three retries is considered OK, then when the test fails at any of these activities (debug, diagnose, etc.,) it confuses the automation developer as he can't distinguish between failures that are the fault of his recent changes and faults that were considered OK before. If he needs to run and debug everything three times, then it lengthens his work considerably.

- Because issues are deferred and swept under the rug, then in the long run, more and more issues cause more and more tests to become flickering and in a higher frequency. This makes the three retries insufficient, and the natural reaction is to increase the number of retries, which only makes things worse...

Using Fixed Delays (Thread.Sleep)

A typical cause of flickering tests is timing. As in most cases, the SUT is running in a different process than the test, it also means that it is running on a different thread. This implies that whenever you perform an option on the SUT (e.g., click a button, sending a HTTP request, etc.), the operation completes on a thread in the SUT while the thread of the test continues in parallel.

This doesn't mean that operations cannot be synchronized, however, by waiting for some kind of an acknowledgment from the SUT that the operation completed. In fact, Selenium always waits for the browser to complete its operation before the method returns, and so are many HTTP/REST libraries, which wait for the HTTP response to be received before continuing. But still, the notion of what's considered a "complete operation" is debatable. For example, if the browser sends an asynchronous HTTP call to the server (known as AJAX or XHR), and displays a wait spinner, then Selenium will return as if the operation has completed, even though in most cases the user considers the operation as complete only when the asynchronous call returns and the result is displayed on the UI. A similar situation occurs when a REST API returns a "200 OK" response after it pushed a message to a queue, which another service should process asynchronously. In these situations you should explicitly tell the test to wait until the operation completes, which usually depends on the specific scenario.

Knowing what to wait and how is often challenging, and therefore some automation developers choose the easy way of waiting for a fixed period of time, using a the Thread. Sleep method. While this solution often resolves the problem in the short term, it has serious drawbacks:

- Suppose that 50% of the times the operation completes in 3 seconds or less. Then it's not suffice to wait for 3 seconds, as in the other 50% of the times the operation won't complete yet. Theoretically, you can never reach 100%, but it's OK to put some threshold above which the time is considered unacceptable and the test should indeed fail, reporting that the operation didn't complete in an acceptable period. However, the closer you want to get to 100%, the time you have to wait increases more rapidly. This means that if you want the operation to succeed 99% of the times, you might need to wait 10 seconds. Figure 13-9 shows a Gamma Distribution graph of the time an operation may take. This means that in 50% of the cases you're waiting 7 seconds *more than you really need!*

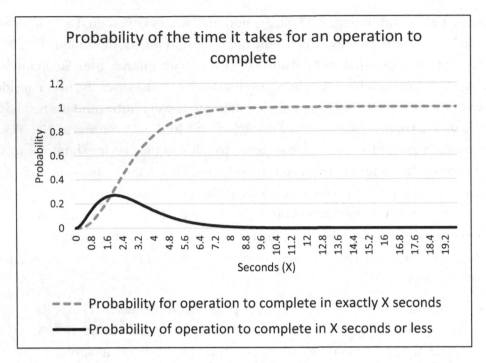

Figure 13-9. *Gamma Distribution for completing an example operation*

- When you're just waiting for a fixed period of time, when that time elapses, you typically don't know whether the operation really completed or not. If you don't check that, then your test may fail only later on. When investigating the failure, this distracts you from the root cause. As you should already understand, the time and ease of investigating failures are crucial to the reliability and the overall value of the test automation. If you do check whether the operation completed successfully after the delay, then it should be very easy to convert the fixed delay to wait for the operation to complete.

TIMING ISSUES AND SELENIUM

Unlike what many automation developers believe, each method call in Selenium returns only when the operation has completed on the browser in a completely deterministic fashion. In many cases it means there's no need for any delays or waits. However, the question is how you define "the operation has completes." In order to answer this question, we need to understand how the browser works.

In the browser, every page (browser's tab or window) is capable of running JavaScript code, and also perform some other internal operations only on a single thread. However, asynchronous operations can still take place while the page is idle, waiting for input from the user or from the server. For example, AJAX calls (also known as XHR or XmlHttpRequest) are performed asynchronously, but when they return, the callback function that handles their results is executed again on the same thread, only if it's idle. If it's not, then the callback will remain in a queue until the thread is idle and then the callback will be executed. Asynchronous operations can also be performed in JavaScript using the setTimeout function.

Because Selenium communicates with the web page, then its calls are also synchronized with this thread. This means that if the JavaScript code that is executed on a click event is synchronous (does not initiate AJAX calls or use setTimeout), it is guaranteed that the Click method that you call through Selenium will not return until the JavaScript event handler has completed its execution. Only if the handler initiates an asynchronous operation explicitly (using AJAX or setTimeout), then the method may return before the operation is completed.

Some JavaScript frameworks, like AngularJS and KnockoutJS, as well as some homegrown architectures, make more use of asynchronous operations, and therefore are more susceptible to timing issues than websites that don't use them.

Selenium provides two main mechanism for waiting for asynchronous operations to complete, often referred to as *implicit wait* and *explicit wait*. Implicit wait is a timeout value that you can set via the IWebDriver.Manage().Timeouts().ImplicitWait property, and affects how long Selenium will wait to find an element if it hasn't existed yet before throwing a NoSuchElementException. It is important to note that implicit wait only applies when calling FindElement, and it does not affect any other operations like Click, for example. FindElements (the plural form) is also affected by this value, but it waits only wait until at least one if found. It could be that this is what you expect, but there are cases in which a list is filled asynchronously and then this method may return before all the elements are populated. Explicit wait is a more generic mechanism that lets you wait for various predefined conditions or define your own. You apply Explicit Wait by instantiating a WebDriverWait class (from the **Selenium.Support** library), specifying the timeout value, and calling the Until method, specifying the expected condition. The predefined conditions are defined in the ExpectedConditions class and contain conditions like ElementIsVisible,

`ElementToBeClickable`, `TextToBePresentInElement` and many more, as well as to define your own. Here are two examples:

```
var wait = new WebDriverWait(webDriver, TimeSpan.FromSeconds(30));
// Using predefined condition:
var button = webDriver.FindElement(By.Id("approveButton"));
wait.Until(ExpectedConditions.ElementToBeClickable(button));
button.Click();

// Use a custom condition to wait for a file to be created:
wait.Until(drv => File.Exists(path));
var text = File.ReadAllText(path);
```

Note   WebDriverJS, the JavaScript version of Selenium WebDriver, does return before the operation completes and lets you to use callbacks, known as *promises* to be notified when the operation has completed. This is because JavaScript itself is single threaded and must free the main thread in order to allow it to process the response when the operation completes.

Properly Waiting for an Operation to Complete

The alternative to fixed delays is to wait for an event or a condition to be met, which indicates that the operation is completed either successfully or not. Try to think how the user knows that an operation has completed. For example, while a loader spinner appears, it indicates the user that the data is not ready yet, but when it disappears it should indicate that it is. If you're not using UI automation but any type of API, then you should think how client systems should be indicated that the operation is completed.

When you're waiting for an event or condition, you should always set a timeout, such that if the condition is not met in that period, the operation should fail. This is to prevent a situation in which the test hangs indefinitely. You can set this timeout pretty high, as in most cases the test won't wait for that long, only when the condition is not met (which can either be a bug in the SUT or in the test). The timeout should be high enough to avoid failing the test unnecessarily, but not above a time that the most patient user would reasonably wait for the result.

Even though implementing a mechanism that polls for a condition until it becomes true, or a timeout occurs, is not rocket science, you should rarely develop it yourself. There are many existing libraries that already do that for you. If you're using Selenium you have the WebDriverWait class, TestAutomationEssentials.Common also has a Wait class, and I'm sure that there are plenty of similar implementations out there for any language you use.

Note   Some testing frameworks, including MSTest, have a default timeout for a test to complete, which is usually very high, like 30 minutes or so. Other frameworks don't have a built-in default, but let you specify your own default timeout that applies to all tests. In addition, most frameworks let you specify a timeout value for specific tests that overrides that default, but you should very rarely use that. This means that implementing your own loop that waits for a condition, without taking care to fail the test on a proper timeout, even if it won't hang the test forever, due to the default timeout, it will still take a very long time (e.g., 30 minutes) until it fails. If there is more than one test that will fail for the same reason, then each of these will take 30 minutes…

Properly Handling and Investigating Flickering Tests

Sometimes there's a tendency to blame the test automation for flickering tests. However, it's important to realize and communicate that such failures can be the fault of real bugs just as well. In fact, in my experience it's even more likely, because most systems are asynchronous in nature, which is more prone to random timing issues and race conditions, while test automation is typically single threaded, and therefore more immune from these problems. Having said that, it can also be a matter of an improper isolation, or some other reason. Therefore unless you investigate the root cause, you cannot know where the fault is.

Shortly I'll describe a method for investigating flickering tests. However, if this investigation still takes too long, then you should somehow separate or mark these tests distinctly from other tests, so that other people can know that it's under investigation and understand that the failure is probably not a regression. This is important in order to preserve the perceived reliability of the test automation. Not communicating these cases clearly leaves the impression that the entire test suite is unreliable.

However, you don't want to stop these tests from running regularly, as you want to collect as much data about their failures, in order to be able to investigate it properly. On the contrary, you want to run these tests even more often!

If a test fails on a flickering issue 10% of the time, it is very difficult to investigate. Somewhat counterintuitively, we should prefer that tests will fail more often, as this way it is easier to reproduce and investigate. In order to increase the probability for encountering the failure, we can run the test in a loop, let's say 50 times. This increases the chances that the test will fail to above 99%! (=100%–90%^{50}), which practically means that we can reproduce the failure any time. Then we can start adding diagnostic information, and play the lion in the desert game until we pinpoint the problem.

One particular useful technique to narrow down the scope of the problem, and also to make the investigation process more efficient, is to create a separate test that performs the suspicious operation in a loop and gradually trying to remove code or operations that seem to not be related to the problem, or narrowing the loop only to the suspicious part, performing all the preconditions only once. This shortens the time it takes to run the looping test. If at some point the problem cease to occur, then you know that the last operation that you removed from the loop *is* related to the issue. If this operation is not atomic (can be broken into smaller operations), then you should add it back, and narrow down the loop to perform only some of the suspicious suboperations. If the operation cannot be broken down any further, then you can come to the relevant developer with the narrowed-down loop that reproduces the problem with high probability, and let him continue the investigation from there.

Summary

In order to keep the test automation reliable and trustworthy, it's highly important to investigate each problem thoroughly and find the root cause. We also want to ensure that the investigation is fast and precise, so we can react quickly. For that, we should add any information to the test result that can help us investigate and understand what happened. This can come in the form of clear error messages, logs, screenshots, and more.

Some cases are more challenging to investigate, but a systematic approach of eliminating possible factors, as opposed to randomly guessing and trying things without aiming for clear conclusions, can help investigate the root cause of these cases too. Even flickering tests, which most people feel puzzled by, can be systematically investigated by narrowing down the problem domain and looping through it to significantly increase the probability of reproducing it.

CHAPTER 14

Adding More Tests

In Chapters 10 to 12 we created the first test and its supporting infrastructure. Now it's time to add more tests while enhancing the infrastructure that supports these tests to make it more maintainable. In addition, we'll support running the tests by multiple developers simultaneously and support cross-browser testing.

Writing the Next Tests

We'll add more tests very similarly to the way we wrote the first test:

- Plan the test as a claim and an experiment that proves or refutes it.

- Translate the experiment steps into classes and methods, and make the code compile, even though the methods are not really implemented yet (they just throw NotImplementedException).

- Run the test, and implement the first method that throws NotImplementedException.

- Repeat the last step until the test passes.

There's one difference between the first test and the next ones though: While in the first test none of the classes and methods existed, in the next ones, some of them may already exist. In fact, there can be three cases for each step of the test:

1. The class and method already exist and can be used as is.

2. The class or method does not exist. We need to create it exactly as we did in the first test.

3. A similar class and method exists, but it's not exactly what we need in the new test. Most commonly, we need to provide additional or different arguments to the method.

309

© Arnon Axelrod 2018
A. Axelrod, *Complete Guide to Test Automation*, https://doi.org/10.1007/978-1-4842-3832-5_14

The last case is where things become more interesting. We have few alternatives to handle this case:

1. Create a new method (usually an overload, that is, a method with the same name but with different parameters) and duplicate its code.

2. Modify the original method to accept more parameters. In languages that do not support optional arguments, it means adding more arguments to the calls in existing tests.

3. Create an overload with the new parameters, but remove the duplication either by calling the overload with the additional parameters from the overload with the fewer ones, providing defaults for the additional parameters, or by extracting the common code to a private method or base class, which both of the public overloads call.

4. Refactor the method to accept a builder object, in which you can specify values for any parameter.

Clearly, the first option is not ideal for maintainability. You can do it only if you commit to removing the duplication after you completed the test.

The second option is also not advisable for two reasons:

1. If in the first test we didn't think we should specify a value, then it's probably not really relevant for proving the claim of the test. Adding this argument makes the test more cluttered with "noise" and less readable and distracts the reader of the code from the essence of the test. In the book *Clean Code*,[1] Robert C. Martin (AKA Uncle Bob) claims that almost no method should have more than one or two parameters. While he doesn't talk about tests in this context, but about any calling method in general, his reasoning for that is pretty much the same.

---

[1]Robert C. Martin, *Clean Code: A Handbook of Agile Software Craftsmanship* (New Jersey, United States: Prentice Hall, 2008), p. 40.

2. You can claim that the first reason is void if you're using optional arguments, as you can pass only the ones that you're interested in. However, from the side of the method itself, having many parameters implies that the method is probably long and complicated, and it has many `if` statements and in general is difficult to maintain. Depending on the language, usually optional arguments also have other limitations. In addition, often some parameters make no sense in combination with others, or to the contrary, must be specified with others. Having all of them as a flat list of optional parameters contradicts the Poka-Yoke (prevent mistakes) principle, described in Appendix D.

Therefore, I suggest using the second option with an optional parameter, only if you don't see a need for more than two arguments ever. To avoid the limitations of optional arguments, or to support different data types for the arguments, the third3 option (overloads) is better, but still, only if you don't need more than two arguments, or rarely three. Otherwise, I prefer the fourth option of using the builder pattern. This is especially relevant for methods that create business entities. Most entities that you can create in a business application have many parameters, but typically only one or two are important for each particular test. All the rest should either be left empty if they're not mandatory, or use some default or random value if they are mandatory. Random values should generally be used only if the value should be unique. The data builder pattern described in Chapter 12 makes it possible to create an object to which you can assign all of the arguments, and it builds the entity through a composition of methods rather than one big method that has to take all the parameters into account. This makes it easier to maintain.

Planning the Next Tests

For the first test my advice was to find the scenario that demonstrates the value of the system. This also helped us model and build the major blocks of the infrastructure. In general, as described in Chapter 4, choosing the next suite of tests to automate depends on their value and on risk analysis at any given point in time. But just after implementing the first test, when we need to choose the next few tests among all of the tests that have similar business value, I prefer to cover tests that will guide me to enrich the infrastructure and make developing additional tests more easily. However, there's a trade-off: on one hand, if we add tests for a feature with a very small overlap with the previous ones, it will force us to expand the model and build more infrastructure to support this test. On the other hand, if we add tests that exercise more or less the same path as the first one, but with slight changes, we'll probably have to make small adjustments to the model that we already created. When changing the model to support the new tests and refactoring to remove duplication, we should end up with better abstractions and more robust model and infrastructure.

There's no right answer to this trade-off, and usually it's better to implement few tests of each kind. Note that if you're going all the way with the first approach and add tests for a completely different feature (or even a completely different system), you may need to build a completely different infrastructure. There's nothing wrong with that, but it's usually preferable to stay more focused on building the infrastructure for one project before proceeding to another one.

For our tutorial, the next test I choose to add is a test that verifies the ability to filter the discussions by categories. Additional tests that I also considered as appropriate for the first few include testing the badges, which is a differentiator feature for this application, and the votes feature. However, implementing these tests is beyond the scope of this tutorial. Note that all of these tests introduce new concepts from one hand but also make use of existing functionality that we already created in the first test.

After covering the main flows of each feature, you can start to cover specific features more deeply. In this case, most of the tests will be more similar to one another with only small changes between them.

Adding the Test: Discussions Can Be Filtered by Category

In order to test this functionality, we need to have more than one category. We also don't want to use the default "Example Category" because it will be difficult to define what we expect to see in it, as it will be used by all tests that are not concerned with a specific category. Therefore, we'll create two new unique categories, just for this test. Then we'll create a discussion, assign it to one of these categories, and verify that we only see the discussion in that category and not in the other one, which should be empty. Listing 14-1 contains the textual plan for the test.

Listing 14-1. Discussions can be filtered by category

```
Discussions can be filtered by category
=======================================
Create 2 new categories: A and B
```

```
Create a new discussion "discussion1" and assign it to category A
List discussions in category A
Verify that "discussion1" appears in the list
List discussions in category B
Verify that the list is empty
```

As we did for the first test, now we have to define the contexts for each step in order to help us create an object-oriented model of the application in code. Listing 14-2 shows the contexts that we'll use to perform each step.

Listing 14-2. Discussions can be filtered by category – with contexts

```
Discussions can be filtered by category
========================================
Create 2 new categories: A and B // MVCForum.AdminConsole
Create a new discussion "discussion1" and assign it to category A
// a logged-in user
List discussions in category A // MVCForum.Categories
Verify that "discussion1" appears in the list // CategoryView.Discussions
List discussions in category B // MVCForum.Categories
Verify that the list is empty // CategoryView.Discussions
```

Notes:

- In the first line we create two categories. However, in the code it makes more sense to map it to two lines.

- When we create the categories we'll automatically add Create Topic permissions to them in order to make them usable. This is an implementation detail that is mandatory in order for the test to succeed, but still it's not relevant for the essence of the test.

- The AdminConsole property will automatically log us in as "admin" and navigate to the Admin console. Note that we already have this functionality in the TestInitialize method, broken into smaller steps, so we should refactor the existing code to remove this duplication and reuse the functionality. In addition, we'll rename the AdminPage class we created previously to AdminConsole, to better describe its essence, as it's not a mere single page.

- As in the first test, we won't actually use hard-coded strings like "discussion1," but rather create unique strings. We use "discussion1" in the text just to make it clear that we refer to the same discussion at all the relevant places. In the code we have variable names for that instead.

- In the second line, we wrote "a logged-in user" without preceding it with a Login step. This is because in this test, the question which user we're using is not very interesting, as long as it's a registered member. In the code we'll probably still call RegisterNewUserAndLoging() to create that user. Note that because this application is based on collaborations between users, I don't see fit to define a "default user" for the tests, which is something that I do in many other applications that are less collaboration-centric. We may still want to define such "default user" in the future if we'll have many tests that are agnostic to the user, but we first have to see a clear need for that.

- There's one important entity that hides "between the lines," but we'll definitely need it in the code. This is the **Category** entity of course. We'll instantiate this object when we create the category in the first step and pass it as an argument both when we create the discussion and to a Select method on the MVCForum.Categories property. The object itself will hold only the name of the category, but it's still worth creating a class for, for the sake of strong-typing and Poka-Yoke.

Listing 14-3 shows the skeleton of the new test method that we've added to SanityTests.cs. This is of course not compilable yet.

Listing 14-3. DiscussionsCanBeFilteredByCategory test method skeleton

```
[TestMethod]
public void DiscussionsCanBeFilteredByCategory()
{
    var adminConsole = MVCForum.AdminConsole;
    var categoryA = adminConsole.CreateCategory();
    var categoryB = adminConsole.CreateCategory();

    var user = MVCForum.RegisterNewUserAndLogin();
```

```
    var discussion = user.CreateDiscussion(DiscussionWith.
    Category(categoryA));

    var categoryView = MVCForum.Categories.Select(categoryA);
    Assert.AreEqual(1, categoryView.Discussions.Count,
    $"1 discussion is expected in categoryA ({categoryA.Name})");
    Assert.AreEqual(discussion, categoryView.Discussions.
    Single(), $"The single discussion in categoryA ({categoryA.
    Name}) is expected to be the same category that we've created
    ('{discussion.Title}");

    categoryView = MVCForum.Categories.Select(categoryB);
    Assert.AreEqual(0, categoryView.Discussions.Count,
    $"No discussions expected in categoryB ({categoryB.Name}");
}
```

As you can see, some of the classes and methods we already have, some are completely new, and some others exist but will require some modifications, most notably CreateDiscussion should be changed to support the Category parameter that is added through the builder.

Note   CategoryView.Discussions would be a collection of DiscussionHeader objects, just like we have in the LatestDiscussions list. However, this means that in the second Assert statement, we compare a Discussion object to a DiscussionHeader object. In order to make it work, I intend to extract a common base class from these two classes that will hold only the title of the discussion (which is its unique identifier) and implement Equals such that it compares the title's own title with the other object's title, regardless of the concrete type. Comparing a unique identifier of an entity is sufficient for the general use, and it makes the code cleaner.

From here you know the drill: create new classes and methods until the code compiles. Then run the test and fix any NotImplementedException, until the test passes.

Here's the list of classes, methods, and properties that we have to add in order to make the code compile:

- `public AdminConsole MVCForum.AdminConsole { get; }`

Note   We renamed `AdminPage` to `AdminConsole`, so this is in fact an existing class

---

- `public Category AdminConsole.CreateCategory()`
- `public DiscussionBuilder Discussion.Category(Category category)`
- `public CategoriesList MVCForum.Categories { get; }`
- `public class CategoriesList`
  - `public CategoryView Select(Category category)`
- `public class CategoryView`
  - `public IReadOnlyCollection<DiscussionHeader> Discussions`

Note   We still didn't extract the common base class out of `Discussion` and `DiscussionHeader`. We'll do it when we'll need to make the `Assert` succeed.

Remove Duplication Between MVCForum.AdminConsole and AddCreateTopicPermissionToStandardMembers

When we run the test after we've made it compile, the first `NotImplementedException` that we encounter is `MVCForum.AdminConsole`. As mentioned before, we already have the logic of logging in as admin and navigating to the Admin console in `AddCreateTopicPermissionToStandardMembers` method, which is called from `TestInitialize`. Listing 14-4 shows the current implementation of `AddCreateTopicPermissionToStandardMembers`. The bold lines are those that we want to extract to the `MVCForum.AdminConsole` property.

> **Note**   While I added the visual logger to the project in the previous chapter, I also extracted the code that existed in `TestInitialize` to the `AddCreateTopicPermissionToStandardMembers` method in order to separate it from the initialization of the logger itself.

Listing 14-4. AddCreateTopicPermissionToStandardMembers

```
private void AddCreateTopicPermissionToStandardMembers()
{
    using (Logger.StartSection(
    "Adding 'Create Topic' permission to Standard members"))
    {
        var adminPassword = GetAdminPassword();
        var adminUser = MVCForum.LoginAsAdmin(adminPassword);
        var adminConsole = adminUser.GoToAdminConsole();
        var permissions = adminConsole.GetPermissionsFor(
        TestDefaults.StandardMembers);
        permissions.AddToCategory(TestDefaults.ExampleCategory,
        PermissionTypes.CreateTopics);
        adminUser.Logout();
    }
}
```

Trying to extract the accented lines into their own method reveals that we need this method to return two values: the adminConsole, which is obvious; but also the adminUser, which we use at the end of the method to call Logout() on. Returning two values from a method is not a good practice. But the harder question that it raises, is when do we log out the administrator in the new test?

Looking at our test code again, obviously we must log out the administrator before RegisterNewUserAndLogin! In order to avoid adding too much noise to the test code, with all of these login and logout operations, we can change the AdminConsole property to an OpenAdminConsole method, make the AdminConsole class implement IDisposable, and use a using clause around the creation of the categories, so that the administrator will automatically log out when the scope of the using clause ends. It's still a bit noisier than it was, but it's a lesser evil. Listing 14-5 shows the changes to the test method.

Listing 14-5. DiscussionsCanBeFilteredByCategory with automatic admin logout

```
[TestMethod]
public void DiscussionsCanBeFilteredByCategory()
{
    Category categoryA, categoryB;
    using (var adminConsole = MVCForum.OpenAdminConsole())
    {
        categoryA = adminConsole.CreateCategory();
        categoryB = adminConsole.CreateCategory();
    }

    var user = MVCForum.RegisterNewUserAndLogin();
    ...
}
```

After these changes, let's run the test again. We'll see that it fails on
OpenAdminConsole as expected. So now we need to implement it, but we
already saw that we can't just perform an **Extract Method** refactoring on
these lines. So, let's start by duplicating these lines from SanityTests.
AddCreateTopicPermissionToStandardMembers to MVCForumClient.OpenAdminConsole,
and later we'll refactor to remove the duplication.

However, if we copy these lines as is, it doesn't work either. GetAdminPassword
and MVCForum are members of SanityTests and not of MVCForumClient. Regarding
MVCForum, that's a piece of cake to solve, as we just need to use the current instance
(this) instead. Regarding GetAdminPassword, we have to move this method ourselves.
If you're using Resharper, when your cursor is on the GetAdminPassword method name,
press **Ctrl+Shift+R** to open the **Refactor this** context menu, and select **Move Instance
Method**. In the dialog select the MVCForum property, click **Next** twice (the second time
you approve to change the access modifier of the method from private to public,
so it remains accessible to AddCreateTopicPermissionToStandardMembers. After we
remove the duplication, we'll set it back to private inside MVCForumClient), and voila!
The method has moved to MVCForumClient. If you don't use Resharper, then you can
manually cut and paste the code and make the necessary changes; there are not that
much. Listing 14-6 shows OpenAdminConsole as it is now.

Listing 14-6. First implementation of MVCForumClient.OpenAdminConsole

```
public AdminConsole OpenAdminConsole()
{
    var adminPassword = GetAdminPassword();
    var adminUser = LoginAsAdmin(adminPassword);
    var adminConsole = adminUser.GoToAdminConsole();

    return adminConsole;
}
```

The next time we run the test we fail on `AdminConsole.Dispose`. This is where we need to log out the administrator. However, `AdminConsole` doesn't have a reference to the logged-in administrator, so we need to add it in the constructor. Fortunately, the constructor of `AdminConsole` is only called from the `LoggedInAdmin` class, so we can just pass "`this`" as an argument. Listing 14-7 shows `AdminConsole`'s constructor and the `Dispose` method.

Listing 14-7. AdminConsole's constructor and Dispose

```
public AdminConsole(
IWebDriver webDriver, LoggedInAdmin loggedInAdmin)
{
    _webDriver = webDriver;
    _loggedInAdmin = loggedInAdmin;
}

public void Dispose()
{
    _loggedInAdmin.Logout();
}
```

If we run again we'll fail on the `AdminConsole.CreateCategory` method, which means that `OpenAdminConsole` and its `Dispose` counterpart work. But now we have duplicate code that we must eliminate! Fortunately, now it's pretty easy and it also simplifies `AddCreateTopicPermissionToStandardMembers`. Listing 14-8 shows `AddCreateTopicPermissionToStandardMembers` after removing the duplication.

Listing 14-8. AddCreateTopicPermissionToStandardMembers after removing the duplication

```
private void AddCreateTopicPermissionToStandardMembers()
{
    using (Logger.StartSection(
    "Adding 'Create Topic' permission to Standard members"))
    {
        using (var adminConsole = MVCForum.OpenAdminConsole())
        {
            var permissions = adminConsole.GetPermissionsFor(
            TestDefaults.StandardMembers);
            permissions.AddToCategory(TestDefaults.ExampleCategory,
            PermissionTypes.CreateTopics);
        }
    }
}
```

Now we can also change GetAdminPassword back to private, as we use it only from within OpenAdminConsole, which is on the same class (MVCForumClient).

There's one more thing that bothers me regarding OpenAdminConsole: it looks very redundant that we look for the **Read Me** topic in order to get the administrator's password, each time we want to open the **Admin** console. If we did it once, we can store the password for the next times. We can achieve this by promoting the local adminPassword variable to a field and changing it from string to Lazy<string>,[2] specifying GetAdminPassword as the value factory. Listing 14-9 shows the relevant changes in MVCForumClient.

Listing 14-9. Perform GetAdminPassword only once

private readonly Lazy<string> _adminPassword;

```
public MVCForumClient(TestDefaults testDefaults)
{
```

---

[2]The Lazy<T> class in .Net is a generic class that can wrap any object that we want to initialize only on its first use. In its constructor it gets a delegate for a factory method, which creates the object on the first time it's being used.

```
    _adminPassword = new Lazy<string>(GetAdminPassword);

    ...

}

public AdminConsole OpenAdminConsole()
{
    var adminUser = LoginAsAdmin(_adminPassword.Value);
    var adminConsole = adminUser.GoToAdminConsole();

    return adminConsole;
}
```

Reusing Existing Code

Now we can proceed to implement AdminConsole.CreateCategory using our usual top-down process. Similar to when we implement the second test, also when we implement a new method we have the three possible cases for the methods that it calls: we may need to call a method that already exists; we may need to call a method that don't yet exist whatsoever, and we need to create it; or we have a similar method but not exactly what we need, in which case we need to modify existing code to meet our new needs and remove duplication. Listing 14-10 shows how AdminConsole.CreateCategory uses the GetPermissionsFor and AddToCategory methods that we already implemented for the previous test.

Listing 14-10. AdminConsole.CreateCategory uses existing methods

```
public Category CreateCategory()
{
    var categoryName = Guid.NewGuid().ToString();

    var categoriesPage = OpenCategoriesPage();
    var category = categoriesPage.Create(categoryName);

    GetPermissionsFor(_testDefaults.StandardMembers)
    .AddToCategory(category, PermissionTypes.CreateTopics);
    return category;
}
```

Trading Off Duplications

When we reach the failure on CategoryView.Discussions and try to implement it, we realize that it's very similar to the LatestDiscussions class that we already have. It's true that in LatestDiscussions we only needed the top and bottom elements, while in CategoryView we need to return the list of elements, but in essence they're very similar. Both of them represent lists of discussion headers, and in fact, the structure of their contained DOM elements is nearly identical. So, let's try to remove this duplication. Listing 14-11 shows the LatestDiscussions class as it is now.

Listing 14-11. Original LastestDiscussions class

```
public class LatestDiscussions
{
    private readonly IWebDriver _webDriver;

    public LatestDiscussions(IWebDriver webDriver)
    {
        _webDriver = webDriver;
    }

    public DiscussionHeader Top
    {
        get
        {
            var topicRows = GetAllTopicRows();
            return new DiscussionHeader(topicRows.First(), _webDriver);
        }
    }

    public DiscussionHeader Bottom
    {
        get
        {
            var topicRows = GetAllTopicRows();
            return new DiscussionHeader(topicRows.Last(), _webDriver);
        }
    }
```

```
private ReadOnlyCollection<IWebElement> GetAllTopicRows()
{
    Activate();
    var topicRows = _webDriver.FindElements(By.ClassName("topicrow"));
    return topicRows;
}

private void Activate()
{
    var latestMenuItem = _webDriver.FindElement(By.CssSelector(
    ".sub-nav-container .auto-latest"));
    latestMenuItem.Click();
}
}
```

It looks like GetAllTopicRows is something that we can reuse for CategoryView. Basically, we could move it to a common base class and make it protected to enable this reuse. However, while this method is pretty close to what we need, it's not exactly so. There are two issues with the way it's currently implemented:

1.   It returns a list of IWebElement, and we need to wrap it with a DiscussionHeader object. In fact, there's already a duplication between Top and Bottom in that regard, as they both instantiate DiscussionHeader objects to wrap elements returned from GetAllTopicRows

2.   It calls Activate whenever it's being called, to ensure that we're still in the **Latest** tab.

While we can resolve the first issue quite easily, the second one seems to block us from sharing this method between the classes. The Activate method was created to ensure that whenever we try to access any of the elements in LatestDiscussions, we first ensure that this is the active view. However, this is not something that we need in CategoryView, as opening a category is always a proactive action that must be explicitly performed before accessing its discussions.

One way to tackle this difference is to make `Activate` virtual and implement it only in `LatestDiscussions`, while leaving it empty in `CategoryView`. However, this doesn't look right because it's not that we never have to activate the category view, but it just doesn't seem to be the responsibility of the `CategoryView` class itself to do it automatically every time.

So, what we can do is to take the call to Activate out of `GetAllTopics` and put in the beginning of the `Top` and `Bottom` properties. This looks more logical, even though now we duplicated the call `GetAllTopics` in both of these methods. However, now we can extract `GetAllTopics` to a base class and reuse it between the `LatestDiscussions` and the `CategoryView` classes, removing the duplication between these classes. So, we add a bit of duplication in one place to remove a bigger duplication in another.

Looking at it a bit deeper and examining the usages of `Top` and `Bottom`, we can conclude that it's safe to ensure that we're in the right tab only in the constructor of `LatestDiscussions` instead of at each and every relevant member, so we can remove this duplication eventually too.

Eventually, let's rename `GetAllTopicRows` to `GetAllDiscussionHeaders` as it no longer returns just the row elements, but rather full `DiscussionHeader` objects. Listing 14-12 shows the `LatestDiscussions` class after making the above changes, and before extracting `GetAllDiscussionHeaders` to a common base class.

Listing 14-12. LatestDiscussions.GetAllDiscussionHeaders ready to be extracted to a common base class

```
public class LatestDiscussions
{
    private readonly IWebDriver _webDriver;

    public LatestDiscussions(IWebDriver webDriver)
    {
        _webDriver = webDriver;
        Activate();
    }

    public DiscussionHeader Top
    {
        get { return GetAllDiscussionHeaders().First(); }
    }
```

```
public DiscussionHeader Bottom
{
    get { return GetAllDiscussionHeaders().Last(); }
}

private IReadOnlyCollection<DiscussionHeader> GetAllDiscussionHeaders()
{
    var topicRows = _webDriver.FindElements(By.ClassName("topicrow"));
    return topicRows.Select(row =>
    new DiscussionHeader(row, _webDriver)).ToList();
}

private void Activate()
{
    var latestMenuItem = _webDriver.FindElement(By.CssSelector(
    ".sub-nav-container .auto-latest"));
    latestMenuItem.Click();
}
}
```

After this refactoring it's important to run also the first test in order to make sure that we didn't break it with our changes.

Now we need to extract the GetAllDiscussionHeaders method to a common base class. If you're using Resharper you can do it automatically by standing on the method name, pressing **Ctrl+Shift+R**, and choosinh **Extract Superclass**. If you don't, you'll have to create the base class and move the method manually. We also need to move the _webDriver member to the base class and make it protected so it can be accessed both from the base class and from the derived classes. We'll call the new base class DiscussionsList and make CategoriesView derive from it. Listing 14-13 shows the implementation of CategoriesView deriving from the new DiscussionsList class.

Listing 14-13. CategoriesView implemented by deriving from DiscussionsList

```
public class CategoryView : DiscussionsList
{
    public CategoryView(IWebDriver webDriver)
```

```
        : base(webDriver)
    {
    }

    public IReadOnlyCollection<DiscussionHeader> Discussions
    {
        get { return GetAllDiscussionHeaders(); }
    }
}
```

Implementing Equals

The next failure we see looks a bit daunting at first: **Test method MVCForumAutomation.SanityTests.DiscussionsCanBeFilteredByCategory threw exception: OpenQA.Selenium.StaleElementReferenceException: stale element reference: element is not attached to the page document.** StaleElementReferenceException means that an element that we already found is no longer available in the DOM. However, if we look at the test code and the stack-trace, it becomes clear: we try to read the discussion title from a Discussion object, which represents an open discussion page, while we're currently viewing the list of discussions in the categories. While we can see the title of the discussions from the list, the way to extract this value from the DOM is different. Anyway, going back to the note from the beginning of the chapter regarding CategoryView.Discussions, we intended to move the Title property to a common base class and implement Equals on it. This should solve our problem as the Title property should also be initialized in the constructor and stored in memory instead of being read from the screen each time, which will prevent the StaleElementReferenceException that we get.

Extracting the base class with the Title property and implementing the Equals method also makes the test pass! Listing 14-14 shows the new base class DiscussionIdentifier with its Equals implementation.

Listing 14-14. DiscussionIdentifier.Equals

```
public class DiscussionIdentifier
{
    public DiscussionIdentifier(string title)
    {
```

```csharp
        Title = title;
    }

    public string Title { get; }

    public override bool Equals(object obj)
    {
        if (obj == null)
            return false;
        var other = obj as DiscussionIdentifier;
        return other != null && Equals(other);
    }

    protected bool Equals(DiscussionIdentifier other)
    {
        return string.Equals(Title, other.Title);
    }

    public override int GetHashCode()
    {
        return Title.GetHashCode();
    }
}
```

Now that this test passes, we should verify that the first test still passes too. Fortunately, it does.

Summary for Adding the Second Test

During the implementation of the second test, we've created more classes and methods but also used some existing ones. The most challenging situations were when we had a similar implementation in a different place and had to refactor to remove the duplication. In a few of the cases, we ended up creating class hierarchies to achieve this. As you can see, writing well-maintainable automation is not a simple programming task that every beginner can easily do. On the contrary, it requires advanced programming and design skills.

Making Additional Improvements

After we've completed the test, it's a good time to improve things that were not directly related to making the test pass.

Creating More Comprehensible Identifiers

For example, one thing that annoyed me when I developed the last test, but wasn't important enough to stop and change, is that it was difficult to distinguish between identifiers of different types of entities, because we use GUIDs for all of them. This especially annoys me when reading the log or error messages. If we'll just add a prefix with the entity type to each GUID, it will make our life much easier.

As always, instead of duplicating this logic, let's create a special class and method to do that. Let's name them UniqueIdetifier and For respectively, so when we use it, it will read:

```
var discussionId = UniqueIdentifier.For("Discussion");
```

Now we only need to find all references of Guid.NewGuid and replace them with this method call. Listing 14-15 shows the UniqueIdentifier class.

Listing 14-15. UniqueIdentifier

```
public static class UniqueIdentifier
{
    public static string For(string entityType)
    {
        return $"{entityType}-{Guid.NewGuid()}";
    }
}
```

Arrange the Code in Folders

If you look at the Solution Explorer, you'll see that all of the classes that we've created were created as one long list of 28 code files, and this is after implementing only 2 tests... This makes finding and understanding the code base for newcomers a daunting task. If you know the name of a class or even part of it, it's not a big problem to find it (you can use the **Search** box in the **Solution Explorer** pane, or press **Ctrl+T** in Resharper to quickly find any symbol). However, if you don't know exactly what class to look for, or just want to understand the high-level structure of the code, it's very difficult to do that when all the files are in a one long, flat list.

If we were trying to do this in advance, we wouldn't know yet which kind of classes we'll need. But now we can look at the classes and try to search for common categories of classes. We can then create a folder for each of these categories and move the relevant classes to that folder. The two most trivial categories are **Tests** and **PageObjects**. Sure, currently we have only one test class, but soon we'll have many. I can also identify a category for **Entities**, such as `Category`, `Role` and `PermissionTypes`, and a fourth one for all of the generic infrastructure code, like the `VisualLogger`, `SeleniumExtensions` and `UniqueIdentifier`. We'll call this folder **Infrastructure**. Note that some classes don't fall nicely into one of these category folders, and that's OK. Either put them in one of them, or even leave them outside at the root. For example, `FormPage` is a base class for any form-based Page Object, so it can either be under the **PageObjects** folder or under the **Infrastructure** folder. `TestDefaults` is also related to Infrastructure, but it's also very specific to MVCForum, so it may be better suited in **Entities**. I'll just leave that one out of any of these folders and keep it directly on the root folder of the project.

Extract a Base Class for Tests

One more improvement along those lines is to extract a common base class for all the tests. In fact, right now it may not seem necessary, as we only have two test methods that reside in a single test class. However, even at this stage we can identify that `SanityTests` has two distinct responsibilities: first, it is a container for test methods; and second, it contains a lot of infrastructure code that is related to MSTest, and mainly deal with the initialization and cleanup of the tests. So that's a good enough reason to extract all of the infrastructure stuff in this class into its own `MVCForumTestBase` class, which `SanityTests` will derive from. Obviously, when we'll have more test classes, they should all derive from `MVCForumTestBase` in order to avoid duplication. In order to maintain a consistent folder structure, we'll put the new class inside the **Infrastructure** folder. In addition, we must decorate the base class with `[TestClass]` too in order for the `[AssemblyInitialize]` and `[TestInitialize]` attributes to take effect. The Git tag **ExtractBaseClass** contains this change.

Supporting Multiple Users and Browsers

Currently the tests run great on our machine, but in order to gain more value out of them, we must allow other developers to run them too, before they check in their changes. Allowing others to run the test may also reveal some hidden assumptions that are true only for our machine. We need to fix those. Soon, we'll also want to run the tests in a CI or nightly build, which also runs the tests on another machine (see Chapter 15 for more details about CI). If we solve the problem for other users, adding the tests to the build will be much easier.

In fact, we didn't use any hard-coded paths, so it shouldn't be too hard to support other environment. However, when we try to run it on another's developer's machine we see that his web server doesn't use port 8080 as ours do, but rather 8090. Other developers may use https instead of http, with a certificate issued to a specific domain name, which prevents users from using localhost or an IP address as the hostname. We can support all of these scenarios if we extract the entire URL to a configuration file.

Tips for Using Test Configuration Files

As you see, configuration files are often necessary in order to allow different users of the automation (developers) to run the tests, or in order to support different environments. However, it's important to keep these configuration files short and simple; otherwise using them becomes its own mess. Here are some tips for using these configuration files:

- Because we want the tests to be consistent and repeatable as possible, we want to include as little detail as we can that may be different between environments. Therefore, avoid adding any values in there except of those that you expect that people will really need to change. Typically, a URL, path to an executable, etc., are the only really important things. Sometimes a username and password for the default user are also convenient if the system doesn't start from barebones on every run. However, having Ids of many entities that different tests use is not a best use of a configuration file. Isolation techniques that create the data are usually better and save the need to configure many entities in an external file.

- Keep in mind that these files are meant to be used by people, and not only by the software. This means that it should be easy to use and configure as possible, so whenever someone wants to run the tests on a new machine or environment, he should be able to do it as easily as possible. In addition to having as few as needed entries, creating an XSD (XML Schema Definition) file that describe the structure of the configuration file helps a lot in composing and editing these files. Most modern IDEs (including Visual Studio and Eclipse) provide auto-completion of elements in an XML file that has an XSD associated with it. An XSD file can also be used to add annotations and restrict the user from providing wrong values.

- Another thing that makes configuration easier is to have default values for most keys. Having default values saves the effort of thinking and deciding what to configure for anything that is not obvious. However, as the developer who chooses the default values, you're responsible for coming up with default values that are actually the correct ones for most of the users. Default values are especially important if you want to introduce a new configuration key after people already have existing configuration files. In this case, the default value should usually cause the system to behave in the same manner that it did before introducing the new key. Adding a key without a default value in this situation forces everyone to go and add the configuration key with the correct value.

- If you can't find a proper default value and you believe that every user should explicitly set this value, then in the code that reads this value, you should first check if it exists or not, and if it doesn't, provide a clear message specifying exactly which key to add and how to choose its value. This way, on the first time that users run the tests after you've added the mandatory key you inform them exactly what they need to do in order to proceed successfully. The same rule applies for the first time you introduce the existence of the configuration file as a whole: first, check if the file exists; and if it doesn't, provide a clear message describing how to create it. A good practice is to provide a template or an example file and instruct the user how to modify it for his needs.

- Finally, as the content of the configuration files should be different
  for every developer, it shouldn't be put in source control. As
  suggested above, you can put a template or an example file and clear
  instructions on how to create it, so the first time a user runs the test
  he's instructed how to create the file. Note that for build environments,
  you should make sure to copy the file with the correct value from a
  predefined location as part of the build process, or somehow create it
  in another manner, before running the tests. If you're using Git, you
  should add this file to the **.gitignore** file (most other source control
  systems have similar ways to ignore changes in a file).

To simplify reading and parsing the XML from the configuration file, I used the
TestAutomationEssentails.Common library. For more information about the Test
Automation Essentials libraries, see Appendix B.

Supporting Multiple Browsers

Occasionally websites behave somewhat different on different browsers, so it's important
to run the tests on multiple browsers. Selenium allows us to run the same tests on
multiple browsers, with a very small change to our code base.

In the central build, usually we'll want to run the tests on all of the browsers in
parallel. However, even before we have a build, we'll benefit if we could manually
choose to run the tests on a particular browser, by specifying the browser type in the
configuration file. When we create the build, we'll simply use the same capability and
invoke the tests several times, using different configuration files, once for each browser.

In order to tell the tests which browser to use, we'll use the same configuration file
that we've created in the previous step. We'll add a new key `BrowserType`, to this file
(and the corresponding XSD file) that tells which browser to use. Currently we'll support
Chrome, which is also the default, Firefox and Edge. Listing 14-16 shows the change to
the constructor of `MVCForumClient` and the new `CreateDriver` method that instantiates
the correct implementation of `IWebDriver` according to the configuration file.

Listing 14-16. Instantiating the correct IWebDriver object according to configuration

```
public MVCForumClient(TestDefaults testDefaults, TestEnvironment
environment)
{
    _adminPassword = new Lazy<string>(GetAdminPassword);

    _testDefaults = testDefaults;
    var parentDriver = CreateDriver(environment);
    var eventFiringDriver = new EventFiringWebDriver(parentDriver);
    VisualLogger.RegisterWebDriverEvents(eventFiringDriver);
    _webDriver = eventFiringDriver;
    _webDriver.Url = environment.URL;
}

private static IWebDriver CreateDriver(TestEnvironment environment)
{
    switch (environment.BrowserType)
    {
        case TestEnvironment.BrowserTypes.Edge:
            return new EdgeDriver();

        case TestEnvironment.BrowserTypes.Firefox:
            return new FirefoxDriver();

        case TestEnvironment.BrowserTypes.Chrome:
            return new ChromeDriver();

        default:
            throw new NotSupportedException($"Browser {environment.
            BrowserType} is not supported");
    }
}
```

The first time you run a test after these changes, you'll see an error message: **Assert.Fail failed. Configuration file TestEnvironment.xml not found. In order to create one, copy the file TestEnvironment.Template.xml from the project folder to TestEnvironment.xml (in the same folder), edit it according to the contained instructions and rebuild the project.** If you follow these instructions, the test should pass. If you open TestEnvironment.xml in Visual Studio, you should have auto-completion support that guides you for the valid keys and values that you can specify. Don't forget to rebuild the project or solution in order for these changes to take effect. You can see all of the changes made to support the configuration file in the Git commit tagged **Listing 14-16** and its preceding one.

Note   An alternative solution for cross-browser testing is to use Selenium Grid or one of the test cloud providers like BrowserStack and SouceLabs, which host Selenium Grid on their servers and give you access to a wide range of browsers and operating systems. From the point of view of the code, there's not much difference between the solution I showed above and Selenium Grid, but Selenium Grid also gives you some means to manage the different environments, and the cloud providers also give you a broader range of browsers and operating systems. However, the details for using Selenium Grid are beyond the scope of this book.

Additional Improvement Opportunities

After we have few working tests, we can experiment with additional improvements. Constantly running the tests tells us whether the improvements that we just did didn't break anything. You don't have to implement or even experiment with all of these improvements all at once. You can create a backlog of improvement ideas and interleave them with the development of additional tests. When prioritizing these tasks, especially if you need to report to your manager about your progress, think how much time it will save you in writing, debugging, maintaining, and diagnosing the tests, and how it can affect the reliability of the tests. Don't wait for your manager to tell you to make these improvements – either convince why they're important and how much time it will save, or just do them along the way if they're small enough.

Automatically Re-create the Database

Currently we assume that we're running on a virgin database. As I mentioned before, occasionally I delete and re-create the database in order to ensure this assumption. While doing it only occasionally and manually doesn't take too much time, if other people use the tests and they're not minded to this need, they might work against a dirty database, which at some point may cause their tests to fail without a clear reason, eventually hurting the reliability of the automation. In addition, when we integrate the tests in a build process, we'll have to do that anyway. There are few alternatives to tackle this problem, as usual, each with its pro's and con's. I leave it to you to experiment and consider the best approach. Here are a few alternatives that I can think of:

- Write code in [AssemblyInitialize] that automatically re-creates the database. While this only take a couple of seconds, when you're working on a new test or debugging an existing one, rapidly running the test again and again, this initialization time can become disturbing. In addition, in order to re-create the database, you must specify additional parameters, like the name of the database, username, and password for the database, etc., in the TestEnvironment.xml file. While these details exist in the web.config file of the application itself, the test doesn't have access to it directly, so at the minimum, we need to specify the path to the web.config file and parse the connection string from there.

- In order to save the time of re-creating the database on each run while debugging, we can add a new Boolean key RecreateDatabase, in the TestEnvironment.xml file that determines whether to re-create the database in AssemblyInitialize or not.

- Because we normally want to re-create the database only once in a while, adding this Boolean flag to TestEnvironment.xml is not very convenient either, because after we'll set it to true, we'd most likely want to change it back to false before the next run, but we need to remember to do that each time... Instead, we can extract the functionality of re-creating the database to an external program, batch file or script (e.g., PowerShell on Windows or Bash on Linux), and run it whenever we want. In the central build we'll run this script before each run, of course. This script also has to take parameters or a configuration file containing the name and credentials for the database, but you rarely have a reason to change it, and it can be kept separated from the TestEnvironment.xml data.

Cleanup

If we re-create the database at every run or every few runs, we probably don't have a reason to clean up every entity that we create, like category or discussion. However, in other situations where re-creating the database isn't feasible for whatever reason, you might want to clean up these entities in order to avoid "littering" the database with a lot or "junk" data created by the test automation. These cases also usually imply that part of the data in the database was not created by the test automation. For example, legacy systems often rely not only on the schema of the database but also on specific data, but these dependencies are not documented well enough and no one really knows which feature relies on which data. Therefore, re-creating only the schema is not enough but it's also infeasible to create an empty database and only add the minimum necessary data, because we simply don't know what it is. Therefore, in these cases we must use a copy of a real database (typically the existing "test" environment), and it's not feasible to re-create it from scratch.

There are generally two approaches to clean the data that the automation creates, and you can also combine the two if needed, as described in the following topics.

Cleaning All Entities Created by Test Automation in a Batch Process

You can create a batch file or program that cleans up all of the entities that the automation creates and run it on a scheduled basis, or before the test run starts. In order to do that, you must somehow distinguish between entities that the test automation created to other data that it shouldn't touch. If certain types of entities are created only by the test automation, then this is not an issue, but if the database contains entities from the same kind where some of them are created by the automation and some not, then we must distinguish between them somehow to prevent this program from deleting entities that it should not. This can usually be done by adding a known prefix or postfix to the Id or name (e.g., title) of the entity.

If the environment may be used by different automation users simultaneously (including the build process), one important challenge that you should address if you choose this approach, is not to delete entities of tests that are currently running. If you don't address this issue, tests may fail unexpectedly, and it will be very hard to diagnose why. If the entities have a built-in field that contain the time of their creation, you can use it to filter the entities that were created recently and may already be in use, e.g. in the last 24 hours. If there's no such creation time field, then you may add it to the Id or name, though it may be difficult and inefficient to filter it out directly from SQL.

Yet another option, though a bit more complicated, is to create a separate table that the test will write to whenever it creates an entity. This table will contain the Id of the entity and its creation timestamp. Whenever the test creates an entity, it writes the Id and type of the entity along with the timestamp to this table. The batch process can join this table with the actual entity table and easily filter the records that may still be in use.

Cleanup When the Test Finishes

The second option is to create a cleanup mechanism like the one mentioned in Chapter 7 and described in Appendix B, which cleans every entity that the test creates when the test finishes. In this case you don't have to use any special Id or name to distinguish between entities created by the automation and other entities, because each cleanup action deletes only the one specific entity that was created, and of course that you don't have an issue with deleting entities that are in use, because you delete the entities exactly when they're no longer in use.

One drawback of this approach though is that when the test run stops abruptly, the cleanup mechanism won't kick in, and the entities that were created during the last test won't be cleaned. This is particularly relevant when you debug the tests in the IDE and stop the debugger, because stopping the debugger is like killing the test process abruptly, without running any cleanup code. For this reason, it may be worthwhile to combine the two approaches.

Note   You might want to apply this mechanism as an isolation technique between individual tests while applying a more robust isolation technique before each run, like re-creating the entire database. This can be useful especially if you have many tests and limited resources.

Improve Performance

Currently each of the tests that we wrote takes between 30–60 seconds each on my machine. That's not a whole lot for an end-to-end test, but still it's not very fast. Considering that we're going to have hundreds of tests, this starts to become a significant burden. From the test log we can see that a significant portion of the time is taken in the `TestInitialize` method and in creating entities like users and categories. Doing these operations from the UI does not add a lot of value if any to the tests. We can try to perform these operations directly through the database, or through the DAL. Obviously, doing so introduces another dependency for the test automation as we should consider whether it is worth it or not, but it's a viable option. Another thing to take into consideration is whether the Admin UI changes more often than the DAL or database schema. These considerations are described in greater detail in Chapter 6.

Adding More Tests

Going forward, the more tests you add, more of the infrastructure should be in place. If you pay attention to removing duplication, your code should be easy to maintain, and it should be easy to adopt them almost to any feature or implementation change. Typically, after completing the sanity suite (which is usually in the order of few dozen tests), additional tests should be pretty similar to existing ones, with only minor variations. In most cases you'll still need to add a little bit of infrastructure code to support the new cases, but it should be pretty trivial. However, from time to time you'll need to cover an entirely new feature that was not covered by the sanity suite before, and you may need to create new test infrastructure code to support it.

Data-Driven Tests (DDT)

While most new tests still require us to add a bit of infrastructure code, there are cases where the tests differ only in values that are passed to some of the methods, or used as the expected result in the `Assert` statement. In these cases, the entire test method logic is a duplication, and the way to remove this duplication is to use a feature that most testing frameworks support, which is called *Data-Driven Tests* (DDT). Different frameworks implement this feature differently, but the idea is the same: you define the test method once, and you provide the data for the test from an external table. This external table can be in the form of attributes (annotations in Java) above the test method, or an external data source, like a CSV file, Excel file, a database table, etc.). When the test runs, the framework treats it as a series of tests and runs the test method once for each row in the table. This makes each row in the table a separate test case.

For example, suppose that when a new user registers to our SUT's website, he needs to choose his password. When he types the password, the system indicates whether the password is valid or not, and if it is, it indicates its strength. So, in total, for any given password the system indicates whether it is Invalid, Poor, Medium, or Good. In order to test these rules and conditions, we can give a table that contains two columns: the given password and the expected indication. Each row is a test case that verifies the indication for a given password. The test method navigates to the registration form, types in the password, and verifies that the indication is as expected. Listing 14-17 shows an example for this test method using MSTest.

Listing 14-17. Data-driven test example

```
[TestMethod]
[DataRow("", PasswordStrength.Invalid)]
[DataRow("abc", PasswordStrength.Invalid)]
[DataRow("abcdefg1", PasswordStrength.Poor)]
[DataRow("abc123@$#", PasswordStrength.Medium)]
[DataRow("$g62D*&a244dfle*)]", PasswordStrength.Good)]
public void PasswordValidation(string password,
PasswordStrength expectedInidication)
{
    var homePage = WebSite.NavigateToHomepage();
    var registrationPage = homePage.EnterRegistrationPage();
    registrationPage.Username = GenerateRandomUserName();

    registrationPage.Password = password;

    Assert.AreEqual(expectedInidication, registrationPage.
    PasswordStrength);
}
```

Anti-patterns in DDT

While DDT is very useful for removing duplication between similar tests, there are a few common anti-patterns that people use DDT for:

- Some people abuse DDT in the excuse of allowing testers to add more scenarios without writing code. They do that by adding many parameters (columns) to the data and complicate the logic of the test method to support all the possible combinations. The unfortunate outcome of that attempt is poor maintainability of both the test method (the code) and of the data, which inevitably contains a lot of duplicate values in each column and multiple rows.

- Sometimes people use DDT, especially with an external data source by using a large set of real-world data, in order to verify that there are no regressions. While this sounds like a good idea, whenever the logic is changed by design, you would probably need to update the entire dataset. The most convenient and feasible way to update the entire dataset is simply to take the new results and use them to be the new expected results. But the moment you do that, you lose the safety net that you were expecting from this test, as you don't have a way to tell whether the new results are correct or not. Speaking more generally, the reasons this is an anti-pattern are that much of this "test cases" (rows) actually verify the same thing, and that you can't tell what the "claim" is for each row.

- DDT often aims to exercise a single unit (e.g., class, method, component, etc.) with different parameters. Doing that as a system test or at any scope beyond the unit where this logic is implemented makes the test slower, less reliable, harder to run, harder to maintain, etc. In fact, the above example does exactly that and should better be written as a unit test that directly calls the method that evaluates the strength of the password.

Summary

After completing one test, we can add more and more tests in the same manner, though we can now reuse relevant pieces of code that already exist. Some pieces we can use as is, but others we have to refactor in order to reuse without adding more noisy details to the existing tests.

In addition, after we have one or more tests, we can make additional improvement to the infrastructure. We use the tests that we wrote in order to verify that our changes work correctly. We simply run them in any of the conditions that we want to verify and see if they pass correctly. One critical improvement is to support running the tests simultaneously from different machines. This is necessary in order to allow developers to run the tests after every change they make, which provides the most significant value of the test automation.

Finally, don't wait for anyone to tell you to improve the infrastructure of the test automation. Take ownership and do whatever it takes to do the right thing, while communicating the value that it provides.

CHAPTER 15

Continuous Integration

Now that we have at least one test, and we made it possible to run the tests from more than one machine, it's time to integrate the tests into an automatic build process, preferably a continuous integration (CI) build. This build process can be extended to also deploy the built version to the Test or Stage environments (continues delivery). The process may even be configured to deploy directly to production to create a complete continuous deployment pipeline. In this chapter, we'll focus mainly on the continuous integration part as this is where the automated tests usually run.

Note Sometimes CI is considered to run only unit tests, while a continuous delivery process deploys the new version on the Test environment, and then runs the integration and system tests against it. However, continuously deploying every build to the Test environment while testers may be performing manual tests is not always desired. In addition, as discussed in Chapter 7, due to isolation concerns, I advocate using different environments for the manual tests and the automatic ones. If you do that, the distinction between CI and CD becomes somewhat blurred. Therefore, I prefer to refer to any build process that runs automated tests and provides fast feedback to developers as CI and use the term CD (continuous delivery) to refer to the process whose purpose is to ensure that the same version that was tested throughout the CI pipeline (and beyond) is deployed correctly and safely to each environment, and eventually to production. In that sense, the automated tests are mainly part of the CI rather the CD pipeline.

© Arnon Axelrod 2018
A. Axelrod, *Complete Guide to Test Automation*, https://doi.org/10.1007/978-1-4842-3832-5_15

Is It Really Necessary?

Having a source-control system combined with a build server ensures that everyone is working on consistent versions of the source and prevents the infamous saying, "but it works on my machine!" If developers only synchronize (check out) with versions whose builds passed, then everything should work on everyone's machines.

Most development organizations today don't get started developing real production code before having a build server in place. Setting up a build server these days is pretty simple and cheap, so there's no good reason not to do it early on. Only a few years ago it wasn't that easy, and also today there are cases where teams don't yet have a build server, or don't have the knowledge and capacity to establish a proper build process in the near future, possibly due to technical challenges that are specific to their project. In these cases, if the team is small, it is possible to start using and getting value from the test automation even before having a build process in place. It takes a bit of discipline and cooperation, but if you make sure that the tests can run on different machines, then every team member can still run the tests on his own machine before checking in the code. This by itself allows you to harvest most of the value of the test automation, even without having a build server and an automated build process.

However, people make mistakes, and when they're under pressure, they tend to cut corners and can avoid running the tests, even if they're usually disciplined and cooperative. This become more noticeable as the team grows beyond two or three people and also as the length of running the entire test suite rises.

Creating the Test Build Process

The exact technical details of how to create a test build process depend on the technology of the build management system, be it Jenkins, TFS, TeamCity, etc., and on the specific structure of the SUT and the tests and is beyond the scope of this book. However, the idea, which will be explained soon is more or less the same. Thankfully, these days most tools are pretty easy to use, and there are many resources online if you need to learn how to use them in general or how to do something more specific.

All of these technologies allow us to define a process that is composed of concrete actions. These actions typically run in sequence, but some of them can be parallelized as necessary according to the process definition. The build process can also be distributed among several dedicated machines (agents), also according to the process definition.

A typical build process that is designed to run automated tests includes the following steps:

1. Retrieve the most recent sources of the application and of the tests from the source-control system.

2. Compile the application and the test executables.

3. If unit tests exist (that don't need any special prerequisites), they are typically run right after compiling the project.

4. Deploy the compiled application on one or more existing environments. These environments can either be existing ones, like a typical "Test" environment, or be a new environment that is created automatically by the build process. Using containers technology makes this option much more applicable.

5. Prepare the test environment for the test automation. This step depends on the isolation strategy but can include things like deleting old test data and/or creating new data, configuring the application according to the test's needs, setting up simulators, etc.

6. (Optional) deploy the compiled test executables to one or more test execution environments (agents) where they'll run. In simple cases, the tests can run directly from the build agent so there's no need to deploy them to another machine.

7. Run the tests against the deployed environments.

8. Gather the results and generate a report. Depending on the integration between the testing framework technology and the build management system, the report may be integrated and displayed as part of the build outcome, or simply be added as a file to the build outputs. In addition, if one or more tests failed, the build is usually marked as failed. This report can also be sent by email or other means to relevant people.

Scheduling the Test Build Process

If the entire process is in the realm of 15–30 minutes or less (depending on your team's willingness to wait for feedback), and given that the tests are stable, then it's worthwhile keeping it as one consolidated process and running it in a CI mode, which means that the build is triggered automatically upon every check-in. However, if it takes longer or tests are not stable, this can significantly hinder the productivity of the development team. In these cases, it's common to split the build process into two: the first one performs only the first three steps as a CI build process; and another separate build process runs all the rest, which includes the automated tests (excluding unit tests). Below are descriptions of typical options for scheduling the second part. Later in this chapter we'll discuss techniques for stabilizing the test suite and shorten its duration, so it will be more feasible to run everything in the CI process.

Running the Tests on Demand

One approach for scheduling the second part of the process, which is more common when the tests are less reliable and also when the test automation is considered to be owned solely by the QA team, is to run the tests on demand. This "demand" is usually before or in parallel with a manual testing cycle, typically before a release or milestone, but may also be when a quick fix or a risky change needs to be tested more thoroughly. The upside of this approach is that it takes less time for the automation developer to investigate the failing tests, as he needs to do this only once in a while. However, its downside is that due to the exact same reason, stabilizing the tests gets harder and harder. As there can be many changes to the SUT between every two runs, many tests can fail on legit application changes, which can make the investigation of a single run longer and also be less effective.

Nightly Builds

The next approach, which is probably the most common for system tests, is to run the tests every night. In this case the build is scheduled to run automatically at a specific hour every night. Compared to the previous approach, this approach requires that someone, typically an automation developer, will investigate the results every morning, fixing the tests as needed and reporting the relevant bugs to the developers.

Similar to the previous approach, in this approach too, the developers rarely look at the test results themselves, but only at bugs that they report. Please refer back to the topic "Handling Bugs That Are Found by the Automation" in Chapter 5 for a more complete discussion on the approaches for treating these bugs, and their corresponding consequences. Note that with nightly builds, the developers get feedback about their changes about one whole day after they checked in, which is enough to require a significant context switch from new work that they already started. This is in contrast to CI where the feedback comes after a few minutes.

Right After the CI Build

The third approach is to run the tests, still as a separate build, but right after the CI build (which does not run the system tests) has finished successfully. As mentioned before, the idea is that failing tests won't fail the "main" CI build.

In fact, this approach is pretty useless, because on one hand, an automation developer probably won't keep pace with investigating the results; and on the other hand, developers would probably not bother to do that either, because as far as they're concerned, the CI build itself passed. It may only be useful as a transition state before adding the tests into the main CI build. This can help people gain more confidence and visibility while the automation developers and DevOps people, which maintain the build processes, make sure that the process works fluently. Once this build is proven to be stable, there's no reason to keep it separate from the CI build.

Running the Tests as Part of the CI

If we really want to take full advantage of the test automation and the fast feedback loop it can provide, we need to run the tests as part of the CI build itself. From a technical point of view, running the build on every check-in instead of nightly, is only a matter of flipping a switch. However, from a process point of view, we can only do that if the tests are highly reliable and fast enough, otherwise it will either block developers from checking in valid changes or be completely ignored and useless. For this reason, the process of adding the tests to the CI build is something that should be done thoughtfully.

Creating the Automatic Deployment Process

Creating the first part of the CI build, which only compiles and runs unit tests, is usually pretty easy, and most development teams do it without any problem. However, especially if there are no unit tests, it makes a very small difference: it only ensures that developers don't check in code that doesn't compile, but nothing more than that.

If only that first part of the CI build is implemented, deploying the application is probably a manual and error-prone process. Often teams in this situation create nightly builds that only run the tests on an existing, manually deployed environment. The problem in these cases is that it's hard to tell the exact version of the source code that was compiled and used in the deployment. This lack of traceability brings significant challenges when investigating failing tests, most notably the challenge of reliability and trust.

Therefore, it's critical to deploy the application automatically as part of the build process and run the tests on the deployed version. For web applications or services, deploying the application generally means at least copying the executables to an existing environment. For desktop or installed server applications, it usually means running an installation wizard on a VM after reverting it to a clean snapshot, or creating a new one. For web applications and services, containers can be leveraged and used to deploy the application on a new environment each time, instead of updating an existing one. This also ensures better isolation for the tests.

Updating the Database Schema

While ideally we should deploy a completely new and clean environment every time, it's not always feasible, as creating a new instance of the database each time may be complicated and expensive, typically due to tight coupling between the application logic and some data in the database. This is true especially for centralized applications like web applications or internal business critical apps. However, even without creating a new instance of the database, from time to time the schema of the database and even static data has to be changed along with corresponding changes to the application code in order for the application to work correctly.

While deploying a new version of the executables to a Test or Staging environments and to the Production environment is basically the same, deploying database changes to production is much more sensitive, as we can't afford to lose any existing data, and we also want the application to be able to use the existing data without any problems after deploying the new version. But in order to ensure that we can do it safely to production, we should first ensure that we can do it safely in the Test and Staging environments. This means that we should build it to be an integral part of the normal deployment process that we use for the Test environment too. As Martin Fowler says in his blog:[1] *if it hurts, do it more often!*

---

[1]https://martinfowler.com/bliki/FrequencyReducesDifficulty.html

Relational databases are especially challenging to update, as their structure is much stricter. Because this challenge can sometimes be a pretty hard one, often it is left as a manual operation. While not ideal, if the database schema changes much more rarely than the code and you're facing this challenge, don't let it hold you from building the rest of the process. Create the process as if the database schema never changes, and update it manually at the rare occasions when it does. Later on, consider automating this process too.

The exact solutions to this challenge are beyond the scope of this book. *Refactoring Databases: Evolutionary Database Design*[2] by Scott Ambler and Pramod Sadalage is an excellent book that covers this topic and provides great techniques for making changes to the database in small steps and a safe manner. But here are a couple high-level approaches to keep the source code, database schema, and deployed application synchronized:

1. Use SQL change scripts: for every change to the schema and/ or the data, create an SQL script that will make that change. Run these scripts by order as part of the deployment process (first to the test environment and later to production).

2. Use tools that compare databases and create change scripts automatically: Some tools can compare the desired schema with the existing one and create those change scripts automatically. While it is easier, you have to be careful and review the scripts it creates, as it doesn't always know what you intend to do with the data. If needed, you can make the appropriate changes manually.

Make a New Build Process First

If you already have a CI build that is in regular use, but doesn't run tests or run only unit tests, don't touch it just yet. Make all of your experiments with deployment and running the tests in a new, separate build process. Only at the end, when tests are running stably on the new build, either disable the original build and enable the new one to replace it, or if it's simpler, copy the necessary parts from the new build to the existing one.

---

[2]Scott J Ambler, Pramod J. Sadalage, *Refactoring Databases: Evolutionary Database Design* (Menlo Park, CA: Addison-Wesley, 2006).

When you believe that your process sets everything up to create the environment for the tests, try to access the environment manually (e.g., using a browser, remote desktop, or whatever means that is appropriate for the SUT). If you can't access it as planned, go back and fix whatever that needs to be fixed in the build process, and run it again until you can. Most often, the problems are related to configuration files, file system paths, permissions, environment variables, etc.

Adding the Tests to the Build

After you managed to prepare the environment automatically through the build process and you can use it manually, you have to add two build steps:

1. First you need a step to compile the test executables. This step should come at the beginning of the build process, because if the compilation step fails, there's no point in proceeding. If you already have a compilation step for the SUT, it may only be a matter of adding a parameter to compile the tests. Sometimes you don't even need that if your test code is in the same folder in the source-control repository.

2. Then you need a step to execute the tests against the deployed environment.

Note   In case the source files of the test automation reside in a different source-control repository or different location than those of the SUT, and therefore weren't retrieved already, then you should retrieve the sources of the test automation too before compiling them.

Most popular build systems have dedicated plug-ins to run tests written in the most popular testing frameworks. If you're not sure whether your build system supports your testing framework, or just don't know how to integrate them – the web is your friend. Simply search for the name of your build system and the name of your testing framework, and you'll most likely find all the details that you need. If you're using a rare combination of build system and testing framework that don't have a special plug-in, you should be able to run the tests from the command line. Any build system supports executing an external command-line process. Incorporating the test results may be more challenging if there's no dedicated support, but in most cases the results are either written to the console and/or to a file that you can add to the output of the build. Usually testing frameworks also provide exit code that indicates whether all the tests passed successfully or there was a failure or other problem. While this is not enough for understanding what exactly went wrong, it can be used by the build process to determine how (or if) to proceed.

Running the Tests on the Build Server Itself or Remotely

Depending on the type of application, and also on resource utilization, you may run the tests either on the build server itself, or on another dedicated machine. For example, UI automation tests for a desktop application must run on a machine on which the build process installs the desktop application, which is typically not the same machine that runs the build process itself. This means that the machine on which the application is installed should also be configured to run the tests. Consult the build process documentation (or the web...) on how to configure a remote machine to run tests as part of the build process. The same idea applies for applications that require special hardware or software. One common example for such case is that you need a Mac with a connected iOS device to run tests on a physical iOS device. Selenium tests can either run on the same build server, as it only opens a browser that connects to the application, which is deployed somewhere else, or on another build machine.

Experiment with One Test First

If you have many tests and running all of them takes a significant time so far (compared to the overall build process time), first configure the build to run only one test, until you see that it works as expected and stably. While you're testing and stabilizing that build, you'll probably have to run it many times, and the longer the build itself takes, the longer it will take you to stabilize. This test must be one that you already verified to be stable on different machines and environments. As with deploying the application, when integrating the tests, you may also need to deal with issues such as configuration files, file system paths, permissions, environment variables, etc. While you try to make this work, instead of running the entire build process, which includes redeploying the application anew, you can try to run the tests from the command line of the build machine (e.g., using Remote Desktop or Windows, or `ssh` on Linux). In most cases you'll be able to see the exact command that invokes the tests in the logs of the build process. Copy this command to the command line of the build agent, and you may see more clearly what the problem is. You can try to run the same command on your local computer and see the differences. Note though that there may differences in paths and/ or environment variables, both between the actual build execution and when running it from the command line of the build server, and also between running it on the build server and locally on your machine. While bridging these differences can be dull work, usually it involves no special technical challenge. Printing some log messages can help you with that.

Completing the Build Process

Congratulations! You have one test that passes the complete build process cycle! This is really a significant milestone as it proves that the entire process works end to end. Now you have to add the rest of the tests.

If you know that the entire test suite is stable (or there's simply not that many more tests), you may add all of them all at once. Otherwise, especially if you intend to use the build process as a CI build, add only the ones that you know to be stable, and leave the rest to a nightly build or handle their issues locally first before adding them to the build. If the build is not intended to be used as a CI build, you may add all of the tests at once whatsoever, but make sure to start a stabilization process right away, to prevent the failing tests to "rot."

Changing the Development Processes and Culture

Creating a CI process (or even a CI/CD pipeline) as described so far is a technical task. But on its own it doesn't give much value. Its real value comes from incorporating it into the development process and culture. As mentioned in the beginning of the chapter, the process and culture can be changed to take advantage of automated tests even before the automated CI process is ready. While having it makes the change a lot easier, changing business processes and all the more so, changing business culture, is still the real challenge.

Aiming for the "Holy Grail"

If you refer back to the topic "Getting the Most Out of Test Automation" in Chapter 2, you'll recall that the Holy Grail we aim for, is to have a fully automated pipeline, and business processes that prevent bugs from creeping in. In my opinion, this is what we should be aiming for, though it can be a very long journey. It could be that your goal is not there yet and is much more modest, but anyway, every goal that gets reached is only the baseline for the next goal, so it doesn't really matter if your goal is different. The important thing is that you'd have an idea of what are the benefits you can gain from test automation and then aim for that.

What It Takes to Change the Culture

Introducing new business processes is always a big challenge, as naturally most people are reluctant to changes. A cultural change is even much more challenging, as it requires to change people's presumptions, values, and beliefs. However, attempting to change business processes without causing people to *believe* that it will help them, will likely cause more friction and resistance than good and is doomed to fail.

Changing the culture can sound like a huge thing that's beyond the ability of most mere mortals. But in fact, a culture is like the center of gravity of all the personalities of the people in the group. The smaller the group is, the bigger the influence each individual has on the overall culture. Also, a culture, like people personalities, has countless aspects, and each individual has stronger affect and influence on some aspects and weaker ones on other aspects. People that have a significant effect even on one particular aspect, are often considered "leaders" in that area. Most people that have a weaker effect on a subject usually just follow a leader. But different people can be leaders in different aspects or areas and followers in other aspects.

For test automation to be used successfully, it usually takes only one leader. And there's no excuse that this leader won't be you! You don't have to be a manager or a very charismatic person. If you took the time to read this book, it already a sign that you care a lot about getting the most out of test automation, most probably way beyond anybody else in your team, including your manager. You must surely care to learn and broaden your knowledge on this topic much more than them. Continue this way and it won't take long until you become the expert at least among your teammates. Once you're the "go to" person in the subject of test automation, your influence will increase and more and more people will listen to you. It probably won't happen overnight, and it might take a pretty long time until you're able to reach the Holy Grail that you're aiming for.

Even more realistically, you'll probably *never* really reach that Holy Grail. That may sound very disappointing, but the point is to keep striving for it, and gradually influencing other people to get closer and closer to it. Most probably the Holy Grail itself will change and evolve over time, so even if at some point you'll reach your original Holy Grail, by the time you'll reach it you'll be aiming for something new. So be prepared for a long ride but a very satisfactory one!

Convincing and influencing people can be done in many ways, which mostly depend on your strengths and choices. Some people are better convincing while talking to people informally. Others do it better by writing documents or gathering a formal meeting and giving a presentation. But probably the most effective way to convince people is by showing and giving them a concrete value or solving a problem they have. Just like in the Agile methodology (and philosophy), giving value in small chunks is the way to go. This way you see what's working and what's not. You can and should listen to people and understand what bothers them the most and try to solve the next problem accordingly. The key to success here is to communicate the value of each change with your manager and colleagues and also the course of action that you plan to take. In most cases, you should coordinate anything that you plan to do with your manager beforehand. If you show him the potential value and how small the cost is, he probably won't object to the change. However, there are cases where your manager may not see the immediate value, though others will. For example, a QA manager may not see the immediate value that developers can gain from using the test automation. In these cases, you may slowly and quietly try to show the value to few key people who can see it (e.g., developers) and have them come to *their* manager to ask for your help. In turn, their manager will come to your manager and ask him to allow you to help them. If necessary, their manager can even involve their common higher manager to convince your manager to cooperate. Once your manager will get positive feedback about you and your work from his peers and managers, he'll see the value too.

Lastly, another very important mean for changing a culture is information. Information has a very strong influence on most people's beliefs, as it shows them an objective truth (or at least one aspect of it). Lack of information leads to speculations, biased assumptions, and even personal conflicts, while more information leads to transparency and cooperation. Information can be in the form of data, but also of knowledge. In the sense of data, this is where the CI process and tools, as well as the source-control system and other development life-cycle tools help make a difference. They provide transparency and data regarding the state of a version, bug density, help rationalize the root cause of problems, etc. However, beware that every metric can have severe side effects if it is used too widely or aggressively to measure people's performance. People will naturally strive to maximize the metric they're being measured upon but may neglect many other important aspects of their work along the way, which can sometimes be completely disastrous.

In the sense of knowledge, code reviews, courses, books, blogs, and even informal conversations are what helps make the difference. Gaining and transferring the knowledge regarding test automation in your team is your main tool to make a difference!

Identifying the Starting Point

Back to the ground, making a change to the processes and culture depends on the current situation and the most bothersome problem that you try to solve. Following are a few common situations that you may found yourself in, and the possible course you can take to change it. As pointed out earlier, don't try to fix everything at once. Tackle each issue one at a time, in a way that provides the most value in the smallest effort.

Not Having an Automated Build

As mentioned in the beginning of the chapter, a team can take good advantage of the test automation without an automatic build. However, in the situation described there, the assumption was that the team is small, collaborative, and understands how to get the most value from test automation. But if you're a single automation developer that works as part of a QA team far away from the developers, then chances are that the potential value the team gets from test automation is far from being realized.

If you don't get buy-in for creating an automated build that runs the tests (even though with today tools there's really no good excuse for that), you can simply create a scheduled task on your machine (e.g., using Windows Task Scheduler) to run all of the tests each night. With a few lines of script, you can make the results be sent to the relevant people automatically by mail. But even without that, sending the results yourself every morning is a good starting point. As I'll describe in the next topic, you should also elaborate on the results in your own words.

Expectations Gap

Very often, test automation developers either report to a nontechnical manager, or a manager who's just too busy to get into all of the details and intricacies of the test automation project. These managers often have a hard time seeing the bigger picture and the status of the project, which causes frustration and gaps between their expectations and the actual state of the project.

One of the main reasons to this is that the results of the test automation and consequently the value that they provide are pretty opaque. The reports tell how many and which tests passed or failed, but the failure message is too technical for these managers to understand. Even if you have a visual log and everything that helps you investigate the results quickly, it's still not something that your manager would probably look into for each failure. Assuming you're given the time to investigate and fix the tests as needed, often your manager doesn't get into the technical details and has a hard time understanding what exactly you're spending your time on. (If you're not given the time to investigate and fix, refer to the topic "Having Many Unstable Tests" later on.) Because there can be other reasons for failures that are not bugs, managers sometimes only see a high cost of developing and maintaining the tests, but very little value in the sense of bugs that are found by the automation. They simply don't have the means to estimate whether it's reasonable or not, and where the root causes lie in order to try and improve it.

Assuming that you're already investigating the results every morning, continue to do that, but also write a report in your own words, and send it to your manager, and possibly also to relevant peers. The report can either be in the form of a table, or a more flexible, textual format – whatever you feel suits and best conveys the information.

For each failed test, investigate and try to come to a conclusion whether the failure is due to (a) a bug in the application, (b) a change in the product, (c) an environmental issue, or (d) an unexpected condition in the test (i.e., a bug in the test). For each of these cases, describe the problem in one or few sentences, which are not too technical but are also clear enough and not vague. In addition, describe what you have done and/or think that should be done in order to solve or mitigate that problem. For known bugs, clearly distinguish between them and new bugs. If you can't completely identify the root cause of a failure and determine whether it's a bug or a different problem, describe what you have investigated so far and your interim conclusions. In addition, describe what diagnostics you have added or think should be added (if you need more time or help from other people for that), in order to help you investigate the problem next time. Again, write only the relevant details in a concise but understandable way.

When you investigate failures, one of the common first steps is to try and reproduce the problem on your local machine both by running the same automated tests, and by trying to reproduce it manually. The results of these investigations are often interesting to mention directly, as it tells a lot about the nature of the problem.

Finally, group identical issues together in the report, so that the focus is on the *problems and their solutions*, and not on the tests themselves. **This is also your opportunity to highlight issues that needs to be fixed, including more general and long-term ones that impede your work, and push toward additional process and cultural improvements.** This report will be much more valuable to your manager than any automatic report he may have asked for, and I'm sure he'll appreciate it.

Having Many Unstable Tests

Let's make it clear: unstable tests are useless! With unstable tests you can't determine whether the tested scenario works correctly or not, and whether a failure is caused by a bug or some other reason. This only adds noise to the process and wastes time rather than helping anyone in any way. That's why tests must be stable at all times. For the sake of our discussion, unstable tests are not necessarily flickering tests. Even tests that pass on one machine and fail on another, or simply tests that fail consistently, but no one had the time to investigate the root cause and fix it, should be considered unstable, even though they're not flickering.

While this is not desired, too often I saw situations where the automated test suites became unstable, having many unexplained failing tests. These situations usually come about from ignorance, mainly of managers who don't understand the maintenance demands of test automation and are more concerned about covering more scenarios rather than stabilizing existing ones (probably because they committed to a certain deadline to their own manager). If you report to such a manager, try to communicate the uselessness and cost associated with these unstable tests to your manager, and if needed also to his manager too. Assert that stabilizing tests must be a constant and high priority effort.

As always, information, both in the form of data and knowledge are your best tools. In the sense of knowledge, communicating the cost and value of unstable tests, as well as the differences between manual and automated tests in that regard, is the important thing. In the sense of data, the test run results from the build is the basic source of information. However, if there are many failures, chances are that you're not given enough time to thoroughly investigate and fix the issues, and as time goes by, the problem only gets worse. Because it gets worse, you'll need even more time to investigate and stabilize the tests and chances are your manager will want to postpone it until after some arbitrary milestone (that will probably be postponed too).

While you should coordinate with your manager the solution I'm about to suggest, it is so cost-effective, that it's pretty unlikely that your manager will object it. Instead of trying to stabilize all the tests at once, start from the tests that are already pretty stable. Even if most of the tests are unstable, almost always there are a few tests that pass almost regularly. If there are not, then start with the test you're writing now, and as soon as it works, consider it as stable. Make a list of these relatively stable tests, even if the list is very short. Each morning, instead of investigating the failures in all of the tests, only focus on the tests in that list. Because the list contains the tests that are relatively stable, they should usually pass, so the time you invest in investigation and fixing is very minimal. However, when some of them fail nonetheless, investigate these failures thoroughly and fix them to make them stable again. Report to your manager every day about the status of the tests in that list, just like I described in the previous topic. Slowly, when all of the tests in the list pass, add to the list one or a few more tests that you notice to be pretty stable lately too, or select one test that fails regularly with the same message, and try to investigate and fix it. It is likely that some of your fixes, either of tests in the list of stable tests, or fixes to tests that used to fail regularly, would have fixed other tests too. Apply the ideas mentioned in Chapter 13 for investigating and stabilizing the tests. Gradually expand the list of stable tests until all of the tests are stable.

Even if eventually there are a few "stubborn" tests that are difficult to stabilize, they remain the exception rather than the norm, and they are also clearly distinguished from the rest, so it's easy to notice regressions. For these few problematic tests, you may postpone treating them to a less stressed period, or even completely delete them if you realize that their intended value is not so clear and questionable in the first place.

Notice how the gradual approach helps you avoid having to invest too much time investigating many failures, while still making constant progress toward a stable test suite. This gradual approach is a much easier sell to your manager, as the time needed for investigation and fixing becomes much less intimidating, and the value he'll see from it is much more immediate. Communicating the progress of the stabilization progress to your manager ensures that he's aware of this progress and sees your contribution to the success of the test automation journey.

Inheriting a Legacy Test Suite

In companies, over time, people come and go, and test automation developers are no exception. When the test automation changes hands, especially if it was developed, maintained, or even led by a single person, it's common that the new automation developer that inherits the test automation has a hard time maintaining it. Because the new automation developer is less familiar with the code of the test automation, he may not be aware of decisions and reasons that led to the way the automation is written, and simply because no two developers have a common coding style and skills, he'll feel uncomfortable maintaining the tests and will probably even consider the automation that he inherited like a piece of crap that must be replaced (BTW, this is true almost for all developers inheriting someone else's code, not only automation developers). Moreover, while many of these reasons are subjective, it's often true that during the time the automation was developed and maintained, the SUT has changed, technologies have changed, and the knowledge of the automation developer has changed. Even with best intents, there are probably traces of the old technologies and implicit knowledge spread all over the code, making it harder to maintain. It could also be that the tests are objectively unstable or difficult to maintain due to bad coding skills or lack of isolation.

Before throwing everything away and starting from scratch, answer the following questions:

1. Is it possible to understand the intent of each test, or at least of some of them? If at least some of the test names, steps or descriptions are understandable (maybe even by domain experts or relevant developers), or the relationships between the test methods and manually written test case are maintained, then chances are that you can still stabilize and get value out of them.

2. Can you point at some isolation or architectural problem that hinders the reliability of the tests? If so, is it possible to change the infrastructure code to fix it, or will most of the tests should be changed in order to fix it?

If the tests are unreliable due to an isolation or architectural issues that you can clearly point to, but are hard to fix, then chances are that there's probably no reason to keep maintaining these tests. However, even if the tests are unreliable, but it's possible to understand the intent of the tests, then you can apply the technique of gradually stabilizing the tests, which I described in the previous section.

If you can't point at an inherit problem with the isolation or architecture, but the intent of the tests is not understandable, you can continue to run the tests, but when a test fails, only invest a reasonable time in the investigation. If you can easily fix it, then go for it, and if you can also change the name or description of the test method to better explain its intent, the better. If you think that the test is too long and verifies too many things, then you can also break it down to shorter tests that together cover the same functionality of the original one. However, failing tests that are both hard to maintain and also their intention is unclear, are really worthless. If the developers of the feature and the product owner (PO) also think like you, then you can probably delete these tests.

Now the question is what to do about new tests. The first impulse of most developers is to write a new infrastructure that will be easier to maintain. The thing is you have to balance between the cost of using and maintaining code which you feel less comfortable with, and the cost of developing all of the infrastructure anew. In many cases, you can reuse only the parts of the infrastructure that make more sense to you and write other parts anew. Especially if you take the approach described in Chapters 10 to 12, and the previous automation wasn't written using this approach, chances are that you'll want to write some of the infrastructure yourself. But still, if there is usable code in the old infrastructure that you can reuse, then go ahead and use it.

Eventually, if you do decide to write a new automation system from scratch, consider running the new tests side by side with the old ones, at least until a proper coverage and trust was gained in the new system.

Chasing After the Application Developers

The last problem and improvement technique I want to mention has many different symptoms:

1. Automation developers feel that their work isn't getting enough management attention,

2. Bugs whose priority are not high enough to be fixed immediately, but that affect the test automation are postponed, making the automation less reliable.

3. Necessary changes to the SUT to make it more testable are not given enough priority.

4. The automation often fails on legit changes of the SUT, because the automation developer hasn't been prepared in advance for the changes. The automation developer feels that he has to chase after the application developers in order to understand what has changed and why.

All of these symptoms are typically an outcome of the belief that the automation is part of the QA team's responsibility, and that application developers shouldn't be concerned too much about it. This belief is usually bound also to another belief that the main communication channel between the QA and development teams is the bug tracking system. Almost always in these situations the tests are being run only on nightly builds and not in a CI.

This is where changing the culture takes the most significant place. In order to solve these problems, the responsibility for running and maintaining the tests should eventually be moved to the hands of the developers, or at least they should be closely involved with the test automation efforts. In fact, it should be a team responsibility, but the developers should definitely be actively involved. The challenge of course is how to make this transition...

The interesting thing I found over and over again, is that while most developers don't like to test their changes and new features thoroughly, or write tests for their code, they *are* willing to be able to run the automated tests themselves. If you give them automated tests that have already been written, and which they can run in a click of button, they'll feel much more confident that their changes didn't cause any significant harm. Eventually, developers don't like it when bugs are found in their code, as it creates more work for them (and also beats their ego...).

The trick to make it work is to talk to developers, preferably unofficially at first, and tell them what your automation does and how it works. Then, suggest to show them how they can run one, few or all tests (depending on the overall time it takes). Chances are that at least a few of them will get excited by the possibility. In my experience, these are usually the more senior developers, technical leads, and even team leads, though it greatly depends on the people themselves. When you find a developer who's willing to run the tests, on his own will at first, offer your help in any problem he might encounter, and be very willing to actually provide this help. Try to do this "trick" with as many developers you can, focusing on these senior, tech leads and hand-on team leads. Most probably every now and then a developer will encounter a failure and call you to help him. When it happens, show him how you investigate the failure and find the root cause together. If the cause is a bug that the developer just introduced, that would be a great win in many respects. Let him fix the bug, and then make sure that the test passes. If the cause is a legit change in the SUT, show him how you fix the test (assuming the fix is quick, which in most cases it should if you kept the rule of avoiding duplication). Run the test again to make sure that the fix was successful. This way you gradually transfer the knowledge and responsibility to the developer, while the developer sees the value that the fast feedback that he gets from the automation gives him.

After some period of doing the above practice and a number of cooperating developers, when a test fails in the nightly build, try to identify the developer who checked in the code that failed the test, by looking at the build details and the source-control history of the last day. Note that the fact that the test failed in the nightly build indicates that this developer hasn't run that test before he checked in his changes. Assuming that this developer already knows how to run the tests, and that this test is one of the tests that you'd expect him to run, come to that developer directly, and show him that if he'd run the tests before checking in his changes, then he would have caught that bug before he checked in the code. You can take note each time this happens, and after some time, communicate with the team (as well as with your manager) the time that would have been saved if the tests were run by the developers before check-in. Needless to say, you should do it politely and practically, and suggest it as a process improvement and not blame the developers for not doing it. The point is to use the data to provide transparency, and to show the value in changing the process.

Eventually, someone will already suggest to add the tests (or a subset of them) to the CI build, in order to prevent such regressions from reoccurring. Obviously, you shouldn't only wait for that someone to suggest it but be preaching for it all along. By preaching, you prepare the ground for that moment of consensus in which you can make it work without major objections.

Note   According to my experience and observations, most developers don't like to develop tests for their code, mostly due to lack of experience and knowledge of how to do it right. After they gain some experience and get better at it, it becomes obvious to them that they should do it as an inseparable part of their work. Naturally, some people get it more quickly while others struggle more. However, at the beginning, many developers perceive writing automated tests as having a very low technical challenge, which makes them feel that it's not the best use of their busy time. As a result, they think that this should be done by someone else, namely a tester. The common excuse that they're too busy writing code and don't have time for also writing tests, is perceived as true by most people. But the truth is that the same amount of work is divided by the same amount of people, be it application developers or automation developers, whether everyone does both types of tasks, or each only does his own thing. Needless to say that the bigger the communication overhead is, the more time consuming it is, and the time spent on finding, investigating and fixing bugs is a huge cost that is saved when each change of code is immediately covered by relevant automated tests. In the next chapter we'll cover increasing the collaboration between the application developers and automation developers even further.

Decreasing the Test Run Duration

Before you expect developers to run the tests and/or adding the test to the CI build, you should ensure that the entire test run don't take too long; otherwise you'll never get their cooperation to use it regularly. Some people say that the entire test run should take no more than few minutes or even seconds, but most developers accept waiting up to 30 minutes to get a valuable feedback on their changes. There are two main reasons for that:

1. Even though the developer can continue to work on other things while the build runs as a result of his check-in, only when it finishes is when he truly has the peace of mind to work on the new stuff. This is because if the build fails, then he needs to do a context switch back to fix it.

2. Depending on the size of the team and rate of check-ins, the longer the build takes, the more check-ins are likely to be merged into a single build, and the more likely it is to fail due to integration conflicts.

This is the main reason why unit tests are more commonly used in CI builds than full system tests. However, in many cases the option to run tests that are more than pure unit tests is often rejected prematurely. There are a few techniques that can help keep the CI speed under control even while enjoying the safety of the broader automated tests.

Improve Isolation

While the main purpose of isolation (which is described in greater detail in Chapter 7) is to improve the reliability of the tests, it can also affect their performance. A shared database with a lot of data makes the application run slower. The amount of simultaneous connected users can lead to locking, which slows that system down, and the amount of data can affect the performance of queries that the application performs as part of the tests. However, if each test environment has its own small database, then you remove the bottleneck and also make the tests more reliable. In addition, if you put the database and the application server together on the same machine, then you also eliminate the overhead of communicating over the network, which is likely to affect the performance of the tests significantly too.

Besides isolating the database, you should isolate the test environment from any external dependencies (e.g., external web services, external hardware, etc.). These external dependencies should either be simulated (as described in Chapter 6) or be cloned and used separately for each environment. By doing that you remove the latency and the load on these services, which consequently also improve the performance.

Perform Prerequisites Through API

Creating the prerequisite data of tests through the UI usually takes long; may make the tests less reliable, harder to maintain, and don't serve the purpose of the tests. Consider doing it directly through API or even directly to the database. APIs are designed to be used by code, while UI isn't. See Chapter 6 for the trade-offs between the different test scopes.

Parallelization and Virtualization

If you already optimized for isolation, then running multiple tests in parallel is straightforward. The level of isolation and the exact architecture dictates whether you need different threads, different process, different machines, or completely different environments to run the tests safely in parallel. Containers, whether used locally or on the cloud, especially with an orchestration tool like Kubernetes, greatly help creating multiple environments that can be used to run tests in parallel well isolated from each other. While containers and VMs are excellent for this purpose, if your application doesn't lend itself well to this technology, or even if you don't have the knowledge and time to learn how to use it, don't let it hold you back from finding other ways. I used to create isolated environments for running tests in parallel long before I first heard about containers...

364

Once you solve the parallelization problems, you can scale out more and more by adding more hardware. While it may be somewhat more costly in terms of hardware or cloud resources, in terms of reducing the overall test time, parallelization gives an order or magnitude of improvement!

Run Only Sanity Tests in CI

While improving isolation and parallelizing brings the most value out of the performance improvements, it's not always the easiest thing to do. If you already have many tests that run on a nightly build and take hours, and the isolation requirements are too complex, it may seem that using these tests in a CI build is impractical. Well, it's true that it's impractical to run the entire test suite, but a small subset that don't take more than 30 minutes can still make a big difference. The obvious (and mostly correct) choice for this subset is the sanity suite. The sanity suite should cover most features, but just a bit of each of them, and not all permutations and edge cases. While it doesn't provide the most value out of the entire test suite, at least it catches major breaks early. These major breaks are bugs that prevent the application from starting or to perform one of the important use cases of the system. Such failures can waste a lot of time for testers and other developers that are trying to get the latest changes. Moreover, adding the sanity suite to the CI helps start the cultural shift toward a greater involvement of the developers in the quality and test automation aspects.

Actually, the highest direct benefit of this approach is for you: the developers will have to help you keep the tests stable and adopt the tests to their changes before they even break the build. Having a stable "always green" sanity suite running in the CI build greatly helps stabilizing and make the full nightly build green too. If a bug is caught at the nightly build, the developers will be much more cooperative in fixing this too, because they already familiar with the test automation in general.

Breaking the CI Pipeline to Stages

Instead of waiting for the nightly build to run all the non-sanity tests, it's also possible to create a chain of builds, each triggering the next one on successful completion. Some stages can trigger multiple other builds to run in parallel also. For example, the first build only compiles and run unit tests (which are very fast and don't require deployment). If it completes successfully, it triggers the next build that deploys the application and runs the sanity suite. If that one completes successfully, then it triggers yet another build that execute the rest of the tests which may take, let's say, three hours. In addition, it can also trigger two more builds in parallel on separate environments: one that executes long-running load tests and one which tests installations and upgrades. If one of the first builds fail, it doesn't trigger the next ones. Finally, there should be an indication for the overall status of the version and a notification if the whole process completed successfully or not. Obviously, this entire process can be easily extended to create a Continuous Deployment pipeline.

In fact, because the overall duration of the entire process is much longer than the average gap between check-ins, if the pipeline is based on the idea that each build triggers the next one, the result will be a queue overflow. Instead, in order to avoid this, the common practice is that each of these builds run continuously in a loop, taking the results of the latest successful build that precedes it. If there's no new preceding successful build, then the current build just waits until there is.

The idea of creating a chain of builds has the advantage of providing the fastest feedback possible about every suite of tests. The drawback, however, is that it makes the work process somewhat more complicated, as developers should look at the results of all of these builds in order to determine whether they can check in their changes or not. Let alone that failures in one of the longer builds may also take longer to fix, which can block all developers if the process is that strict. Common sense and practices that fits the specific organization should be applied in these cases to determine who can check- n what whenever one of these builds fail.

Write Mostly Integration and Unit Tests

As described in Chapter 6, the decision about the scope of the tests (e.g., end-to-end, integration, or unit tests), has many considerations, performance being one of them. The general rule is that the smaller the test scope is, the faster the tests are. Therefore, after taking all considerations into account, it may be a good idea to run only a few end-to-end tests (e.g., the sanity suite), and leave all the rest as integration tests. Obviously, the smaller that the test scope gets, they do a lesser job of testing the integration between the components, so you have to find the right balance between that risk, the speed of the tests, their reliability, and their maintainability. But all in all, putting most of the weight on integration tests is often a good balance, which makes it possible to run thousands of tests in a few minutes. Again, Chapter 6 has much more details about the considerations and options in that regard.

Run Tests Only for Relevant Components

A good architecture is one in which different components (or micro-services for that matter) have different and distinct responsibilities. If these responsibilities also correlate to different business features, then it makes sense to write most of the tests as component (or service) tests, and only use end-to-end tests to test a few cross-feature related functionalities. Unlike typical integration tests, where the scope is narrowed by *skipping layers*, these component tests may exercise all of the layers (though not necessarily), but test and rely only on a single component that contains all of the functionality of the feature at hand. These tests can use simulators or mocks to mimic the interaction with other components, but these should be pretty rare, as the integration between the components should typically be tested in a higher scope.

If the architecture is indeed that modular and the modularity is aligned with the business features, then it makes sense that most tests only need to exercise one component, and only the fewer tests that need to verify cross-feature scenarios need the bigger scopes. In this case it also makes sense to have different builds for each component, each running only the tests that are relevant to that component. Because the components are naturally mostly independent from each other, then the risk that a change in one component will cause a problem in another is pretty low. This way if a developer makes changes to one component, then he doesn't have to care about all of the tests, but rather only the tests of that component. Accordingly, the builds of each component are also faster. The few tests for the cross-feature scenarios can then be run at a separate build in the CI pipeline.

Today, with the growing trend toward a micro-service and modular architecture, this becomes more and more prevalent. However, the fact that a system is composed from multiple services does not guarantee that the services are indeed independent from the perspective of business features. If most user stories (which should give real value to a customer or end user) involve changing more than one service, then it's probably an indication that the services are not independent enough for that purpose. While this sounds pretty logical and straightforward, in reality it's hard to say that the architecture of most systems actually allows most user stories to give value by changing only one component or service.

Optimizing Test Performance

Even though optimizing the speed of the tests themselves (and their underlying infrastructure) may sound like the first thing to consider, I wouldn't recommend you to put too much focus on that before considering the above approaches. In fact, in the context of most software development nowadays, it's considered a bad practice to optimize every bit of performance while writing the code, because it often complicates the development and testing, and eventually comes to the expense of maintainability. Back in 1974, Donald Knuth, one of the founding fathers of computer sciences, referred to this phenomenon as "premature optimization" and even stated that "premature optimization is the root of all evil."[3] The recommended approach is to write the code in the most readable and maintainable way first, and only after measuring and profiling the performance, identify the bottlenecks and optimize them. Without profiling and measurements, you'll very likely be wasting a lot of time optimizing negligible things. The same rule applies to test automation as well.

If after profiling the application you found a "guilty" piece of code that needs to be optimized, you may need to compromise the structure and maintainability of the code in order to fix it. However, in other cases, a reasoned decision can be made to compromise isolation in order to improve the performance of all the tests. For example, if every test opens the application anew and logs in, you may find that if you keep the application open and the user logged in, and only returning to the main screen at the beginning of every test, saves a lot of time. While you increase the risk for instability, you can consider some remedies to overcome this risk. For example, in case of a test failure, or tests that perform log out, reopen or log in to the application nevertheless. Reiterating the first point, consider these options only as a last resort and after measuring the time it will save.

Covering a Broader Matrix

One of the biggest benefits of test automation is that it can be run on different environments. For example, making sure that the application works correctly on various operating systems and versions, various browsers, different types of databases, different hardware, etc. These days, mobile applications often need to be tested on multiple devices, where services like PerfectoMobile, Xamarin Test Cloud, SauceLabs, and others play an important role.

---

[3]http://pplab.snu.ac.kr/courses/adv_pl05/papers/p261-knuth.pdf

A pure CI pipeline (without CD) typically runs the tests only on one configuration that acts as a reference. As most of the code in the application shouldn't be affected by the type of OS, browser, etc., this is sufficient to give fast but valuable feedback to developers whether they checked in something that broke an existing behavior. Having one reference configuration makes it a lot easier to reproduce, debug, and analyze most regressions caught by the CI process.

The rest of the matrix can be run after the CI has completed, as it will probably take longer and/or be more expensive in terms of resources. It can even be running nightly or even weekly only, if the rate of defects it detects is pretty low and the release cycle allows it (e.g., in life-saving applications). Because most of the regressions and problems are detected in the CI process, and the tests are stabilized using it, then problems occurring at the broad matrix run are most probably limited to problems that are actually related to the specific configuration where the test failed. This makes the investigation much easier, and the overall process much easier to stabilize.

A mistake that many teams do is to run the entire matrix nightly without having a reference configuration on which the tests are stabilized and defects are handled more rigorously and more often. This makes it very hard to distinguish between unstable tests and configuration-specific problems.

Summary

In order for a test automation suite to be effective, we need to run it regularly and as often as possible. Technically, creating the build process is pretty straightforward using the most popular build tools, but the real challenge is how to use it properly. The main reason that this is more challenging is that it requires many people to adopt new processes and even a new mindset.

The common belief that such changes can happen only if it comes from management is false. While it can be easier for a manager to lead these changes, it doesn't have to. Everyone with the right passion and just enough knowledge can lead this change. The trick is to improve one thing at a time, demonstrating immediate value, and to be persistent striving toward your goals.

In order to get the cooperation of developers, the main value that they need to get from this is fast feedback for their changes. In order to be able to provide them with that value, the tests should not take too long to run. A bunch of techniques and ideas were provided in the chapter to help you optimize the length of the test run to fit well in the CI process.

CHAPTER 16

Acceptance Test Driven Development

Having a good CI/CD pipeline helps a lot in providing fast feedback to the development team about regressions. This is an important part of being agile but is far from enough. For a team to be agile, it needs to be able to respond to customer feedback quickly and do so constantly for the entire life span of the product. In this chapter we'll discuss the Acceptance Test Driven Development (ATDD) methodology (which was introduced briefly in Chapter 5) and see how it helps the team to be much more agile.

Note Kanban (one of the Agile methodologies) advocates the use of a metric called *Lead Time*. This metric measures the time it takes for a user story to advance from inception to realization (use in production). Minimizing this time is arguably the most desired outcome of agility, as it shortens the feedback cycle with the customers, but it should also be kept low over time. While this metric is mainly used in Kanban, shortening the feedback loop is an important goal of any Agile methodology. ATDD helps achieve that.

Overview on ATDD

As described in Chapter 5, ATDD, which is also known (arguably with some nuances) as *Behavior Driven Development* (BDD) and *Specification by Example* (SbE) is a methodology that complements Agile. In this methodology, for each user story, the team defines together with the product owner the acceptance criteria in a form of few representing scenarios. These scenarios are used both as documentation and as the basis of automated tests. These tests can be implemented even before implementing the application code to support that user story. When the application passes the newly developed acceptance

A. Axelrod, *Complete Guide to Test Automation*, https://doi.org/10.1007/978-1-4842-3832-5_16

tests, as well as all existing tests, the user story can be considered done. Later in the chapter we'll describe the process much more deeply, but for now, that's the gist of it.

Being More Agile

Before discussing what makes a team agile, let's clarify the term "Technical Debt" as it's a key concept to understand for this discussion.

Technical Debt

The term *Technical Debt*, coined by Ward Cunningham in a short report he wrote in 1992,[1] is a metaphor that describes the idea that taking shortcuts today, incur more work, in the context of programming and software development, in the future. The further we postpone fixing these shortcuts, the more work it becomes, similar to the interest that a monetary debt gains.

Technical debt has no strict and universally accepted definition. In the paper that Ward Cunningham wrote, he talks about the technical debt in the context of the maintainability of the code. However, you can think of it more broadly like anything that we postpone and takes more time and effort later. In that sense, writing code that is not testable is also a technical debt, as it will take us more time to test, or even cost us more if not tested properly and bugs are found in production.

But probably the most prevalent form of technical debt is bugs. The further we postpone finding and fixing them, the more it costs to fix them.

What Makes a Team Agile?

As mentioned above, for a team to be agile and minimize lead time, it needs to be able to respond to customers' and other stakeholders' feedback quickly and do so continuously for the entire life span of the product. For this to happen, a couple of conditions have to be met:

1. The team must avoid technical debt as much as possible. A team that works on a new project may feel as they're really agile because they release features and respond to feedback quickly, but this feeling is false if at the same time they incur a lot of technical debt.

---

[1] http://c2.com/doc/oopsla92.html

As time goes by, this technical debt slows them down and they can no longer continue to be really agile anymore (even if they're keep following all of the "Agile" methodology ceremonies).

2. The entire team, and I mean here the *entire* team in the sense that encompasses everyone that brings value to the company through the developed product, starting from the salespeople, through the product managers, developers, testers, operations and up to the customer support, needs to be aligned and work collaboratively toward the same business goals, which may change frequently.

Of course, that there's much more to agility than ATDD, and in some cases a team can be very agile and meet the above conditions without implementing ATDD, but as you'll see throughout this chapter, implementing ATDD correctly usually makes a big difference in that sense.

"DOING" AGILE VS. BEING AGILE

The term "Agile" (with the capital 'A'), is the family of methodologies that was influenced by the Agile Manifesto and its 12 principles, with Scrum being the most popular one, followed by Kanban and eXtreme Programming (XP). Any methodology (not just Agile) provides a set of guidelines for what and how things should be done. In recent years, the adoption of the Agile methodologies was very rapid, and today most companies adopt at least some of the guidelines of these methodologies. Unfortunately, often companies in our industry that implement these methodologies, even those who try to implement one completely "by the book,", focus too much on the guidelines and practices and often miss the ideas and values behind them. It's often said that these companies are *doing* Agile but *are not* themselves agile.

Avoiding Technical Debt

In order for a team to stay agile for a very long time, they should avoid having technical debt. This means that every new feature and every change should be deployed to production and be treated equally to a major version, including all of the important aspects of the release life cycle, leaving no open ends like testing, security, monitoring, etc. for later.

Of course, it's impossible to develop every new complex feature in its entirety in a very short cycle. The thing is that almost all complex features can be decomposed into many smaller features, and the trick is to spit the complex features into these smaller ones in a way that each of them still gives some value to the end user. For example, a report generator can be a feature of a business application. However, instead of implementing the entire report generator as one piece, it can be split to multiple user stories, each supporting only one type of report or a more advanced way of customizing an existing one. As explained in Chapter 2, this is the concept of a user story. There are many techniques to split big features into small user stories and is also something that requires a different mindset (and sometimes creativity) than the common practice of writing a complete specification for an entire feature as a whole. (You can think of it as dividing the development and the design "vertically" rather than "horizontally.") If you want to learn more about these techniques, I recommend the book *Fifty Quick Ideas to Improve Your User Stories*[2] by Gojko Adzic and David Evans (2014).

While decomposing features may look also like just another form of technical debt (because we may release before we've completed the *entire* feature), as long as the smaller user stories each have a value on their own, it's not a technical debt because whatever was developed remains completely useful at least to some users, even if the plans have changed and the originally planned "big" feature will never be completed.

For our purposes, the main implications of avoiding technical debt are:

1. The code and the design must be kept clean continuously. We can't plan on having the time to clean it later.

2. There's very little room for misunderstandings and miscommunications about the requirement. Such misunderstandings mean that work should be redone. Note that a feature developed according to requirements may still turn out to have a bad impact on the user, which may still require rework (in the form of another user story), but at least we gained invaluable knowledge and understanding about our actual customer needs.

3. New features should be delivered when they're already tested and as bug-free as possible.

These implications pose nontrivial challenges, but we'll soon see how ATDD helps us deal with them better.

---

[2]Gojko Adzic and David Evans, *Fifty Quick Ideas to Improve Your User Stories* (Neuri Consulting LLP, 2014).

The Process

Here's the high-level description of the process, followed by a detailed explanation of each step:

1. The team, including the product owner, create and elaborate the user story collaboratively, defining one or few scenarios as the acceptance criteria for the user story.

2. Write a failing test for each scenario defined in the acceptance criteria.

3. Write the application code to make the new tests pass, and make sure that all of the existing tests still pass too.

4. Deliver the application and get feedback.

Create and Elaborate the User Story

Many teams treat User Stories as mini features, which the product owner should specify in a detailed manner, so the developers know exactly what to develop. However, I subscribe to another school of thought, which claims that user stories should only convey a need, while the solutions themselves and their elaborated specifications should be done collaboratively by the (inclusive) development team. In the first chapter of *Fifty Quick Ideas to Improve Your User Stories*, authors Gojko Adzic and David Evans put it this way:

> *"To make things crystal clear, if a team passively receives documents in a hand-over, [...], that's not really working with user stories. Organizations with such a process won't get the full benefits of iterative delivery,"*

and in the second chapter they state that

> *"[...] user stories are discussion reminders that have served their purpose after a conversation."*[3]

It's a team responsibility, including and primarily of the product owner, to identify the customer needs that once met, will bring the highest value to those customers (and therefore will be willing to pay for respectively). This is also how the user stories should be prioritized. These needs are typically formalized as user stories in the format:

> *As a [role]*
> *In order to [solve a problem, fulfill a need or provide more value]*
> *I want [the proposed solution]*

---

[3]Adzic and Evans, *Fifty Quick Ideas to Improve Your User Stories*.

Or some variation of it. Gojko and David even go further to suggest that whoever formalizes the user story (which is usually the product owner), should only specify the "who" and the "why" (the first two sentences), because the proposed solution should be the result of a team discussion. At most, the product owner should come up with a suggested solution, but the final decision should be the team's.

Coming Up with a Solution

When the need is understood and prioritized, the team should have a meeting in which they suggest solutions collaboratively. It's important to note that at this context, the problem is how to satisfy the customer's need, and not how to implement an already specified behavior. Accordingly, **the solution should only specify the behavior that affects the user, and not the technical and implementation details**. The team should seek the most effective solution to the problem, which can be delivered quickly, but at the same time provides the highest possible value to the customer (by solving the main problem or need). Further improvements to the solution can be split to other user stories that solve smaller problems that the chosen solution didn't address. However, these user stories should be weighted and prioritized against all other user stories.

It is recommended that the participants in this conversation include all the relevant people who are going to work on this user story, but if not feasible, at least the product owner, one developer who's going to actually implement the solution, and either a tester or an automation developer. Each of these roles typically brings a different angle to the table:

- The product owner, as the representative of the business or customer, has the best understanding about the need of the customer and can ultimately decide which solution brings the most value.

- The developer usually knows best what solution is the most feasible and how costly a solution may be. He can think of the possible designs for each proposed solution and estimate (even if very roughly) how complicated they are, and how will they affect the maintainability of the code going forward. Note that while this is not a design meeting, different solutions can have implications on the design that can have different effects on the delivery times as well as on the long-term maintainability.

- The tester or test automation developer should think how the suggested solutions can be tested and how long it will take to test them. In addition, testers tend to have a broader view of the product and can often foresee potential problems and conflicts with other features that both the developers and the product owner may be blind to.

Defining the Acceptance Criteria

Once the team reaches consensus about the chosen solution, they continue to collaboratively define its acceptance criteria. This acceptance criteria can serve a few purposes:

1. As the guidance to the developers about what they should develop. In other words, it serves as a lightweight specification for the user story.

2. As acceptance tests for the developed feature or changes (this is where the name "Acceptance Test Driven Development" comes from). Most of these acceptance tests can then be automated (more on that later).

3. As a scenario for a demo that can be shown to customers and stakeholders, and of course to the product owner.

4. As a documentation for the intended behavior of the developed feature.

Defining the acceptance criteria collaboratively as examples of usage scenarios and their expected outcomes have the following advantages:

1. It helps envision the solution from the eyes of the user, and how it solves the problem at hand. Contrast this with how people often talk about traditional specifications, where they tend to be caught up on details and miss the big picture.

2. It ensures that everyone has a shared understanding of the solution. When people talk, they happen to use generic and ambiguous terms, making all sorts of assumptions that they believe to be common to all participants, but are often not. However, when talking about concrete examples and concrete expected outcomes, these assumptions and ambiguities are often exposed.

377

3. It helps to flush out issues with the suggested solution. Because free text specifications, and even more so freestyle conversations, are prone to ambiguities and presumptions, then even if everyone understands the same thing, it could be that they all miss an important detail or issue with the suggested solution. Here again, writing down concrete examples helps flushing out these issues.

4. It bounds the scope of the solution. Every idea can be interpreted and implemented in many ways, from the most minimal and even "quick and dirty" ones, to the most comprehensive and even overly complicated. Flushing the ambiguities and issues help draw the bounds of the minimal viable solution. For example, if a user story talks about the need for a text editor, one may imagine something as simple as like Notepad, while another may envision a full-blown word processor, like Word. The usage scenario implies what's the minimal solution that addresses the immediate need. Further improvements should be extracted to additional user stories.

Some user stories are not about adding new functionality, but rather about changing or removing existing ones. In such cases, we have to identify the existing scenarios (tests) that need to be changed, and modify them accordingly, and also remove the unneeded ones. These modified scenarios become the acceptance criteria of the user story, and we should treat them as new tests for the rest of the process.

Writing the Automated Tests

At this point, the acceptance tests can be implemented as automatic tests. While writing the acceptance criteria as usage examples helped flush most of the ambiguities and vagueness, it can still have some of those, because they're still written in a natural language after all. Implementing the tests in code leaves much less room for ambiguity, as all technical details affecting the test, and accordingly the user, should be defined in order for the test to run. The process of implementing the code of the test can reveal any last hidden issues and ambiguities.

If the team uses different types of automated tests (e.g., system, integration, and unit tests), then they should first decide what's the most appropriate type for each test. Once it's been decided, the appropriate test or tests should be developed. If different people write the automated tests and the application code, then in fact the automated tests can be written in parallel to the application code and don't need to come before. However, they have to work closely together to flush out the details that will allow the test to interact correctly with the SUT. Both developers should aim to agree about these details as soon as possible to avoid unnecessary rework down the line.

If the same developer writes both the application code and the tests, or a pair (or more) of developers writes both the tests and the code together (in a pair-programming or mob-programming fashion; see sidebar), then it's highly recommended that the tests will be written first. This ensures that the SUT will be written in a way that ensures testability and reveal any last-minute ambiguities.

If there's more than one test, then the team can decide whether all of the tests should be developed prior to start working on the application code, or if for each test the necessary application code should be written before proceeding to write the next test. Each of these approaches has their pros and cons, but in general the answer to this question is highly contextual. Writing all of the tests first help flush all potential issues, though writing the code can also reveal some limitations that will force to make adjustments to the tests. In most cases the recommended way is to implement the code for the simplest test and gradually proceed to the more complex ones. This gives us faster feedback that we're on track, and helps the developers evolve their design as needed. It also prevents developers from developing unnecessary code and keep it simple.

It's also possible to develop the skeleton for all of the tests first (as we did in Chapter 11), then develop the code to make the first one pass, then proceed to the next one until all of the tests pass.

PAIR-PROGRAMMING AND MOB-PROGRAMMING

One of the more controversial concepts of the eXtreme-Programming methodology, is that all (or most) code, both of the application and of the tests, is written in pairs. One programmer is "driving" the keyboard and mouse, and the other one looks over his shoulder and reviews his work at real time, tracing errors, and suggests better ways to write the code. These two roles should be switched from time to time. Also, it's recommended that the partners of different pairs will switch from time to time to foster better team collaboration and knowledge transfer. The benefits of this approach are faster feedback and better and faster knowledge transfer and alignment across the team. In fact, if a team attempts to have a mandatory code review process, then they should seriously consider encouraging pair-programming. Most teams that I met which attempt to enforce a code review process (without encouraging pair-programming) either end up not really enforcing it, do it perfunctory, or really spending more time than it would take for the reviewer and reviewee to sit together and implement the whole thing together. Let alone that the knowledge transfer between them is much more valuable this way. In addition, many people report that when they exercise pair-programming they're much more focused than working alone.

The main objection to this approach, of course, is that every feature costs almost double to develop. In fact, most experts agree that pair-programming should be exercised when appropriate and not as a mandatory practice. It's most valuable when the skills of the two partners complement each other, but when a task is too trivial or when the partners don't get along, then it's probably not a good idea. Also, some people feel more comfortable doing pair-programming, while some don't.

An even more controversial idea takes this concept one step further and suggests that an entire team should work collaboratively on all programming (and other) tasks. The idea is pretty much the same as in pair-programming, with the advantage that all participants are synchronized and participate in all decisions. As in pair-programming, there's always one "driver" (which switches routinely), and the others review and make suggestions at real time. Unlike in pair-programming though, the reviewers can also use their laptops to look for alternative solutions or to search for existing pieces of code that can be reused, making the collaboration more effective. Samuel Fare wrote a very nice blog post about it.[4]

Implementing Tests for a Nonexisting Feature

When some people first hear about the idea of writing the tests before the application code, they're often left puzzled, not understanding how it's even possible to test something that doesn't exist. Well, obviously the test should fail if it's supposed to verify functionality that wasn't implemented yet. In the case of writing unit tests first (which is the classic TDD), the code wouldn't even compile. In the case of UI automation or API testing, there shouldn't be any problem to write the test code to compile, but it will fail at runtime. But I think that what really puzzles those people is the question: How can I write the test if I don't have all of the technical details that I need for it? The answer is that, instead of deciding about these details when you (or someone else) writes the application code and adapts the test to match these details, you do the opposite: you decide (together with the application developer) about these details when you write the test code, and then he writes the application code to match these details.

---

[4]https://medium.com/comparethemarket/i-did-mob-programming-every-day-for-5-months-heres-what-i-learnt-b586fb8b67c

As a simple example, suppose we're about to develop a user story for adding a button to calculate the square root of a number, in an online calculator application. One may think that we can't write the test before the code because need to know the id of the new button, as well as the result of the calculation. Regarding the id, the answer is that you can decide what the id should be when you write the test, and coordinate it with the application developer, so he'd use the same id when he creates the button. Regarding the expected result, first, it should be defined as part of the acceptance criteria. For example, you should know in advance that the square root of 16 should be 4. But the question gets a little more complicated when we want to test the result of the square root of 2, because now we need to discuss precision and maybe rounding issues. If these questions are important from a business perspective and were not addressed in the acceptance criteria, then we must involve the product owner and possibly the rest of the team to decide what should be the *exact* expected result and write both the test and the application code to follow the decision. In case it doesn't have an important business impact, we're likely use whatever the standard library of the programming frameworks provides (e.g., the .Net framework's Math.Sqrt function). In this case it's indeed hard to know the *exact* result in advance (in this simple example it is, but if the calculation is a bit more complex, then we may not). So, either we write the test to allow for a marginal precision error, or we write the test with an arbitrary precision, which will fail even after the application code is implemented correctly, and then we'll fix the test to match the exact number after you verified that it's indeed correct. This approach shouldn't be the default, but as long as it's done sensibly (only the exact value is fixed in this case), then it's still OK. Note that in this example, the approach of tolerating a marginal error is preferred, because the test would be more robust and less prone to failures due to minor implementation details.

Another challenge we might have is when the scenario has more than one step that can't work until the application code is complete. The problem is that we can't verify the correctness of the test until the application is ready, because the test will always fail on the *first* incomplete step, and we won't be able to exercise the rest of the steps that we've implemented in the test code. There are a few ways to overcome this challenge:

1. Work closely with the application developer and plan the work such that the first step should work first, and only then continue to the next one, and so forth, until the whole test passes.

2. Work closely with the application developer, but instead of planning to implement the first step completely, only implement a stub that will allow the test to continue and fail on the final assertion.

3. Use the debugger to jump over methods that are not working yet, or comment out these lines temporarily, in order to get to the later steps of the test.

Sometimes the first approach flows very naturally, but on others it's not feasible or can complicate the development of the feature too much. The third approach is something that the automation developer can do for the sake of feeling confident about his changes, but it's not a good systematic approach for the problem. It's also risky in the sense that you may forget to uncomment the lines and keep the test passing without really doing whatever it should do. Therefore, in general, if the first approach doesn't fit, then the second approach is the most recommended one. There are two common use cases for the second approach that is worth mentioning specifically:

1. For UI applications and UI automation (including web UI and Selenium), a preliminary, nonfunctioning UI can be created first. Even though it shouldn't be functioning at this stage, the ids (or other identifying attributes) at least for the elements that the test should use, should still be defined. This allows the automation developer to write and run the test code, while the developer can start implementing the functionality that makes the test pass. Creating a preliminary UI first also makes the idea of the final solution more tangible. The final style of the UI can be polished later on, as long as the Ids and the functionality remain unchanged.

2. For REST or SOAP services, or any other message exchange format for that matter, the exact structure of the messages should be defined first. This allows both the automation and the application developers to start working on their code. Moreover, creating the service to accept any message and respond with a predefined message that satisfies the test needs, except of the final assert, lets the automation developer proceed with the implementation of the test without having to wait for the full implementation from the application side. The application developer can then proceed developing the functionality of the service, including validating the request and building the response according to the actual functionality. When the developer completed his work, the test should pass.

Implementing the Code to Make the Test Pass

> **Note**   As this topic is oriented more toward application developers, I use second person (you) to refer to the application developer.

Once the acceptance criteria are implemented as one or more automated tests, your job as a programmer is very straightforward and clear. No more vague and ambiguous requirements. The scope of the task is crystal clear: make the new tests pass, and don't fail existing tests. If the project is developed with ATDD from its start, or you reached a high-enough coverage of functional tests, then it really should be that easy. If the test coverage is not that high, then in addition to "make the new tests pass, and don't fail existing tests," you must try not to break anything that works, even though you don't have tests for them.

Obviously, because tests are always only specific examples, and not the rule itself, one may take my advice too far and make all the tests pass by returning the specific values expected in the tests. Clearly you shouldn't do that. Actually, even if you do, you'd "get caught for bluffing" in the next step in the process. However, you should really be focused on the scenarios defined in the acceptance criteria, and don't try to address all sorts of nontrivial edge cases. If you identify such edge cases that are not trivial to handle, communicate them with the product owner and relevant team members, but as long as it doesn't invalidate the original solution, the simplest solution should be used for now, and the solution that addresses these rare cases should be added to the product backlog to be handled as an additional user story.

For other edge cases that are fairly trivial, even if they were not covered specifically in acceptance tests, handle them appropriately. However, these cases can usually be covered by unit tests, so it's recommended that you write unit tests for them, so that this behavior will also be covered and documented (in the form of unit tests). This will help you ensure that you really didn't break anything if you do a major refactoring or rewrite of the code.

Refactoring the Code as Needed

If you have coverage of acceptance tests for each user story from the beginning of the project, then you are really free to modify the structure of the code however you like. The tests give you a very robust safety net on which you can rely on, making all sorts of experiments and changes. The adage "if it ain't broke, don't fix it" is no longer relevant!

You can and should improve anything that you don't like in the way the code is written, as long as you make sure that all the tests pass. Moreover, because Agile allows and even encourages clients to change the requirements every so often, yesterday's design assumptions may no longer be valid today, so the design *has* to change to accommodate for these changes in requirements.

If you're starting with ATDD on a brownfield project, then refactoring may not come as easy, because you don't have that safety net of full acceptance test coverage (and nearly full code coverage). Later in this chapter I'll explain how to mitigate this challenge.

You should always strive to make the refactoring in small steps, where after each such step you can run the tests and make sure that everything that worked before continues to work (i.e., all the tests except of the acceptance test of the new user story, in case you haven't finished it yet). It takes some practice, planning, and mind shifting to do a major refactoring this way instead of rewriting big portions of code at once. But doing so reduces the risk of getting into a "rabbit hole" of changes that can take you a few days or even weeks to get out of, and get the code to work correctly again. I usually start by adding a `// TODO:` comment with the intention of my refactoring, and then plan how to do it in small steps. While the refactoring is not complete, I may create temporary duplications and detours in the code in order to keep the code working (and passing the tests), but I also add comments near these duplications and detours, so if I have to jump to another task and in the future either me or someone else looks at it, he can understand why this duplications and detours exists and how to continue the refactoring. When I complete the refactoring, hopefully before I check in the changes, I should be able to safely remove all of these duplications and detours along with their corresponding comments. At this point, the code should look like what I intended, which should be shorter and cleaner. Obviously, I should make sure that all of the tests continue to pass.

It's important to note that you should avoid starting a refactoring journey while your code is not compiling or some tests are temporarily broken. First bring your code to compile and these tests to pass, and only then start the refactoring. Often the best timing to start refactoring is either before or after (or simply – in between) working on implementing a user story. Though sometimes you notice the need for the refactoring while in the works, and implementing the user story without the refactoring will take longer.

Identifying Conflicting Requirements

Given that the tests are fast enough, whenever your code compiles and you expect the existing tests to pass, run them (if they're too slow, consider running only a relevant subset as often as you can). If you expect them to pass and they don't, it could be due to one of the following reasons:

1. You introduced a bug. Given that you expected the test to pass, it means that your implementation (or design) is incorrect. In this case, you should fix the bug (fixing the design if necessary), and you'd better do that right on, even before completing implementing the new user story. Anyway, as long as you can think of a way to fix the bug, then you should do it before considering the user story "done." This is in fact where the value of test automation really shines – you prevent the bugs from creeping in, even before you checked in any code. If you can't think of a way to implement the new user story without introducing a regression in another functionality that was previously working, then it probably means that the new requested functionality conflicts the existing one, and it's not a mere implementation bug, but rather a problem with the solution that was chosen for the user story.

2. You changed some technical details that the automated tests rely on. For example, you removed a class name that your Selenium tests relies on, from an HTML element. In this case you should fix the test code to make it pass. Note that if the code of the tests is well structured, then the changes should not be in the test methods per se, but only in the infrastructure code. If a test method should be changed, it might mean that the scenario itself, as accepted between the product owner and the team when it was written, is changed, and this means that it's no longer a technical detail. If you think that these changes are indeed technical details, but they still require you to change test methods, then it's probably an indication that the test methods are lacking an abstraction and should be refactored. Just make sure that you don't change the meaning of the tested scenarios (consider asking someone for a review on that to make sure).

3.   The current user story conflicts with some previous requested behavior. In large and complex projects, sometimes different requirements may conflict each other, without anyone noticing it, until some user who expects and relies on the old functionality complains. In even worse cases, like in a consumer facing websites, the affected users may simply move to a competitor's website without even complaining... One of the big strengths of ATDD and BDD is that they allow you to detect these conflicts very soon. When you detect such a conflict, you should involve the product owner and the team immediately in order to find a solution that can satisfy both the old requirement and the new one. If business metrics (or even estimations) shows that the old functionality is not worth maintaining, then the broken test, as well as the code of the obsolete feature can be removed, and you can continue to develop the new user story as planned. But otherwise, either the acceptance criteria for the new user story has to change, the existing test and its tested functionality have to change, or in some extreme cases the new user story even has to be completely cancelled.

Deliver the Application and Get Feedback

Once the new acceptance tests, as well as all existing tests, pass, the user story can be considered "done." But this doesn't mean yet that everything is perfect and there are no additional hidden bugs. Even if no bugs can be found, we still don't know if the solution we've implemented is usable and actually solves the actual problem that the user story was supposed to solve. In order to find that out, we need to put the software in the hands of people that can provide feedback.

In projects that implement continuous deployment, having the changes checked in and passing all the tests implies that the functionality is automatically delivered at least to some portion of the users. It's usually preferred that these users are first internal people or beta testers that are expected to provide more constructive feedback in case of problems. But even without that, actual usage and logging information should be measured and monitored to find out if the users actually use the new functionality and whether they experience problems with it.

In more conservative projects (mainly in conservative and critical industries like medical and avionics), with longer release cycles, the new functionality should first be exposed to people internal to the project, like manual testers, but also to the product owner and other domain experts. These people should try to use the new functionality and provide feedback to the development team. Small bugs can be reported directly to the developers, which can fix them immediately. More complex usability or business issues, including edge cases that were not covered by the original user story, should go through the product owner first for prioritization. Issues that require more time and planning, and do not pose a threat on the value of the user story, should be added to the product backlog as new user stories.

As the main scenarios were already tested automatically as part of the acceptance criteria of the user story, the chance for finding critical bugs by manual exploratory testing is much lower, and even if one is found, chances are it should be easy to fix. In addition, for UI-related changes, because automatic tests cannot actually measure usability, it's advisable that a manual tester, or even the product owner have a look and see that the look and feel is acceptable and there are no usability bugs (like, for example, unreadable font size or color, truncated texts, etc.). If there are regression tests that don't lend themselves to automation, then they should be run by the tester if these tests are relevant for the user story. Other than that, the manual tester should mainly perform exploratory tests, to try and find out potential issues that didn't emerge in the elaboration phase of the user story. Again, small bugs can be fixed immediately, and more complex ones should usually be treated as separate user stories as long as they don't threaten the value of the user story.

If a demo meeting is customary at the end of each sprint, the same acceptance scenarios can be used for the demo. The demo meeting is also a great place to get feedback from stakeholders, and it's ok to try out new scenarios together with the stakeholders in order to explore the edges of the solution, and identify additional needs and ideas for improvements that should be added to the product backlog in the form of new user stories.

Using the Acceptance Tests as Documentation

If the textual description of the acceptance tests is kept and somehow linked to the automated tests, then these descriptions can be used as documentation for the functionality (or behavior) of the system. What's special about this documentation is that it's always up to date! For this reason, it's often called "living documentation."

Whenever an existing functionality is changed, either it is done consciously as part of the elaboration of a new user story, in which case the description of the test should have been changed to reflect this change of functionality; or it should be revealed unintentionally when the developer runs the test, as described above (under the "Identifying Conflicting Requirements" topic). As mentioned, the team then decides together with the product owner about the expected change, and the description of the test should be updated accordingly.

While small inaccuracies may still creep in the descriptions of the tests, all in all it's much easier to keep these descriptions up to date than it is for a formal documentation document. While scenarios are very valuable as examples in the context of documentation, it's not always enough, so obviously it's recommended to combine, and bind them with more traditional documentation, mainly if this documentation is also valuable for customers.

Binding Steps Rather Than Tests

Binding the textual descriptions of the acceptance scenarios to the automated tests is very valuable by itself, but there's still a little room for vagueness and inconsistencies between the descriptions and the tests. In order to minimize these vagueness and inconsistencies even further, some tools make it possible to bind *sentences* to *test steps*. The most popular tools in this category are those that use the Gherkin syntax, like Cucumber and SpecFlow. There are other tools like the Robot Framework that use a freer style language, but the idea is pretty much the same. When you write tests using these tools, instead of writing test methods in which the entire test is implemented, the tests themselves are written as sentences in a special text file, with minimal syntactic rules, and each sentence is bound to a method that implements this particular step. A step can be reused by multiple tests, helping to minimize the code and reduce duplication. In addition, a step method can be bound to multiple sentences to allow for different formulations of the sentence in different contexts. The step methods are typically bound to the sentences using Attributes (in C#) or Annotations (in Java), containing the sentence string or a regular expression that the sentence should match. A regular expression is especially useful for methods that accept parameters. Each parameter should be matched by a group in the regular expression, which makes these methods more generic and allows better reuse.

The Gherkin Syntax

In Cucumber, and its port to other languages (including SpecFlow, which is its .Net version), you compose the tests and the sentences that describe their steps, in files with **.feature** extension. While these files contain text in natural language, they still have a well-defined structure and few keywords. This structure is described by the Gherkin syntax.[5]

Each feature file in Gherkin language starts with the `Feature:` keyword, followed by a free text description of the feature, which can span multiple lines (all lines except the first one should be indented). In addition, each feature file can contain multiple scenarios. Each scenario is denoted by the `Scenario:` keyword, followed by the title of the scenario on the same line. The following lines (which should be indented) should all start with one of these keywords: `Given`, `When`, `Then`, `And`. and `But`, each followed by a plain text sentence that describes the step. As far as Cucumber is concerned, all of these five keywords are pretty much the same, but the idea is to use them to structure the test in three main parts:

- **Given** – describes the preconditions for the scenario, or what should be done in order to bring the system to the desired state before invoking the operation we want to test.

- **When** – describes the operation that we want to test.

- **Then** – describes the expected result.

The `And` and the `But` keywords are used as conjunctions and semantically continue the meaning of the previous sentence. Technically though, all of the five keywords can come in any order; however, the order of the sentences in the scenarios determines the order of the steps in the execution of the test. The Gherkin language has some more to it, but that's the main idea. Listing 16-1 shows an example of a feature file.

Listing 16-1. Example of a Gherkin feature file

```
Feature: ATM
        As a bank manager,
        In order to increase my income from commissions
        I want to allow my customers to withdraw cash from ATMs
```

---

[5]For a full documentation of the Gherkin syntax, go to `https://docs.cucumber.io/gherkin/`

```
Scenario: Cash withdrawal charges commission
        Given the commission is $1
        When I withdraw $50
        Then the charged commission should be $1
```

In order to bind the first sentence to a method, the method should have a signature and an attribute as shown in Listing 16-2.

Listing 16-2. Method template for the first sentence

```
[Given(@"the commission is \$(.*)")]
public void GivenTheCommissionIs(decimal commission)
{
  /* implement here the code that sets the commission to the given value */
}
```

Similar methods should be created for the other sentences in order for the test to run successfully.

The Trade-Offs Between Reusability, Granularity, and Readability

Binding steps instead of tests to their textual descriptions helps to ensure that the test indeed performs the described steps. However, there can still be a gap between the description of an individual step and its implementation (i.e., the textual representation of a step can say one thing, but the implementation of its bound method does another thing). In fact, even when the test is written completely in code, we can have similar problems, where the name of a method doesn't necessarily match what it actually does (in good, clean code this shouldn't happen, but in reality it might). So, if we want to take it to the extreme, that is, write the test method in a way that leaves as little ambiguity as possible, then we must describe every little detail specifically in the test method itself. But this of course limits its reusability and even its readability.

By contrast, if we want our tests to be as readable as possible, then we might want to formulate similar sentences a bit differently according to its context in the overall sentence (looking at the entire scenario as one long sentence here). As mentioned above, it is possible to bind more than one sentence to a step method, so technically this can be done without hurting reusability. However, without looking at the code, one cannot be sure that the two formulations are actually bound to the same operation, which makes more room for ambiguity.

On yet another hand, if you want to emphasize reusability (in the sense of the sentences themselves, not only the code), and to avoid ambiguity, then the sentences may sound awkward at times and therefore less readable.

Bottom line: there's no one right answer, but usually if you don't try to maximize any of these traits too extremely, and simply use the Gherkin language naturally, you'd be fine most of the time. Just be aware that occasionally you'll have to make these trade-offs. Having said that, in my opinion, while associating complete scenario descriptions to test methods rather than binding sentences to step methods leave some more room for ambiguity, it also has a slight advantage in terms of maintainability. To do this, the test descriptions can reside in a test management system, like TFS, MicroFocus Quality Center, and alike, and their IDs can be specified at the test method level using an attribute or an annotation. I usually tend toward the later approach, but it's definitely not clear-cut.

Introducing ATDD in an Existing Project

Because ATDD is not a trivial mind shift, as well as a cultural shift, and because its value in existing projects is somewhat lower than in greenfield projects (due to the lower code coverage), it's often not a very easy sell. Here are a few tips that can help you introduce this idea to your team (in addition to the more general tips from Chapter 15 about changing the culture and incorporating better usage of test automation in the team, which are mostly relevant here too).

Start Without Automated Tests

Even if you don't have any automated tests in place yet whatsoever, you can start making use of the practice of defining the acceptance criteria as a team. At first (and maybe for a long period of time), you won't have automatic tests out of it, but the manual regression tests will be more valuable as they'll be testing the value that the use stories should provide to the customers or to the business. Doing only that practice have other benefits too:

- It ensures that the testers are involved at an early stage and can have a real impact about the solution and its quality.

- It improves the communication between developers, testers, and the product owner and promotes a shared understanding of the requirements and the scope of the user stories. It even fosters an attitude of shared ownership and responsibility.

- It leads the team to think about testability before implementing. This makes it possible to test more scenarios easier, even if only manually at first. The need to describe the acceptance criteria unambiguously also drives building simulators for manual testing, which later may be used also by the test automation.

Implementing the Automation Retrospectively

Continuing the previous course, if you do have test automation in the project, but it's not yet mature and stable enough to be used in CI, then you may still need to implement the automatic tests in retrospect and allow user stories to be marked as "done" before having automated tests for them. However, implementing the automation no later than the next sprint (iteration) can be a significant step forward. This is especially relevant when the test automation is developed by a separate and independent team.

The benefits mentioned above for manual tests apply also to the automated tests written in retrospect. When the automation developers will come to implement the tests for a functionality that was defined with clear acceptance criteria, they'll be able to use the same acceptance criteria as the scenarios for their tests. Because the team should have already thought about testability when they defined the acceptance criteria, it should make these scenarios better suited for automation than scenarios that were designed without testability in mind.

One step further down that path could be to involve one member of the test automation team (preferably a senior) in the elaboration meetings. Not only it will allow the automation team to prepare for the changes in advance, but it will also give a chance for that member to provide further inputs about the testability and the clarity of the expected results.

From this state to fully implementing the ATDD process, it should be mainly a matter of following the advice I gave in the previous chapter about stabilizing the tests and transitioning the responsibility for them more toward the developers. Once the tests are stable and fast, and an automation developer participates in the elaboration meetings, nothing should stop the automation developer from implementing the tests for the new user stories immediately and not wait for the next sprint.

Start from Bug Fixes

A different approach, which developers often engage with more easily, is to start by writing tests for bugs before fixing them. While it's a different direction than the previous approach, it doesn't contradict it, and you can definitely apply them both concurrently. However, this approach works best if there's already an infrastructure for test automation in place, and at least few stable tests that run CI or nightly.

Defining tests for scenarios that weren't implemented yet is a big mind shift. But with bugs, the expected behavior should already be specified in the bug description or at least be commonly known. For that reason, I find that many developers are able to adopt it somewhat more easily.

The idea is to enforce developers to write automated tests that reproduce each bug before fixing it. (Unlike most of my advice, in this case, mainly in large organizations, it may have to be enforced by managers at the beginning, because the benefits for the developers may not be immediately obvious.) The test should first fail because of the bug and the developer should be able to see that the failure matches the actual result in the bug report. After he investigates and fixes the bug, he can use the test to ensure that it now passes, which means that he fixed the bug correctly. In addition, while the developer debugs and investigates the bug, he can use the automated test to do it more quickly. When the bug is fixed and the test passes, the developer should check in the test code together with the bug fix, and the new test should be added to the CI or nightly build.

Over time, the developers should feel more comfortable writing and relying on the test automation, which puts the team in a better position to adopt the ATDD methodology completely.

Enriching Regression Coverage

Because the benefits of ATDD are smaller on a brownfield project with little or no coverage to support safe refactoring, we should consider how to enrich the coverage of regression scenarios to reduce this deficiency.

On large, monolithic projects, reaching high coverage may not be feasible in a timely manner. The strategy to overcome it is to create "islands" of high coverage. In these islands, refactoring could be done more safely than outside of them. It's recommended to plan and prioritize to cover these islands according to the needs for refactoring. These islands can be aligned to a structural component (class, DLL, etc.) or to a business feature, which may span multiple components. Ideally, the structural components and the business features themselves should be aligned, but unfortunately with legacy monolithic projects it's rarely the case, and you'll have to assess how these islands should look like so they'll reduce most of the risk involved in refactoring.

Another way to enrich the coverage in a somewhat less planned manner, but which generally provides good value, is to plan where to enrich the coverage as part of each user story. In other words, in addition to defining the scenarios for the acceptance criteria for a user story, the team decides how to enrich the coverage of existing functionality around the area of the change as to reduce the risk of breaking anything.

Summary

To me, the highest value of test automation is reached when the automated tests are used to cover the scenarios that bring business value and improve collaboration and agility by reducing the lead time and keeping it low over time. One of the important enablers for agility is refactoring, which requires high test coverage in order to be done safely. ATDD (which as mentioned above, is basically the same as BDD, Specification by Example, and other related names), provides the methodological framework to provide these values.

The main challenge with this methodology is that it requires a significant mind shift and a cultural change. Hopefully this and the previous chapters gave you some tools to meet this challenge.

CHAPTER 17

Unit Tests and TDD

While both acceptance-test-driven development (ATDD) and test-driven development (TDD) are methodologies that advocate writing the tests before the code, ATDD (or BDD) is usually considered to lend itself better to bigger test scopes and to scenarios that describe how the users use the system, while TDD is considered to lend itself more specifically to unit tests, which uses the smallest test scope (of a single class or even a method), and therefore tests more technical details. For that reason, unit tests and TDD are considered practices that are done directly by the same developer that implements the code under test (CUT[1]). While toward the end of this chapter we'll question the distinction between TDD and ATDD, we first need to understand more about unit tests and TDD in general.

Learning Unit Tests and TDD

While almost everyone agrees that developers should write unit tests for the code they write, during my career I saw many more developers avoiding or struggling with it than those who do it properly, let alone doing it the TDD way. Even among those who write unit tests or even do TDD, there are often strong debates around the most effective way to do it. An excellent example for such a debate is the series of video recorded conversations titled "Is TDD Dead?"[2] on Martin Fowler's blog. So, let's face it: the reason that people struggle with it means that it's not an easy thing to master. There are many excellent books on unit testing and TDD, but even these are not enough. A lot of real-world practice and experience but also continuous learning (controlled practice like katas, reading blogs, watching screencasts, attending workshops, and conferences, etc.) are required in order to master it, and probably the journey never ends. Speaking

---

[1]CUT can either mean "*code* under test" or "*class* under test." I use this acronym interchangeably whenever the difference is not important or the meaning is clear from the context. Otherwise I'll use the explicit term.

[2]https://martinfowler.com/articles/is-tdd-dead/

© Arnon Axelrod 2018
A. Axelrod, *Complete Guide to Test Automation*, https://doi.org/10.1007/978-1-4842-3832-5_17

for myself, it took me several years from the first time I heard about TDD and tried to apply it, until I really felt that I got it. Even since then I keep learning and improving this skill. In fact, my perspective about unit tests and TDD and how it relates to other test automation as well as to some coding practices have changed many times along the way, and probably will continue to change.

KATAS

Kata is a Japanese word, borrowed from the martial arts domain, which means choreographed patterns of movements that one does as a practice in order to improve their skills in the martial art. In the context of software, these are exercises that programmers can practice in order to improve their programming skills. The goal of a kata is not just to implement something that works, but also to emphasize different aspects and practices of how you write the code. For example, a kata can be something like developing the calculation engine for the score of a bowling game but emphasize aspects like TDD, functional programming, avoiding 'if' statements, and even things like avoiding using the mouse. Some people do the same kata over and over again to improve their skills. You can find many Katas on the web.

Note that learning the technical details required to write unit tests is very easy and straightforward. Even learning the concept of TDD is very easy. But the hard thing is to apply these techniques in the real world. I like to compare learning TDD with learning to play the piano. You can learn pretty quickly how to read notes and play each of them on the piano including flats and sharps. You may also master all of the special symbols and can play staccato, legato, forte, piano, and even use the sustain pedal. But knowing all of these details doesn't even bring you close to be able to play Chopin's music, let alone call yourself a pianist. For this you need to practice, practice, and practice some more. The same goes for TDD. Therefore, in this chapter I'll only teach you how to "read the notes" but also talk about the "challenges of playing the piano for real" and the role of the piano (i.e., unit tests) in the symphony called "Software development."

The Mechanics of Writing a Unit Test

Let's start by describing the mechanics of the unit test framework, and then we'll learn how to use it to write unit test, but in a technical fashion at first.

Unit Test Framework Mechanics

We already used a unit test framework (MSTest) when we created the test project in Chapter 11. The unit test framework is actually a very simple technology but is still very useful.[3] There are many unit testing frameworks for many languages and runtimes, like NUnit and xUnit.Net for the .Net Framework, JUnit and TestNg for Java, PyTest for Python, etc., but the basics of all of them are pretty much the same.

While in a regular console application, you have only one method as an entry point, which is the "Main" method that is called when the program starts, a unit testing project lets you create as many entry point methods as you like and invoke any of them separately, all of them sequentially, or any subset of them at your will. The idea is that each unit test has its own entry point. As we saw in Chapter 11, in MSTest you create such a method by decorating it with the [TestMethod] attribute. Other frameworks have different ways to denote a test method, but the idea is similar. This allows the framework to discover the test methods in the project in order to list them, so you can choose which ones to run, and then to run them. MSTest also requires that we decorate each class that contains test methods with a [TestClass] attribute, to let it know whether to look for test methods in it or not. Note that some other frameworks don't have a similar requirement.

When Visual Studio runs the tests, it also shows a pass/failed status for each of them at the Test Explorer pane. The way it determines whether the test passed or failed is very simple: if the test completed without throwing an exception it passes; otherwise (if it did throw an exception), then it fails. This means that an empty test method always passes.

Asserts

Because tests should verify some outputs of the SUT (or CUT) against some expected result, it means that every test method should contain at least one statement similar to this: `if (expected != actual) throw new Exception("...");`

In order to make this repetitive code a bit more elegant and signify the special intent of these lines in the test, MSTest, as well as most common unit testing frameworks, provide the `Assert` class, which we already used in Chapter 11 as well.

The `Assert` class in MSTest, as well as most of its cousins at the other frameworks, also provides methods for directly failing the test (`Assert.Fail`), for failing the test if a condition is expected to be `false` but it isn't (`Assert.IsFalse`) or expected to be `null`,

---

[3]As Martin Fowler said about the JUnit framework: "Never in the field of software development was so much owed by so many to so few lines of code."

(`Assert.IsNull`) and a few other similar methods. MSTest also provides more specialized assert classes for strings (`StringAssert`) and collections (`CollectionAssert`). There are also third-party assertion libraries for different frameworks that provide additional assertion methods often using a fluent and extensible API.

Test Execution Life Cycle

Having multiple entry points (test methods) in the same project or even in the same class allows us to share code easily between these methods. However, because often multiple tests need to perform the same initialization sequence, it would be helpful if we would also have a way to eliminate the code duplication of invoking this sequence from each test method (even if you put all of the initialization sequence in one shared method, you'd still need to call it from each test). In addition, there could be cases where we'd want to initialize something only once, regardless of whether you run only a single test, multiple tests, or all of the tests in the project. The same goes for cleanup (AKA teardown) code – both per test and per execution.

Fortunately, all of the standard testing frameworks let us do these things, and in pretty similar manners. In an MSTest project we can decorate a method in a test class with the [`TestInitialize`] attribute to tell the framework to run it before *each* test method in that class, and with [`TestCleanup`] to tell it to run after each test method. In addition, we can use the [`ClassInitialize`] and [`ClassCleanup`] attributes to tell the framework to run these methods once before and after all test methods in that class, and [`AssemblyInitialize`] and [`AssemblyCleanup`] to run once before and after all of the methods in the entire project (.Net Assembly).

Note   The various cleanup methods are invoked regardless of whether the tests passed or failed. In most cases this is desirable, but it also entails some nontrivial cases. Appendix B describes a mechanism that you can build to overcome most of these cases, and Appendix C describes the Test Automation Essentials utilities library that I developed for .Net that already includes an implementation for this mechanism.

To summarize the execution order of these methods, let's suppose we have three test classes: `ClassA`, `ClassB`, and `ClassC` with test methods A1, A2, and A3 in `ClassA`; B1, B2, and B3 in `ClassB`; and C1 and C2 in `ClassC`; and we choose to run only tests A1, A2, A3, and B1. The execution order will be as follows:

```
AssemblyInitialize
    ClassA.ClassInitialize
        ClassA.TestInitialize
            ClassA.A1
        ClassA.TestCleanup
        ClassA.TestInitialize
            ClassA.A2
        ClassA.TestCleanup
        ClassA.TestInitialize
            ClassA.A3
        ClassA.TestCleanup
    ClassA.ClassCleanup*
    ClassB.ClassInitialize
        ClassB.TestInitialize
            ClassB.B1
        ClassB.TestCleanup
    ClassB.ClassCleanup*
AssemblyCleanup
```

Notes:

1. In MSTest, the ClassCleanup methods are not guaranteed to run exactly in this order, but rather it's only guaranteed that they run not before all test methods and TestCleanup methods in that class have completed, but also before AssemblyCleanup is called. In fact, the framework actually calls all of the TestCleanup methods just before it calls AssemblyCleanup.

2. As you can see, ClassC.ClassInitialize and ClassC.ClassCleanup haven't been called whatsoever because we didn't include any test method from that class in the execution. If we had chosen to run all of the tests, then these methods would have been called.

3. All of the *Initialize and *Cleanup methods are optional and you don't have to implement them if you don't need to.

MSTest has many more features to offer, and so do all other frameworks (though those features may be totally different). However, these features are more specific and are less important to most cases and therefore are beyond the scope of this book.

The Mechanics of Writing a Unit Test

The unit testing framework does not limit or even provide much guidance for how to write a unit test. It will simply execute any piece of code that you'll write inside the test methods (and inside the initialization and cleanup methods in the appropriate order), will mark the test methods as "passed" if they don't throw an exception and as "failed" if they do. From the unit test framework standpoint, whatever you do inside these methods is your own business.

But in order to really write a unit test, we need to call one or few methods on a class inside the SUT and verify its result. In order to do that, our test project must reference the project (or a compiled class library), which is the component of the SUT that contains the class or classes that we want to test. If the method(s) that we want to test is non-static, then we must instantiate an object from that class first, and then call the methods. Calling the methods of the SUT directly from the test is one of the important properties that distinguish unit tests from integration and systems tests, which use a network protocol or UI automation technology to interact with the SUT. Because it's common that multiple tests in the same test class need to instantiate an object from the same class at the beginning of the test, the instantiation is usually done in the `TestInitialize` method (though if different tests need to instantiate the object with different constructor arguments, then there's no point in doing that). Note that you can only instantiate public classes and call public methods this way. These are techniques to call internal or even private methods of the SUT from unit tests, but that's usually discouraged as these are considered to be technical details that are more likely to change (though this is sometimes also a topic of debate).

Finally, a test should also verify some expected result, typically using one of the `Assert` methods. The simplest result that a unit test can verify is the return value of the tested method. But some methods have no return value (they're declared as returning `void`), or we simply want to verify something else. In these cases, we should understand what this method affects and how we can observe that. For example, a method can change the value of a property or to change the internal state of the object in a way that affects the result of some other method. In this last case we must call the other method and verify its result in order to test that the first one changes the internal state of the object as expected. We'll soon look at a more concrete example.

Structuring the Test: Arrange – Act – Assert (AAA)

A typical structure of a unit test consists of three parts: Arrange, Act, and Assert. In fact, these parts are very similar to the Given, When, and Then terms described in the previous chapter. As their names imply: Arrange is where we prepare the prerequisites for the test, including creating the instance of the tested class; Act is where we call the method or the sequence of methods that we want to test; and Assert is where we call the `Assert` methods to verify the result. If the Arrange is common to few tests, it can be moved to the `TestInitialize` method to avoid the duplication. Sometimes also the Act part is sharable and can also be moved to the `TestInitialize` method, leaving only Asserts in the test methods, for verifying different and independent outcomes of the same operation, but this is much less common.

Example – Simple Calculator

Suppose that we're developing a simple, standard calculator. In the project we've implemented a class named `CalculatorEngine`, which manages the state of the calculator after every button click and provides the value to be displayed (this class doesn't handle the UI itself, it is only being used by the UI layer as described). Listing 17-1 shows the public members of this class.

Listing 17-1. CalculatorEngine class

```
public class CalculatorEngine
{
    public enum Digit { Zero, One, Two, Three, Four, Five,
                        Six, Seven, Eight, Nine };
    public enum Operator { Plus, Minus, Multiply, Divide}

    public void ProcessDigit(Digit digit);
    public void ProcessOperator(Operator op);
    public void ProcessDecimalPoint();
    public void ProcessEquals();
    publi void Clear();

    public double DisplayedValue { get; }
}
```

Listing 17-2 shows a test class with a few test methods that test this class:

Listing 17-2. Unit tests for the CalculatorEngine class

```
[TestClass]
public class CalculatorEngineTests
{
    private CalculatorEngine _calculator;

    [TestInitialize]
    public void TestInitialize()
    {
        // Arrange
        _calculator = new CalculatorEngine();
    }

    [TestMethod]
    public void CalculatorCanAcceptMultipleDigitNumbers()
    {
        // Act
        _calculator.ProcessDigit(Digit.Eight);
        _calculator.ProcessDigit(Digit.Five);
        _calculator.ProcessDigit(Digit.Two);

        // Assert
        Assert.AreEqual(852, _calculator.DisplayedValue);
    }

    [TestMethod]
    public void CalculatorCanAcceptDecimalFraction()
    {
        // Act
        _calculator.ProcessDigit(Digit.Four);
        _calculator.ProcessDecimalPoint();
        _calculator.ProcessDigit(Digit.Seven);

        // Assert
        Assert.AreEqual(4.7, _calculator.DisplayedValue);
    }
```

```
[TestMethod]
public void CalculatorCanMultiplyNumbers()
{
    // Act
    _calculator.ProcessDigit(Digit.One);
    _calculator.ProcessDigit(Digit.Four);
    _calculator.ProcessOperator(Operator.Multiply);
    _calculator.ProcessDigit(Digit.Three);

    // Assert
    Assert.AreEqual(42, _calculator.DisplaycdValue);
}
}
```

Unit Tests and I/O

Up to here, things look pretty simple. But the above example is a very simplistic one. The class that we've tested is completely self-contained, with no dependencies on any other class and more importantly, it does not perform any I/O by itself. If we had to create a UI for it, the UI layer would simply call the methods in the `CalculatorEngine` class and update the display according to the value of the `DisplayedValue` property, but the class itself wouldn't have to know anything about the UI. However, most classes in the real world are not self-contained. They depend on many other classes, and usually do some kind of I/O, whether it's UI, database, file system, networking, etc., either directly or indirectly through other classes it depends upon.

The thing is, testing I/O in unit tests is usually discouraged for a few good reasons:

1. Unit tests are meant to be very fast. Almost all I/O operations are an order of magnitude slower than pure CPU and memory access operations.

2. Unit tests should be able to run anywhere, anytime. Performing I/O usually requires prerequisites that are not necessarily available on every machine.

3. Even if the prerequisites are available, the test code should take care about synchronization and isolation, which makes it much more complicated and slow, and may also be somewhat less reliable.

4. Often I/O uses some limited resource, which prevents the tests
    from running in parallel. Pure unit tests (which don't perform I/O)
    can be safely run in parallel and is only limited by the CPU and
    memory of the machine. Some frameworks and IDEs (including
    Visual Studio 2017 and above) make it possible to run the tests
    in the background, while you're coding. Doing it with tests that
    perform I/O is not likely to work correctly in that fashion.

Mocks

Suppose that our CalculatorEngine class also needs to write the performed calculations
to a log file that the user can then open in a standard text editor, how would we test that?
One way would be to read the file at the end of the test and verify its content. But that
wouldn't be such a good idea for the reasons mentioned above. If writing to the file is
done directly from the CalculatorEngine class itself, then we don't have any other way,
unless we'll refactor the code (which we'll cover later). For now, let's suppose that our
CalculatorEngine class only calls another class, LogWriter, that actually writes the
content to the log. In other words, CalculatorEngine tells it what to write (the arithmetic
expression performed, e.g., "12+3=15"), and the LogWriter class only appends that line
as is to the log. In addition, let's suppose that the CalculatorEngine does not reference
the LogWriter class directly but only through an interface ILogWritter that LogWriter
implements, and that the CalculatorEngine accepts this reference in its constructor. All
of these assumptions may sound very cumbersome, and you may wonder why we need
to complicate things so much just in order to write a line to a file, but you'll soon see
why. Listing 17-3 shows the relevant declarations and pieces of code that clarify these
details and the relationships between the CalculatorEngine and the LogWriter classes.

Listing 17-3. The interaction between CalculatorEngine and LogWriter

```
public interface ILogWriter
{
    void WriteToLog(string line);
}
```

```csharp
public class CalculatorEngine
{
    private readonly ILogWriter _logWriter;
    public CalculatorEngine(ILogWriter logWriter)
    {
        _logWriter = logWriter;
    }

    // ...

    public void ProcessEquals()
    {
        // ...
        expression = ...

        _logWriter.WriteToLog(expression);
    }
}

class LogWriter : ILogWriter
{
    private string _filePath;

    // ...

    public void WriteToLog(string line)
    {
        // Perform the actual I/O (append the line to the file)
        File.AppendAllLines(_filePath, new[] { line });
    }
}
```

Given this design, we can now create another implementation of the ILogWriter interface that we'll use only in the test (it will be part of the test project) and will allow us to test that our calculator writes the right messages to the log, without actually writing anything to any file. Listing 17-4 shows this class. As the name of this class implies, this is what's typically called a *Mock* object.

Listing 17-4. MockLogWriter

```
class MockLogWriter : ILogWriter
{
    public string LineWritten { get; private set; }

    public void WriteToLog(string line)
    {
        LineWritten = line;
    }
}
```

Now we can write a test, that although won't actually verify that the expressions are written to the file, it will test something very close to it: it will verify that CalculatorEngine sends the correct expression to the LogWriter class (which should in turn write it to the file). Listing 17-5 shows what this test looks like. Note that because we've added a constructor argument to CalculatorEngine, we also had to change our TestInitialize method to pass this parameter. We'll use the new MockLogWriter class as the value for this argument.

Listing 17-5. Testing that CalculatorEngine sends the correct expression to the log

```
[TestClass]
public class CalculatorEngineTests
{
    private CalculatorEngine _calculator;
    private MockLogWriter _mockWriter;

    [TestInitialize]
    public void TestInitialize()
    {
        // Arrange
        _mockWriter = new MockLogWriter();
        _calculator = new CalculatorEngine(_mockWriter);
    }
```

```csharp
// ...

[TestMethod]
public void CalculatorWritesTheExpressionToTheLog()
{
    // Act
    _calculator.ProcessDigit(Digit.Two);
    _calculator.ProcessOperator(Operator.Plus);
    _calculator.ProcessDigit(Digit.Three);
    _calculator.ProcessEquals();

    // Assert
    Assert.AreEqual("2+3=5", _mockWriter.LineWritten) ;
    }
}
```

Mocking Frameworks

In a real-world application code, often the interactions between classes are way more complex than in this example (though if it's way too complex, it may probably indicate a design problem). In these cases, implementing the mock objects as we did can become complicated and error prone. To tackle this problem there are plenty frameworks out there that let you create mock objects more easily, without having to declare and implement a special class for them. Listing 17-6 shows the previous test but using the Moq[4] mocking framework, instead of the handwritten MockLogWriter class.

Listing 17-6. Using the Moq framework instead of the MockLogWriter class

```csharp
[TestClass]
public class CalculatorEngineTests
{
    private CalculatorEngine _calculator;
    private Mock<ILogWriter> _mockWriter;

    [TestInitialize]
    public void TestInitialize()
```

---

[4]https://github.com/moq/moq4

```
    {
        // Arrange
        _mockWriter = new Mock<ILogWriter>();
        _calculator = new CalculatorEngine(_mockWriter.Object);
    }

    [TestMethod]
    public void CalculatorWritesTheExpressionToTheLog()
    {
        // Act
        _calculator.ProcessDigit(Digit.Two);
        _calculator.ProcessOperator(Operator.Plus);
        _calculator.ProcessDigit(Digit.Three);
        _calculator.ProcessEquals();

        // Assert
        _mockWriter.Verify(
            writer => writer.WriteToLog("2+3=5"), Times.Once);
    }
```

Mocking External Dependencies

In addition to mocking dependencies that perform I/O, we usually want to isolate also third-paryt libraries, classes from other layers, and even collaborating classes from the same component, in order to test the specific behavior of a single class. The collaborating classes may affect the outcomes of the CUT in ways that we cannot easily control from the test, or without creating a maintainability overhead. In these cases, we can also create mocks for these dependencies of the CUT, even if they don't perform I/O, to be able to have better control over the expected result and the maintainability of the test.

The Mechanics of TDD

By now, you know all of the "mechanics" of how unit tests work and the technical aspects of writing unit tests. Before we'll get into the discussion about the challenges of applying these techniques in the real world, let's understand also the mechanics of the TDD method.

Red-Green-Refactor

The way TDD is typically described is as a cycle of the following three steps:

1. **Red** - write the *simplest* test that fails or don't even compile.

2. **Green** - write the *simplest* code that make this test and all other tests pass.

3. **Refactor** – refactor (change the implementation details of) the code and "clean" any "litter" that you left in the code in the previous step. Make sure that all tests still pass.

You already saw in Chapter 11 how it looks like to write a code for something that doesn't exist yet. The only difference is that in Chapter 11 we used the test code to drive the creation of the infrastructure code for the system tests of the MVCClient application, which itself was already fully implemented, while in TDD we use this technique to create and implement the actual code of the application.

This technique may also look similar to the ATDD process we discussed in the previous chapter. There are significant commonalities indeed, but while in ATDD we write acceptance tests for user stories in a cycle that normally takes a few days, TDD guides us in the more granular journey of implementing the code, in cycles of mere minutes.

What "Refactor" Really Means?

I believe that one of the reasons that people often struggle with TDD is the fuzziness around the "refactor" step. In the book *Test-Driven Development by Example*[5]by Kent Beck, he clarifies that this step means "refactor to remove duplication. According to Beck and the examples in that book, a duplication can be anything from a "magic number" that appears twice in the code, to entire code components that repeat themselves with small variations. In fact, duplication can even mean pieces of code that looks completely different but have the same purpose. For example, if we've implemented and used two different sorting algorithms in our code for no particular reason, then this is a duplication and we should remove one of them. By contrast, code that may look the same but is used for different purposes (and may evolve in different directions over time) is not a duplication.

---

[5]Kent Beck, *Test-Driven Development: By Example* (Menlo Park, CA: Addison-Wesley, 2002).

Also, in the examples he gives, Beck clarifies a very important aspect of this step that many people miss: duplication should be removed not only from the CUT, but also from the test code, and even **duplication between the test code and the CUT**. When I read that book, realizing the last sentence was a moment of revelation for me! Duplication between the test code and the CUT indicates that there is coupling, or hidden knowledge, between the CUT and its clients, which violates the basic principle of object-oriented programming: encapsulation. It can also indicate that the class violates the Single Responsibility Principle (SRP) or simply that the test is not well defined, if the test has to calculate the expected result in a similar manner to the calculation that the CUT itself should do. Either way, that duplication should be removed.

Beck also emphasizes that the code, both of the test and of the CUT should "reveal its intent." On the face of it, this is another way to say that the code should be readable. But the word "intent" implies that the code should reveal *what* the code should do rather than *how*. This is especially relevant to method names, but it also implies that most method implementations should include as little technical details as possible. This leads to very short and concise methods, which call few other methods with intent-revealing names, or only hide one specific technical detail. These aspects of design: no duplication, clear names, and short methods all have a vast impact on the maintainability of the code.

Lastly, a very important notion to understand about refactoring, especially in the context of TDD, is that it should be done in tiny little transformations, which each of them keep the code working and all the tests pass. Automatic refactoring transformations like those that exist in most modern IDEs and their plug-ins (e.g., Resharper), like "Extract method," "Introduce variable," "Extract base class, etc., help a lot with that, but even without it, you can do most refactoring transformations pretty safely in small and safe steps. It may require some change of a mindset, practice, and creativity, but it's almost always possible. The general rule of thumb is that instead of simply changing everything to how you want it to be, you first create the new stuff, then route the old stuff to use the new one, and only then remove the old one. It may mean that you have to *create duplication* in the interim, but you remove it afterwards. For example, suppose that you have a class `CustomerDataWriter` with a method `WriteData` that writes some data about customers to a file, accepting the filename as a parameter, and you notice that whenever this method is called multiple times on the same object instance, the same filename should always be used. Therefore, you decide to move the `filename` parameter to the constructor of the class, store it in a field, and remove it from the method. Here's a way to go about this refactoring, without ever breaking existing code:

1. Create a new constructor overload that accepts the `filename` parameter and saves it to a new `_filename` field. Also call the original constructor from the new one (in case it existed and wasn't empty). Because no code calls this constructor yet, all tests should still pass.

2. Find all references to the old constructor and change them to call the new constructor overload providing the appropriate filename argument. (You should know the value of this argument from the calls to `WriteData` invoked on that object.) All tests should still pass, because the new field is still not in use. You can even change these references one by one and everything would work. Notice that you now created a bit of duplication, because now the same parameter is passed both to the constructor and to the method, but this is only temporary.

3. After you changed all of the references from the old constructor to the new one, you can copy the content of the old constructor into the new one instead of calling it, and delete the old one (this transformation is called *inlining*). All test should still pass because the old constructor is not called anymore, and the new one does exactly what the old one did.

4. Create an overload of the `WriteData` method, without the `filename` parameter, and call the old overload with the value of the new `_filename` field as the argument. All tests should pass because the new overload is not called yet.

5. Find all the references of the old overload of `WriteData`, and one by one remove their argument, to actually call the new overload. Because we already changed the calls to the constructor to pass the filename and store it in the `_filename` field, and the new overload of `WriteData` calls the old one using this field's value, then the behavior should not change and all tests should still pass.

6. Once all references to the old overload of `WriteData`, which has the `filename` parameter, have been migrated to the new one (which doesn't have the parameter), you can inline the body of the old overload into the new one, and remove the old one. Because no one uses the old overload anymore, all tests should still pass. We now reached the destination of our refactoring maneuver: we pass the filename only on the constructor and we don't have to pass it in every call to the `WriteData` method anymore. Obviously, the behavior remains the same.

Note that steps 2 and 5 result in changing some test code, if this test code calls the class that we're refactoring. But that's not a problem, as we already mentioned that we should remove duplication from the test code as well as from the production code.

Jumping Back and Forth Between the Steps

While in theory these three steps (red-green-refactor) should be done in a nice clean loop, I often find it practical to do some refactoring between any of the steps, and even in the midst of the each of them. However, when I do so, I first make sure that the code compiles and that all the tests, except the new one, pass. I never leave the tests broken or implement new functionality before writing a test for it first though.

Why Should We Write the Tests First?

Starting to implement a feature by writing the test first is counterintuitive for most people, so why should we do it anyway?

- The code is written with testability in mind. Because the unit tests should test the smallest possible unit and avoid calling methods that perform I/O, most unit tests need to use mocks, and for that the CUT needs to reference its dependencies through interfaces. The way most of us write our code normally does not do that and therefore is not unit testable.

- Thinking about the tests first drives us to think and design the API of the CUT in way that is easy to use. Often when people write the code first, the resulting API is bound to the implementation rather than being a nice and clean interface that hides all of the technical details.

- Making sure that the test we write fails at first, and passes after we implement the CUT, ensures that we've written the test properly (which is the answer I like to give to the common question: "*should we write tests for our tests?*"). If for example, we forgot to write the `Assert` statement, or asserted on the wrong thing, then the test may pass before we implemented the CUT, which tells us that we did something wrong.

- Developers are usually pressed to complete and deliver their work as soon as possible. When we write the test after the fact, we'd probably be pressed to complete it quickly and may cut some corners. Especially if we didn't write our code in a unit-testable manner but already tested the functionality manually, we'd probably feel that it won't be effective to refactor the code and write the "right" unit tests for it at this point. When we write the tests first, we'll be less pressed to cut these corners, because they drive development rather than come as an afterthought, and also the tests prevent us from cutting corners when implementing the CUT.

The Real Challenges in Unit Testing and TDD

By now, in addition to knowing all of the mechanics that you need in order to write unit tests, you also know the mechanics of doing TDD. I also explained to you the motivation for writing the tests first. But as mentioned earlier, this only allows you to "read notes" but not to "play Chopin" or master the practice of TDD for that matter. While you won't be able to master TDD by reading this book alone, I'll first explain the reason why this is so challenging, but then also give you some tips on how to get there somewhat faster.

Main Challenges with Unit Testing

Most software systems, at least those that are important enough for writing tests for, are built from large amounts of classes and methods with many interdependencies. Many of these classes also perform I/O, depend on third-party libraries, and often make various assumptions regarding one another (which are probably correct in most cases, otherwise they would be bugs...). The way that most programmers write software, including experienced and talented ones, typically does not adhere to the testability requirements of unit tests. Almost any class and method that was not written with unit tests in mind needs some decent refactoring effort before you can write unit tests for it. But refactoring without the coverage of (unit) tests is also dangerous of course. Thankfully, Michael Feathers's excellent book *Working Effectively with Legacy Code*[6] provides a wealth of hands-on techniques and practices for doing small refactoring transformations safely for the sake of making "legacy" code (i.e., code without testing) testable. However, besides reading that book, it also takes practice to know what technique you should apply when. Below are the most common challenges in my opinion when working with legacy code, and how to refactor them. Naturally, Feathers's book cover these techniques much more in depth.

Main Challenges with TDD

While TDD promises to solve many of these challenges, it also imposes some challenges of its own:

- It's a very big mind shift to think about tests for each class and method before implementing it.

- It's very rare to start working on a truly greenfield project. That means that virtually all code is "legacy" and was not designed with unit tests in mind, which brings us back to the drawbacks of writing tests after the fact. In fact, most greenfield projects start as a quick and dirty POC (Proof of Concept) that gradually evolves into a real software project. So. you really have very tiny chances to start a greenfield project using TDD.

A common idea to resolve the second challenge, is to do it only for new features added to an existing system. Generally. this is a good idea, and I strongly advocate it, but it's also not that simple, because the new code should usually integrate into the existing code too, and this usually still requires us to refactor the existing code.

More Specific Challenges

Behind the above-mentioned challenges lie many, more specific, technical challenges. Here are just some them, which I found to be the most prevalent ones, and some hints regarding the way to resolve them. If you're not a programmer, you may want to skip this topic.

---

[6]Michael Feathers, *Working Effectively with Legacy Code* (Englewood Cliffs, NJ: Prentice Hall, 2004).

Big Classes and Methods

Often the important classes and methods, which are good candidates for unit testing, are pretty big. When the project was young, these classes were probably pretty small, but over time, more and more behavior was added to them and made them bigger. Such a big class or method often do a lot of things, which makes testing just one aspect of it very hard (this is often referred to as the "God Object" anti-pattern, and a violation of the Single Responsibility Principle). In order to resolve this, you need to break the big method or class into smaller methods and classes. The "Extract method" automatic refactoring, which exists in most modern IDEs, helps a lot in that. But you need to think about how to split the big method to smaller ones, and you're likely need to perform more refactoring than just "Extract method" in order to safely get to the result you want.

I/O

As we saw in the previous example, in order to isolate the I/O operations in our code, we need to refactor it and abstract it behind an interface, so we can mock it in our unit tests. In order to isolate these operations, we should first extract them into their own methods, and then take all related methods that perform I/O and extract them into their own class. We then need to extract an interface from that class and pass it through the constructor of the CUT that stores its reference to a field. The result should be similar to what we saw in Listing 17-3.

While the test always passes the mock to the constructor, we should also fix the production code that uses this class to work with the actual I/O class. You can do that by leaving the default constructor (or the existing constructor that does not accept the new interface as a parameter), and change it to call the new one that does take the interface parameter. The constructor with the old signature (without the parameter) should instantiate the new concrete class that actually performs the I/O, and should pass it as an argument to the new constructor overload.

Alternatively (or later on), especially if the CUT is instantiated in the production code only at one place, you can remove the old constructor, instantiate the new I/O class before you call the constructor of the CUT, and pass the new instance of the I/O class to it.

Singletons

Singleton is a pattern described in the classic book *Design Patterns: Elements of Reusable Object-Oriented Software*[7] (AKA known as the "Gang of Four" or "GOF" book) back in 1994, as a way to restrict the instantiation of a class to just one object instance. However, these days it's usually considered to be an anti-pattern.[8] Nevertheless, it's still pretty prevalent in many application's code bases. In Chapter 9 I briefly mentioned that Singletons prevent reuse, but I didn't mention there that they also prevent testability, especially of unit tests.

Whenever you write a unit test for a class or method that use a singleton, the internal state of this singleton is preserved between different unit tests, which breaks isolation. This means that you need to use the initialization and cleanup methods of the test to somehow make sure that they reset to a well-known state before each test. But the more severe problem is that often a code base that contains Singletons contains many of them, and many of those are interdependent. These interdependencies are a fertile ground for hidden assumptions that "all developers in the team know" (except those who don't...). Besides the high potential for bugs in such code bases, the code tends to be a tightly coupled spaghetti of dependencies and hidden assumptions, which makes the code very resistant to unit testing.

But if we only have one or two singletons that we want to isolate using mocks, we can usually resolve that pretty easily. First, extract an interface out of the methods of the singleton that the CUT uses. Then, in the CUT (which uses the singleton), create a field from the type of this interface, and initialize it in the constructor, like we did in the case of an I/O dependency. Now, wherever the CUT calls a member of the Singleton, replace it with a call to interface using the new field. If you don't have any hidden assumptions about interdependencies with other singleton objects, then you're good to go.

Note that if you have classes that use mutable static fields, and don't implement the singleton pattern, then your situation is even worse. But you can first refactor the class that use these fields to use a singleton internally, (assuming they're `private` or are used only inside that class), then refactor the CUT to use the singleton instead of the static methods, and then apply the previously described refactoring. In case these fields are

---

[7]Erich Gamma, Richard Helm, Ralph Johnson, and John Vlissides, *Design Patterns: Elements of Reusable Object-Oriented Software* (Menlo Park, CA: Addison-Wesley Professional, 1994), p. 124.

[8]In the Software-Engineering Radio podcast, episode 215, around minute 56 onward, the authors of the GOF book themselves discuss the problems with the Singleton pattern (`http://www.se-radio.net/2014/11/episode-215-gang-of-four-20-years-later/`).

also `public` and are manipulated from other classes, then it's a much more complicated problem, because the code that manipulate them can be spread all over the code base. In this case you should first find all the usage of these static fields and then move and group the logic that manipulates them into the class where the field is declared. Only then you can make it private and continue as described above.

Instantiating a Dependent Object from the CUT

Every object needs to be instantiated by using the `new` operator and the object's constructor before it can be used. This is basic, and we do that all the time. But the thing is, if we instantiate a concrete class (i.e., not an interface) inside the CUT, we can't isolate it in the test using a mock object. Because the CUT explicitly specifies which class to instantiate, the test doesn't have a chance to inject the mock object. For example, suppose that some business logic class instantiates an object from the DAL (Data Access Layer) that retrieves some data from the database, which it needs to process, and we want to isolate this class in order to test the business logic class alone. Suppose that this DAL object opens a connection to the database inside its constructor and closes it on Dispose. In order to keep the connection to the database short, the DAL object is instantiated only when needed, inside the relevant Business Logic (BL) method, and then disposed right after retrieving the relevant data from the database. Currently we don't have a way to pass the mock object to the method, and refactoring the class and passing the DAL object in the constructor is also not an option because we don't want the connection opened before we actually need to retrieve the data.

In order to resolve it, we should use the Factory design pattern. The Factory pattern consists of an object that has a method that instantiates and returns another object. This method is declared to return an interface that the created object should implement, instead of the concrete class of that object. In order to mock the dependent object, we need to extract an interface both from the DAL object and from the factory object that creates it. Then we should inject the factory to the CUT as an interface through the constructor and use this factory interface inside the BL method to instantiate the class. Listing 17-7 shows a pseudo-code that can give you an idea for what this would look like. Note that in the test we need to create a mock factory object that returns our DAL mock object, and pass this factory to the constructor of the BL class.

Listing 17-7. Pseudo-code for using a factory

```
public interface IDataProviderFactory
{
    IDataProvider CreateInstance();
}

public interface IDataProvider
{
    Data RetrieveData();
    void CloseConnection();
}

public class BusinessLogicClass
{
    private readonly IDataProviderFactory _dataProviderFactory;

    public BusinessLogicClass(IDataProviderFactory dataProviderFactory)
    {
        _dataProviderFactory = dataProviderFactory;
    }

    public void DoSomethingImportant()
    {
        // ...

        var dataProvider = _dataProviderFactory.CreateInstance();
        var data = dataProvider.RetrieveData();
        dataProvider.CloseConnection();

        // ... use data
    }
}
```

Mastering Clean Code and the SOLID Principles

As you can see, unit tests (whether written using TDD or not), require that almost no class should have a direct dependency on another concrete class. This makes these classes small and independent, and therefore modular and reusable, also often referred to as *loosely coupled*. One of the biggest benefits of TDD is exactly that: it leads you to write good, modular object-oriented code that tends to be easy to maintain. Because of this, it is often said that TDD actually stands for Test Driven *Design* rather than Test Driven Development.

However, because in most cases legacy code is a fact that we need to live with, it's not enough to let the tests guide us toward this design. We need to know how to write loosely coupled code regardless of TDD. In addition, some people "succeed" to write badly designed code using TDD too, ending not only with code that is hard to maintain, but also with many unit tests that bind the CUT to that bad design and make it even harder to change. While the "remove duplication" rule can prevent most of these cases, identifying duplication is also a practice that one needs to master. Some duplications are easy to spot, but others are more elusive.

Uncle Bob (Robert Martin) defined five principles that provide guidance for loosely coupled design, known by their acronym SOLID (see sidebar). These principles make it somewhat simpler to understand how to write loosely coupled code, but then again, mastering these principles is not trivial either.

THE SOLID PRINCIPLES

Robert C. Martin, widely known as Uncle Bob, introduced in the early 2000s (in various documents[9]), the following five principles that deal with managing dependencies between classes in an object-oriented design, practically making these classes loosely coupled from each other. These five principles are:

- **Single Responsibility Principle (SRP)** – *A class should have one, and only one, reason to change.* In my words: classes should be small and focus on just one thing. Any auxiliary behaviors should be extracted to other collaborating classes.

- **Open/Close Principle (OCP)** – *You should be able to extend a classes behavior, without modifying it.* Extending a behavior of a class without modifying it can be done by overriding virtual methods, or by depending only on interfaces that the client can supply, usually

---

[9]In his website, `http://butunclebob.com/ArticleS.UncleBob.PrinciplesOfOod`, there are links to the major documents where these principles originally appeared.

through the constructor. The behavior can then be extended by providing other classes that implement the required interface and that extend the original behavior. Another way to implement this principle is using events: the class fires events, and the collaborators can register to these events to extend the original behavior.

- **Liskov Substitution Principle (LSP)** – *Derived classes must be substitutable for their base classes.* In my words: neither the base class nor its clients should be aware of any specific detail of derived classes or even their existence. This means that adding or changing derived classes should work without changing the base class or its clients. In addition, when you access an object through an interface, you should not rely on specific implementation details that you may know about the classes that implement it.

- **Interface Segregation Principle (ISP)** – *Make fine grained interfaces that are client specific.* In my words: if a class is designed to be used by two (or more) different clients for different purposes, the class should expose separate interfaces, one for each of these clients. For example, a buffered memory stream object may expose separate interfaces for a reader and for a writer, as the reader doesn't need the functionality of the writer and vice versa.

- **Dependency Inversion Principle (DIP)** – *Depend on abstraction, not on concretions.* This means that the class in question should not reference other concrete classes, but rather only interfaces that those classes should expose. For example, for a BL class, instead of referencing a DAL class directly, it should only reference and use an interface that the DAL class exposes. This makes both of these classes depend on the interface, but none of them depends on the other, and therefore can be changed, extended, or replaced independently from the other.

Uncle Bob's website (mentioned in the footnote) has links to full documents describing each of these principles in detail. Also, in 2011 I wrote a series of blog posts[10] about the relationships between these principles and TDD.

---

[10]http://blogs.microsoft.co.il/arnona/2011/08/26/tdd-and-the-solid-principles-part-1-introduction/

Mastering Refactoring

Even if you master the SOLID principles and can spot the most elusive duplications, it's still not enough. In order to master TDD and unit testing, you also need to master refactoring. As mentioned above, refactoring is best done as a series of small and safe steps that leave the code working. Martin Fowler has written a whole book about this topic, called *Refactoring: Improve the Design of Existing Code,*[11] but in order to be effective, you should also master the available refactoring tools that your IDE provides. In addition, once you master these techniques, you may come up with your own refactoring techniques and may even be able to extend your IDE to perform these transformations automatically, like the built-in ones.

The Biggest Challenge: What to Test?

The challenges we've discussed up until now are pretty technical. But probably the biggest challenge for doing TDD is to decide what we should test. If we really test each and every class separately, abstracting it from all of its collaborating classes through interfaces (and using mocks in the tests), then we might end up with *loads* of tests, but many of them will be very technical and not directly related to a user scenario. While TDD and unit tests promise to drive a design in which the classes are loosely coupled and easy to maintain, these technical tests (e.g., tests that verify that specific arguments were supplied to a specific method on a specific interface, or tests for a class that handles a low-level data structure) end up being tightly coupled to the details of the many *interfaces* that are created to satisfy the testability of these classes. When you want to *refactor the interactions* between a few classes, you'll need to change the interfaces between them (and probably some of their implementations). Consequently, you'll also have to change most of the tests of classes that implement them or mock them. You may then find out that these fine-grained unit tests not only are not helping you but even hinder your maintainability!

This means that it's not always effective to write unit tests with a test scope of a single class, and sometimes it's better to test a few classes together. The question then becomes: How can I decide? The short answer is that it's mainly a matter of practice and experience. But below you'll find some guidelines that will hopefully help you through.

---

[11]Martin Fowler, Kent Beck, John Brant, William Opdyke, and Don Roberts, *Refactoring: Improving the Design of Existing Code* (Menlo Park, CA: Addison-Wesley Professional, 1999).

While all of these challenges may look daunting, mastering all of the above-mentioned challenges, makes you a better programmer, even without TDD. But TDD also becomes arguably the most powerful tool in your tool belt, as it leads you to write cleaner, more maintainable code, which you can also easily verify to do what you expect.

TDD the Way It Was Meant to Be

In fact, no formal definition of unit tests that I'm aware of, especially by the Extreme Programming (XP) thought leaders like Kent Beck and Martin Fowler, says that a unit tests (or any test done in a TDD fashion) must be of a single method or class, but somehow this has become the common notion. As Martin Fowler tells in his blogpost titled UnitTest[12] and also in the "Is TDD Dead?" series mentioned earlier, ever since they first came up with this idea of unit testing and TDD, they were not concerned so much about isolating every class, and mostly tested the collaboration among a bunch of classes. They only used test doubles (mocks) from time to time when it was awkward to test it with the real collaborators.

Note   Martin Fowler refers to tests of a single class that use mocks for all other classes as *Solitary Tests* and the advocates of this style of tests as "mockist style xunit testers," while to tests that include few classes together as *Sociable Tests*, and to their advocates as "classic style xunit testers."

In fact, when you remove the restriction that a unit test can only test one class, you find that TDD with "sociable" unit tests is very similar to ATDD, except maybe for the following nuances:

1. In TDD, usually the person that writes the tests is the same developer that implements the code. However, TDD advocates usually also advocate pair programming, so in fact you can say that the two persons that write the tests are the same persons that implement the code together.

---

[12]https://martinfowler.com/bliki/UnitTest.html

2. The tendency is to choose somewhat smaller scopes than you'd likely to choose in ATDD, and the emphasis on faster tests and tighter feedback loop is stronger.

Outside-In vs. Inside-Out Approach

The second nuance is also related to another kind of style that different practitioners have: the "outside-in" approach claims that you should start from broader-scoped tests that cover the scenario closer to the user's perspective, and fill in more details using more fine-grained (smaller-scoped) unit tests. The broader-scoped test may keep failing until all of the smaller-scoped tests pass.

The "Inside-out" approach claims that you should start from a narrow-scoped unit test, which covers the essence (business logic) of the scenario, and then write more tests that stretche the scope more widely until the entire user scenario is implemented. In fact, you can refactor the narrow-scoped test code, extract all calls to the SUT to virtual methods in the test class, and then derive a new test class for the broader-scoped test and override these virtual methods to invoke the same behavior from a broader scope (e.g., through REST API, and even through Selenium). This is actually an implementation of the Abstract Test Scope pattern described in Chapter 6.

In my experience, most features should start from a user story whose behavior is relatively simple and straightforward, and mostly only moves some data from one place to another, possibly performing some pretty simple manipulations on that data, while later user stories mostly thicken the internal business logic of that feature, which gradually makes it more complex. In these cases, there's not much justification to start with a narrow-scoped unit test, as the CUT will be pretty simple (especially if there's not much manipulation of data). The larger-scoped test is justified as it can show that the data flows correctly throughout the system. As later user stories dealing with the same feature make the internal business logic more complex, and as we already have tests that verify the data flow, then we can focus our efforts on covering that business logic using smaller-scoped unit tests. If we do it this way, we'd typically end up with many unit tests and fewer integration and system tests, which adheres to the test pyramid paradigm. But that does not mean that it's always like that, and you shouldn't aim to form a pyramid but rather choose the appropriate scope mainly on a case-by-case basis.

Summary

If we don't write our code with Unit Testing in mind, then chances are that it won't be unit testable as is. In order to make it unit testable, we need to refactor it and extract the external dependencies and I/O operations outside from the CUT to external classes and reference them through interfaces. Doing it properly requires some skills that we need to master. Doing TDD helps direct us in the right way but does not solve all of the problems, and practice and experience are needed in order to master it. But once you master these techniques and TDD itself, it will improve the maintainability of your code greatly and make you a better programmer. When you do it properly, you'll probably realize that TDD and ATDD are pretty much the same thing after all.

CHAPTER 18

Other Types of Automated Tests

All of the chapters so far have dealt only with functional tests. But there are a few other types of automated tests, and this chapter covers the most common ones.

Performance Tests

The purpose of performance tests is to measure the time it takes for the system to complete various operations. Usually the reason to test it is that the performance of the system greatly affects the user experience, and sometimes it even maps directly to revenue, as in the case of e-commerce websites that have numerous competitors, which users can easily switch to if they have a bad experience.

Note   Some people confuse Performance Testing with Load Testing, which tests how the system handles many concurrent users. While these types of tests are somewhat related, they serve different purposes and use different techniques. Load testing is discussed later in this chapter.

Measuring Performance in Production

Most web applications, especially those hosted in the cloud, can use the canary releases paradigm (mentioned in Chapter 5), where each release is first distributed only to a small portion of the users (can be a distinct group of users like opted-in Beta testers, or it can be just arbitrary users selected randomly by a load balancer) , and gradually takes

© Arnon Axelrod 2018
A. Axelrod, *Complete Guide to Test Automation*, https://doi.org/10.1007/978-1-4842-3832-5_18

over the older release. In this case, you can avoid having extensive performance tests, as you can measure the actual performance of the users directly. In business applications, sometimes you can first distribute the application only as a pilot for one team, on which you can measure the performance and gradually improve it, before you extend the distribution to the entire organization.

Note that in web and client/server applications, the time an operation takes is combined from the time the client processes the user action and prepares the message to send to the server, the time it takes the message to be sent from the client to the server, the time it takes the server to process and handle the request and prepare the response, the time it takes the response to be sent back to the client, and the time it takes the client to process the response and render the result on the screen. This description is even pretty simplistic, as there can be multiple messages sent between the parties and some intervals may be overlap or be completely parallel. In addition, these intervals can be broken down to more granular ones. Figure 18-1 shows the timing intervals of a simple client/server operation.

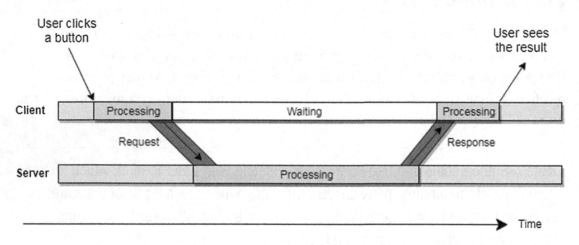

Figure 18-1. *Timing intervals of a client/server operation*

If you want to collect performance statistics of actual user operations in production, and the client-side processing time may be significant enough to measure, then you have to instrument the client to measure and collect this data and send it back to the server. There are many sophisticated monitoring tools these days that allow you to analyze, query, and drill down the performance both of the client side as well as of the server side. You can find not only which operations take long time, but also the exact scenarios in which it happens, and how frequently.

But not all applications lend themselves well to canary releases, as some applications must be performant on their first release or may not have so many users to gather statistics on. For example, medical applications that should pass the FDA certification before going to production don't have the privilege to make these rounds of measuring the performance in production and fixes the bottlenecks before going live. Another example where measuring performance using tests can still be very important is in applications that should be used mainly in rare emergency situations. In most cases where canary releases are not feasible, regular dedicated performance tests are needed before going to production.

What Not to Do

A common misconception about measuring performance is that you can leverage the existing functional tests to measure the performance of the operations it performs. Indeed, technically this is possible, and sometimes even very easy, especially for HTTP API-based tests, where the time between each request to its response can be measured automatically and seamlessly and saved to a database. While indeed this way you gather a lot of performance data, it doesn't help you much in making reasoned decisions about the performance of the system. In addition, when the measurement is not as transparent to the tests as with HTTP API-based tests, mixing between testing functionality and testing performance often makes the test code more complex and less maintainable.

The main reason that measuring performance as part of functional tests is not so valuable is that functional tests often run in isolated, sterile environments that don't reflect the real production environment. But in order to not just gather data, but really test, you need to define an expected result – just like in functional tests. The difference though is in the way you define the expected result.

Note that often people think that they can still leverage the performance data measured by the functional tests and define the expected result (regarding the performance) as the threshold on the percentage of degradation in performance related to a previous build or version. In other words, the tests will warn them when the performance of each operation was significantly worse than in the previous build. There are a couple of main caveats for this idea:

1. There can be many factors that affect the measured time of an operation. Without considering all of these factors in the tests, there can be many false positives, which makes this data unreliable.

2. The tests themselves can be changed to do things differently, in order to improve the reliability or the maintainability of their functional aspects, without taking into consideration the effect on the performance measurements. Taking these effects into the considerations can conflict with the maintainability and reliability of the functional tests so that's not the solution.

Defining the Expected Result

In order to define the expected result, you should first decide what's the operation that you care to measure the most and in which scenario. Note that the same operation, like check-out from an e-commerce site, can go faster or slower according to the number and the type of items in the shopping cart and other similar factors.

After defining the operation that you want to measure and the scenario in which it's being used, you should define the environmental conditions under which the test should run: on which hardware profile (number of CPU cores, memory, type of hard drive, etc.), networking profile, size of the database, etc. While using the exact environments as in production is best in terms of the accuracy of the measurement, it's not always feasible. This can be because the hardware used in the production environment is too expensive to be duplicated just for testing performance, or because the application is intended to be installed on customers' hardware (be it a server, a desktop, or a mobile application) that can have a wide variety of hardware profiles and capabilities that you don't have control over. In these cases, you may even want to have multiple environments to measure performance on some of these different hardware profiles.

Note that Virtual Machines (VMs) usually share physical resources with other VMs on the same host. This often adds significant "noise" to the measurement, as another VM can suddenly make use of a lot of resources, leaving to the tested application only a small portion and thus affect its performance. Therefore, it's preferable to configure the VM with minimal allocated resources that can't be shared with other VMs.

Lastly, the thresholds of the expected performance should be defined. Unlike functional tests where you run each test once and determine whether it passed or failed, with performance tests you typically have to run the same test a few times, or make a loop inside your test that invokes the tested operation, and gather a few results. If you visualize the performance results on a graph (e.g., using Excel), you should see something similar to a bell curve (actually a gamma distribution as described in Chapter 13, but you don't have to care too much about the mathematics of that). The expected results should be defined in terms of the thresholds in which some high enough percentage of the results don't exceed a specified duration. For example, you can define that if at least 90% of the results were under five seconds, then the test should pass. You can also calculate the mean or the median, but these are usually less important. By the way, this is how typically service-level agreements (SLAs) are defined. If your company obligates to a specific SLA regarding the performance of the application, then you should simply use these numbers. If not, you can define together with your product owner (and your team) these thresholds and make them your internal "SLAs," upon which you decide whether it's appropriate to release or not. In case you have a continuous delivery (CD) pipeline, you can make this test a part of its gates.

Reusing Code Between Functional and Performance Tests

While I advised against using the same tests both for functional and performance tests, I do advise you to reuse their common code. In fact, as performance tests typically perform operations that are used also in functional tests, then it makes a lot of sense to reuse the relevant common parts.

Investigating Performance Bottlenecks

There are a whole lot of books on this topic alone, but as an introduction to this topic, it's worth mentioning that there are profiling tools that allow you to analyze and drill down how much time each method call has taken, how long the database transaction took (and why), what was the network latency, etc. Sometimes analyzing these results can be straightforward, but other times it can be pretty complex. But anyway, beware of premature optimization! Recall Donald Knuth's quote from Chapter 15: "*premature optimization is the root of all evil.*" Don't assume you know where the bottleneck is until you measured and performed a root cause analysis.

Perceived Performance vs. Actual Performance

It's important to note in the context of performance, experts often distinguish between actual performance and perceived performance. While the actual performance is easier to measure, the perceived performance is what's important in the context of user experience. For example, if the application takes five seconds to retrieve a bunch of data, and then it shows it to the user all at once, it can seem longer than if it takes seven seconds, but the most important data is presented after two seconds, and only the rest of the details appear after additional five seconds.

Load Tests

While load tests are related to performance tests (and many people get confused between them for that reason), it measures a completely different thing. Load tests measure how much hardware resources the server uses for a given amount of **concurrent users**. The test can simulate the maximal amount of expected users if it's not too high, or only a percentage of it, which can then be used to extrapolate in order to assess whether the production environment has sufficient resources to handle the full load, or how many resources (e.g., number of servers) are needed to handle full load. Note that testing only a percentage of the maximal load and extrapolating the results is less accurate, but sometimes is the only feasible way. Load tests should also ensure that there's no single bottleneck that adding more hardware resources cannot solve, for example, due to bad architecture. Note that load tests are only relevant for servers, as clients don't need to handle multiple concurrent users.

Like in performance tests, this type of test becomes less relevant in the cloud era, as resources can be dynamically spun up or down according to real-time production monitoring measurements of the utilization of the resources. However, there are still scenarios where these tests are important, mainly:

- When going live cannot be done incrementally, as the site must go up for a particular event.

- When not using the cloud or even a private cloud, or when using special hardware resources. This is especially relevant for older, "monolithic" applications.

- In fact, in the first case, the load tests can be done as a one-time effort, without having to add the load tests to the CI/CD pipeline. But the ideas are pretty much the same.

How Load Tests Work

There are various tools for load testing, with different features and advantages (most known are JMeter, SmartBear's LoadUI Pro and LoadComplete, Visual Studio Load and Performance, LoadRunner and Gatling), but the basic idea is the same. You either record or write tests that send requests to the server, and the load-testing tool simulates many concurrent users running in parallel, by running the tests from different threads or processes on the same machine.

Note that the test machine itself should be pretty powerful itself in order to run so many threads or processes, and beyond a certain number of concurrent simulated users (according to the power of the test machine), you may have to use more than one test machine (agent) in order to simulate the desired load. These days it's also common to run these test agents from the cloud, to simulate load from different geographical regions. Note that the tested application itself doesn't have to run on the cloud in order to use the cloud for running the load test agents. Another thing to note is that there's no point in running the client application, as it will only take resources from the test machine without generating more load. Therefore, it is better that the test sends the requests and receive responses directly and not through the client (e.g., with Selenium). However, sometimes the costs of writing and maintaining separate tests for the server side just for the sake of load testing are not justifiable, and reusing client-side functional tests, or at least their infrastructure, is nonetheless the preferred choice.

Defining the Expected Result

As always, before implementing any kind of automated tests, we first need to define our expected results. The expected result of load tests is typically defined to be that the server can handle the maximal expected number of concurrent users successfully. But there's a lot more to it:

- What's the most common operation that these users perform?

- What other operations users are expected to perform and what's their distribution in a given moment? For example, we can say that in an e-commerce website we expect that in a given moment, 60% of the users are searching and browsing for products, 25% perform the checkout process, 10% are new users that are currently registering to the site, and another 5% are sending "contact us" requests.

- How long a typical user waits between one operation and the other?

- What is the expected response time for each request?

- What percentage of error responses or timeouts is acceptable? The desirable answer to this question is always 0 obviously, but this is very rarely achievable. Therefore, it's important to define this threshold realistically

- Etc.

Note that all of these parameters are about the users or the interaction of the server with the client, but similarly to performance tests, we should also define the characteristics of the server (or servers) that should handle the load. Generally speaking, the success criteria for a load test is that the server continues to operate and serve users in the expected response time and percentage of errors.

Defining the Thresholds

Because it's not always feasible (or simply too expensive) to have a load test environment that allows for the actual maximal load that is expected in production, typically the load is tested on a smaller, less powerful environment with a proportionally lower load. Moreover, we want to run the test for a period of time (usually a few hours) to make sure that the system's resource utilization is stabilizing and not increasing, under a constant load. Memory leaks, which is a term that describes the situation that memory usage increases over time with for no justifiable reason, is the most common type of bug that cause an increase in resource utilization. But it can happen with other resources too (disk, network, CPU, and more). For these reasons, we usually don't settle only for the criteria mentioned above, but also want to measure the resource utilization, like CPU, memory, and other health metrics, over time, and make sure that they remain under a certain threshold. Some of the load testing tools have these metrics built in, but normally the production, and production-like environments where the tested application runs, should employ health and diagnostics monitoring tools anyway.

Because the load test agents themselves are stressed when running the tests, it's important to monitor their health metrics too. If we see that they are nearing their limits, we should consider adding more agents or more hardware resources to the existing ones, to prevent the agents themselves from crashing.

Creating the Tests and Their Environments

In order to know what these thresholds should be, we need to first measure those at least once as a reference. As mentioned above, sometimes we only want to run load tests once in order to measure these things. But even then, if you'll try to run the test for the first time with all of the criteria mentioned above and with the maximum load, you're likely to fail pretty fast. There can be many factors that limit the scale that the test tries to reach, and you need to identify and remove those limits first. For example, if the test was created by recording the network traffic, or it uses Selenium, the test may cause requests to be sent to third-party services. These requests are needed by the real application (for example, the website needs to retrieve fonts from Google Fonts), but because they are sent from the same machine (the load test agent) many times in a very short period, these third-party services may identify these requests as a denial-of-service (Dos) attack and block further requests that will cause the tests to fail. Similar issues can be caused by firewalls and other security mechanisms in the organization, by bugs in the tests, by limitations of the test or production environment, etc. Therefore, we would usually try to run the tests first for a small number of users, and for a short period of time, and as we identify and fix these issues, we can add more and more users and lengthen the time of the test. Sometimes during this process, a bottleneck in the SUT's is identified, which is in fact a bug that prevents scalability, and needs to be fixed.

If it's desired to add the load tests to the CI/CD pipeline, then after the first time the test has passed and the environment is prepared, it's possible to rerun the same test cycle against new builds. However, if you first run the test against the production or a preproduction environment that you may want to use for other purposes, then you need to construct a dedicated environment for the load tests first. This environment can be less powerful than the production environment, but in that case the thresholds and expected load should be adjusted proportionally. Note that like functional tests, these tests will need maintenance as the application evolves.

Combining Performance with Load Tests

When you first reach the desired load, it's useful to open a browser and try to use the website manually, to experience the impact of that load on the perceived performance. But if you want to add the load tests to the CI/CD pipeline, then it can be useful to run the performance tests alongside the load tests, in order to make sure that the performance characteristics are still within the expected threshold even when the system is loaded.

The performance of an operation in a client/server (including web) application is combined from the processing time on the client + communication time + processing time on the server. It's important to understand that the client-side processing is not affected whatsoever from the server load, and the communication time also shouldn't be affected as long as the server's bandwidth is not saturated, in which case the load test should fail. Therefore, if you can reliably infer from the architecture of your application that it's performance is affected mostly from the client-side processing, then there's no point in running the performance tests under load, but if you know or suspect that the time an operation takes is mostly affected by to the server-side processing, then there's a lot of value doing so. If the client-side processing is negligible or is constant and not expected to change over time due to future developments, then it suffices to run performance tests as server-side only tests.

Running Tests in Production

Until a few years ago when someone suggested to me to run tests in production, I would ask: What's the point? If the tests pass in CI, why would they fail on production? But over time I realized that there are some good reasons to do that.

Testing Deployment

In theory, your CI/CD pipeline should be fully automated and reliable and should prevent you from deploying a build that destined to fail. But reality is always more complex. Even if the CI/CD pipeline is fully automated, new features may require new dependencies, the pipeline's scripts themselves may have changed, and database schema updates is always a tricky part that can be error prone. In addition, in systems that compound from several services that are deployed independently, or systems that need to interact with other systems, it could be that the version of one of the other services or systems that were used in the test environment is not the same as the one currently in production. This could happen for several reasons:

- The test environment has a newer version of a related service that was not yet deployed to production.

- The test environment used the same version of a related service that was in production when the tests ran, but then a newer version (that was tested on another environment) was deployed to production before our system was.

- An external service was updated. Even though such external services should normally maintain backward compatibility, we may run into an edge case in which compatibility was broken.

Therefore. running a few tests just after deploying a new build can give us confidence that the system is functioning properly and that nothing was broken during the deployment

Testing the Health of the Production Environment

The second reason for running tests in production is to monitor the health of the application and of the production environment. There are many monitoring and diagnostic tools these days that give the DevOps (or just Ops) guys a pretty clear picture about the health of the system in production. While these tools are invaluable, they are not aware of the expected functional behavior of your system. You can usually customize them to measure some parameters that indicate it, but it may not be as reliable and as easy as running a test that performs a selected and known business scenario routinely and reports in case it failed.

Which Tests to Run

If you're about to start planning a new automation test suite and considering to use them in production, I advise not to mix these concerns. For CI you should first consider the isolation aspects that may not fit so well in production, like the use of simulators or controlling the configuration of the system. However, for production tests, you must ensure that the tests don't do any harm to real data or invoke business processes that you don't want them to invoke because they may have unwanted consequences in real life, like ordering more goods from suppliers.

Having said that, sometimes existing functional tests' isolation requirements make them suitable for production too as is. But you would probably want to select only few of them specifically and make sure that they're safe for production. If you're not sure, want to be on the safe side, or you know that the isolation requirements of your functional tests don't fit the production environment, then you should write a dedicated suite of tests for that purpose. Clearly you can reuse some of the infrastructure of the tests.

Like in performance tests, we'd probably don't want to send an alert to the DevOps guy whenever a test failed once. Unlike in CI, where we should run the tests in a sterile environment, here we probably want to give the test another try or two in case of a failure and only then send the alert.

Cleaning Up Test Data

Most tests create some data when they run. It may not be much in terms of storage, but because these tests run periodically, this data can affect statistics and reports about users. One way to do clean up this data is using the cleanup mechanism described in Appendix B. Otherwise, it's better to create a batch job that deletes this data once a day or few days. But in order to delete that data easily, we must distinguish it from other real-user's data. We can decide on a known pattern, like prefix everything with "AUTO," but we also need to know from which tables to delete the data. In other words, it may be feasible but you need to give some proper thinking to make it right.

One more thing to pay attention to is to ensure that when the job that deletes the data runs, it doesn't delete the data of a test that is currently running; otherwise this test will probably fail. This can be achieved either by synchronizing this job with the job that runs the tests: after the test has completed, pause the test's job, run the job that deletes the data, and then resume the tests job. Alternatively, you can make the job to delete only data whose date is yesterday or older to ensure that you don't affect any test that is currently running.

Visual Testing

Visual testing grabs a lot of attention lately. In general, visual testing is a way to test the actual image presented on the screen, much like the user sees it, against a previously saved template. While Selenium and other UI automation tools test the application from the UI layer, they don't verify that the UI appears correctly. The colors, sizes, shapes, etc., of the elements are not tested, even though they have a significant effect on the usability and user experience. Obviously, the reason that these UI automation tools don't rely on the exact location, size, colors, etc., is that these things can change more frequently and thus fail the test. But sometimes verifying the appearance of the UI can be very valuable, *in addition to* regular functional tests.

Currently the dominant product in this area is Applitools Eyes. The Sikuli open source project uses visual object recognition, but it uses it more as a way to identify elements rather than strictly for visual testing. Another new tool in this area is Chromatic, though it also takes a different approach that is based on comparing the look of individual components and is specifically tailored for the React framework.

Note   Because strict pixel-by-pixel image comparison is very error prone due to issues like aliasing and resolution, these tools use smarter image comparison techniques that can compensate for these limitations.

The Visual Testing Workflow

Visual testing provides an API that you can integrate with your functional tests to take screenshots in relevant moments in the test, either of the entire page or of a specific element. The first time your run the tests, these images are saved as a reference.

The following times you run the tests, it compares the screenshots with their corresponding reference images and reports the differences. It also marks the exact locations of the differences on the image. For each of these differences, you can then choose to exclude their region from the next comparison, to update the reference image, or, if the difference is a bug, then you can choose to keep the original reference image as is (and fix the bug in your application).

Note that the amount of attention and maintenance that this workflow requires varies (examining the differences and updating the baseline), mainly according to the frequency of UI changes, and the number of screenshots that the tests take. Though as we already know from Chapter 2, if it doesn't change then there's probably not much value in testing it. I believe that in the future these tools will be smart enough to recognize the same type of change in many places, so when you choose what to do regarding one difference, the tool will suggest to you to do the same for all similar differences, reducing the maintenance costs significantly. Though I believe that even then, occasionally an all-encompassing change to the appearance of the page (which can be done by a pretty small change in CSS) may affect all of the reference images, and they all should be taken anew.

Visual Testing and Cross-Browser/Cross-Platform Testing

One area where visual testing really shines is cross-browser and cross-platform testing. Today the sheer number of browsers, operating systems, and moreover, mobile devices, is tremendous. Performing manual visual testing on the entire matrix of tests and platforms in short release cycles is far from feasible. While applications that are designed to be cross-browser and cross-platform should look the same everywhere, they don't always do. These different browsers and operating systems have each a different rendering engine that can have an effect on the outcome. Sometimes small variations are expected, but other times these small variations in the rendering engines are multiplied and amplified to cause a real bug. Thankfully, Applitools Eyes and similar tools allows you to control the level of accepted variations, which can overcome the legitimate differences between browsers from one hand, but still catch more severe rendering problems on the other hand.

Installation Tests

Some applications that are designed to be installed on the customer's machine have a complex dedicated installation program. While the need for such installation programs is gradually going down (as most applications today can be installed simply by copying a folder or extracting a Zip file), there are still applications that require them. These are typically client or server applications that interact with special hardware or software and need to install device drivers, or they require complex configuration processes in order to operate.

Approaches for Installation Tests

You can look at these installation programs as separate programs that you need to test on their own. The problem is that the output and the purpose of the installation program do not stand on its own (i.e., no one uses the installation program for any other purpose other than to use the installed application). There are a few approaches to testing installation programs.

Testing the Direct Outcome

The direct outcome of an installation program is that the relevant files are copied or extracted to their correct locations, and that certain configurations are saved in a configuration file, the Registry, or alike. Accordingly, you can write a test that invokes the installation program and then verifies that the correct files and settings are written to their correct locations.

There's an important drawback to this approach though: maintaining the list of required files and settings can be cumbersome and error prone and make the test very fragile. The fact that the test passed does not mean that the application is installed correctly. It could be that all of the *expected* files were copied and settings were written, but the application cannot start because it requires another new file or setting that the test was not aware of. Similarly, the test may fail because a file is missing, but that file is not really needed anymore.

Installing the Application Before Running All Tests

The second approach is to install the application once on the test environment before running the tests. The preferred way to do that is to use a VM with a clean snapshot. Before the test run starts, it reverts the VM to that clean snapshot, runs the installation program, and then starts to run the tests. If the installation was not successful, probably all of the tests, or at least most of them, would fail. The failure would typically be pretty fast because the application won't even start, but you can also condition the run of most of the tests on the success of the first few sanity tests. If all or most of the tests have passed, it probably means that the installation was successful.

The drawback of this approach is that it only verifies one positive scenario of the installation program. It does not verify all of parameters and their combinations, error conditions (e.g., out of disk space), different platforms, and the existence or inexistence of prerequisites, etc.

Testing That the Application Can Run Correctly After Every Installation

The last approach treats testing the installation application like testing any other application, but in order to verify that the installation was successful, it runs one sanity functional test. Some more specific tests of the installation program may need to also run a more specific functional test as a verification. For example, if the installation program lets you configure a mail server that it uses to send reports, you may want the installation test to run a functional test that verifies that the report is sent (and received) by email. Naturally, negative tests should not run any functional test but need to verify that the correct error message is displayed, and possibly that the installation folder does not exist after the installation has failed.

This approach allows to test the installation program with different parameters and preconditions. Like in the previous approach, you should also use a VMs with a clean snapshot for these tests, but in addition, you can use different VMs to test the installation on different operating systems and use snapshots for testing different preconditions. You may even need several groups of VMs to test different network topologies, like having the database and server on different machines.

While this approach is theoretically preferred, it's the most complex and expensive to write, and takes the most time and compute resources to run. Of course, you can also mix and match the different approaches in order to optimize the balance between reducing the risk and reducing the costs.

Testing the Installation Through UI or Through Silent Install

Most installation programs allow us to run them interactively, with the typical installation wizard, but also to run them with no UI, where the parameter values are specified as command-line arguments or through a dedicated file. Running the installation silently requires no UI automation technology, which is typically faster and easier to maintain. But sometimes you may want to test the installation UI too, in which case you must use UI automation.

Testing Uninstall

Usually the same program that is used to install an application is also used for uninstall. Testing the uninstall feature is pretty similar to testing the installation, though you should obviously first install the application before you can uninstall it. The expected result of uninstall should usually be that all files were deleted, but it can get somewhat more complicated than that. Sometimes files that the user created or even changed (e.g., configuration files) need to remain. And sometimes files are locked and will only be removed after restarting the system. In order to test the last scenario properly (though other scenarios may also require it), the test should be run from a machine other than the installation machine, in order to be able to restart it, and check that all the files were deleted after restart.

Upgrade Tests

If installation tests sound complicated, then upgrade tests are much more. There are two additional dimensions to the test matrix over for upgrade tests over installation tests:

1. **The source version** – upgrades are not always performed from the latest version. Users can skip one, two. or more versions when they upgrade. In addition, each major version can have few minor versions and even a few Beta versions.

2. **User data** – while the user was working with the old version, he probably created some data (in the form of files, database records, etc.). He may also change some configuration data to customize the system to his preferences. When he upgrades, he would probably expect to be able to use his data with the new version and preserve the configuration values, given that they're still relevant in the new version.

Approaches for Upgrade Tests

Similar to the installation tests, upgrade tests can be tested using the following approaches.

Testing the Direct Outcome

Similar to the corresponding approach for installation, after installing the old version and optionally creating or changing some data, the test should run the upgrade program, and verify that the new files were copied. Similarly, if new configuration entries should have been added, then this should be verified as well. It's possible also to test that the data that was created or changed after installing the old version is still intact (or has transformed to a newer format as necessary).

Upgrade the Application Before Running All the Tests

Similar to the corresponding approach for installation, we perform the upgrade only once before running all the tests. We can either explicitly install an older version, run some functional tests in order to create some data, then upgrade, and then run the functional tests again; or we can preserve the environment from the previous build

441

or version, and directly upgrade and run the tests. Note that if we upgrade from the previous build, and some tests (or the installation itself) failed, then the environment is no longer clean, and we may not know if failures that we experience after the upgrade are trailing errors or new ones. In addition to the downsides of the corresponding installation approach, testing upgrade this way pretty much misses the point of testing the upgrade of the data. Because functional tests typically create the data they need (for isolation purposes), then they never verify that data that was created in the previous version is still usable.

Explicit Upgrade Tests

This is also similar to the "Testing that the application can run correctly after every installation" approach, but here it's not enough to run a sanity test in order to verify that the new version is installed correctly. Most tests need to create or change some data before the upgrade and run a more specific test after the upgrade to verify that the data is still usable. In addition, while in the installation tests we could reuse existing functional tests, here we probably can't, because we need that the test that runs after the upgrade will verify the data that was created by another test that was run before the upgrade.

To sum up the upgrade tests topic: the test matrix and the complexity of implementing these tests properly is huge. Therefore, trade-offs must be made according to risk and cost analysis in order to decide what to test.

Testing AI, Statistical, and Non-deterministic Algorithms

These days the term AI (Artificial Intelligence) starts to become very popular, if not to say the next buzzword. The term "AI" itself is very loaded with many philosophical meanings and implications, which makes it too broad for any effective discussion. A somewhat more specific term is "machine learning," which means that the machine can "learn by itself" without being specifically programmed to solve a specific task, by looking at previous examples or by looking for patterns in the data. One particular technique for machine learning that started to gain a lot of traction lately is "deep learning." Deep Learning is based on a technique called Artificial Neural Networks (ANN) that was well known for several decades and was pretty widely used in areas like handwriting and speech recognition. But Deep Learning also takes advantage of tremendous compute power and access to vast amounts of data available on the Internet, which makes it capable of solving new problems that were not considered to be solvable by computers before. A canonical example for this technology are the computer vision offerings of the big cloud vendors (Mainly Microsoft Azure, Google Cloud Platform, and AWS) that can recognize the content of any arbitrary image and tell you what's seen in it. The common thing about all of the "AI" and deep learning techniques is that they heavily rely on statistics.

There are seemingly two main challenges with testing algorithms that are based on statistics:

1. You need a lot of data in order to get a meaningful result.

2. The exact results may vary with small changes (and improvements) to the algorithm.

In addition, some of these algorithms make use of random numbers, which makes them nondeterministic.

Approaches for Testing Statistical Algorithms

Following are few approaches to consider when testing an application that makes use of statistical algorithms. As always, you can mix between them as appropriate.

Mocking the Algorithm Altogether

Most systems that make use of statistical algorithms contain the algorithm in one specific component. While this component typically contains the core value of the product, it is usually wrapped with a lot of other components that contain normal application code and business logic. When we want to test that business logic we'd often hit a challenge trying to define the expected result, if that result relies on the outcome of the algorithm.

For that reason, it's often wise to mock the component that contains the algorithm altogether when we want to test the result of the business logic of the application. Note that the mock doesn't have to simulate the logical behavior of the algorithm, and it can even return absurd results. For example, suppose that our application allows the user to upload a few images and to specify a name of an object to look for in those images, and the application tells the user how many of the images contain the specified object. For example, the user might upload four images, three of them containing a cat (with possible other objects in the image), and one of a car, and specifies the term "cat" as the object to look for in the images. The user should then get the result "3" because only three images contain a cat. Let's assume that the algorithm we're using accepts only one image at a time and returns a list of objects that it recognizes in the image. The mock should not care what's actually in the image and therefore you can feed it with the same 1x1 black pixel image all the time, and only tell it to return different results each time it's called. In the test, we can specify the results that the mock should return to be [cat, table] the first time it's called, [cat] the second time, [bottle, cat] the third time, and [car] the fourth time. This way we can test the business logic of our application without having to use the real algorithm whatsoever and be affected by its fuzzy results.

Obviously, in this approach we don't test the algorithm itself, only the code that surrounds it, but in many cases, this is what we actually need.

Using Absurdly Trivial Results

If you do want to test the application end to end, including the algorithm, but don't want the fuzziness of its results to affect the reliability of your tests, you can use absurdly trivial cases. Following the previous example, instead of using a mock, and instead of using a "cat" as the search term, you can use a "black rectangle" search term and provide it with simple images drawn in MS-Paint that contain a black rectangle and optionally other geometrical shapes in different colors over a white background. Recognizing these shapes should be a lot "easier" for the algorithm and there shouldn't be any surprises as to the results of the algorithm. (If you'll use real cat images, small changes in the algorithm or its training data may result in identifying one of the cats according to its breed and return "Ragdoll" instead of "cat," for example.)

Using Thresholds

Most "deep learning" algorithms, as well as other statistical algorithms classify their inputs to a set of possible outputs, returning one concrete result. But other algorithms return one or more values, like percentages, estimations of quantities, date and time, etc. Small changes in these algorithms or the use of random values may produce slightly different results at each test run. Whether you want to test the algorithm itself or the end-to-end application, you should consider defining the expected result as a range. In some cases, this range can be the same for all cases, but in others it should be different for each case. For example, suppose that the previous computer vision algorithm also produces the certainty level of its results, and we also want to test that. Then for a black rectangle over a white background we can assume that the certainty level should be very high (e.g. 99%), and we can use a narrow range (e.g. 98%–100%) for our tests. But for a specific image of a cat which is not very clear, where the confidence level that we get is 65%, we'd probably also want to use a wider range as the expected confidence level, of let's say, 50%–90% to allow for future changes in the algorithm.

The thresholds can be used for other results that are not percentages. For example, we may use an algorithm that attempts to predict the number of participants in a particular event. Suppose that under certain circumstances it currently predicts that 120 people will attend the event. If we'll determine the expected result to be exactly 120, then small changes in the algorithm will likely fail our test. So, we can use a range of 110–150 to be safe. You should consult with the product owner about the range, because sometimes either the upper bound or the lower bound should not be too far from the current result, while the other bound can vary more.

Using Test Sets or Regression Data

When you want to test the algorithm itself, you normally need a volume of data, along with their expected results. Machine learning algorithms are typically categorized into *supervised learning* and *unsupervised learning* (and sometimes also semi-supervised, but that's beyond our scope). With supervised learning, the algorithm is fed with a set of training data, which contains both the input data and the expected outcome of the algorithm (often referred to as "labeled data"). For example, for handwriting recognition, the labeled data can contain a big set of images of handwritten letters along with the actual letter (character). The common practice is to split the available labeled data into three parts:

- **Training set** – this set of data is used by the algorithm to "learn" the patterns.

- **Validation set** – this set of data is used by the algorithm engineer (AKA data scientist) to validate the accuracy of the algorithm and fine-tune its parameters to improve its results.

- **Test Set** – this set of data is used to verify the final effectiveness of the algorithm. The reason that this step is important is to avoid a phenomenon called *overfitting*, where the algorithm can identify the data in the training and validation sets very accurately, but identifies any other input data much poorly

The last part can be implemented as a data-driven test (DDT), or as a single test that loops over the data and invokes the algorithm. This test can constitute the regression test for the algorithm. Note, however, that in many cases it is not expected that 100% of the rows in the test set will actually pass. A threshold should be put on the number, or the percentage, of failures to determine the success criteria of the algorithm.

For unsupervised learning, and for algorithms that are not classification algorithms, you'd probably won't have a predefined test data. In these cases, you can probably take some historical data, feed the algorithm with it, and save its results as a reference (i.e., expected results) for future test runs. As mentioned above, you should also take some reasonable thresholds either for each result, or a fixed threshold for all results, and use that data for a data-driven test. Given that your current algorithm does its job pretty well and that your thresholds are appropriate, then this data can make a good use of regression testing for the algorithm.

Testing Applications That Use Random Numbers

Regardless of AI, applications use random numbers for various purposes. Obviously, games are the most common example, but some business applications use them too. There are few approaches to tackle the challenge of testing these applications.

Mock the Random Generator

In most cases, using a mock for the random generator is the best approach, as it gives the test full control over the "randomly" generated values. If you want to use this mock outside of a unit or component tests, then you need to have a way to inject that mock into the process of the SUT. This can be done by means of dependency injection mechanisms, a dedicated configuration flag, and so on. In fact, this is similar to how we go about simulating the system's data/time as described in Chapter 6.

Use a Known Seed

Random generators use a special algorithm to generate a sequence of numbers that has a more-or-less uniform distribution. In order for the sequence to be different each time, they normally use the number of milliseconds or system ticks since the computer has started or of the current date/time as the initial value for this sequence. This initial value is called the *seed*, and you can typically provide it directly to the random generator, instead of using the system's clock. Providing the same seed in different invocations of the application causes the exact same sequence to be generated.

Therefore, you can add a "hidden" option in your application to provide this seed value from a configuration file or any other external source and use it in the tests in order to ensure consistent and deterministic results.

Even though this approach also requires a change in the SUT, this change is usually much simpler. However, it doesn't actually give you control over the generated values, which you may need to simulate some edge cases, as it only ensures that the sequence is consistent. Moreover, small changes in the application code, including refactoring which should not affect the behavior of the application, may nonetheless cause the application to produce different results with the same seed. For example, if a game needs to initialize the player to a random location on the screen, it should draw two random values: one for the X coordinate and the other for the Y coordinate of the player. If the application draws the X value first and then the Y value, or the other way around, it does not matter from the user standpoint (because both of them are random), but if this order is changed, it will fail the test if it relies on the seed to produce the same location each time.

Testing Business Intelligence (BI) Applications

The term Business Intelligence (BI) is used to describe technologies and applications that help the organization analyze data stored in its systems, in order to provide business information and insights about it for the sake of helping decision makers make better business decisions. While this is a wide topic, which sometimes also involves machine learning, in many cases it's comprised mainly from a bunch of ETL processes and corresponding reports. ETL, which stands for Extract, Transform and Load basically mean to take data from one place (Extract), transform it to better suit the format we need, and/or extract the relevant information, and the load it to another database, from which it can be queried more easily. While normally these ETL processes and reports work on large volumes of data, mostly they don't use complex statistical algorithms to produce their results. Therefore, in order to test these ETL processes, or the BI application altogether, you can usually treat is as testing any other application and use *small* amounts of data, dedicated precisely for the needs of each test. The database can be reverted to a clean backup before each test and filled only with the relevant data by each test according to its needs.

For example, if a report should show the percentage of employees that work in the company, classified by their seniority, in ranges of 0–1, 1–3, 3–5, 5–10, 10–20 and 20+ years, you can generate between 1 and 3 employee records for each of these categories (which total as about 10 records altogether), and verify the results accordingly.

While most BI applications are pretty complex, performing many transformations and allowing the user to slice the data in the reports in various manners, you can usually test each of these features separately as you would normally do with regular applications.

Summary

In this chapter we saw different uses of test automation other than the normal functional tests. For each of these uses, we discussed the challenges that they pose. For each of these challenges, we saw one or few ways to tackle them. But this is only a sample. There are many other unique uses for test automation and reality imposes many more challenges on any unique use. Eventually you'll be left on your own to find the appropriate solution for your unique problems. I hope though that you gained some ideas and insights that will help you face any such challenge to come.

CHAPTER 19

Where to Go from Here

First, I want to thank you for reading this book to its end! But your journey for learning about test automation doesn't end here, rather it has only started. Actually, it will also probably never end. Here are some general tips for the journey.

Make Mistakes

As with all important things in life, so it is with test automation: there's no one right way, and even if there is, you may not know what it is. But if you're afraid to make mistakes, you'll go nowhere. Mistakes and failures are invaluable learning resources. Over time, you'll learn from your mistakes and be able to improve. You'll probably make new mistakes but hopefully won't repeat the same ones that you made before.

One important tip in that regard, is that if you can do a quick experiment that will tell you whether you're in the right direction or not, then do it! It's much better to fail fast than to stick to a mistake for a long time.

Listen, Consult, and Take Advice

Because there's no one right way for most things, you can learn a lot from the mistakes, experiences, or even the ideas of *others*. Consult the people whose opinions you value the most, but also listen carefully for those who you usually don't. Even if you don't accept their opinion, at least you'll understand their different point of view better, which can be very valuable too.

Also, don't afraid to ask for help, ask for review, or to ask questions. Remember: the only stupid question is the one you don't ask. Reviews (code reviews, design reviews, or even reviewing ideas) are an invaluable way to learn, which cannot be overrated. And finally try to get help whenever you need it. You may find help on the web, including

A. Axelrod, *Complete Guide to Test Automation*, https://doi.org/10.1007/978-1-4842-3832-5_19

on this book's website (`www.TheCompleteGuideToTestAutomation.com`), but sometimes, if you feel that you lack enough knowledge in a specific domain, you should probably look to hire someone to help you, whether it's a part-time consultant or a full-time employee. Obviously, you're always welcome to hire me as a consultant as well (you can contact me through LinkedIn at `https://www.linkedin.com/in/arnonaxelrod/`).

Having said that, I'd recommend that at least for specific technical questions, you should first try to find the answers yourself before asking someone, either by reading the docs, searching the web, or even better – by experimenting. When you find the answer for yourself, you're more likely to remember the answer and get a better understanding of the issue.

Understand and Align to Your Business's Goals

At the end of the day, test automation is just a means to an end. If used properly, this tool usually helps the organization to release stable versions much more rapidly and do that for a long time. But each organization has different goals and ways to reach those goals; and at different phases, the organization may have different goals or strategies to achieve them. Understanding your organization's needs and goals should guide you when you plan, develop, or use test automation, to best serve your current organization's goals.

Get to Know Your Tools

No matter how you've built your automation solution, you're using a set of tools. For example, Selenium, MSTest, Visual Studio, and C# may be your primary tools. For the tools you're using the most, try to get to know them in depth and expand your knowledge about them. Often people use a tool for a long period of time, but they only know and use a small portion of its capabilities and features. Knowing the tool that you're using on a regular basis deeply usually can make you much more efficient! The primary way to learn a tool in depth is to read its docs. Another useful way to learn more about tools is simply by exploring their features. You can explore features of a code library (like Selenium and MSTest) by using code-completion and inline tooltips, explore IDEs by traversing its menus, etc. Whenever you encounter something that you didn't know about, take some time to experiment with it or at least to read more about it. For open source projects, you can even clone their repositories and look inside their code.

In addition, you can subscribe to relevant topics on StackOverflow[1] to get a feed of questions specific for the tools you're using the most. Reading other people's questions, with or without their answers, exposes you to different features and problems that you were not aware of. Trying to answer some of these questions presses you to check your answer and to formulate it in a clear way, which strengthens your understanding of it (as the old saying goes: teaching is the best way to learn). If you also take the time to research some of these questions that you don't know the answer to, you'll probably learn something completely new.

Gaining knowledge about your tool not only makes you more productive but will eventually make you the go to person about this tool, which will make you even better at it. Moreover, when you know one tool in depth, you have a better understanding on how it works. When you come to learn another tool that works in a similar manner (e.g., another test automation framework, another UI automation technology, another programming language, etc.), you'll quickly identify the similarities and differences compared to the tool you already know and you'll learn the new tool very fast. The more tools you'll know, the quicker you'll learn new ones.

Improve Your Programming Skills

As stressed enough throughout this book, test automation is primarily programing. Therefore, treat yourself as a software developer. Get to know your programming language and IDE in depth; ask for code reviews; take some programming tasks; learn new programming languages and paradigms (e.g., functional programming, actor model, etc.); go to developer's conferences, etc. See Appendix D for some tips and practices to improve your productivity as a programmer, like working effectively with the keyboard, understanding some language features, writing error-proof code, handling exceptions properly, etc.

Throughout this book I reference few other books and paradigms about programming that I believe that every programmer should master, such as Clean Code, the SOLID principles, Design Patterns, Refactoring, and TDD.

I even believe that in order to be a good test automation developer, you should spend a couple of years as an application developer. Not only will you improve your programming skills, but you'll also have a better understanding of the developer's work and the challenges they're facing, both from the technical standpoint, but also from aspects like organizational processes and workflows. When you return to develop automated tests, you'll have a whole new perspective on it.

---

[1]www.stackoverflow.com

Improve Your QA Skills

While I mostly stress that automation is programming, it is definitely also about QA. Analytical and critical thinking are key to test planning and failure investigation. But first and foremost, you should be primarily focused on *quality*, and not on the test automation per se. Remember that test automation is just a tool, that testing goes way beyond automation, and that QA goes way beyond testing. Try to acquire a broader view on the tested application, its users, and the development life cycle, in order to be able to assess where the real risks are and the ways to mitigate these risks most effectively. Try to define what quality really means for your organization and for the users, and try to find ways to measure these things effectively, in order to make a real change.

Similar to improving your programming skills, you should also improve your QA skills by reading about different and new QA paradigms, talk to people, listen to podcasts, and go to conferences. Clearly, spending a couple of years as a tester will help you know their challenges, standpoints, and the way they think better. But instead of spending a couple of years in each role, probably the best way is to spend a couple of years in a team where everyone does everything (dev, testing, DevOps, etc.) or at least a multidisciplinary team that works in a tight collaboration.

Broaden Your Horizons

In our day-to-day work we're only being exposed to a specific problem domain, specific organizational structure, processes, architecture, etc. If you really want to be a professional, you should know more about what happens in other places, domains, technologies, and so on. A great way to gain this knowledge is by going to conferences and local meetups (AKA User Groups), but also to read and participate in forums and groups on social media, reading blogs, listening to podcasts and similar things. Reading books is also an excellent way to expand your knowledge and also to deepen it in the areas you're already familiar with.

Once every few years, looking for and taking new opportunities inside your organization, or outside – if you don't find what you're looking for inside – can also broaden your horizons a great deal.

Share Your Knowledge

Finally, whenever you gain some knowledge about something, even if you think that it's not much and that probably most others already know it, share it nonetheless. You'll be surprised how much value this knowledge can be to others. Today it's very easy to share your knowledge though LinkedIn, or to open a blog. Writing down something to explain it makes you understand it even better. Getting comments from the community will give you ideas for improvement and can pretty quickly make you a domain expert in a particular area.

Beyond writing a blog, you can share your knowledge by speaking at conferences and meetups. Local meetups are typically more suitable for less experienced speakers, which makes it a great way to start. But it can also give you invaluable experience and confidence for later speaking at conferences.

Sharing your knowledge with the community (whether it is blogs, meetups, conferences, or any other way) makes you a known personality among your colleagues and potential future employers or customers, and it can give your career a significant boost. Even if your blog remains pretty anonymous, pointing potentials employers to it can give you a big advantage even before the interview process, over similar candidates that don't write blogs.

Share the Tools You Build

One way to share your knowledge in a very helpful way is by sharing reusable code and tools that you developed, as an open source project (or as a tool that you can download or use online). If this code or tool is indeed useful for other people, they'll probably appreciate it much more than if you only shared your plain knowledge. Also, managing a successful open source project has all the benefits for your career as sharing knowledge does.

This is what I did with the Test Automation Essentials project (described in Appendix C). I simply took everything I built that can be reusable by other projects and shared it on GitHub.

Don't Forget to Enjoy!

Take whatever advice you feel like from this chapter and from this book in general, but most importantly – don't forget to enjoy whatever you do! Oh, and wear sunscreen!

APPENDIX A

Real-World Examples

In Chapter 6, we've discussed how to design the test automation to fit the architecture of the specific application. This appendix describes three examples based on real-world applications that I was involved in designing test automation solutions for.

Note that these examples are only *based* on real-world cases. Some details have been changed for clarity purposes, to protect Intellectual Property, and for anonymity purposes. A couple of ideas that are presented here did not come to full fruition in the real projects, mainly due to priority changes, internal politics, etc., but the technical feasibility of all of them were at least proven.

Example 1 – Water Meters Monitoring System

One of my clients develops electronic water meters and a system for controlling and monitoring the meters in towns and districts. The meters themselves, including the electronics and the embedded software, are developed and tested separately from the control and monitoring system for the towns and districts.

They called me to help them build a test automation infrastructure for the control and monitoring system. This system is a website that can display information about the meters and their statuses over a Google Maps widget, in addition to more standard ways like tables, forms. and charts. The system has the architecture depicted in Figure A-1.

© Arnon Axelrod 2018
A. Axelrod, *Complete Guide to Test Automation*, https://doi.org/10.1007/978-1-4842-3832-5

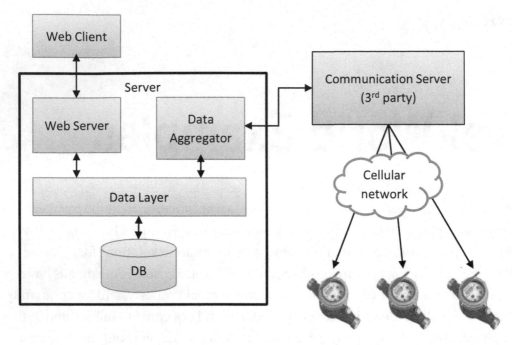

Figure A-1. *Architecture diagram for water meters monitoring system*

Here's a description of the components and the interactions between them:

- The Web Client is the HTML pages along with JavaScript and CSS files that the browser uses in order to show the UI and interact with the user. Like any other website, these HTML pages and related files, as well as the data to display are retrieved from the Web Server on the server side. The main page also displays a Google Map widget and uses the Google Maps JavaScript API to add markers in the locations of the meters on the map.

- The server side contains the following components:

    - The Web Server is the server side of the website, which provides the HTML, JavaScript, and CSS files to the clients' browsers, as well as Web API that provides the data that needs to be displayed. The Web Server mainly retrieves the data and receives events on important updates from the Data Layer. In addition, it can send commands to the meters, also through the Data Layer.

- The Data Layer manages the access to the data and provides relevant notifications to the layers above it about updates of data. The Web Server uses the Data Layer to retrieve data from the database, get notifications and send commands, while the Data Aggregator uses it to store and update data in the database and receive commands to send to the meters.

- The Data Aggregator component receives a stream of near real-time data from all of the meters throughout the district, through the Communication Server. It aggregates it and transforms it to the structure that the Data Layer requires. In addition, it sends commands to the meters according to requests from the Data Layer. Before sending a command, the Data Aggregator first translates it from the internal data structures of the application to the protocol that the meters can understand.

- The Communication Server, which was developed for my client by a subcontractor, behaves like a specialized router between the application and the meters. The Communication Server itself doesn't read or change the content of the messages but only dispatches them to and from the right meter, through a cellular network.

- Finally, the meters themselves are the physical electro-mechanic devices that measure the water flow, alert on problems, and accept commands like open or close the tap. These devices are equipped with a cellular antenna to communicate with the Communication Server. Even though these devices also have software in them, this software is developed in a completely separate group in the company and in different cadence. Therefore, for the purpose of testing the Control and Monitoring system, the software on these devices can also be considered as 3rd party, and not an integral part of the system.

When I was called to help the QA team establish a framework for their automated tests, I asked them what was important for them to test. The initial response was: "end to end." However, when we dove deeper, it turned out that what they really care about are the UI and server pieces, which are all the software that they build themselves in that group, while the Communication Server and the Meters themselves are of less interest as they were considered stable and reliable.

Simulating the Communication Server

Then I asked them how they performed their manual tests today, and it turned out that they're using a database that is a copy of one of their clients and performs all of the tests through the Web Client's UI. Only at our meeting they realized that they're not testing the Data Aggregator component at all, even though a big part of the logic is there. When we discussed how we should approach it from a test automation perspective, we came to the conclusion that we need to create a simulator for the meters and the Communication Server. This is the only way we can also test the Data Aggregator component and also is necessary in order to create reliable tests that cannot affect one another.

At first it seemed like an unrealistic mission, because the QA team and their manager were stressing that on one hand, because only the developers have the knowledge of the protocol, then they're the ones that should develop the simulator; but, on the other hand, the developers are too busy and will have no time for that in the foreseeable future. But then I suggested that the developers will only provide the documents of the protocol and a little bit of knowledge transfer, and that the automation developers will actually develop the simulator. So, the QA manager called the relevant developer and asked him if he can help us with that, and he promptly agreed! It turned out that they have a very detailed document of the protocol, and for any unclear or outdated details he was happy to assist us. Figure A-2 shows the final architecture of the test automation.

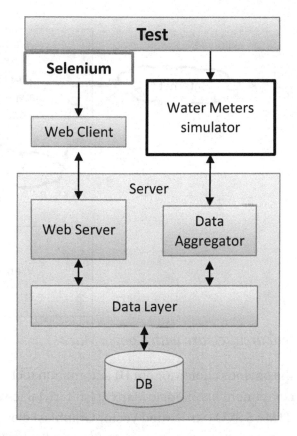

Figure A-2. *Final test architecture for water meters monitoring system*

Dealing with Google Maps

The other architectural challenge was with the Google Maps component. Like any web page that contains a Google Map component, the architecture is as shown in Figure A-3.

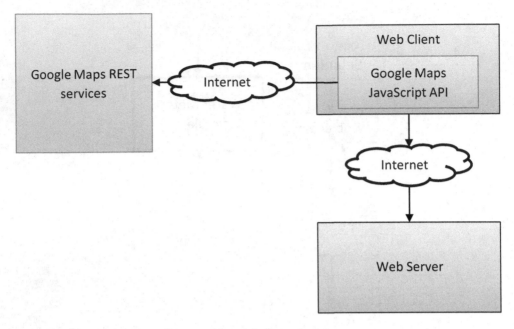

Figure A-3. *Web Client architecture with Google Maps*

As Selenium was the obvious choice for our UI automation technology, when it comes to a graphical component like Google Maps, it isn't trivial to work with. Google Maps is based on an HTML 5 SVG (Structured Vector Graphics) element, which contains all the raw data that represents lines and shapes required to display the map. While Selenium has access to this data, it's unfeasible to reason about it and to identify the *meaning* of what the user sees. However, Google Maps also uses a JavaScript API behind the scenes that provides more meaningful information and operations. Selenium on its part can send any JavaScript code that we'll give it to be executed directly in the browser and get the result back, so we can use Selenium to query and manipulate the JavaScript API of Google Maps, and thus we can get a meaningful notion of what the user sees.

Figure A-4 shows the architecture of the solution with regard to the Google Maps component.

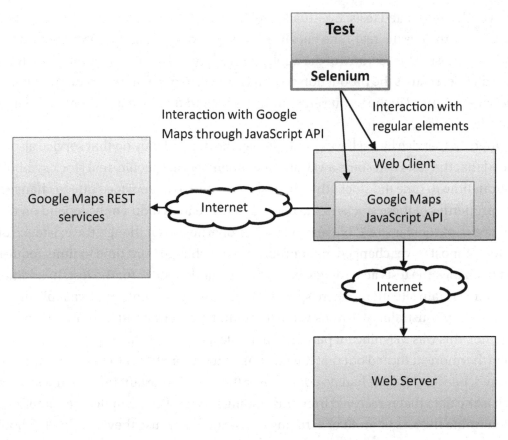

Figure A-4. *Test architecture for Web Client with Google Maps component*

Example 2 – Forex Trading System

To the customer of my second, example I came after they have started implementing automated testing, but they reached out to me because they had some issues, mainly with the stability of their tests. After investigating and fixing some apparent issues, we started discussing the business processes that they use around the automated testing. Pretty late in the conversation, I realized that they don't run the tests on Sundays. It may look obvious to you, but if you consider that in Israel the work week is Sunday to Thursday (i.e., Sunday is just another regular working day), you'd probably understand why I was surprised. The people I talked to took it for granted that tests cannot be run on Sundays, because the stock exchanges don't operate on Sundays. Obviously, I understood why the real system doesn't work on Sunday, but I still didn't understand why tests cannot run on Sundays, and this was true both for manual tests as well as the automated tests. Eventually I realized that they depend on a third-party service that provides the real-time data from various stock exchanges throughout the world, and most of the features of the application are unavailable when there's no trade. This is all fine as far as the production system is concerned, but it turned out that the same service is used in the testing environment too, and that's what prevented them from testing on Sundays.

While this service by itself was pretty stable, the dependency on that service also implied that the tests had some awkward dependencies on specific, real stock symbols, and from time to time the stocks that the tests used had to be replaced due to changes of some properties of these stocks in the real market. The tests didn't only depend on the existence of particular stock, but also on their properties. Even though the existence of the stock almost never changed, their properties did change from time to time, requiring them to change the tests accordingly or to choose another stock for the test. In addition, there were certain situations where specific stocks were temporarily unavailable due to real trading constraints. Obviously, the test didn't have any control over that, and altogether, this was a significant part of what made the tests unstable.

Furthermore, it turned out that the most basic functionality of the system cannot be validated, because the test had no control over the most important input of the system, which is the data that is received from this trading service. For example, they couldn't predetermine the loss or profit of a trading transaction, because they couldn't tell how the stock would behave.

After that conversation I realized I must have a better understanding of the architecture of their system and so I asked them to show me an architecture diagram. The architecture diagram that they showed me was similar to the one in Figure A-5.

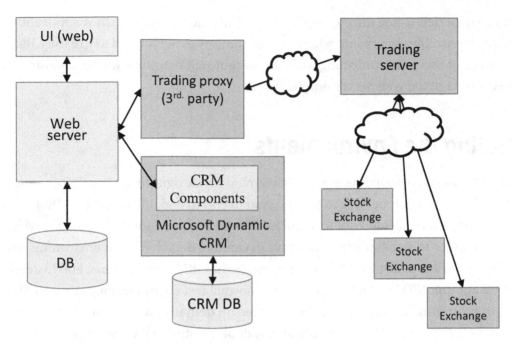

Figure A-5. *Forex trading system architecture*

The Solution

Due to the conclusions from that discussion, we decided to implement a simulator for the Trading Server (and its proxy). This allowed us to have better control of what's going on in the tests and to simulate scenarios (including the very basic ones!) that we couldn't test before. Obviously, it made the tests more reliable and allowed the tests to run at any time, including Sundays.

Instability Caused by CRM

Another component that affected the stability of the tests was the CRM application. The main system was connected to a Microsoft Dynamic CRM system that stored the information about their users. The Microsoft Dynamic CRM application was also extended and tailored to their needs (the "CRM Components" in the diagram). The team that worked on this part of the system was separated from the team that worked on the main Web Server, but the testing environment of the main Web Server was configured to work with the same testing environment of the CRM team. Due to technical constraints, the CRM Components developers used their testing environment not only for testing per

463

se, but also for debugging during development. This meant that the CRM application was mostly unstable. As a result, whenever the main Web Server had to use the CRM component, it was communicating with the unstable CRM application that, in turn, made the tests of the Web Server unreliable too.

Isolating the Environments

Because the CRM components are tightly coupled (by design) to Microsoft Dynamic CRM, and because the goal was to test the system end to end, including the CRM Components, we've decided not to simulate the CRM as done for the Trading service. Instead, in order to stabilize the tests, we've decided to detach the test environment of the Web Server from the test/dev environment of the CRM Components, and instead to create another CRM installation inside the normal test environment. An automated build (that runs nightly but can also be triggered on demand) was created to build the code in the source control, and upon success, deploy both the Web Server *and* the CRM Components to the test environment. This allowed the developers of the CRM Components to debug their code on their original environment, and only after they verified their changes, check in the code to the source control system, thus leaving the test environment clean and stable enough to run the automated tests. Figure A-6 shows the final architecture of the test environment.

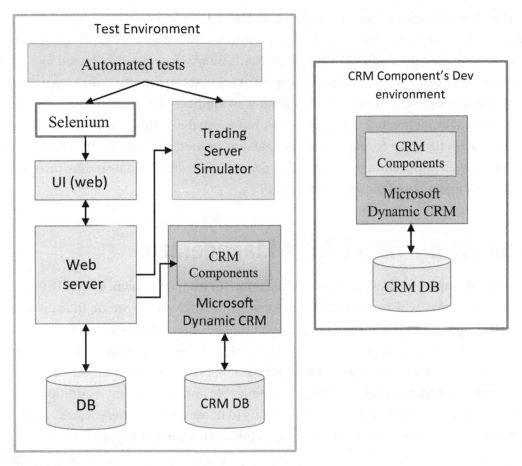

Figure A-6. *Final architecture of test environment*

Testing the Mobile Application with Abstract Test Scope

In addition to the normal web application, they started to develop a new mobile application. The mobile application has basically provided the same functionality, but the UI was organized differently to fit to the smaller form factor of a smartphone. The UI technology that was used for the mobile application was of a hybrid application, meaning that it's like a web browser embedded inside a shell of a native application. That means that technically we could use Selenium also to test the mobile application, but because the UI was organized differently, then we couldn't reuse the existing tests as is.

Therefore, in order to support testing both the regular web application and the mobile one, we decided to refactor the test code to use the Abstract Test Scope pattern that was described in Chapter 6: The test methods themselves shouldn't need to change, but we extracted a set of interfaces for every class and method that represented a business functionality (that uses the regular web application), and created a new set of classes that implemented these interfaces, but using the mobile application. We've also added a setting to a configuration file that determined whether we should use the normal web application or the mobile one, and according to that setting, the test automation instantiated the appropriate classes.

Example 3 – Retail Store Management

Our third example is of a client/server application for managing retail stores. Unlike the first two examples, which are central web sites with a single deployment, the application in this example is an off-the-shelf product that retailers can buy, install, and run on their own hardware. Because this software was an off-the-shelf product, and because it was a major and important software that the retailers used to run their businesses, it was important that it would be highly customizable and extensible. In addition, we supported several different deployment options to fit retailers of different sizes and needs. Figure A-7 shows the architecture for a full deployment of the system.

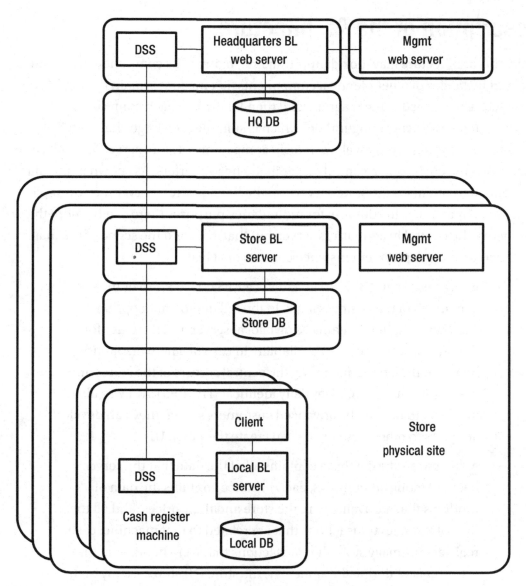

Figure A-7. *Architecture of the application in full depoloyment*

Description of the Architecture

While this architecture may look daunting at first, many of its components are simply different instances of other identical components. Let me first explain the high-level architecture described in the diagram, and then I'll explain each component.

In a full deployment configuration, which is suitable for a large chain retail store, the application is deployed on all cash register machines, a store server for each store (branch) in the chain, and a central server in the headquarters. As shown in the diagram, different components of the store server and the headquarters server may be deployed on separate machines. In addition, for redundancy purposes there can be more than one instance of the central headquarters server, but that's beyond the scope of the diagram. In particular, each deployment instance consists of at least:

- A Business Logic (BL) server – this is a REST/HTTP server that contain all of the business logic. In the full deployment option, each cash register contains its own local server and database for the sake of scalability and availability in case of a network failure. All of the BL servers, including the central servers of the stores and the headquarters. are essentially identical. The REST API was also intended to be used by advanced customers so that they can develop adopters to other systems or even create their own UIs.

- A database – the database contains all of the data that the server needs. Among other things, each instance contains the data of all products that are available in the store and their prices, and all the data of the sales transactions that are related to that machine: cash registers normally store the transactions that were handled at that same register during the same day, the store DB stores a copy of the transactions that were handled by all the cash registers in that store (branch), and the headquarter DB stores a copy of the transactions of the entire chain. In the Headquarters and Store servers, the database can be deployed on separate machines.

- Data Synchronization Service (DSS) – this component is responsible to synchronize the data between the different servers. Generally, most data changes (e.g., updates to products and prices) are transferred from the higher tiers (Headquarters, Store) to the lower tiers (cash registers), while sales transaction logs are transferred upwards. The DSS has dedicated business logic that allows it to decide which data it should transfer to which other server and which it shouldn't. For example, some products and prices can be applicable only to some stores and not the others.

Because that in the full deployment configuration the BL server is deployed both on the cash registers, at the store levels and at the headquarters, it was also called a "3-tiers" deployment.

In addition to the components that exist in every instance, the cash register machines have a dedicated UI client application that the cashiers use. This component is mostly a thin UI layer that talks to the local server that is installed on the same machine.

Lastly, the Management web server can also be deployed and connect to Store and Headquarters servers. This server provides a web interface for managing all data, including products and prices and also viewing and querying sales transaction logs and some analytical dashboards.

Minimal Deployment

As mentioned above, the application supports different deployment configurations according to the size and the needs of the particular customer (store). So above I explained the most complex configuration, and now I want to describe the simplest one.

The most minimal deployment consists of only one BL server, a database, and one client, all on one single machine, which is the cash register. Typically, one Management server will also be present, but even that's not obligatory as instead the data can be transferred from a third-party management system using the REST API. Figure A-8 shows the minimal deployment configuration.

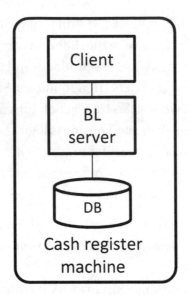

Figure A-8. *Minimal deployment configuration of the application*

The internal structure of the Server and Cash Register applications were very similar to the typical client/server architecture mentioned at the beginning of Chapter 6. However, it's important to note a few things:

1. The Service Layer was used as the public REST API. Customers used this API mainly for integrating this system with other systems and automating business processes.

2. The Business Logic layer was also exposed as a .Net API, mainly to allow customers to extend, customize, and override the default behavior of the system. This layer was made out of many components, some of which had interdependencies.

3. Each data entity (e.g., Product, Price, Sales, Customers, Cashiers, and many more) that had to be transferred to other servers using the DSS, had implemented an interface for serializing and de-serializing itself as XML. We'll talk about its consequences a little later.

Organizational Structure

In order to understand the considerations for the different test automation solutions, it's also important to understand the organizational structure (in Chapter 8 we've discussed the relationships between the organizational structure, architecture, and test automation). The application was developed by a group of about 200 people: about half of them are developers, others being mainly testers and product managers. There was a dedicated team for the Management web application, another team for the Cash Register client, and yet another one for the DSS. The BL server was developed by a few other teams, more or less corresponding to the different components in the Business Logic layer, but each of them was also responsible for the corresponding parts in the Service and Data Access layers. The project was managed using a Scrum methodology.

Test Automation Solutions

Because the Business Logic layer was exposed as a public API it was important (and natural) to write most of the tests as **component tests**. For each component, its tests would mock the other components. In addition, these tests were mocking the DAL, while other tests would test the DAL of each component separately. Naturally, as these tests were very light and fast, they were being run as part of the CI build (see Chapter 15). This build compiled and ran all of the tests of all the components together.

However, because of the interdependencies between the components, and because the Service Layer also exposed a public REST API, it became important to test the integration of the entire server as a whole on a regular basis. For this reason, an infrastructure for **integration tests** was also created. The general guideline was that for each User Story the teams should write at least one integration test in addition to the few component tests that they were doing anyway. These integration tests were testing the entire server and database as one unit, by communicating with it only through the REST API. The infrastructure of these tests created a dedicated empty DB before all the tests started to run for isolation purposes (see Chapter 7 about isolation) and used this DB throughout the tests. This allowed developers to run these tests on their local machines before check-in. These tests were also added to the CI build by installing the new version of the server on a dedicated test machine and running all the tests there.

While these tests were slower than the component tests, they were still pretty fast. While tens of component tests were executed in a second, most integration tests took between 0.5 seconds to 1 second. At the beginning it wasn't an issue, but when the number of tests raised to thousands, it took 30–40 minutes to run all the tests, and that started to become an obstacle. Even though it doesn't sound much, when developers were under pressure to release a new feature, they often skipped running all the tests before check-in, and then, mostly due to a conflict with a change of some other developer, the build failed. At that moment no one (of 100 developers!) was allowed to check- n their changes until the build was fixed. This was a huge bottleneck and time waster. Add to that the build itself took even longer due to the overhead of compilation and running the component tests (which was summed up to about 50 minutes) and you'll see how frustrating it could be.

The solution was to allow the tests to run in parallel. On developers' machines the tests were split between 4 threads (which was the number of cores on each dev machine). In the build, we split the tests to 10 different machines, each running 4 threads! That allowed us to reduce the local run time to about 10 minutes and the overall build time, including the compilation and component tests, to about 15 minutes! Of course, that each thread had to work with a separate instance of the application and with a separate instance of the database. Because the tests always started with an empty database – it wasn't a big issue.

Date/Time Simulator

There was a bunch of features that were dependent on dates and times. Fortunately, mainly due to the extensibility requirements, the system incorporated a dependency injection (DI) mechanism. In addition, partly thanks to the component tests, but also thanks to a proper architectural decision that was made early on, all uses of the `System.DateTime` class in .Net were abstracted behind an interface that a singleton object has implemented. This allowed us to develop a date/time simulator component that was injected into the system using the DI mechanism and control it from the tests through a specifically created REST end point. Figure A-9 shows the architecture of integration tests including the Date/Time simulator.

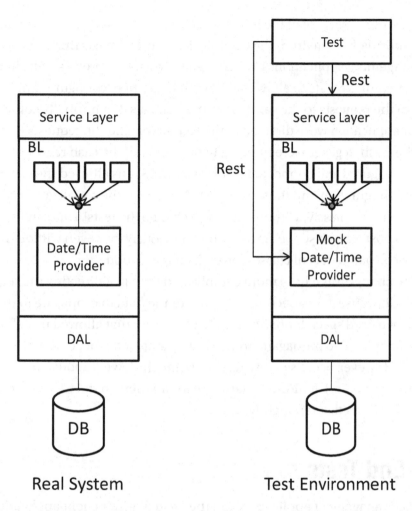

Figure A-9. *Architecture of the integration tests including Date/Time simluator*

3-Tiers Tests

The Management web application, Cash Register client and DSS teams were writing unit tests but no higher scope tests. However, manual testers often found bugs that were happening only in a full (3-tiers) deployment. This was mainly because of the special serialization and de-serialization code that should have been implemented separately for each entity and was not being used in the single-tier integration tests nor in the component tests.

Luckily, the infrastructure of the integration tests distinguished between REST requests that normally come from the Cash Register and requests that normally come from the Management application. This allowed us to make a pretty small change in the infrastructure of the tests to allow them to run in a 3-tiers configuration. Instead of directing all of the requests to the same URL, the requests that normally come from the Management application were directed to the HQ server, and the requests that normally come from the Cash Register were directed to the server of the cash register. Because the 3-tiers were configured and connected through the DSS, this allowed the existing tests to run in this configuration and thus test the DSS and all of the serialization and de-serialization code seamlessly, without having to change the tests! This can be considered as a form of an abstract test scope, as described previously, but even without having to implement two separate sets of classes for each configuration.

In fact, the change was a little more complicated than just directing the requests to different URLs, because it was necessary to wait for the data to propagate to the other tiers. For that, we used special monitoring API of the DSS that allowed us to know when the data has completed to propagate, so we could wait just the necessary amount of time and not more. However, because these tests were much slower (about 1 minute per test, as opposed to 1 second...), it didn't make sense to run them in the CI, so we created a different build process that ran nightly.

End-to-End Tests

Regarding the Management application and the Cash Register client application, even though they were covered by unit tests, it wasn't enough to make sure that they're working correctly along with the server. Occasionally there were discrepancies between the content of the requests that the clients were sending to what the server has expected, or similarly between the responses that the server sent and what the client was expecting. Therefore, at some point we decided that we cannot avoid automatic end-to-end tests. These tests were using Microsoft Coded UI for the Cash Register client, and Selenium to interact with the Management web application and were also running in a dedicated nightly build process. In most cases, a dedicated team (reporting to the QA manager) were writing these tests. Because the integration tests were already testing the 3-tiers deployment, it was enough for the end-to-end tests to test a single server but with the combination of the Management server and the Cash Register client. So, a single server gave us the missing coverage that we needed.

Cleanup Mechanism

As explained in Chapter 7, writing robust test cleanup code is not trivial and can be error prone, though it's possible to create a mechanism that solves the majority of these problems. This appendix explains how to create such a mechanism step by step and the recommended way to use it. Note that this mechanism already exists built in the Test Automation Essentials project (see Appendix C), so at least for MSTest you can use it almost out of the box, while for other frameworks for .Net (e.g., NUnit or xUnit), you should adopt the mechanism to the framework yourself. For any other language outside the .Net framework (like Java, Python, JavaScript, etc.), you should be able to implement a similar mechanism according to the explanations in this appendix.

Understanding Callbacks and Delegates

The cleanup mechanism is based on a programming concept called *Callback*. Different programming languages implement callbacks in a different ways and syntaxes, but all general-purpose languages have some way to implement it. A callback is a way to reference a function or method and keep it for a later use. In C# this is achieved through *delegates*, in Java through an interface with a single method (typically `Consumer` or `Function`), in JavaScript and Python you can simply assign a function to a variable without calling it (i.e., without the parenthesis after the function name). After you store a reference to a function in a variable, you can call the function through the variable. This allows you to assign different functions to the variable according to different circumstances and then call the chosen function simply by calling what the variable references. Some languages have a short syntax for declaring short inline anonymous functions, often called *Lambdas*, so you don't have to create and declare a whole new method if you just want to store a reference to that simple method in the callback variable.

© Arnon Axelrod 2018
A. Axelrod, *Complete Guide to Test Automation*, https://doi.org/10.1007/978-1-4842-3832-5

In c#, the predefined delegate type System.Action is defined as follows:

```
public delegate void Action();
```

This definition means that a variable of type Action can reference any method that takes no argument and doesn't return a value (i.e., return void) as a callback.

Listing B-1 shows an example of delegates and lambda expressions in C# that use the Action delegate type.

Listing B-1. Example of the concept of Callbacks using Delegates and Lambdas in C#

```
private static void Foo()
{
    Console.WriteLine("Foo");
}

public static void Main()
{
    // The following line doesn't call Foo, just stores the callback for
    // later use.
    Action x = Foo;

    // do other stuff...

    // The following line actually calls Foo
    x();

    // Assign a lambda expression (anonymous inline method) to x for later
    // use. The empty parenthesis mean that it takes no arguments, and the
    // code between the { } is the body of the method.
    x = () => { Console.WriteLine("This is a lambda expression"); };

    // do more stuff...

    // Now the following line calls the body of the lambda expression.
    x();
}
```

Building the Cleanup Mechanism

Let's get back to our cleanup problem. I'll describe the full solution step by step, in order to explain the need of each nuance of the final solution. But before discussing the solution, let's recall what's the problem is that we're trying to solve.

The Problem

If, for example, the test performs five operations that should be undone (e.g., creates entities that should be deleted), and the fourth operation fails, then we want only the first three to be undone, because the fourth and fifth operations didn't actually happen. Let's take a more concrete example: suppose we're building an e-commerce website, and we want to test that when buying three items and adding a coupon, the system will give the user the appropriate price reduction. In order to test this scenario, we should first add three products to the catalog and also define the coupon details. Listing B-2 shows the original test method. The first four statements perform the operations that we'll want to clean up when the test ends.

Listing B-2. The original test method, without the cleanup code

```
[TestMethod]
public void CouponGivesPriceReduction()
{
    var usbCable = AddProductToCatalog("USB Cable", price: 3);
    var adapter = AddProductToCatalog("Car AC to USB adapter", price: 7);
    var phoneHolder =
                AddProductToCatalog("SmartPhone car holder", price: 20);
    var coupon = DefineCouponDetails("12345", percentsReduction: 20);

    var shoppingCart = CreateShoppingCart();
    shoppingCart.AddItem(usbCable);
    shoppingCart.AddItem(adapter);
    shoppingCart.AddItem(coupon);

    var totalBeforeCoupon = shoppingCart.GetTotal();
    Assert.AreEqual(30, totalBeforeCoupon,
                    "Total before coupon added should be 30 (3+7+20)");
```

```
    shoppingCart.AddCoupon(coupon);

    // Expect 20% reduction
    decimal expectedTotalAfterCoupon = totalBeforeCoupon * (1 - 20 / 100);
    var totalAfterCoupon = shoppingCart.GetTotal();
    Assert.AreEqual(expectedTotalAfterCoupon, totalAfterCoupon,
                    "Total after coupon");
}
```

The Basic Solution

In order to leave the environment clean, we need to delete the products we added to the catalog and the coupon definition. But as we said, if one of the operations failed, we don't want to perform its cleanup code or the cleanup code of the operations that didn't happen yet. Therefore, the basic solution is to manage a list of callbacks (Action delegates) that each does an atomic cleanup operation. Immediately after successfully performing an atomic operation that creates an entity or changes the state of the environment, we should add to that list a delegate of a method (or lambda) that undoes that operation. In the cleanup method of the testing framework, we'll loop over the list of delegates and invoke them one by one. As we're using MSTest, we'll do it in the method that is decorated with the [TestCleanup] attribute (virtually all other unit testing frameworks for any language have a similar method). Let's first define the generic cleanup mechanism inside our test class, as shown in Listing B-3.

Listing B-3. Basic cleanup mechanism

```
private readonly List<Action> _cleanupActions = new List<Action>();
private void AddCleanupAction(Action cleanupAction)
{
    _cleanupActions.Add(cleanupAction);
}

[TestCleanup]
public void Cleanup()
{
    foreach (var action in _cleanupActions)
    {
```

```
        action();
    }
}
```

Now we can use it inside of our test method as shown in listing B-4.

Listing B-4. Using the cleanup mechanism inside the test method

```
[TestMethod]
public void CouponGivesPriceReduction()
{
    var usbCable = AddProductToCatalog("USB Cable", price: 3);
    AddCleanupAction(() => RemoveProductFromCatalog(usbCable));
    var adapter = AddProductToCatalog("Car AC to USB adapter", price: 7);
    AddCleanupAction(() => RemoveProductFromCatalog(adapter));
    var phoneHolder =
                AddProductToCatalog("SmartPhone car holder", price: 20);
    AddCleanupAction(() => RemoveProductFromCatalog(phoneHolder));
    var coupon = DefineCouponDetails("12345", percentsReduction: 20);
    AddCleanupAction(() => RemoveCouponDefinition(coupon));

    var shoppingCart = CreateShoppingCart();
    shoppingCart.AddItem(usbCable);
    shoppingCart.AddItem(adapter);
    shoppingCart.AddItem(coupon);

    var totalBeforeCoupon = shoppingCart.GetTotal();
    Assert.AreEqual(30, totalBeforeCoupon,
                "Total before coupon added should be 30 (3+7+20)");

    shoppingCart.AddCoupon(coupon);

    // Expect 20% reduction
    decimal expectedTotalAfterCoupon = totalBeforeCoupon * (1 - 20 / 100);
    var totalAfterCoupon = shoppingCart.GetTotal();
    Assert.AreEqual(expectedTotalAfterCoupon, totalAfterCoupon,
                "Total after coupon");
}
```

479

If, for example, adding the "phone holder" product (the third3 statement) fails, then the only cleanup action that we've added so far is for removing the "USB cable"(in the second statement), and therefore this is the only cleanup action that will be called by the Cleanup method. Note that the AddCleanupAction method-calls in the test code *don't call* the RemoveProductFromCatalog and the RemoveCouponDefinition methods. AddCleanupAction only *adds a reference to these methods* to the _cleanupActions list, which is used to invoke them only in the Cleanup method.

However, there are two problems with this cleanup approach:

1. The test method is now cluttered with a lot of technical code, which makes it much less readable.

2. Whenever we want to call AddProductToCatalog or DefineCouponDetails, we need to remember to add the appropriate cleanup action. This is very error prone and introduces duplication because each call to AddProductToCatalog or DefineCouponDetails should be followed by a call to AddCleanupAction with the corresponding cleanup callback method.

Gladly, the solution to both of these problems is very simple: Just move each call to AddCleanupAction to inside the appropriate method that creates the entity that we need to clean. In our case, we should move these calls to AddProductToCatalog and DefineCouponDetails. Listing B-5 shows how to add the call to AddCleanupAction to AddProductToCatalog:

Listing B-5. Adding the call to AddCleanupAction to AddProductToCatalog

```
private Product AddProductToCatalog(string name, decimal price)
{
    Product product = ... /* original code of AddProductToCatalog comes
    here (e.g. send HTTP request or add the data directly to the database,
    as appropriate, and returning a new instance of an object that
    represents the new product) */

    AddCleanupAction(() => RemoveProductFromCatalog(product));

    return product;
}
```

Now we can revert the test method back to exactly how it was in Listing B-2, but still have the cleanup code execute appropriately when the test completes.

Reusing the Cleanup Mechanism

Because we probably need this mechanism in most or even all of our test classes, it makes sense to extract this behavior to a common base class. Listing B-6 shows the cleanup mechanism in the base class.

Listing B-6. Moving the cleanup mechanism to a common base class

```
[TestClass]
public abstract class TestBase
{
    private List<Action> _cleanupActions = new List<Action>();

    public void AddCleanupAction(Action cleanupAction)
    {
        _cleanupActions.Add(cleanupAction);
    }

    [TestCleanup]
    public void Cleanup()
    {
        foreach (var action in _cleanupActions)
        {
            action();
        }
    }
}
```

And make all test classes derive from TestBase.

Handling Dependencies Between Cleanup Actions

That's all nice and fine, as long as the changes we're doing to the environment are independent from one another. Let's modify our example a little: suppose we want to support a different type of coupon, one that is associated with a specific product, and grants a discount only if that particular product is purchased *n* times. In this scenario, we have to define a coupon that refers to a particular product, and therefore the product must be created first, and when we define the coupon we specify the previously created product to be associated with it. If the application enforces referential integrity between the coupon definition and the product, then it should throw an error if you would try to delete the product while there's still a coupon definition associated with it. The test code in Listing B-7 shows this scenario. Notice how the usbCable object is passed as an argument to DefineCouponDetailsForProduct, which associates it with the new coupon. Assuming that DefineCouponDetailsForProduct adds a cleanup action for deleting this coupon, this code would throw an error in the Cleanup method, saying that "Product 'USB Cable' can't be deleted because there are active coupon definitions associated with it." Note that the exact line that throws the exception is not shown in the listing, but we can conclude that it should be thrown from RemoveProductFromCatalog (shown earlier in Listing B-5), which is called implicitly from the Cleanup method (shown in Listing B-6) using the delegate, because it would be called before the delegate that deletes the coupon is called.

Listing B-7. A test method that should fail due to the order of cleanup actions

```
[TestMethod]
public void CouponGivesPriceReduction()
{
    var usbCable = AddProductToCatalog("USB Cable", price: 3);
    var coupon = DefineCouponDetailsForProduct("12345", usbCable,
                               minimumCount: 4, percentsReduction: 20);

    var shoppingCart = CreateShoppingCart();
    shoppingCart.AddItem(usbCable, count: 4);

    var totalBeforeCoupon = shoppingCart.GetTotal();
    Assert.AreEqual(3 * 4, totalBeforeCoupon,
                "Total before coupon added should be 12 ($3 * 4)");
```

```
    shoppingCart.AddCoupon(coupon);

    // Expect 20% reduction
    decimal expectedTotalAfterCoupon = totalBeforeCoupon * (1 - 20 / 100);
    var totalAfterCoupon = shoppingCart.GetTotal();
    Assert.AreEqual(expectedTotalAfterCoupon, totalAfterCoupon,
                    "Total after coupon");
}
```

Fortunately, the solution to this problem is also pretty simple: we just need to **call the cleanup methods in the reverse order to which they were added.** It may look like this solution is accidental and specific to our case, but if you think about it, whenever we create a dependency between entities, we either first create the independent entity (i.e., the entity upon which the other entity depends), and only then create the dependent entity, or we create both entities independently (in any order), and only then create the dependency between them, as a separate operation. In the first case, which is like we saw in the example, deleting the entities in reverse order first removes the dependent entity (which also eliminates the dependency itself) and then deletes the first (independent) entity, which we don't have any dependency on already. In the second case, when we create the dependency between the entities, we should add the cleanup action that removes this dependency (without deleting any of the entities). When the cleanup actions will be called in reverse order, then the dependency itself will be removed first, and only then the entities will be deleted. Listing B-8 shows a very simple implementation of this solution.

Listing B-8. Reversing the order of cleanup actions to resolve dependencies

```
[TestCleanup]
public void Cleanup()
{
    _cleanupActions.Reverse();
    foreach (var action in _cleanupActions)
    {
        action();
    }
}
```

Now the cleanup will be done in the right order, and no exception will occur.

Note   You can obviously implement the cleanup mechanism using a Stack instead of a List, and avoid calling `Reverse`. This will probably be slightly more efficient, but it's pretty much negligible.

Handling Exceptions in Cleanup Actions

The basic idea of the cleanup mechanism is to perform exactly the relevant cleanup actions, no matter if the test failed or not, and if it failed, no matter in which line. However, what happens if one of the cleanup actions themselves fails? Unfortunately, nothing can be 100% safe, and the cleanup actions may throw exceptions too. In some cases, for example, if the test changes a global setting that affects all tests, and the cleanup action that should have reverted this setting to its original state, have failed, then it may cause the rest of the tests to fail because of it. But in most cases, it's not, and it's safe to continue to run the other tests. In addition, sometimes a failure in one cleanup action may cause *other cleanup actions* to fail as well. But nonetheless, because we can't be sure, then it's still worthwhile trying to call the other cleanup actions anyway.

In any case of failure, we must report all of the details of the exception in order to be able to investigate and fix the root cause (as described in Chapter 13). In case an exception is thrown *out* from the `Cleanup` method, the unit testing framework will report it automatically as part of the test results. But because we want to continue running the other cleanup actions, then we need to catch each exception. Therefore, we need to collect all of the exceptions that were thrown from cleanup actions and throw them only at the end of the `Cleanup` method, wrapped together using an `AggregateException` if there's more than one. If there was only one exception, then we can throw that particular exception as is. Listing B-9 shows the `Cleanup` method with the proper exception handling.

Listing B-9. Cleanup method with proper exception handling

```
[TestCleanup]
public void Cleanup()
{
    _cleanupActions.Reverse();
    var exceptions = new List<Exception>();

    foreach (var action in _cleanupActions)
    {
        try
        {
            action();
        }
        catch (Exception ex)
        {
            exceptions.Add(ex);
        }
    }

    if (exceptions.Count == 1)
        throw exceptions.Single();

    if (exceptions.Count > 1)
        throw new AggregateException(
            "Multiple exceptions occurred in Cleanup.", exceptions);
}
```

Note   in .Net, it's recommended to use a list of `ExceptionDispathInfo` class instead of list of `Exception`, in order to preserve their original stack-traces. I didn't use it here in order to keep the example simpler. You can look at the implementation of this mechanism in the Test Automation Essentials, project on GitHub to see how `ExceptionDispathInfo` is used. See Appendix C for more details about the Test Automation Essentials project.

Summary

As described in Chapter 7, one technique to help achieve isolation is to clean everything that the test created when it's finished. But we also discussed the reasons why it's difficult to write cleanup code that would work correctly in all situations. The cleanup mechanism described here ensures that the exact relevant cleanup actions are called whether the test passed or failed, regardless of the exact line in which the test failed. It also ensures that cleaning up entities that depend on one another are cleaned in the right order to avoid data integrity problems and exceptions. Finally, we made sure that any exception that might occur inside a cleanup action does not prevent other cleanup actions to run, and that all of the exception details are reported so that we can investigate and fix the root cause.

Test Automation Essentials

This appendix describes the Test Automation Essentials open source project that I created, which contains various useful utilities for developing test automation in C#.

Background

When I started to work as a consultant and had to establish the infrastructure for test automation for multiple clients, I noticed that many things that I had implemented for one client was useful to other clients as well. As you probably realized by now, I hate writing duplicate code, so I looked for a way to share this code between my clients. Because naturally my clients don't share the same source control repository, I determined to make it an open source project, hosted on GitHub, for the benefit of all. Over time, whenever I wrote something that I though could be beneficial for other clients or other people in general, I added it to the project. The source code of the project can be found at `https://github.com/arnonax/TestEssentials`.

Most of the public classes and methods in these libraries have pretty extensive XML comments (similar to JavaDoc comments in Java), which Visual Studio displays as tooltips when you hover over them, in order to make it easy to use. Gradually I'm trying to cover with XML comments the rest of the classes and methods that I still haven't.

© Arnon Axelrod 2018
A. Axelrod, *Complete Guide to Test Automation*, https://doi.org/10.1007/978-1-4842-3832-5

Project Structure

Because my clients and the projects I was involved in use different test automation technologies, I divided the project into small and modular libraries, so that anyone can use only the libraries that fits his needs and the technologies he's using.

Accordingly, the solution consists of several C# projects:

- **TestAutomationEssentials.Common** – this project contains very generic and reusable utilities. It has no dependency on any specific technology (except for the .Net Framework itself) or library, and therefore can be used in any project. In fact, many of the utilities in this project are not even specific to test automation and can serve any .Net project. Most other projects in the solution have a dependency on this project.

- **TestAutomationEssentials.MSTest** – this project provides utilities that are useful for projects written using MSTest version 1, which has been in use up until Visual Studio 2015.

- **TestAutomationEssentials.MSTestV2** – this project provides functionality identical to **TestAutomationEssentials.MSTest**, but for **MSTest V2** (MSTest version 2), which is used since Visual Studio 2017, or as a NuGet package for projects created using Visual Studio 2015. In fact. this project does not contain any C# source files of its own, but rather links all the source files of **TestAutomationEssentials.MSTest**. Therefore. these projects are essentially always identical, except for the version of MSTest they reference.

- **TestAutomationEssentials.CodedUI** – this project provides utilities for Coded UI (Microsoft's UI Automation framework) based projects.

- **TestAutomationEssentials.Selenium** – this project provides utilities that are useful for projects that use Selenium.

In addition to these five projects that provide utilities that are useful for any project, the solution contains also the following projects that are used only internally:

- **TestAutomationEssentials.UnitTests** – contains unit tests (and some integration tests) for the TestAutomationEssentials.Common and TestAutomationEssentials.MSTest projects.

- **TestAutomationEssentials.MSTestV2UnitTests** – contains unit and integration tests for the TestAutomationEssentials.MSTestV2 project.

- **TestAutomationEssentials.TrxParser** – an internal project that is is used by the unit test projects.

Tip   Looking at the unit tests can sometimes help you understand some of the utilities better. In addition, you may find it interesting to look at and debug the tests in `TestBaseTest` (and its base class) and try to understand how they work. As these tests test the integration of the `TestBase` class in `TestAutomationEssentials.MSTest` with the MSTest framework itself, they generate test code on the fly, compile it, and run the compiled code using MSTest – all within the test itself. Pretty complicated and tricky, but cool...

Note About the Unit Tests and XML Comments

Most of the code in this project was first written as part of real projects, and only then was extracted from these projects into Test Automation Essentials. As the original projects were all test projects, the code was covered (indirectly) by the tests of my client's application. When I moved the relevant code to Test Automation Essentials, I tried to retrofit unit tests for most of it to ensure that I don't break compatibility whenever I change something. However, that takes some time and in some cases it's not trivial. For that reason, by now I mainly covered with tests only the Common and MSTest (and MSTestV2) projects, but I'm working on covering the Selenium project as well.

I do a similar thing with the XML Comments, though it's typically easier and faster to do than writing unit tests.

NuGet Packages

In order to use these utilities, you don't need to get the source code from GitHub (even though you can do that as well), but rather use these libraries as NuGet packages (similar to the way we've added the Selenium WebDriver library to the project in Chapter 12). There are five libraries available, one for each project, which you can easily add to your project and start using what you need.

Features and Utilities

Following is the description of the main features and utilities contained in each of these libraries.

TestAutomationEssentials.Common

This library contains various small but very useful utility methods (mainly extension methods that were mentioned in Chapter 13), plus a few bigger features:

1.   Support for configuration files. This was explained and was used in Chapter 14.

2.   A `Logger` class that implements the concept of nested logging, described in Chapter 13.

3.   A generic implementation of the Cleanup mechanism described in Appendix B.

4.   A `Wait` class (pretty similar to `WebDriverWait` in Selenium) that provides a few methods for waiting until a given condition occurs.

Here's a more detailed explanation of the more interesting classes and methods in this library.

ExtensionMethods Class

This class contains many general-purpose extension methods, which can make your code a bit simpler and easier to read. Listing C-1 demonstrates a few usage examples.

Listing C-1. ExtensionMethods examples

```
// SubArray example:
string[] cartoons = {"Mickey", "Minnie", "Goofy", "Pluto", "Donald" };
string[] dogs = cartoons.SubArray(2, 2);

// Dictionary.AddRange example:
var numbers = new Dictionary<int, string>
{
    {1, "One" },
    {2, "Two" },
    {3, "Three" }
};
var moreNumbers = new Dictionary<int, string>()
{
    {4, "Four"},
    {5, "Five"},
    {6, "Six"}
};
numbers.AddRange(moreNumbers);

// IEnumerable<T>.IsEmpty() example:
IEnumerable<int> values = GetValues();
if (values.IsEmpty())
{
    // Do something...
}
```

DateTimeExtensions

This class also contains useful extension methods but mainly around date and time manipulation. I especially like the extension methods that makes the code read more fluently, like for example, instead of writing: `var duration = TimeSpan.FromSeconds(3);` you can simply write: `var duration = 3.Seconds();` The difference is pretty small (and a few people even find it confusing at first), but when you get used to it and read the code, it makes it much more fluent.

TestExecutionScopeManager

This class implements the cleanup mechanism that is described in Appendix B but it's not bound to a specific unit testing framework; and it allows you to nest execution scopes, to support multiple levels of cleanup, like [TestCleanup], [ClassCleanup], and [AssemblyCleanup]. If you're using MSTest there's no need to use this class directly, as TestAutomationEssentials.MSTest (and MSTestV2) already use this class internally and provide a single AddCleanupAction method. However, you can use this class if you need it for other unit testing frameworks or for any other purpose.

This class also uses the Logger class to write whenever an execution scope begins and ends.

Wait

This class exposes a few static methods for waiting for a given condition to be met. These methods throw a TimeoutException in case the condition didn't get met after a specified timeout. The condition is provided as a delegate, or a lambda expression (explained in Appendix B) that returns a Boolean, which indicates whether the condition has been met or not.

This class has a few overloads of methods named Wait.Until and Wait.While, which as their names imply, the first one waits *until* the condition is met, and the second one waits *while* the condition is met (i.e., until it is *no longer* met). Some of the overloads of these methods accept an error message to use in the TimeoutException, though if you're using a lambda expression, then you can use another overload that doesn't take an error message and automatically parses the expression in order to use it in the description. Listing C-2 shows two usage examples of the Wait class.

Listing C-2. Examples of using the Wait class

```
// Wait.Until example
Wait.Until(() => batchJob.IsCompleted, 2.Minutes());

// Wait.While example, with error message
Wait.While(() => batchJob.InProgress, 2.Minutes(), "Batch job
is still in progress after 2 minutes");
```

In addition to the `Until` and `While` methods, there are also `If` and `IfNot` methods. These methods correspond to the `While` and `Until` methods respectively but do not throw a `TimeoutException` when the specified period elapses. Instead they simply continue normally. This can be useful in cases that you want to wait for something to occur but may as well miss it. For example, let's consider the case where clicking a button starts an operation that may take fa ew seconds, during which a "please wait" message should appear, and we want to wait until the operation completes. But the same operation may also be very fast at times, in which case the message appears only for a blink of an eye, and the test may miss it altogether. So, in order to prevent the test from failing if the operation was very fast, you can use the `Wait.IfNot` to first wait for the message to appear, providing a short timeout (e.g., 1 second), followed by a `Wait.Until` to wait for the message to disappear, with a longer timeout (e.g., 1 minute). If the test missed the message because it was too fast, then the `Wait.IfNot` will wait in vain for the message to appear, but only for 1 second and without failing, and then the `Wait.Until` will return immediately because the message no longer appears.

TestAutomationEssentials.MSTest

The most significant class that this library provides is the `TestBase` class. This class is designed to be used as the base class for all of your tests. In case you already have a class hierarchy of tests, simply derive the lowest ones (your own test base classes) from this class.

This class adapts the MSTest specific initialization and cleanup methods to the `TestExecutionScopeManager` class from TestAutomationEssentials.Common. In addition, it exposes a virtual method that you can override and which is called only when the test fails (`OnTestFailure`), something that MSTest does not provide out of the box. This is very useful for adding any information that can help you investigate and diagnose the failures. In fact, if you import the namespace `TestAutomationEssentials.MSTest.UI`, then you'll get a slightly different implementation of `TestBase` whose default implementation of `OnTestFailure` takes a screenshot upon a failure (the screenshot is of the entire desktop, not of a browser page as it in Selenium).

LoggerAssert

In addition to the `TestBase` class, this library also contains few other utility classes. One of them is the `LoggerAssert` class, which writes a message to the log whenever the assertion is evaluated, whether it passes or fails. While generally there should only be no more than a couple of asserts at the end of each test, there are cases where few asserts in the middle of the test may still be useful (e.g., inside a loop, which is also generally discouraged in a test, but there are exceptions...). In these cases, it's useful to see in the log the assertions that passed, and not only the one that failed. Note that in order to use it properly, you should phrase the messages as expectations, (e.g., "x should be 3") and not as error messages ("x was not 3"), because these messages would appear in the log also in case of success.

TestAutomationEssentials.CodedUI

The primary goal of this library is to make working with Coded UI, through code and without UIMaps (see Chapter 3) much easier. TestAutomationEssentials.CodedUI exposes an API that resembles the one of Selenium WebDriver. Listing C-3 shows a usage example.

Listing C-3. Example of using TestAutomationEssentials.CodedUI

```
var customerDetailsPanel =
    mainWindow.Find<WinPane>(By.AutomationId("CustomerDetails"));

var customerNameTextBox =
    customerDetailsPanel.Find<WinText>(By.Name("CustomerName"));

var text = customerNameTextBox.DisplayText;
```

In addition, it provides few useful extension methods lik: `myControl.RightClick()`, `myControl.DragTo(otherControl)`, and the very useful method `myControl.IsVisible()`, which for some reason Coded UI does not provide out of the box.

TestAutomationEssentials.Selenium

This library wraps Selenium WebDriver to make the use of Selenium somewhat easier in most cases and much easier in more specific ones.

Note   Currently this library is a bit too "opinionated," which makes it hard to add it retroactively to existing projects. I'm considering changing or at least softening some of these constraints, but I have no specific details about it yet. Stay tuned…

WaitForElement

To use most of the features of this library, you need to create an instance of the `Browser` class, which wraps your `IWebDriver` object. Using this object (and though other classes that derive from `ElementsContainer`, more or that later), you can find elements using the `WaitForElement` method. This method is similar to the familiar `FindElement` method of Selenium, but with two main differences:

1. It always waits for the element to appear (and not just to exist). You can specify the timeout or use the default of 30 seconds.

2. It takes a `description` argument, which is used for automatically logging click operations, typing, etc. Providing a descriptive name in this argument helps make the log very readable.

`Browser.WaitForElement` returns a `BrowserElement` object, which on one hand implements Selenium's `IWebElement` interface, but on the other hand, it also derives from `ElementsContainer`, which means that you can use `WaitForElement` to look for child elements inside of it, with the same benefits over the standard `FindElement` method.

Handling Frames and Windows

In my opinion, the case in which this library is most compelling is for web applications that use multiple windows or iframes (which is a web page displayed within another web page). Normally with Selenium you need to use `driver.SwitchTo().Window()` and `driver.SwitchTo().Frame()` to use other windows or frames, but the annoying thing is that if you want to use an element you already found in one context (i.e., a window or a frame, including the main page), you can't use that element after you switched to another context, unless you switch back to the original one. If you don't do that, you'll get a StaleElementReferenceException (see Chapter 14), but managing the active context can be cumbersome and complicate your code. Listing C-4 demonstrates this problem.

Listing C-4. The problem with SwitchTo

```
// Navigate to a website that contains an iframe
webDriver.Url = "http://www.some-site.com/outer.html";

// find an element on the outer page
var outerButton = webDriver.FindElement(By.Id("outerButton"));

// switch to the inner frame
webDriver.SwitchTo().Frame("frame1");

// find an element on the inner frame
var innerButton = webDriver.FindElement(By.Id("innerButton"));
// clicking the inner button works normally
innerButton.Click();

// (See next comment)
//webDriver.SwitchTo().DefaultContent();

// Clicking the button on the outer page now would throw a
// StaleElementReferenceException because the outer page is not the current
// context. You must uncomment the above statement, which switches back to
// the outer page, in order to avoid the exception
outerButton.Click();
```

Note that in this example the problem doesn't look so severe, but in more complex situations, managing the current context can make the code very cumbersome and error prone.

The Solution of Test Automation Essentials to the SwitchTo Problem

The classes that derive from ElementsContainer (including Browser and BrowserElement) contain a method GetFrame that finds a frame and returns a corresponding Frame object (which is part of the TestAutomationEssentials.Selenium library). The Frame class also derives from ElementsContainer, so you can look for nested frames within the frame that this object represents (i.e., to find an iframe within another iframe). In addition, `Browser` has an `OpenWindow` method that invokes an operation that you provide to it (e.g. ,clicking a button), which should result in a new window being opened and returns a `BrowserWindow` object that represents the new window. As you might have guessed, `BrowserWindow` also derives from `ElementsContainer`. The cool thing is that Test Automation Essentials manages the current context for you, so you don't have to worry about it. Whenever you want to use an element that you found on any window or frame, you should be able to do that, even if it's not on the active context (though given that this element still exists of course). Test Automation Essentials will take care of switching for that context for you. Listing C-5 shows how the previous example would look with Test Automation Essentials.

Listing C-5. Working with Frames using Test Automation Essentials

```
// create an instance of Browser that wraps our webDriver object
var browser = new Browser(webDriver, "Site with iframe");

// Navigate to a website that contains an iframe
browser.Url = @"http://www.some-site.com/outer.html";

// find an element on the outer page
var outerButton = browser.WaitForElement(By.Id("outerButton"), "Outer
button");

// Find the inner frame
var frame = browser.GetFrame("frame1", "inner frame");

// find an element on the inner frame
var innerButton = frame.WaitForElement(By.Id("innerButton"), "Inner
button");
// clicking the inner button works normally
innerButton.Click();

// Clicking the outer button now works seamlessly!
outerButton.Click();
```

Contributing to the Project and Porting to Other Languages

The nice thing about open source projects is that anyone can help improve it and influence its direction. Because of the nature of this project, I mostly added to it things that *I* needed, and therefore there could be many things that should have been right there but are not. Likewise, while this project is very modular, it doesn't have a very clear boundary for what should be included in it and what shouldn't. So, any good idea that can benefit others can be included in it. Obviously, like any other software, this project can also have bugs that need to be fixed. Therefore, you can contribute to this project by many different means.

It is always advisable that before you go on and send a pull-request (see Chapter 13), you discuss it first by posting an issue though GitHub, or by contacting me directly. Note that posting an issue is not necessarily a bug report, as it can also be an idea for improvement or a request for a new feature. If you do send a pull-request, please make sure that it has clear XML comments for its public API; and at least for the Common and MSTest libraries, I expect nearly everything to be covered by unit or integration tests.

I also consider porting some of the stuff to other programming languages, mainly Java, but maybe also Python or any other language that I see a need for. I'll probably do it when I'll have a real and significant test automation project that needs it, but you're welcome to add it too. Note that some things, especially in the Common library are relevant specifically to C#, though other utilities may be useful for other languages.

Tips and Practices for Programmer's Productivity

As a consultant who has worked with many test automation developers, I found that many of them are thirsty for tips and practices for working more effectively and for improving their programming skills. In this appendix, I gathered some of these tips and practices that I believe will be valuable to most people.

Some of these tips are relevant to all programmers, not just test automation developers, and some are more specific to test automation and even to Selenium.

Prefer Using the Keyboard

If you want to work more efficiently when working with code, I suggest that you get used to using the keyboard, much more than the mouse. It takes some time to get used to it, but once you do, you'll be much more productive when writing and reading code! Here are some tips that can help you get used to it. Most of these tips assume that you're using Microsoft Windows. If you're using Mac, Linux, or any other operating system, there are probably equivalent shortcuts, but they may be different. Searching the web for equivalent shortcuts in these operating systems will likely yield the desired results.

1. As it's difficult to change habits, you must put some constraints on yourself at first in order to get used to use the keyboard instead of the mouse. Therefore, I suggest that you deliberately put the mouse farther away from you. Only grab it when you don't find how to achieve your task with the keyboard, and then put it back away.

© Arnon Axelrod 2018
A. Axelrod, *Complete Guide to Test Automation*, https://doi.org/10.1007/978-1-4842-3832-5

2. Pressing the **Alt** key, highlights shortcuts for menus and buttons, by adding an underline under the letter of shortcut. To activate the shortcut, press **Alt** + the highlighted letter. For example, to open the **File** menu in virtually all applications, press **Alt+F.**

3. After the menu is open, you'll see the shortcuts of the menu items. When the menu is open, you can simply press the highlighted letter, even without pressing **Alt**. For example, after pressing **Alt+F** to open the **File** menu, press **O** to activate the **Open...** menu item.

4. Once the menu is open, you can navigate the submenus using the arrows. Press **Enter** to select the menu item. The arrow keys are useful also for navigating most tree controls. For example, to expand a folder in File Explorer, you can press the right arrow.

5. Many menu items also have additional shortcut keys displayed next to them, usually with the **Ctrl** key + some other key. These shortcuts can be invoked directly, without first opening the menu. For example, to open a new file, directly press **Ctrl+O**.

6. Most UI controls (elements) in most applications are capable of being "focused," which means that they're the first control to receive the keyboard input. There's only one focused control at any given moment. The concept of "focus" is most noticeable with textboxes, but other controls, like buttons, checkboxes, drop-down lists, etc., can also have the focus, allowing you to interact with them using the keyboard. Use the **Tab** key to move the focus between elements on a window. Use **Shift+Tab** to move in the opposite order. Press **Enter** or the **Space Bar** to press the focused button. Use the **Space Bar** also to toggle checkboxes, or select items in a multiselect list-boxes. Press **Esc** to click the "**Cancel**" button on dialogs.

7. Most keyboards have a **Context Menu** key (typically located between the right **Alt** and **Ctrl** keys), which is similar to a right-click with the mouse. Note though that when you use the mouse, right-clicking opens the context menu that corresponds to the location where the *mouse cursor* is, while pressing the Context Menu key on the keyboard opens the context menu where the keyboard focus currently is.

8. Use **Alt+Tab** and **Alt+Shift+Tab** to switch between open windows back and forth. In many applications, including Visual Studio, you can use **Ctrl+Tab** and **Ctrl+Shift+Tab** to switch between open documents. Keep the **Alt** (or **Ctrl**) key pressed to see the list of the open applications or documents.

9. In a text editor or textbox, use **Ctrl+→** and **Ctrl+←** to move the caret (the text entry cursor) whole words at once. Use the **Home** and **End** keys to move to the beginning and end of a line. Use **Ctrl+Home** and **Ctrl+End** to move to the beginning and end of the document.

10. Use **Shift+→**, **Shift+←**, or **Shift** + any of the navigation combinations described above to select the text between its current location and the location where the navigation keys will take you to. For example, **Shift+Ctrl+→** will select the next word.

11. Press **Shift+Del** and **Shift+Backspace** to delete the next or previous word (or from the middle of a word to its end or its beginning).

12. Search the web for a list of shortcuts for your favorite IDE or other applications that you work with often. Print these and put it in from of you. Also search the web for specific keyboard shortcuts for actions that you can't find the shortcut to. If you're using Resharper, I highly recommend you to search for "Resharper Default Keymap PDF" on the web, print it, and put it near your keyboard. From time to time examine this document to find useful shortcuts and try to use them often until you start using them naturally. You'll also likely learn addition features of Resharper (or of your IDE) when you examine this list.

13. The keyboard mappings for many applications, especially programming IDEs are customizable. So, you can assign direct keyboard shortcuts to actions that you use often and that don't have ones by default.

Poka-Yoke

In Chapter 11 I declared MVCForum as a read-only property and not as a regular property (with public setter). Declaring a property as read-only is more restrictive than declaring it as read/write, and therefore may seem like an inferior option. Well the thing is that I don't want that anyone to ever change this property from outside of the class. (Note that changing the value of a reference-type, means replacing the reference with a reference to another object, and not making changes to the existing object.) Similarly, there are many other design decisions that a programmer can make to restrict or allow the usage of some code construct, and some programmers mistakenly think that the more you allow – the better. So why should I prefer to restrict? To answer that question, I'll tell you what "poka-yoke" is and why it's so important.

Poka-yoke is a Japanese term that means "mistake-proofing" or "inadvertent error prevention." The term is part of the Lean manufacturing philosophy developed by Toyota in the middle of the 20th century. A poka-yoke is any mechanism that helps an equipment operator to avoid (*yokeru*) mistakes (*poka*), as it turns out that preventing mistakes is often much easier and cheaper than inspecting and fixing defects later on. While originally the term and the idea were used in industrial manufacturing, it holds very true for software design as well.

There are countless examples of language features and techniques in software design that enable poka-yoke. In fact, the first principle of object-oriented design – encapsulation – is one. Encapsulation is what allows you to specify whether a member of a class will be **private**, so only other methods of the same class would be able to access, or **public** if the member is planned to be used by methods in other classes too. Using strong typing (i.e., having to specify the exact type explicitly) is a very strong Poka-yoke mechanism in the languages that support it (e.g., C# and Java). In addition to this, using strongly typed collections that take advantage of the **Generics** language feature are more error preventing than collections of objects. Another technique to avoid mistakes is to avoid using null as a valid value, as I'll explain shortly.

While using poka-yoke sometimes limits flexibility, I strongly prefer to allow flexibility only in places and manners that I explicitly choose, and not by default. This is the reason I preferred to make the MVCForum property read-only.

Avoid Nulls

Most object-oriented languages allow object variables (be it local, field, static, etc.) to have a special value of null, indicating that it references no actual object. This is usually also the default value of an uninitialized object variable. However, probably the most common *unexpected* exceptions (which actually represent a problem in the code, or better put: bugs) is NullReferenceException in .Net (and NullPointerException in Java), which is caused by the use of null values. Especially if you treat nulls as valid values, these bugs can be difficult to investigate, because their cause is often in a different place from where the exception itself is thrown. Not only that, but the cause is that the assignment of a real object *didn't happen!* Investigating why something didn't happen is much harder than investigating why something did happen... Note that if you avoid using nulls as a general rule, but you get a NullReferenceException nevertheless, then it's usually very easy to find the variable that you forgot to initialize.

For these reasons, many modern languages (especially *functional* languages, like F# and Scala) intentionally prevent the use of nulls by default. In some of these languages, you can still use nulls, but only if you explicitly declare the variable to allow it.

Because most of us are still using "regular" object-oriented languages (C#, Java, Python, Ruby, etc.), the compiler doesn't hold us from using nulls. However, with a little self-discipline, we can avoid it ourselves. Simply initialize every variable right when it's declared (or in the constructor), and avoid assigning null or returning a null from a method. If you get a value from "outside" that may be null, (somewhere that you don't have control over, like arguments in a public API, or a return value from a third-party method), then you should check it for null as soon as possible and handle it appropriately. This can be done by throwing an exception if you can't handle it, or "translating" it to a different object that represents an empty object (AKA the "null object pattern." A simple example is an empty list rather than null).

Adhering to these rules will help you avoid many potential bugs!

Avoid Catching Exceptions

Most beginner and intermediate developers use `try/catch` blocks much too extensively, because they think that this makes their code more robust and reliable. Well, it's true that when you catch an exception, you prevent it from propagating to your caller (and if your code is the "main" method or a test method, then you prevent the exception from crashing your application or failing the test), but that only gives the *illusion* that the code is more robust. The reason is that if something went wrong and without knowing exactly what and why, and you just ignore it, you'd very likely be hit by a ricochet of that problem later on. If you ignore all exceptions, the program will never crash, but it also may won't do whatever it's expected to do! Catching an exception just in order to ignore it (i.e., using an empty `catch` clause) is often called "swallowing exceptions," and in 99% of the cases, it's a very bad idea...

Moreover, if you swallow an exception, it will make your life much harder when you come to debug or diagnose a problem. This is even worse if it happens only occasionally in production! Therefore, the most naïve approach to this problem is simply to write the exception to a log file. This is significantly better than swallowing the exception completely, and in some cases it's a good idea, but in general, as far as the user (either the end user or the caller of a method) is concerned, this has the same effect of swallowing the exception, because you normally won't look at the log until a user experiences and reports a problem. If you decide to write an exception to the log, make sure to log all of the information about the exception, including the stack-trace and original exception if it's different from the one that got caught (`InnerException` in .Net or `getCause()` in Java). In .Net, it's best to use the `ToString()` method because the string it returns already contains all of the relevant information.

So how *should* you handle exceptions? In most cases, the correct answer is "you shouldn't"! For exceptions that you expect to happen at times (e.g., "file not found" when the application tries to read from a file that the user might have deleted or renamed), you better avoid the condition by checking for it in advance and handle it appropriately (e.g., check if the file exists, and if not, advise the user what to do). For general exceptions that you can't predict and you can't specify why they may happen, or in case you have nothing to do about it (like "out of memory"), let them propagate down the stack. If you let the program crash immediately (or let the test fail due to the exception), you automatically get most of the information that you need in order to investigate the root cause. If you do it properly, then you'd most likely find the fault and fix it quickly.

Clearly, if it was *always* such a bad idea, the try/catch construct wouldn't make it into all modern languages. So, when does it make sense to catch exceptions? There are a few cases:

- You're able to specify exactly what could go wrong, and handle it gracefully, but you can only do it after the fact. In many cases, runtime conditions may change during the operation (e.g., the file is deleted *while* you try to write to it). At other cases you do have a way to check for the condition before starting the operation, but it simply doesn't pay off, for example, due to performance (i.e., checking if you can do something that takes a long time may require that the check itself take the same time by itself). Other cases may be due to technical limitations (e.g., you don't have an API that can tell you in advance if the operation is about to succeed or fail).

- In these cases, you should catch the most specific type of exception, and narrow the scope of the try block to only the specific operation that you expect to throw that exception. This way you avoid catching exceptions that you don't expect and only catch those you do. The catch block should perform the specific handling that is expected to resolve the issue or advise the user or the caller of the method *how to resolve it*.

- Adding a global error handling that presents all unexpected failures to the user in a special way and/or attaches additional information to the exception. For example, some teams prefer to use a proprietary reporting mechanism for test results and want all the failure information to be written to it, along with the exact date and time. In addition, you may want to add some system information or specific information about the SUT.

- In this case you should have only one try/catch block, but in contrast to the previous case, in this case the try block should encompass the entire program (or test case) and you should catch *all* exceptions. In this case, make sure to report all the information you have about the exception to allow efficient investigation.

- You should also think about a fallback exception handling, in a case where an exception occurred *inside* your normal exception handling code. For example, if you fail to write to a custom report, you should still fall back to writing the failure to the console, or to the normal exception handling that the testing framework provides. Usually the handling should simply be throwing a new exception containing the information of both the original exception and the information about the secondary exception that happened inside the exception handler. This way you'll be able to investigate both the reason for the original failure, and also the problem in the exception handler. Obviously, the secondary exception handler should be much simpler than the first one, so the chances that *it* fails should be very small.

- You have valuable information to add to the exception that may be useful for the investigation. For example, you have a complex method that performs multiple operations on the database, calls external REST services, etc. In such a method a lot of things can go wrong, but the native exceptions that may be thrown may be too low level to be useful and won't tell you how to reproduce the error. In this case you can catch all exceptions (or a more specific but still general exception) and re-throw a new exception that wraps the original exception but adds information about the parameters that the method received, or some internal state of the current object.

- You should very rarely write such handlers in advance. In most cases, you should first let the exceptions handled normally, and only if you see that you're missing some important information that you need in order to find the fault, then you need to add the additional information to the exception for the sake of the next time. Needless to say, you should keep all the information about the original exception, especially its stack-trace.

- You perform an operation on a large number of rows (or other form of data that contain independent entities), and you don't want a failure in one row to stop the process and prevent it from doing the operation on other rows. In such case you should wrap the operation for a single row in a try block, and inside the catch block, add the exception to a list. When the loop completes, you should throw an exception that contains all of the caught exceptions (.Net has an `AggregateException` class just for that), or report the failures to the user by other means.

One common use of exception handling is for retrying the failed operation. This is a valid reason to use try/catch, and it falls into the first category above. However, it's important to note that you understand exactly why and on what you retry. For example, if you try to read from a file and the file does not exist, retrying won't help without a human intervention! If you catch too broad exceptions and retry the entire operation, you create two new problems:

1. You're wasting a lot of time retrying something that has no chance to succeed.

2. You're very likely to miss other problems (including bugs in the SUT!) and lose valuable knowledge and information about the nature of these problems. As mentioned above, you'll have a harder time investigating the problem, and it may cause secondary problems that will just confuse you.

Occasionally I hear about test automation projects that introduced a mechanism that automatically retires a failing test. In my opinion this is a smell for a bad architecture, lack of isolation, or simply a poor test design. **Implementing an automatic retry of tests implies that you trust the tests less than you trust the SUT**, and you assume that most failures will be caused by the test (or its environment) and not by the SUT. An automatic test should be predictable and repeatable. If it fails, you should be able to investigate and fix the problem as fast as possible.

Until now we only discussed when to catch exceptions but haven't mentioned when to throw your own exception. This one is simpler – always throw an exception from methods if you detect a condition that prevents the method from doing whatever it was intended to do. When you do that, make sure to provide all the relevant information that can help whoever needs to understand what happened. Note that in object-oriented languages (that support exceptions), you should never return an error code or a Boolean to indicate success or failure. This is what exceptions are for!

In addition, avoid throwing an exception for the purpose of normal program flow. Exceptions should only be used to indicate some kind of problem! If in order to understand the normal program flow, one should follow the `throw` and `try/catch` constructs, then you're probably doing it wrong. The most obvious case that you should avoid is throwing an exception that you catch inside the same method.

Choosing the Most Appropriate Locator

The following tips are specific to Selenium. However, the main ideas and tips are relevant to all UI automation and may also be applicable for other cases in which the test needs to identify a piece of data from the application, like retrieving values from JSON, XML, or a database.

Selenium finds elements by matching a string value to a specified locator type. Selenium supports the following locators:

1. **Id** – identifies elements whose **id** attribute matches the specified value. According to the HTML standard, if this attribute exists, its value must be unique across all elements in the page. So, theoretically, if an element has an **id** attribute, it should ensure that we can uniquely identify it using this locator. However, this requirement is not being enforced by browsers and sometimes pages contain more than one element with the same **id**

2. **Name** – identifies elements using their **name** attribute. The name attribute should uniquely identify an element within an HTML form

3. **LinkText** – identifies elements by matching their inner text to the specified value

4. **PartialLinkText** – same as **LinkText**, but also matches elements in which their text *contains* the specified value, even if the value is only a substring of the link text

5. **TagName** – identifies elements whose tag name matches the specified value. Tag names are rarely unique, but in case they are, this locator can be used

6. **ClassName** – identifies the element using any of its class names. The `class` attribute of an HTML element can contain zero or more names of CSS classes, separated by a whitespace. This locator can take *only one* class name and only find element(s) that have this class

7. **XPath** – identifies elements according to the XPath specification.[1] The XPath specification provides a special query syntax to locate elements within an XML or HTML documents

8. **CSS Selector** – identifies elements according to the CSS selector pattern.[2] CSS Selectors were originally used to identify elements in a CSS document in order to apply a given style to them. However, the jQuery JavaScript library also makes use of this syntax to identify elements.

If you want to find a single element, you must use a locator and value that matches only that one particular element. If a locator matches more than one element, Selenium returns the first one, but this is not necessarily the one you want. Anyway, while the locator you use must identify the element uniquely, this is not enough: in order to keep the tests reliable and easy to maintain, we must also ensure that the **locator that we choose will always identify the relevant element, or at least which is least likely to be changed**.

Id and **Name** are considered the best locators if they exist, because they uniquely identify the elements (or at least *should*). This is indeed true in the majority of cases. However, some frameworks, or even proprietary JavaScript code, sometimes generate these ids at runtime, randomly or sequentially. While they ensure uniqueness, these values are most likely to change between runs if they're generated randomly. If they're generated sequentially, then they'll probably change only if elements are added or removed, either at runtime or due to a change in the code. So, my advice is to use an id or name locator only if its value is a *meaningful* name that is related to the business functionality of the element that you're looking for. In other words, use it only if its value was apparently chosen by a human. For example, if the id of an element is `submitButton`, then this makes a perfect locator. However, if the id of an element is `button342`, then this would probably mean that this is a *bad* locator!

---

[1] https://www.w3schools.com/xml/xpath_syntax.asp
[2] https://www.w3schools.com/cssref/css_selectors.asp

The same rule also applies to class names: if the class name is meaningful and is related to the element that you want to find, then it's great to use it. But if the class name has nothing to do with the `meaning` of the element, then avoid it if you have a better way.

While the **XPath** and **CSS Selector** locators have the most complex syntax, they provide the most flexibility. These locators allow you to specify a combination of characteristics of the element itself as well of its ancestors and even siblings, all as one string. Chrome can generate these strings for your and copy them to the clipboard, directly from the context menu of the element in the Develop Tools. You can then use these strings with your Selenium code to identify the element you want with it. While this sounds very compelling, and indeed many Selenium automation developers use it, it's often **not a good idea** whatsoever. Chrome attempts to find the best locator using a heuristic that searches for the simplest combination of characteristics that is also unique. However, this heuristic cannot predict what's likely to change in the future or even in the next time the page will be loaded and may even suggest a locator that is currently unique, but in another run won't be. Locators that are less likely to change are locators that contain strings that represent the real meaning of the element. For example, if a button has a `button-login` class name on it, even though class names need not be unique, its name suggests that it identifies a Login button. Therefore, you should learn the CSS Selector and XPath syntax and use your own judgment when combining the most appropriate pattern to use.

The last (but not least) tip is to limit the scope of the search to only a specific container. In other words, you should first identify a unique element that contains the element you're looking for, and then identify the element you're looking for inside of it. The famous `FindElement` method in Selenium works both on the `IWebDriver` object as well as on any `IWebElement` object, so you can use it to identify an element within another element. You can have as many levels of such nesting, and the typical approach is to use a Page Object for each such container that the end user can identify. The advantage of identifying elements only within their containers is that you only have to worry about the uniqueness of the elements within the container and not among all elements on the page, and in addition it removes the duplication from the locators of all the elements that reside in the same container. While this duplication is usually only of a substring (e.g., the start of an XPath expression), if it will need to change it will need to be changed for all of the elements inside this container.

Hard-Coded Strings in Test Automation: Yea or Nay?

Many developers treat hard-coded strings as a bad practice. There are some good reasons for it but also some misconceptions around it. In fact, in most cases you cannot avoid completely the use of string literals (AKA string constants, or hard-coded strings) in the code. For example, even if you want to keep these strings in an external file, you'd probably need to have the name of the file somewhere in your code. But then again, one can keep this limited set of constants in one source file, in order to keep it separated from the actual logic of the application. However, it is important to understand why and when it is a bad practice to use string literals mangling inside the source code, and when it is acceptable or even a good thing.

There are several reasons why hard-coded strings are considered bad practice:

1. Separation of concerns – strings are mostly used for some kind of human interaction, while the algorithm itself is not. The wording or spelling of a string that should be displayed to the user may need to change separately from the algorithm.

2. Localization (Internationalization) – applications that are localizable (i.e., applications that are designed to support multiple languages and cultures), or even may need to be localizable in the future should extract any string that the user may be exposed to, to some external resource that can be easily switched (either at runtime or at compile time).

3. Configuration – in many cases, global string values that are not intended for user interaction (at least not directly), tend to have different values for different environments or configurations. A database connection string is a good example. Hard-coding these strings make the code inflexible and won't be able to run on different environments.

4. Duplication – if you need to use the same string in multiple places in the code and you don't put it in a common place, then you introduce a duplication. If at any point you need to change this string, you would now need to change it in all places.

5. Length – sometimes strings can get quite long. and if they're mingled with the algorithm, they hinder the readability of the code.

Those reasons take some developers to the conclusion that *all* strings literals should be extracted from the code into a separate file. The most common claim I hear for that, is that it allows them to change these values without re-compiling them. However, re-compiling is an issue only for an end user who doesn't have access to the source code and development environment or is not proficient in the programming language and is afraid to change something that he doesn't understand.

Let's consider three common usages for string literals in test automation, and let's analyze where it makes the most sense to put them:

1. Environment information – Depending on your isolation strategy (see Chapter 7), some of this information may be different for every environment that you want to support running the automation on, though some values may be fixed for all environments (or there's only one environment you're supporting). Even though re-compiling is not a big deal in test automation, you'd probably want to keep the information that varies from one environment to another in a configuration file, or at least in a separate source file. This will help you manage their changes separately from the source files in your source-control system. As a rule of thumb, these configuration files should be kept small with very few, easy-to-understand values; otherwise it will soon become a nightmare to maintain by itself.

   The "fixed" values however are anything that is common to all environments and should not change for a predictable reason in the foreseeable future. It doesn't mean that it *can't* change in the future, but for now there's no reason to assume that it will happen soon – for example, a URL of a third-party service provider. In my opinion, it's fine that such data will be kept directly in the code, as long as it appears only at a single place and close to its usage, for example, as a named constant. If this URL will change at some point in the future, it shouldn't be difficult to find the place in the code where it's defined and change it. By contrast, if you put that value in a configuration file and you need to change it after couple of years, you probably won't remember that it's there anyway, and you'll have to debug or analyze the code in order to find where the value comes from in order to know where to change.

Therefore, if the value will be read from a configuration file, it will be less obvious to find it than if it is directly in the code. If you have multiple instances of this configuration file (e.g., for different environments) hanging around, probably not under source control, then even when you know what to change, you still need do it for every instance of this configuration file. After all, because you can never know what would change and when, you'd probably have lots and lots of such configuration values that will just be more difficult to manage and maintain. Bottom line: keep things simple!

2. Locator values (Ids, XPath, CSS Selectors, etc.) – Whether you're doing UI automation (e.g., using Selenium) or REST API tests (or maybe some other kinds of tests), you need to refer to elements on the screen or in the response message. In order to do this, you need to specify the id, name, XPath, etc., of these elements. Some people think that putting these strings in an external configuration file makes their code more maintainable. Frankly, I may be able to see how it makes the "code" more maintainable, but the maintenance of these files often becomes a headache in and on itself. If more than one automation developer works on the project, such a big file that contains all of these elements soon becomes a merge hell. In fact, such files don't solve anything, but rather move the maintainability problem from one place to another, which is less appropriate for it. Keeping the locators with their string literals close to their usages is much easier to maintain than having all of the locators defined in one place while their usages are spread across the entire code base. Encapsulating the details inside the class or the method that use it is the solution to make your code more maintainable, and the Page Object pattern is the most common way to encapsulate the locators inside a class.

3. Input values – Tests typically have to type in or otherwise pass strings as inputs to the SUT (like entering the discussion heading in Chapter 11). Some people like to keep these values in a separate file to give them flexibility over the values of these strings. If you're creating a data-driven test, then that's fine. But if you don't intend to run the same test with different values, which you specifically define to verify different cases, then there's probably not a good reason to extract it from the code. The need to extract such values to an external file is often a symptom for a design that depends on specific data that exists in the database. So, if at some point the data will change, then you won't have to change the code, only the external file. But again, this is just moving the maintenance problem from one place to another. This file becomes a contention point and will be harder to maintain than if the test used its own data.

4. Expected results – Similar to input values, the expected results are values that we expect as outputs from the SUT. The exact same considerations that apply to the input values apply also to the expected results.

5. SQL statements or JavaScript snippets – Sometimes you need to invoke an SQL statements, a JavaScript command, or something along these lines from the test code. If these scripts are long, putting them in separate files will indeed improve the maintainability of the code. However, for sparse one-liner statements, embedding them directly in the code, close to their usage, and not duplicated, improves encapsulation and makes the code easier to understand and to follow.

All in all, in the majority of cases, strings used in test automation code better be in the code, as long as they're not duplicated and appear close to their usage in the code, rather than in an external file. Use external configuration files only for values that *have to be different* for different environments.

Index

S

Printed in the United States
By Bookmasters